# Thomas' Sentencing Referencer

# THOMAS' SENTENCING REFERENCER

## 2019

By

### LYNDON HARRIS
*LLB (Hons), LLM,*
*Gray's Inn,*
*Barrister*

And

### PROFESSOR NICOLA PADFIELD QC (HON)
*Consultant Editor,*
*Master, Fitzwilliam College,*
*Cambridge*

SWEET & MAXWELL

 THOMSON REUTERS

Published in 2018 by Thomson Reuters, trading as Sweet & Maxwell.
Thomson Reuters is registered in England & Wales, company number
1679046.

Registered Office and address for service: 5 Canada Square, Canary Wharf,
London E14 5AQ.

For further information on our products and services, visit *http://
www.sweetandmaxwell.co.uk*

Computerset by Sweet & Maxwell. No natural forests were destroyed to
make this product: only farmed timber was used and replanted.

A CIP catalogue record for this book is available from the British Library.

Thomson Reuters, the Thomson Reuters Logo and Sweet & Maxwell ® are
trademarks of Thomson Reuters.
Printed and bound by CPI Group (UK) Ltd, Croydon, CR0 4YY


ISBN 9780414068407

# FOREWORD TO THE 2019 EDITION

The need for the *Sentencing Referencer* as an essential resource for those working in the criminal courts is as strong as ever. Sentencing legislation remains so voluminous, complex and technical that it has become almost unworkable as a scheme of law and yet it must be used and understood by judges and practitioners on a daily basis. It is vital that it can be properly applied because sentencing represents a crucial step in the criminal justice process: the fair and just determination of a criminal penalty on conviction and the clear, confident declaration of that penalty by the sentencing court.

The *Referencer* is now in its 14th edition. It remains as popular as ever. With legislation that is so impenetrable, it is no surprise that the *Referencer*, which provides such clear and practical guidance, has become so well respected and so heavily used by even the most experienced criminal justice practitioner. It contains the essential information that is so hard to find in the legislation itself or elsewhere. These include the all too elusive commencement dates and guidance on avoiding the numerous pitfalls created by the prescriptive obligations on judges when sentencing. The material is presented in an accessible manner. The table of contents is crystal clear to enable users to find the relevant information swiftly. There are user-friendly tables and flow charts, including tables on guilty plea reductions by percentage and guilty plea reductions for minimum sentences. For many, it is quite simply the usual starting point from which they can confidently find a path through the maze of legislation.

The enormity of the task in producing yet another edition is not to be underestimated, even in an unusual period in which there has been little legislative change. The new edition incorporates numerous developments including references to all the relevant case law developments.

Lyndon Harris has demonstrated that he is a worthy successor to the late great Dr David Thomas QC. I know, from his work on the Sentencing Code project at the Law Commission, how Lyndon has developed an encyclopedic knowledge of sentencing law. He is to be congratulated for producing yet another edition which maintains the very high standards that readers have come to expect of the *Referencer*.

*Professor David Ormerod QC*
*Law Commissioner for England and Wales*
*October 2018*

# PART 1: SENTENCING TOPICS

## PART 2: MAXIMUM SENTENCES (INDICTABLE OFFENCES)

## PART 3: SCHEDULES

## PART 4: CHARTS AND TABLES

# PART 1: SENTENCING TOPICS

# ADJOURNMENT—POST CONVICTION

*References: Current Sentencing Practice H2-7650; Archbold 5A-230*

## General Matters

A *magistrates' court* may adjourn after conviction to enable enquiries to be made or to determine the most suitable method of dealing with the case. The adjournment must not be for more than four weeks at a time, or three weeks if the offender is in custody, MCA 1980 s.10(3). See also CJA 2003 Sch.8 para.25A in relation to community order breaches.

The *Crown Court* may adjourn after conviction for similar purposes; the power is derived from the common law. There is no statutory time limit. The Crown Court may adjourn part of the sentence only, however it will be necessary to state so at the time, otherwise the 56-day limit specified in PCC(S)A 2000 s.155 will apply, (*Dorian* [2001] 1 Cr.App.R. (S.) 135).

## Particular Issues

The BA 1976 s.4 applies if the court adjourns for inquiries.

## Pre-sentence reports

In light of the statutory obligation to obtain a report in certain circumstances, an adjournment for that purpose (and silence from the court) should not be taken as an indication that a non-custodial sentence would be considered to be appropriate. It was, however, better practice, for the court to explicitly deal with the point, *Renan* (1994) 15 Cr.App.R. (S.) 722.

**Offender's expectation**   On adjourning, the court should avoid giving the offender any reason to expect that they will be dealt with by means of a sentence not involving custody. If the offender is given the impression that the court will deal with him without sending him to custody, it may not be open to the court which adjourns, or any other court dealing with the offender subsequently, to impose a custodial sentence, *Gillam* (1980) 2 Cr.App.R. (S.) 267. The principle in *Gillam* does not apply where no one present at the adjournment could have had an expectation that there would be a non-custodial penalty, see *Horton and Alexander* 7 Cr.App.R. (S.) 299.

A magistrates' court which adjourns after convicting a defendant of an either way offence should avoid giving the defendant any reason to expect that he will not be committed to the Crown Court for sentence, e.g. *Rennes* [1985] 7 Cr.App.R. (S.) 343, however any argument based on the expectation requires that the expectation is legitimately held, *Southampton Magistrates' Court ex parte Sansome* [1999] 1 Cr.App.R. (S.) 112.

# AGE OF OFFENDER AND AVAILABILITY OF SENTENCES

## PCC(S)A 2000 s.164(1)

*References: Current Sentencing Practice F1; Archbold 5A-945 et seq.*

### General rule

For the purposes of the availability of custodial sentences and non-custodial sentences, the general rule is that the age of the offender is his/her age on the day of conviction, PCC(S)A 2000 s.164(1) and CJA 2003 s.305(2). Below is a list of sentencing orders detailing their availability and the relevant point in time for determining the offender's age.

As to the severity of the sentence, the starting point for those aged under 18 at the date of the commission of the offence is the sentence that would have been imposed at that date, *Ghafoor* [2003] 1 Cr.App.R. (S.) 84.

### Custodial sentences

*For the purposes of determining the available sentence(s), the offender's age is his/her age at conviction*

Life sentence (murder) (committed when aged 18+ and sentenced when aged 21+), M(ADP)A 1965 s.1(1).
Life sentence (murder) (committed and sentenced when aged 18–20, PCC(S) A 2000 s.93.
Life sentence (discretionary) (offender aged 18+) CJA 2003 s.225(1).
Life sentence (discretionary) (offender aged under 18), CJA 2003 s.226(1).
Life sentence (automatic) (offender aged 21+), CJA 2003 s.224A(1).
Life sentence (automatic) (offender aged 18–20), CJA 2003 s.224A(1) and PCC(S)A s.94.

Extended determinate sentence (offender aged 18+), CJA 2003 s.226A(1).
Extended determinate sentence (offender aged under 18), CJA 2003 s.226B(1).

Imprisonment (offender aged 21+), PCC(S)A 2000 s.89(1).
Detention under s.91 (offender aged under 18), PCC(S)A 2000 s.91(1).
Detention in YOI (offender aged 18–20), PCC(S)A 2000 s.96.
Detention and training order (offender aged under 18), PCC(S)A 2000 s.100.
Mandatory sentence for threatening with bladed article/offensive weapon in public place/school (offender aged 16+), CJA 1988 s.139AA(7).
Mandatory sentence for threatening with offensive weapon in public (offender aged 16+), PCA 1953 s.1A(5).
Suspended sentence order (offender aged 18+), CJA 2003 s.189.

*The offender's age is his/her age when when the offence was committed*

Life sentence (murder) (committed when aged under 18), PCC(S)A 2000 s.90.

Offenders of particular concern (committed when aged 18+), CJA 2003 s.236A(1).

[5]

Mandatory sentence for third burglary/drug trafficking offence (offender aged 18+), PCC(S)A 2000 ss.110(1) and 111(1).

Mandatory sentence for possession of article with blade or point in public place (offender aged 16+), CJA 1988 s.139(6A).

Mandatory sentence for having article with blade or point (or offensive weapon) on school premises (offender aged 16+), CJA 1988 s.139A(5A).

Mandatory sentence for certain firearms offences (offender aged 16+), FA 1968 s.51A(1)(b).

Mandatory sentence for certain firearms offences (offender aged 16+), VCRA 2006 s.29(3), (6).

Mandatory sentence for possession of offensive weapon etc. (offender aged 16+), PCA 1953 s.1(2A).

## Non-custodial orders

*An offender must be sentenced on the basis of his/her age at conviction*

Bind over of parent or guardian, (when offender aged 10–17), PCC(S)A 2000 s.150(1).

Community order (offender aged 18+), CJA 2003 s.177(1).

Discharge (offender aged 10+), PCC(S)A 2000 s.12.

Fine (offender aged 10+; if offender aged under 16 at conviction, the court must, and if aged 16–17 at conviction, the court may order the parent or guardian to pay the fine), CJA 2003 s.163, MCA 1980 ss.32–33, and PCC(S)A 2000 s.137(1).

Hospital order (offender aged 10+), MHA 1983 s.37(1) and (2).

Hybrid order (offender aged 21+), MHA 1983 s.45A, PCC(S)A 2000 s.89(1) and *Fort* [2013] EWCA Crim 2332, [2014] 2 Cr.App.R. (S.) 24.

Parenting order (offender aged 10–17), CDA 1998 s.8 and 9(1).

Reparation order (offender aged 10–17), PCC(S)A 2000 s.73.

Youth rehabilitation order (offender aged under 18), CJIA 2008 s.1(1).

*The following orders are universally available (offender aged 10+ at conviction)*

Bind over to keep the peace, JPA 1968 s.1(7).

Compensation order if offender aged under 16 at conviction, the court must, and if aged 16–17 at conviction the court may, order the parent or guardian to pay the compensation order), PCC(S)A 2000 s.130 and 137(1).

Criminal behaviour order, ASBCPA 2014 s.22.

Deprivation order/Forfeiture order, PCC(S)A 2000 s.143.

Endorsement of driving licence, RTOA 1988 s.44.

Restitution order, PCC(S)A 2000 ss.148 and 149.

Restraining order, PHA 1997 ss.5 and 5A.

Sexual harm prevention order, SOA 2003 s.103A.

Sexual risk order, SOA 2003 s.122A.

Violent offender order, CJIA 2008 ss.98 and 99.

*The offender's age is as at date of sentence*

Guardianship order (offender aged 16+ at sentence), MHA 1983 s.37(2)(a)(ii).

Referral order (offender aged 10–17 at sentence), PCC(S)A 2000 s.16 (though this would appear contrary to *Danga* and was not construed thus in *Dillon* [2017] EWCA Crim 2642).

## Orders contingent on conviction

Automatic barring (does not apply where the offence was committed when aged under 18), SVGA 2006 s.3.

Notification (sexual offences) (universally applicable where the conditions are met), SOA 2003 s.80(1).

Statutory surcharge (universally applicable where the sentence imposed attracts the surcharge), CJA 2003 s.161A.

## Breaches of orders

An offender who is subject to a community order made under the Criminal Justice Act 2003 in whose case the community order is revoked following a breach or subsequent conviction must be sentenced on the basis of his/her age when the original order was made, CJA 2003 Sch.8 paras 10 and 23.

Where the court revokes a youth rehabilitation order and resentences the offender for the original offence, it may deal with him in any way in which the court could have dealt with the offender for that offence, CJIA 2008 Sch.2 paras 6 and 8.

Where an offender who has been the subject of a conditional discharge is convicted of a further offence convicted of a further offence "*committed during the discharge period and the court decides to re-sentence the offender for the original offence,*" the offender must be sentenced on the basis of their age when re-sentenced, PCC(S)A 2000 s.13(6).

## Committals

An offender committed to the Crown Court for sentence under PCC(S)A 2000 ss.3, 3A, 3B, 3C, 4, 4A or 6, must be sentenced on the basis of their age on the day they appear before the Crown Court, PCC(S)A 2000 ss.5, 5A and 7.

Where an offender crosses a relevant age threshold between committal and the appearance at the Crown Court, the relevant date for determining the offender's age is the date of conviction, *Robson* [2007] 1 Cr.App.R. (S.) 54.

## Determining the offender's age

For the purposes of sentences of imprisonment, detention in a young offender institution, detention under the PCC(S)A 2000 s.91 or detention and training orders, the age of an offender is deemed to be what it appears to the court to be, after the court has considered any available evidence, but where it is apparent that the age of the offender is in doubt or dispute, the court should adjourn and obtain proper evidence of age before sentencing, CJA 1982 s.1(6) and *Steed* (1990–91) 12 Cr.App.R. (S.) 230.

## Determining which custodial sentence applies by virtue of defendant's age

The following table sets out the availability of custodial sentences depending on the offender's age at conviction. The table contains the form of each custodial sentence which must be imposed on offenders in each age category.

| Sentencing Order | Age at conviction | | |
|---|---|---|---|
| | 10-17 | 18-20 | 21+ |
| Mandatory life (murder) | Detention during HM's Pleasure | Custody for life* | Imprisonment for life* |
| Automatic life (s.224A) | Not available | Custody for life | Imprisonment for life |
| Discretionary life (s.225/226/ common law) | Detention for life | Custody for life | Imprisonment for life |
| Extended sentence (s.226A and B) | Extended sentence of detention | Extended sentence of detention in a YOI | Extended sentence of imprisonment |
| Determinate sentence of custody | Detention under s.91 / DTO | Detention in a YOI | Imprisonment |
| Suspended sentence order | Not available | Suspended sentence of detention in a YOI | Suspended sentence of imprisonment |

*Note that where an offence of murder is committed by an offender aged 10-17, the sentence will always be one of Detention during HM's Pleasure; the nature of the sentence is not determined by the offender's age at conviction.*

# AGGRAVATING FACTORS: ASSAULTS ON EMERGENCY WORKERS

ASSAULTS ON EMERGENCY WORKERS (OFFENCES) ACT 2018 s.2

*References: Current Sentencing Practice H3-4500*

## Commencement

Section 2 of the Assaults on Emergency Workers (Offences) Act 2018 applies to offences committed on or after 13 November 2018, AEW(O)A 2018.

## Application

Section 2 applies to listed offences (see below) in which the offence was committed against an emergency worker acting in the exercise of their functions as such a worker, s.2(1) and (7) of the AEW(O)A 2018.

## Listed offences

The provisions of s.2 apply where the court is considering for the purposes of sentencing the seriousness of one of the following offences:

(a) an offence under any of the following provisions of the Offences against the Person Act 1861—
(i) s.16 of the OAPA 1861 (threats to kill);
(ii) s.18 of the OAPA 1861 (wounding with intent to cause grievous bodily harm);
(iii) s.20 of the OAPA 1861 (malicious wounding);
(iv) s.23 of the OAPA 1861 (administering poison etc);
(v) s.28 of the OAPA 1861 (causing bodily injury by gunpowder etc);
(vi) s.29 of the OAPA 1861 (using explosive substances etc with intent to cause grievous bodily harm);
(vii) s.47 of the OAPA 1861 (assault occasioning actual bodily harm);
(b) s.3 of the SOA 2003 (sexual assault);
(c) manslaughter;
(d) kidnapping;
(e) an ancillary offence in relation to any of the preceding offences, s.2(1) and (3) of the AEW(O)A 2018.

## Duty to treat as aggravating factor

Where the listed offence was committed against an emergency worker acting in the exercise of their functions as such a worker, the court must treat that fact as an aggravating factor (that is to say, a factor that increases the seriousness of the offence) and must state in open court that the offence is so aggravated, s.2(3) of the AEW(O)A 2018.

Nothing in s.2 prevents a court from treating the fact that the offence was committed against an emergency worker acting in the exercise of their functions as such a worker as an aggravating factor in relation to non-listed offences, s.2(6) of the AEW(O)A 2018.

## Definitions

*Emergency worker* means (whether paid or unpaid):

(a)   a constable;
(b)   a person (other than a constable) who has the powers of a constable or is otherwise employed for police purposes or is engaged to provide services for police purposes;
(c)   a National Crime Agency officer;
(d)   a prison officer;
(e)   a person (other than a prison officer) employed or engaged to carry out functions in a custodial institution of a corresponding kind to those carried out by a prison officer;
(f)   a prisoner custody officer, so far as relating to the exercise of escort functions;
(g)   a custody officer, so far as relating to the exercise of escort functions;
(h)   a person employed for the purposes of providing, or engaged to provide, fire services or fire and rescue services;
(i)   a person employed for the purposes of providing, or engaged to provide, search services or rescue services (or both);
(j)   a person employed for the purposes of providing, or engaged to provide—
     (i)    NHS health services, or
     (ii)   services in the support of the provision of NHS health services, and whose general activities in doing so involve face to face interaction with individuals receiving the services or with other members of the public, s.3(1) and (2) of the AEW(O)A 2018.

In relation to the above list:

*custodial institution* means any of the following—

(a)   a prison;
(b)   a young offender institution, secure training centre, secure college or remand centre;
(c)   a removal centre, a short-term holding facility or pre-departure accommodation, as defined by s.147 of the IAA 1999;
(d)   services custody premises, as defined by s.300(7) of the AFA 2006;

*custody officer* has the meaning given by s.12(3) of the CJPOA 1994;

*escort functions*:

(a)   in the case of a prisoner custody officer, means the functions specified in s.80(1) of the CJA 1991;
(b)   in the case of a custody officer, means the functions specified in para.1 of Sch.1 to the CJPOA 1994;

*NHS health services* means any kind of health services provided as part of the health service continued under s.1(1) NHSA 2006 and under s.1(1) NHS(W)A

2006; prisoner custody officer has the meaning given by s.89(1) of the CJA 1991, s.3(3) of the AEW(O)A 2018.

*Acting in the exercise of functions of an emergency worker* include circumstances where the offence takes place at a time when the person is not at work but is carrying out functions which, if done in work time, would have been in the exercise of functions as an emergency worker, s.2(4) of the AEW(O)A 2018.

*Ancillary offence* means any of the following—

(a) aiding, abetting, counselling or procuring the commission of the offence;
(b) an offence under Pt 2 of the Serious Crime Act 2007 (encouraging or assisting crime) in relation to the offence;
(c) attempting or conspiring to commit the offence, s.2 of the AEW(O)A 2018.

# AGGRAVATING FACTORS: DRUG/SUBSTANCE SUPPLY

## Misuse of Drugs Act 1971 s.4 and 4A

*References: Current Sentencing Practice H3-4500 et seq.; Archbold 5A-43, 5A-44*

### Controlled Drugs

Where the court is sentencing an offender for an offence under s.4(3) of the 1971 Act (supplying, offering to supply or being concerned in the supply or offering to supply of a controlled drug), the offender was aged 18+ at the time of the offence, and either:

(a) the offence was committed on or in the vicinity of school premises at a relevant time; or

(b) in connection with the commission of the offence the offender used a courier who, at the time the offence was committed, was under the age of 18, at any time when the school premises are in use by persons aged under 18 [or] one hour before the start and one hour after the end of such time, the court must treat that fact as an aggravating factor and must state so in open court, MDA 1971 s.4A(1)–(4).

*"School premises"* means land used for the purposes of a school excluding any land occupied solely as a dwelling by a person employed at the school, MDA 1971 s.4A(8).

*"Relevant time"* means any time when the school premises are in use by persons under the age of 18 and one hour before and one hour after such time, MDA 1971 s.4A(5).

This provision applies to offences committed on or after 1 January 2006.

### Psychoactive Substances

Where the court is considering the seriousness of an offence under PSA 2016 s.5 and the offender was aged 18+ at the time of the offence; and one of the following conditions is met the court must treat the fact that the condition is met as an aggravating factor increasing the seriousness of the offence, and must state in open court that the offence is so aggravated, PSA 2016 s.6(1) and (2).

Condition A: The offence was committed on or in the vicinity of school premises at a relevant time.

Condition B: In connection with the commission of the offence the offender used a courier who, at the time the offence was committed, was under the age of 18.

Condition C: The offence was committed in a custodial institution, PSA 2016 s.6(3), (6) and (9).

[13]

*"Relevant time"* means any time when the school premises are in use by persons under the age of 18 and one hour before the start and one hour after the end of any such time, PSA 2016 s.6(4).

*"School premises"* means land used for the purposes of a school, other than any land occupied solely as a dwelling by a person employed at the school. *"School"* has the same meaning as in s.4 of the Education Act 1996, PSA 2016 s.6(5).

*"Custodial institution"* means any of the following:

(a)   a prison;

(b)   a young offender institution, secure training centre, secure college, young offender institution, young offenders centre, juvenile justice centre or remand centre;

(c)   a removal centre, a short-term holding facility or pre-departure accommodation;

(d)   service custody premises, PSA 2016 s.6 (10).

# AGGRAVATING FACTORS: SEXUAL ORIENTATION, DISABILITY OR TRANSGENDER IDENTITY

## CRIMINAL JUSTICE ACT 2003 s.146

*References: Current Sentencing Practice H3-4500; Archbold 5A-47*

### Applicability

This section does not apply to offences committed before 4 April 2005, or in respect of transgender identity to offences committed before 3 December 2012.

### Mandatory aggravating factor

If at the time of committing the offence, or immediately before or after doing so, the offender demonstrated towards the victim of the offence hostility based on either the sexual orientation (or presumed sexual orientation) of the victim, or a disability (or presumed disability) of the victim, or the victim being (or presumed to be) transgender, the court must treat that as an aggravating factor.

The same applies where the offence was motivated (wholly or partly) by hostility towards persons who are of a particular sexual orientation, or by hostility towards persons who have a disability or a particular disability, or who are transgender, CJA 2003 s.146(1) and (2).

### Duty to state in open court

In any such case, the court must state in open court that the offence was aggravated in this way, CJA 2003 s.146(3).

### Transgender

References to being transgender include references to being transsexual, or undergoing or proposing to undergo or having undergone a process or part of a process of gender reassignment, CJA 2003 s.146(6).

# AGGRAVATING FACTORS: TERRORIST CONNECTION

## COUNTER-TERRORISM ACT 2008 s.30

*References: Current Sentencing Practice H3-4500; Archbold 25-213*

### Determination that an Offence has a Terrorist Connection

**Applicability**   Where:

(a) a person is convicted of an offence listed Counter-Terrorism Act 2008 Sch.2;
(b) committed on or after 18 June 2009;
(c) the court is considering the seriousness of the offence for the purposes of sentencing; and
(d) it appears to the court that the offence has or may have a terrorist connection,

the court must determine whether the offence has a terrorist connection, CTA 2008 s.30(1) and (2).

**Determining the issue**   The court may hear evidence for the purpose of determining whether the offence has a terrorist connection, and must take account of any representations made by the prosecution and defence, and any other matter relevant for the purposes of sentence, CTA 2008 s.30(3).

**Duty to treat as aggravating factor**   If the court determines that the offence has a terrorist connection, the court must treat that fact as an aggravating factor and must state in open court that the offence was so aggravated, CTA 2008 s.30(4).

An *"ancilliary offence"* is:

(a) an offence of aiding, abetting, counselling or procuring the commission of the offence;
(b) an offence under the SCA 2007 Pt.2 in relation to the offence; or
(c) attempting or conspiring to commit the offence, CTA 2008 s.94.

**Definition: Terrorist connection**   An offence has a terrorist connection if the offence is, or takes place in the course of, an act of terrorism, or is committed for the purposes of terrorism, CTA 2008 s.93.

**Definition: Terrorism**   *"Terrorism"* means the use or threat of

(1) action where the action:
 (a) involves serious violence against a person;
 (b) involves serious damage to property;
 (c) endangers a person's life, other than that of the person who is committing the action;
 (d) creates a serious risk to the health or safety of the public or a section of the public; or

[17]

(e)   is designed seriously to interfere with or seriously to disrupt an electronic system; and

(2)   the use or threat is designed to influence the government or to intimidate the public or a section of the public; and

(3)   the use or threat is made for the purpose of advancing a political, religious, racial or ideological cause, CTA 2008 s.92 and TA 2000 s.1(1).

The use or threat of action falling within (1) above which involves the use of firearms or explosives is terrorism whether or not the requirement at (2) is satisfied, TA 2000 s.1(3) and CTA 2008 s.92.

*"Action"* includes action outside the United Kingdom, a reference to *"any person or to property"* is a reference to any person, or to property, wherever situated, a reference to *"the public"* includes a reference to the public of a country other than the United Kingdom, and *"the government"* means the government of the United Kingdom, of a part of the United Kingdom or of a country other than the United Kingdom. A reference to *"action taken for the purposes of terrorism"* includes a reference to action taken for the benefit of a proscribed organisation, CTA 2008 s.92 and TA 2000 s.1(4).

**Notification Requirements**

**Applicability**   Notification requirements apply to a person who:

(a)   has been convicted of an offence to which CTA 2008 Pt.4 applies; and

(b)   was aged 16 or over when sentenced; and

(c)   has been sentenced to:
   (i)     imprisonment or custody for life;
   (ii)    imprisonment or detention in a young offender institution for a term of 12 months or more;
   (iii)   IPP/DPP under CJA 2003 s.225;
   (iv)    detention for life or for a period of 12 months or more under PCC(S)A 2000 s.91;
   (v)     a DTO for a term of 12 months or more under PCC(S)A 2000 s.100;
   (vi)    DPP under CJA 2003 s.226; or
   (vii)   an extended sentence of detention under CJA 2003 s.226B;
   (viii)  detention during Her Majesty's pleasure, CTA 2008 s.44 and 45(1).

Notification requirements also apply to a person who has been:

(a)   convicted of an offence to which CTA 2008 Pt.4 applies which carries a maximum term of imprisonment of 12 months or more;

(b)   found not guilty by reason of insanity of such an offence; or

(c)   found to be under a disability and to have done the act charged against them in respect of such an offence, and made subject in respect of the offence to a hospital order, CTA 2008 s.44 and 45(2).

No express provision is made for suspended sentence orders, however sexual offenders notification applies to suspended sentence orders and so it may be that terrorist notification is interpreted in the same way.

**Offences to which CTA 2008 Pt.4 applies**

(1) TA 2000 ss.11, 12, 15-18, 38B, 54, 56-61 and an offence in respect of which there is jurisdiction by virtue of ss.62-63D;
(2) ATCSA 2001 s.113;
(3) TA 2006 ss.1,2, 5, 6, 8-11 and an offence in respect of which there is jurisdiction by virtue of s.17;
(4) any ancillary offence in relation to an offence listed in (1)-(3) above.
    An "*ancillary offence*" is:
  (a) an offence of aiding, abetting, counselling or procuring the commission of the offence;
  (b) an offence under the SCA 2007 Pt.2 in relation to the offence; or
  (c) attempting or conspiring to commit the offence, CTA 2008 s.94.
(5) offences as to which a court has determined the offence had a terrorist connection, CTA 2008 s.94.

**The notification periods**  The period for which the notification requirements apply are as follows, CTA 2008 s.53.

| | |
|---|---|
| Offender aged 18 at the time of conviction and sentenced to an indeterminate sentence or a determinate sentence of 10 years or more | 30 years |
| Offender aged 18 at the time of conviction and sentenced to a term of at least 5 years but less than 10 years | 15 years |
| All other cases | 10 years |

**Must notify defendant**  The court must tell the defendant that notification requirements apply, and under which legislation, CPR 2014 r.42.3.

**When does notification begin?**  The notification period begins on the day the person is dealt with for the offence, CTA 2008 s.53(4).

**When does notification expire?**  In determining whether the notification period has expired, any period when the person was in custody on remand or serving a sentence or imprisonment or detention, or detained in a hospital, or under the Immigration Acts is disregarded, CTA 2008 53(7).

**Appeals**  A person who becomes liable to notification requirements may appeal against the determination that the offence has a terrorist connection as if that determination was a sentence, CTA 2003 s.42(2).

# ALTERATION OF SENTENCE (VARYING/RESCINDING A SENTENCE)

## PCC(S)A 2000 s.155; MAGISTRATES' COURTS ACT 1980 s.142

*References: Current Sentencing Practice H4-350; Archbold 5A-1228*

### General

As a general rule, the power to vary a sentence should be exercised only in open court and in the presence of the offender after hearing their counsel, who should be advised of the nature of the alteration which the court proposes to make, *May* 3 Cr.App.R. (S.) 165. The case must be properly listed so that all interested parties may attend, *Perkins* [2013] EWCA Crim 323, [2013] 2 Cr.App.R. (S.) 72.

### Crown Court

**Power**   The Crown Court may vary or rescind a sentence which it has imposed or an order which it has made, within specified time limits, PCC(S) A 2000 s.155(1). The power may not be exercised in relation to any sentence or order if an appeal, or an application for leave to appeal, against that sentence or order has been determined, PCC(S)A 2000 s.155(1A).

**Same judge must alter/vary/rescind**   The Crown Court must be constituted as it was when the original sentence was imposed or order was made, except that if the court included one or more justices of the peace, one or all of them may be omitted, PCC(S)A 2000 s.155(4).

**Time limit**   The time limit for the Crown Court is 56 days beginning with the day on which the sentence was imposed or the order was made. Where orders have been made on different dates in respect of the same conviction the period of 56 days begins to run on the day on which the particular order which it is proposed to vary was made, PCC(S)A 2000 s.155(1).

The relevant time limit must be strictly observed, *Commissioners of Customs and Excise v Menocal* [1980] A.C. 598.

There is no power to extend the time limit, *AG's Ref (No.79 of 2015) (Nguyen)* [2016] EWCA Crim 448.

**Adjournments**   If the Crown Court rescinds a sentence within the permitted period for variation or rescission, without imposing a further sentence, it may adjourn sentence for such period as may be appropriate, without regard to the time limit, *Gordon* [2007] EWCA Crim 165, [2007] 2 Cr.App.R. (S.) 66.

**General approach**   The general state of the law is as follows:

(a)   where an error had occurred in the factual basis of sentence, this should be pointed out to the court as soon as possible and consideration should be given to correcting this at the earliest opportunity, preferably by revisiting sentence on the same day rather than on a subsequent day;

(b)   a judge should not use the slip rule simply because there was a change of mind about the nature or length of sentence but the slip rule was available where the judge was persuaded that he had made a material error in the sentencing process whether of fact or of law. It was relevant in considering whether or not he had made a material error that the error might be corrected by the Court of Appeal on the Attorney General's application;

(c)   the sooner the slip rule was invoked in such a case the better. The passage of time from the first decision to its revision was a material consideration as to how the power should be exercised (but there was a 56-day cut off in any event);

(d)   a judge should not be unduly influenced by the prospect of a reference being made to change a sentence that he thought was right at the time by the mere threat of a review by the Attorney General. If the judge concluded that the sentence was not wrong in principle and was not unduly lenient, he should not change his mind simply because there was the possibility of a reference. The judge could then use the opportunity at the further sentencing hearing to give any further explanations for the original decision for the sentence;

(e)   sentencing and re-sentencing should take place in the presence of the appellant and administrative convenience should not be allowed to degrade that principle. But, if for one reason or another, the appellant could not be brought to court within the 56-day period, there was a discretion to proceed in his absence so long as there was an advocate who could fully represent the appellant in the sense of who was properly instructed as to the relevant facts and was able to assist the court to make pertinent submissions on the facts and the law (as clearly W's advocate was able to do on the date of the re-sentence); and

(f)   although *Nodjoumi* no longer identified the basic rule in such cases, the appearance of justice and the impact of the change on a defendant where an error had not been induced by anything that he had said or done were relevant considerations and, in appropriate cases, could be reflected in a modest discount to the proposed revised sentence to reflect that fact, see *Warren* [2017] EWCA Crim 226, [2017] 2 Cr.App.R. (S.) 2.

A variation is permissible where a judge concludes on reflection, not merely that he or she wishes to be more punitive or more lenient, but that the approach taken in a sentence was wrong in principle, indeed wrong as to an important aspect of sentence, such as the protection of the public, *O'Connor* [2018] EWCA Crim 1417.

**Nature of variation**   The power is not limited to the correction of slips of the tongue or minor errors made when sentence was originally passed.

There is no restriction on the nature of the variation in sentence which may be made. In appropriate circumstances the court may substitute a sentence or order which is more severe than the sentence originally passed, *Commissioners of Customs and Excise v Menocal* [1980] A.C. 598. See **Judge considers original sentence too lenient**, below.

Where a sentence has been imposed on the basis of a factual error, the sentence may be increased, *Warren* [2017] EWCA Crim 226, [2017] 2 Cr.App.R. (S.) 2.

**Varying the sentence outside the permitted period**

Where a sentence has been passed or order made which is defective in form, it may be permissible to correct the error after the expiration of the relevant time limit, so long as the correction can be treated as a matter of form rather than substance, *Saville* [1981] Q.B. 12.

The scope of the power to vary a sentence outside of the statutory period appears to have been narrowed by *D* [2015] 1 Cr.App.R. (S.) 23, in which the Court of Appeal held that a judge had not been entitled to vary an extended sentence to correct a defect in the way in which the sentence had been articulated, notwithstanding the fact that the defendant would not have been adversely affected by the variation.

**Magistrates' Court**

**Power**  A magistrates' court may vary or rescind a sentence or order at any time after the sentence has been passed or the order made, unless the Crown Court or the High Court has determined an appeal against the sentence or the conviction on which it is based, MCA 1980 s.142(1) and (1A).

**Time limit**  There is no time limit for magistrates' courts, see e.g. *Holmes v Liverpool City Justices* [2004] EWHC 3131 (Admin).

**Particular Situations**

**Bogus mitigation**  Where the court has been persuaded to pass a particular form of sentence, or a sentence of a particular length, on the basis of the existence of specific mitigating factors, the court may review the sentence and substitute a more severe sentence if it subsequently appears that the court has been misled and that the mitigating factors did not exist, *McLean* 10 Cr.App.R. (S.) 18. Such a decision should not be made without proper inquiry and giving the offender an opportunity to dispute the allegation that he has deceived the court, *Tout* 15 Cr.App.R. (S.) 30.

**Judge considers original sentence too lenient**  The court may increase a sentence merely where it considers that the original sentence was providing considerations of fairness to the defendant and public interest in passing an appropriate, lawful sentence had to be weighed, *G* [2016] EWCA Crim 541. As to this "*flexible*" approach, see also *Jama* [2009] EWCA Crim 2109. There is no objection to reducing a sentence because on second thoughts it appears to have been too severe.

**Misbehaviour in the dock**  It is wrong to vary a sentence which has been passed on the ground that the offender has reacted to the sentence by misbehaving in the dock and addressing abusive comments to the judge or other persons present, *Powell* (1985) 7 Cr.App.R. (S.) 247.

**Part of sentencing postponed**  Where the Crown Court passes part of a sentence and expressly postpones passing some other part of the sentence, the time limits do not apply, see **ADJOURNMENT—POST CONVICTION**, p.3.

**Multiple variations**  It is not clear whether a sentence which has been varied once can be varied a second time.

# ANTECEDENT STATEMENTS

## CDP [2015] EWCA Crim 1567 Preliminary Proceedings 8A

*References: See Archbold 5A-6*

### Copies of record

8A.1 The defendant's record (previous convictions, cautions, reprimands, etc) may be taken into account when the court decides not only on sentence but also, for example, about bail, or when allocating a case for trial. It is therefore important that up-to-date and accurate information is available. Previous convictions must be provided as part of the initial details of the prosecution case under CPR Pt.8.

8A.2 The record should usually be provided in the following format: Personal details and summary of convictions and cautions — Police National Computer ["*PNC*"] Court / Defence / Probation Summary Sheet; Previous convictions — PNC Court / Defence / Probation printout, supplemented by Form MG16 if the police force holds convictions not shown on PNC; Recorded cautions — PNC Court / Defence / Probation printout, supplemented by Form MG17 if the police force holds cautions not shown on PNC.

8A.3 The defence representative should take instructions on the defendant's record and if the defence wish to raise any objection to the record, this should be made known to the prosecutor immediately.

8A.4 It is the responsibility of the prosecutor to ensure that a copy of the defendant's record has been provided to the Probation Service.

8A.5 Where following conviction a custodial order is made, the court must ensure that a copy is attached to the order sent to the prison.

### Additional information

8A.6 In the Crown Court, the police should also provide brief details of the circumstances of the last three similar convictions and/or of convictions likely to be of interest to the court, the latter being judged on a case-by-case basis.

8A.7 Where the current alleged offence could constitute a breach of an existing sentence such as a suspended sentence, community order or conditional discharge, and it is known that that sentence is still in force then details of the circumstances of the offence leading to the sentence should be included in the antecedents. The detail should be brief and include the date of the offence.

8A.8 On occasions the PNC printout provided may not be fully up to date. It is the responsibility of the prosecutor to ensure that all of the necessary information is available to the court and the Probation Service and provided to the defence. Oral updates at the hearing will sometimes be necessary, but it is preferable if this information is available in advance.

# APPEALS

*References: Current Sentencing Practice G1; Archbold 7-119*

## From the Magistrates' Court

**Right to appeal**  There is a right of appeal to the Crown Court. The hearing takes the form of a re-hearing. The Crown Court may therefore impose a sentence greater than that imposed by the magistrates' court, MCA 1980 s.108(1) and SCA 1981 ss.48 and 79.

**Time limits**  The notice of appeal must be served within 21 days of the sentence. Extensions of time may be sought and must be supported by reasons, CPR 2015 r.34.2.

**Powers**  On appeal the Crown Court may confirm, reverse or vary the decision appealed against any part of the decision appealed against, including a determination not to impose a separate penalty in respect of an offence, may remit the matter with its opinion, or make any order the magistrates' court could have made, SCA 1981 s.48(1) and (5).

## From the Crown Court

**Applications for leave**  An appeal notice must be in the form specified in the Criminal Practice Directions, see CPR 2015 r.39.3.

It is not possible to appeal against the mandatory life sentence for murder. It is however possible to appeal against the length of the minimum term, CAA 1968 s.9(1) and (1A).

The single judge may give leave on limited grounds or against part of a sentence only. See *Hyde* [2016] EWCA Crim 1031; [2016] 2 Cr.App.R. (S.) 39 for guidance given by the court on the proper approach to a consideration of applications for leave to appeal.

**CACD targets**  The following target times are set for the hearing of appeals. Target times will run from the receipt of the appeal by the Registrar, as being ready for hearing:

| Nature of appeal | From receipt by listing officer to fixing of hearing date | From fixing of hearing date to hearing | Total time from receipt by listing officer to hearing |
|---|---|---|---|
| Sentence Appeal | 14 days | 14 days | 28 days |
| Conviction Appeal | 21 days | 42 days | 63 days |

| Nature of appeal | From receipt by listing officer to fixing of hearing date | From fixing of hearing date to hearing | Total time from receipt by listing officer to hearing |
|---|---|---|---|
| Conviction Appeal where witness to attend | 28 days | 52 days | 80 days |

**Time limits**   Notice of appeal is to be given within 28 days from the date on which the sentence is passed, CAA 1968 s.18(1) and (2).

Extensions of time may be sought and it is the practice of the Registrar to require an application for an extension of time to be made when submitting the notice of appeal. The application for an extension of time must always be supported by reasons why the notice was not submitted within the time limit, *Guide to Commencing Proceedings in the Court of Appeal* para.A3-3.

**Test and powers**   On an appeal against sentence the Court of Appeal, if they consider that the appellant should be sentenced differently for an offence for which he was dealt with by the court below may—

(a)   quash any sentence or order which is the subject of the appeal; and
(b)   in place of it pass such sentence or make such order as they think appropriate for the case and as the court below had power to pass or make when dealing with him for the offence;

but the Court shall so exercise their powers under this subsection that, taking the case as a whole, the appellant is not more severely dealt with on appeal than he was dealt with by the court below, CAA 1968 s.11(3).

*Note: In practice the court considers whether or not the sentence is wrong in principle or manifestly excessive.*

The court has the power to re-open an appeal in order to correct an error that led to the quashing of a sentence which had in fact been lawfully imposed in circumstances where at the appeal hearing the court had proceeded on the basis of a factual error, *Yasain* [2015] EWCA Crim 1277; [2016] 1 Cr.App.R. (S.) 7.

The jurisdiction identified in *Yasain* is very limited and is not available in cases where it is alleged that the proper construction of the legislation was misunderstood and has been recognised as having been misunderstood in subsequent litigation.

The appropriate procedure (until the CPR makes provision) is:

(i)   If a party (whether prosecutor or defendant) wishes the Court of Appeal (Criminal Division) to re-open a final determination of the court based on the implicit jurisdiction identified in *Yasain* it must:
(a)   apply in writing for permission to re-open the decision, as soon as practicable after becoming aware of the grounds for doing so; and
(b)   serve the application on the Registrar and all other parties to the proceedings.

(ii)    The application must specify the decision which the applicant wishes to re-open and provide reasons identifying:

    (a)  the circumstances which make it necessary for the court to re-open that decision in order to avoid real injustice;

    (b)  what makes those circumstances exceptional and thus appropriate for the decision to be re-opened notwithstanding the interests of other parties to the proceedings and the importance of finality;

    (c)  an explanation and reasons for the absence of any alternative effective remedy and for any lapse of time in making the application having discovered the facts which form the grounds for so doing.

(iii)    On receipt of an effective application, the Registrar will refer the application to the full court for determination on paper. There is no right to an oral hearing unless the full court so directs.

(iv)    The court must not give permission to re-open a final determination unless each other party to the proceedings has had an opportunity to make representations. In making any such representations, the prosecution has a duty to obtain the views of any victim or the family of such a victim, *Hockey* [2017] EWCA Crim 742.

**Function of the court**    The Court of Appeal (Criminal Division) is, in relation to sentencing, a court of review. Its function is to review sentences passed below and not to conduct a sentencing hearing. However, it is also clear that s.23 permits the court to receive fresh evidence on appeal against sentence, provided the conditions set out in the section are met. There are circumstances where the court will consider updates to information placed before the sentencing judge without the conditions in s.23 being applied, but otherwise s.23 is of general application to all sentencing appeals, *Rogers* [2016] EWCA Crim 801; [2016] 2 Cr.App.R. (S.) 36.

**Updated information not before sentencing judge**    Exceptions to s.23 will include updated pre-sentence and prison reports on conduct in prison after sentence, but not fresh psychiatric or psychological evidence in support of an argument that a finding of dangerousness ought not to have been made or a hospital order should have been made, *Rogers* [2016] EWCA Crim 801; [2016] 2 Cr.App.R. (S.) 36.

**Loss of time**    Both the court and the single judge have power, in their discretion under ss.29 and 31 of the CAA 1968 to direct that part of the time during which an applicant is in custody after lodging his notice of application for leave to appeal should not count towards sentence, *CPD* 2015 (Loss of time) 39E.1.

**Prohibition on dealing with appellant more severely**    On appeal against sentence, a defendant may not be dealt with more severely than he was dealt with at the Crown Court, CAA 1968 s.11(3).

In *Thompson* [2018] EWCA Crim 639; [2018] 2 Cr.App.R. (S.) 19 (five-judge court) the court observed that the limit of the power on appeal was that the court had to be satisfied that, taking the case as a whole, an appellant was not being dealt with more severely on appeal. That required a detailed consideration of the impact of the sentence to be imposed in substitution for the original sentence, which had to involve considerations of entitlement to automatic release, parole eligibility and licence. If a custodial sentence was reduced, the addition of non-custodial orders (such as disqualification from driving or sexual offences prevention orders) might be considered but, in every case, save where the substituted sentence was "ameliorative and remedial", that sentence had to be tested for its severity (or potential punitive effect) when compared to the original sentence. For further discussion, see [2018] Crim. L.R. 593 and *Archbold Review* 2018 (7) 4-7.

# ASSISTING THE PROSECUTION ("INFORMANTS")

SERIOUS ORGANISED CRIME AND POLICE ACT 2005 s.73

*References: Current Sentencing Practice H3-1550 et seq.; Archbold 5A-91*

## General

A sentencing court may make a reduction in sentence to reflect assistance provided or offered in relation to his offence or other offences.

In *Z* [2015] EWCA Crim 1427; [2016] 1 Cr.App.R. (S.) 15, the court declined to alter the common law principle that an offender's sentence could not be discounted for assistance given to the police to enable a reduction to be made for assistance given post-sentence.

Material assistance to the prosecution leading to the apprehension and conviction of an offender in circumstances where the conviction concerned an offence where the defendant was a victim might merit a reduction in sentence, *Campbell* [2018] EWCA Crim 802; [2018] 2 Cr.App.R. (S.) 24.

## Written Agreements (The Statutory Scheme)

**Availability**   Where a defendant who has pleaded guilty in proceedings in the Crown Court, or who has been committed to the Crown Court for sentence following a plea of guilty, has entered a written agreement with a specified prosecutor, to assist or offered to assist the investigator or prosecutor in relation to the offence to which he has pleaded guilty or any other offence, the provisions of s.73 apply, SOCPA 2005 73(1).

The reference to *"imprisonment"* in s.73 includes a reference to any custodial sentence within the meaning of PCC(S)A 2000 s.76, notably detention under PCC(S)A 2000 s.90 or 91, an extended sentence under CJA 2003 s.226B, custody for life, detention in a YOI and a detention and training order.

**Procedure**   The discount for assistance provided should be calculated first, against all other relevant considerations, and the notional sentence so achieved should be further discounted by the guilty plea, *P* [2007] EWCA Crim 2290; [2008] 2 Cr.App.R. (S.) 5.

**The level of the reduction**   The court may take into account the extent and nature of the assistance given or offered in determining what sentence to pass, SOCPA 2005 s.73(2).

**General principles**   The Court of Appeal has set down some general principles relating to the reduction:

(a)   no hard and fast rules can be laid down as to what, as in so many other aspects of sentencing, is a fact-specific decision;

[31]

(b)   the first factor is the criminality of the defendant, thereafter, the quality and quantity of the material provided by the defendant will be considered;

(c)   a mathematical approach is liable to produce an inappropriate answer; the totality principle is fundamental;

(d)   only in the most exceptional case will the discount exceed 3/4 of the total sentence;

(e)   the normal level continues to be between 1/2 and 2/3, *P* [2007] EWCA Crim 2290; [2008] 2 Cr.App.R. (S.) 5.

The extent to which the assistance given or offered may affect the sentence is a matter within the discretion of the sentencing court.

**Judge must state reduction given**   If the court passes a sentence which is less than it would otherwise have passed, the court must state in open court that it has passed a lesser sentence than it would otherwise have passed, and what the greater sentence would have been, SOCPA 2005 s.73(3). This obligation does not apply if the court thinks that it would not be in the public interest to disclose that the sentence has been discounted. Where no statement is made in open court, the court must give written notice of the fact that it has passed a lesser sentence, and what the greater sentence would have been, to the prosecutor and to the defendant, SOCPA 2005 s.73(4). Where the duty under subs.(3) does not apply, the duty under CJA 2003 s.174(1)(a) and 270 do no apply to the extent that the explanation will disclose that a discount has been given pursuant to a formal agreement, SOCPA 2005 s.73(8).

**Minimum sentences**   Nothing in any enactment which requires that a *"minimum sentence"* is passed in respect of any offence or an offence of any description or by reference to the circumstances of any offender affects the power of a court to take into account the extent and nature of the assistance given or offered, SOCPA 2005 s.73(5).

**Murder**   In a case of murder, nothing in any enactment which requires the court to take into account *"certain matters"* for the purposes of making an order which determines or has the effect of determining the minimum period of imprisonment which the offender must serve affects the power of the court to take into account the extent and nature of the assistance given or offered, SOCPA 2005 s.73(5).

**Additional mitigation**   Taking account of the assistance given by a defendant does not prevent the court from also taking account of any other matter which it is entitled by virtue of any other enactment to take account of for the purposes of determining the sentence or in the case of a sentence which is fixed by law, any minimum period of imprisonment which an offender must serve, SOCPA 2005 s.73(6).

**Review of sentence**   The review of sentence procedure applies where a defendant has been sentenced in the Crown Court, and:

(a)   has received a discounted sentence after having made a written agreement to give assistance to the prosecutor or investigator of an offence, but has knowingly failed *"to any extent"* to give assistance in accordance with the agreement;

(b)   has received a discounted sentence as a consequence of having made a written agreement, and having given the assistance in accordance with the agreement, in pursuance of another written agreement gives or offers to give further assistance; or

(c) has received a sentence which was not discounted but in pursuance of a written agreement he subsequently gives or offers to give assistance, a specified prosecutor may refer the case back to the court if the person concerned is still serving their sentence, and the prosecutor thinks that it is in the interest of justice to do so, SOCPA 2005 s.74(1) and (2).

Where an offender who has pleaded guilty to murder offers or gives assistance after sentence, the case may be referred if the prosecutor chooses to do so, SOCPA 2005 s.74 (13).

The case so referred must if possible be heard by the judge who passed the original sentence, SOCPA 2005 s.74(4).

If the court is "*satisfied*" that a person whose sentence has been discounted has "*knowingly failed to give the assistance*", it may substitute for the sentence which has been referred "*such greater sentence*" as it thinks appropriate, provided that the new sentence does not exceed the sentence which it would have passed if the agreement had not been made, SOCPA 2005 s.74(5).

On such a reference, the court may take into account the extent and nature of the assistance given or offered (under (b) or (c) above), and substitute for the original sentence "*such lesser sentence as it thinks appropriate*", SOCPA 2005 s.74(6).

The requirement to state the level of reduction specified in s.73 (see above) applies to reviews under s.74, as does the "*public interest*" exception in relation to CJA 2003 s.174(1)(a) and 270, SOCPA 2005 s.74(14) and (15).

Consideration of the interests of justice in that context involved an open-ended deliberation. Section 74(3) imposes no explicit constraint on how the specified prosecutor should approach the question and there was no warrant for implying a fetter on the exercise of the unrestricted discretion for which the statute clearly provided. It was not difficult to envisage a wide range of factors beyond the question of whether or not circumstances had changed that might be pivotal in deciding if the original sentence should be referred back to the court that imposed it, see *Re Loughlin* [2017] UKSC 63; [2018] 1 Cr.App.R. (S.) 21.

**Appealing a review**    A person in respect of whom a reference is made under s.74 and the specified prosecutor may with the leave of the Court of Appeal appeal to the Court of Appeal against the decision of the Crown Court, SOCPA 2005 s.74(8).

The procedure and powers of the Court of Appeal are governed by SI 2006/2135.

**Excluding the public/publicity restrictions**    On the hearing of a reference, or any other proceedings arising in consequence of a reference, the court may exclude from the proceedings anyone other than an officer of the court, a party to the proceedings or legal representatives of the parties, and may give such directions as it thinks appropriate prohibiting the publication of any matter relating to the proceedings, including the fact that the reference has been made, SOCPA 2005 s.75(1) and (2).

Such an order may be made only to the extent that it is necessary to do so to protect the safety of any person, and is in the interests of justice, SOCPA 2005 s.75(3).

## The "Text" Regime

**Assistance provided outside the statutory scheme**　The statutory provisions do not replace the conventional practice by which a defendant who is unable or unwilling to enter onto a written agreement may ask the prosecuting or investigating body to produce a "*text*" setting out the details of the assistance or information provided by the defendant. In such cases, the court may discount the sentence imposed upon the defendant. For details of the "*text*" procedure, see *X* [1999] 2 Cr.App.R. (S.) 294 and *R* [2002] EWCA Crim 267.

**Contents**　A text will set out:

(i)　　the offender's status and whether he is a Covert Human Intelligence Source (CHIS)[1] under the Regulation of Investigatory Powers Act 2000;

(ii)　　the details of the assistance provided, the information or intelligence provided and whether he is willing to be a witness;

(iii)　　the effort to which the offender had gone to obtain the information;

(iv)　　any risk to the offender or his family;

(v)　　an assessment of the benefit derived by the police, including any arrests or convictions or any property recovered;

(vi)　　any financial reward the offender has already received for the assistance provided;

(vii)　　a statement as to whether the offender will be of future use to the police, *AXN and ZAR* [2016] EWCA Crim 590; [2016] 2 Cr.App.R. (S.) 33.

**General principles**　As summarised in *X* [1999] 2 Cr.App.R. (S.) 294:

(i)　　the text is supplied by the police at the request of the offender;

(ii)　　without confirmation by the police, an offender's statement that he has provided assistance is unlikely to be of assistance;

(iii)　　as the courts rely so heavily on police confirmation, the greatest care has to be exercised by the police in the provision of the information;

(iv)　　absent issues of Public Interest Immunity, the text should be shown to counsel for the defence who can discuss it with the offender;

(v)　　there should normally be no question of evidence being given or an issue tried about it. If the offender disagreed, then questioning of the police officer would almost inevitably be contrary to the public interest.

**Extent of discount**　The extent of the discount will ordinarily depend on the value of the help given and expected to be given. Value is a function of quality and quantity. If the information given is unreliable, vague, lacking in practical utility or already known to the authorities, no identifiable discount may be given or, if

---

[1]　　Under RIPA 2000, a person is a "CHIS" if:

(a)　he establishes or maintains a personal or other relationship with a person for the covert purpose of facilitating the doing of anything falling within paragraph b) or c);

(b)　he covertly uses such a relationship to obtain information or to provide access to any information to another person; or

(c)　he covertly discloses information obtained by the use of such a relationship or as a consequence of the existence of such a relationship. Source: CHIS Code of Practice, 2010.

given, any discount will be minimal. If the information given is accurate, particularised, useful in practice, and hitherto unknown to the authorities, enabling serious criminal activity to be stopped and serious criminals brought to book, the discount may be substantial. Hence little or no credit will be given for the supply of a mass of information which is worthless or virtually so, but the greater the supply of good quality information the greater in the ordinary way the discount will be. Where, by supplying valuable information to the authorities, a defendant exposes him/herself or his/her family to personal jeopardy, it will ordinarily be recognised in the sentence passed. For all these purposes, account will be taken of help given and reasonably expected to be given in the future, *A* [1999] 1 Cr.App.R.(S.) 52.

A large-scale police informer can expect a reduction in his proper sentence from about one-half to two-thirds according to the circumstances of the case, but no hard and fast rule can be laid down. The amount of the reduction will depend on a number of variables, such as the quality and quantity of the information, its accuracy, the informer's willingness to confront other criminals or give evidence against them, and the degree of risk of reprisal to himself and his family. The defendant could then expect a substantial mitigation to produce the information, varying from about one-half to two-thirds reduction, according to the circumstances, in what would otherwise be the proper sentence, *King* (1986) 82 Cr.App.R. 120; (1985) 7 Cr.App.R. (S.) 227.

**Information given post-sentence**   Since the Court of Appeal is a court of review, however, assistance given to the police or the Crown post-sentence would normally be too late, subject to certain exceptions, *Emsden* [2015] EWCA Crim 2092; [2016] 1 Cr.App.R. (S.) 62.

**Taking account of information on appeal**   Where assistance has been given by an offender but, by some oversight or misadventure, the judge was unaware of this, the Court of Appeal would consider mitigation which should have been before the Crown Court, *H* [2009] EWCA Crim 2485; [2010] 2 Cr.App.R. (S.) 18 (p.104).

For further details of the "*text*" procedure, see *X* [1999] 2 Cr.App.R. (S.) 294 and *R* [2002] EWCA Crim 267.

As to the obligation of the authorities to provide a text, and the safeguards in place where an offender believes the context of a text is incorrect, see *AXN and ZAR* [2016] EWCA Crim 590; [2016] 2 Cr.App.R. (S.) 33.

# ATTENDANCE CENTRE ORDERS

## PCC(S)A 2000 s.60

*References: Current Sentencing Practice B4-350*

### General

This order used to be available upon conviction, but following a statutory repeal (effective from 30 November 2009) it is now available only in limited circumstances.

### Making the Order

**Availability**    PCC(S)A 2000 s.60(1) Where:

(a)    [*repealed*];

(b)    a court would have power, but for s.89 below (restrictions on imprisonment of young offenders and defaulters), to commit a person aged under 21 to prison in default of payment of any sum of money or for failing to do or abstain from doing anything required to be done or left undone; or

(c)    a court has power to commit a person aged at least 21 but under 25 to prison in default of payment of any sum of money, the court may, if it has been notified by the Secretary of State that an attendance centre is available for the reception of persons of his description, order him to attend at such a centre, to be specified in the order, for such number of hours as may be so specified.

Additionally, those in contempt of court where it appears to the court they are aged 17 or over may be made subject to an attendance centre order, CCA 1981 s.14(2A).

**The order**    The court may order the individual to attend at such a centre, to be specified in the order, for such number of hours as may be so specified, PCC(S)A 2000 s.60(1).

**Order already in place**    An attendance centre order may be made even though the offender is still subject to an existing attendance centre order, PCC(S)A 2000 s.60(5).

### Setting the Number of Hours

**Under 14**    An attendance centre order is normally for 12 hours. The court may specify less than 12 hours if the offender is under the age of 14 and the court considers that 12 hours would be excessive, having regard to his age and any other circumstances, PCC(S)A 2000 s.60(3).

**Under 16**    The court may specify more than 12 hours if the court considers that 12 hours would be inadequate. If the offender is under 16 the maximum number of hours is 24. If the offender is over 16 the maximum number of hours is 36, PCC(S)A 2000 s.60(4).

**Aged 16–25**   The court must not make an attendance centre order unless it is satisfied that the attendance centre to be specified is reasonably accessible to the person concerned, having regard to his age, the means of access available to him, and any other circumstances.

The court cannot require an individual to attend an attendance centre on more than one occasion per day and for more than three hours on any occasion, PCC(S)A 2000 s.60(10).

**Avoid conflict with school/work/religious beliefs**   The times at which the offender is required to attend shall be such as to avoid interference, so far as is practicable, with the offender's school hours or working hours, PCC(S)A 2000 s.60(7).

### Breach

**Further offence**   Commission of an offence while subject to an attendance centre order does not give rise to any power in respect of the attendance centre order.

**Magistrates' court**   Breach of the requirements of an attendance centre order enables a magistrates' court to:

(a)   impose a fine not exceeding £1,000;
(b)   where the original order was made by a magistrates' court, resentence for the original offence (magistrates' court powers apply);
(c)   where the original order was made by the Crown Court, commit him to custody or release him on bail until he can be brought before the Crown Court, PCC(S)A 2000 Sch.5 para.2(1).

**Crown Court**   Breach of the requirements of an attendance centre order enables a Crown Court to:

(d)   deal with him in any way he could have been dealt with for the original offence;
(e)   revoke the order;
(f)   where the individual has wilfully and persistently failed to comply the court may;
(g)   impose a custodial sentence, PCC(S)A 2000 Sch.5 para.3.

# ATTORNEY GENERAL'S REFERENCES

*References: Current Sentencing Practice G2; Archbold 7-437*

## General

**Function**   The function of s.36 of the 1988 Act is not to provide a general right of appeal to the prosecution. It is a means of ensuring by judicious selection of cases, that issues of principle in relation to sentencing can be resolved, and sentences corrected, in cases where public confidence in sentencing could otherwise be undermined, *Reynolds* [2007] EWCA Crim 538; [2007] 2 Cr.App.R. (S.) 87.

**Availability**   If it appears to the Attorney General:

(a)   that the sentencing of a person in a proceeding in the Crown Court has been unduly lenient; and
(b)   that the case is one to which this Part of this Act applies, he may, with the leave of the Court of Appeal, refer the case to them for them to review the sentencing of that person, CJA 1988 s.36(1).

   *"Unduly lenient"* includes a situation where in the view of the Attorney General a judge has:

(a)   erred in law as to his powers of sentencing; or
(b)   failed to impose a sentence required by—
   (i)     ss.1(2B) or 1A(5) of the Prevention of Crime Act 1953;
   (ii)    is susceptible to treatment, but does not warrant his detention under a hospital order;
   (iii)   s.51A(2) of the Firearms Act 1968;
   (iv)    ss.139(6B), 139A(5B) or 139AA(7) of the Criminal Justice Act 1988;
   (v)     ss.110(2) or s.111(2) of the Powers of Criminal Courts (Sentencing) Act 2000;
   (vi)    ss.224A, s.225(2) or s.226(2) of the Criminal Justice Act 2003; or
   (vii)   s.29(4) or (6) of the Violent Crime Reduction Act 2006, CJA 1988 s.36(2).

**Cases to which the scheme applies**   The AG may seek leave to refer the sentence(s) imposed in a limited class of case only. For the list of cases to which the ULS scheme applies, see p.373.

**Deferred sentences**   A deferred sentence may be referred by the Attorney General under the unduly lenient sentence scheme, *AG's Ref. (No.22 of 1992)* (1993) 14 Cr.App.R. (S.) 435.

**Time limits**   Notice of an application for leave to refer a case to the Court of Appeal under s.36 above shall be given within 28 days from the day on which the sentence, or the last of the sentences, in the case was passed, Sch.3 CJA 1988 Sch.3 para.1.

The day on which the sentence was passed does not count for this purpose, *AG's Ref No.112 of 2002* [2003] EWCA Crim 676.

An application to the Court of Appeal for leave to refer a case to the Supreme Court under s.36(5) above shall be made within the period of 14 days beginning with the date on which the Court of Appeal conclude their review of the case; and an application to the Supreme Court for leave shall be made within the period of 14 days beginning with the date on which the Court of Appeal conclude their review or refuse leave to refer the case to the Supreme Court, CJA 1988 Sch.3 para.4.

### Pre-hearing Matters

***Goodyear* indications**   The advocate is personally responsible for ensuring that his client fully appreciates that any sentence indication given by the judge remains subject to the entitlement of the Attorney General (where it arises) to refer an unduly lenient sentence to the Court of Appeal, *Goodyear* [2005] EWCA Crim 888; [2006] 1 Cr.App.R. (S.) 6.

**Registrar writes to sentencing judge**   The standard letter makes plain that it is not for the judge to comment generally on the Attorney General's application. It invites the sentencing judge to provide any information which will not be apparent from the papers and the transcript. One example might be where a *"text"* has been placed before the judge. The Registrar will then consider whether any further such information needs to be placed before the court and counsel. The letter makes clear that it is not permissible for a judge to add to his sentencing remarks. Assistance sought is limited to information of which the judge was aware but which is not before the court, *AG's Ref (Bailey)* [2018] EWCA Crim 1640.

### The Hearing

**Electronic service**   Service of the notification may be conducted via electronic means, *AG's Ref. (Lindley)* [2016] EWCA Crim 1980; [2017] 1 Cr.App.R. (S.) 39.

**Reference does not preclude an appeal**   Where a sentence is referred under the unduly sentence scheme, the offender has not yet exercised the statutory right to apply for leave to appeal, *Hughes* [2010] EWCA Crim 1026.

**Powers of the court**   On a reference the Court of Appeal may—

(i)    quash any sentence passed on him in the proceeding; and
(ii)   in place of it pass such sentence as they think appropriate for the case and as the court below had power to pass when dealing with him, CJA 1988 s.36.1. At the hearing of the Attorney General's Reference the court has, at least in theory, the power not only to uphold or increase the original sentence, but also to reduce it or to impose a different form of sentence, *Hughes* [2010] EWCA Crim 1026.

**Test to apply**   The court may only increase sentences which it concludes were unduly lenient. It cannot have been the intention of Parliament to subject defendants to the risk of having their sentences increased — with all the anxiety that that naturally gives rise to — merely because in the opinion of this Court the sentence was less than this Court would have imposed. A sentence is unduly lenient where it falls outside the range of sentences which the judge, applying his mind to all the relevant factors, could reasonably consider appropriate, *AG's Ref. (No. 4 of 1989)* (1989) 11 Cr.App.R. (S.) 517.

**CACD is a court of review**    It is clear that the power of this court to declare a sentence unduly lenient depends entirely on what was put before the original sentencing court. It is not open to the Attorney General to rely upon further evidence not placed before the sentencing court to justify the Reference, *AG's Ref. (No.79 of 2015) (Nguyen)* [2016] EWCA Crim 448; [2016] 2 Cr.App.R. (S.) 18.

**AG conducting hearing on different basis to that at Crown Court**    It is permissible for the AG to conduct a reference on a different basis to that advanced in the Crown Court. Very often it is that departure which results in the view that the sentence was unduly lenient. The court's function was to decide whether or not the sentence imposed was unduly lenient, *AG's Ref. (Stewart)* [2016] EWCA Crim 2238; [2017] 1 Cr.App.R. (S.) 48.

In such circumstances, however, the court should be cognisant of the potential unfairness to the defendant and a reduction in sentence may be appropriate, *AG's Ref. (Susorovs)* [2016] EWCA Crim 1856; [2017] 1 Cr.App.R. (S.) 15.

Additionally, where the AG sought to depart from a concession made by prosecuting counsel in the context of a *Goodyear* indication, close consideration would be required, *AG's Ref (Powell)* [2017] EWCA Crim 2324; [2018] 1 Cr.App.R. (S.) 40. It is suggested that such a departure at a reference hearing should only be entertained where the court can be sure of no unfairness to the offender.

**Information not before the sentencing judge**    The power to declare a sentence as unduly lenient depended entirely on what was put before the original sentencing court. It is not open to the Attorney General to rely on further evidence not placed before the sentencing court to justify the reference, *AG's Ref. (No.19 of 2005) (WB)* [2006] EWCA Crim 785.

Once the court has concluded that a sentence, as passed, was unduly lenient based on the facts as known to the judge, the responsibility of the Court of Appeal is to pass the appropriate sentence for the case. In those circumstances, it is open to the court to take into account whatever new information is available, whether or not it is adverse to the offender, *AG's Ref. (No.79 of 2015) (Nguyen)* [2016] EWCA Crim 448; [2016] 2 Cr.App.R. (S.) 18.

**Double jeopardy: general**    The practice of making a reduction for so-called "*double jeopardy*" (the fact of being sentenced for the same offence twice) has fallen out of favour in recent years and reductions are increasingly difficult to obtain. See *AG's Ref. (No.45 of 2014)* [2014] EWCA Crim 1566 for more details.

However, the practice is not dead. It is submitted that circumstances giving rise to a submission that a reduction is due must extend beyond the usual arguments surrounding finality of sentence, legitimate expectation and the effect of being sentenced twice. For a recent example of where a reduction was obtained, see *AG's Ref. (Ferizi)* [2016] EWCA Crim 2022; [2017] 1 Cr.App.R. (S.) 26.

**Double jeopardy: murder**    Where a reference relates to the determination of minimum term in relation to the mandatory life sentence, the Court of Appeal shall not, in deciding what order under that section is appropriate for the case, make any allowance for the fact that the person to whom it relates is being sentenced for a second time, CJA 1988 s.36(3A).

# AUTOMATIC BARRING

## SAFEGUARDING VULNERABLE GROUPS ACT 2006

*References: Archbold 5A-1104*

### General

Barring is not an order of the court, it is an automatic consequence of a conviction for certain offences. The offender's name will be included on the children and/or adult barred list, by the Disclosure and Barring Service (DBS).

**Court's duties**   The court before which the offender is convicted must inform the person at the time he is convicted that the Service will include him in the barred list concerned, CPR 2015 r.28.3(1).

**Types of barring**   There are two types of barring; automatic and discretionary. Automatic barring is contingent upon a caution or conviction for a listed offence (see below). Discretionary barring usually follows from a referral by a third party, e.g. an employer, and is not dealt with in this text.

**The lists**   There are two lists; the child list and the adult list. A person included on the adult and/or child barred lists is prohibited from regulated activity in relation to adults or children, see SVGA 2006 Sch.3 para.2.

**Those aged under 18**   Automatic barring applies only to those aged 18+ at the time of the commission of the offence, SVGA 2006 Sch.3 para.24(4). A defendant aged under 18 at the time of the offence will not be automatically barred, but the DBS may consider barring the defendant under the discretionary barring powers.

### The Triggering Offences

There are two types of triggering offence:

(a)   automatic inclusion offences, where the defendant has no right to make representations; and

(b)   automatic inclusion offences, where the defendant has a right to make representations before he is included in the list.

### Automatic inclusion offences with no right to make representations

For automatic inclusion offences with no right to make representations, the DBS will inform the person in writing of his inclusion in the adult and/or child barred lists.

### Automatic inclusion offences with a right to make representations

For automatic inclusion offences with the right to make representations, if the person satisfies the *"test for regulated activity"* (see SVGA 2006 Sch.3 para.2), the DBS will seek representations from the person and consider any representations prior to making a barring decision. If no representations are received the person will be barred. The person will be informed in writing whether or not he is barred.

The list of offences can be found in SI 2009/37 rr.3–6 and Sch.1.

### Any "Connected Offence" of the Listed Offences

*"Connected offence"* means any offence of attempting, conspiring or incitement to commit that offence, or aiding, abetting, counselling or procuring the commission of the offence.

It is uncertain whether the reference to incitement in this provision includes a reference to offences contrary to the SCA 2007 ss.44, 45 and 46.

### Offence of Engaging in Regulated Activity Whilst Barred

An individual commits an offence if he:

(a)   seeks to engage in regulated activity from which he is barred;
(b)   offers to engage in regulated activity from which he is barred;
(c)   engages in regulated activity from which he is barred.

The offence is triable either way and the maximum sentence is five years, SVGA 2006 s.7.

# AUTOMATIC LIFE SENTENCE "TWO STRIKES LIFE"

## CRIMINAL JUSTICE ACT 2003 s.224A

*References: Current Sentencing Practice A2-2600; Archbold 5A-736*

### Availability

The sentence is available where a person aged 18+ committed an offence on or after 3 December 2012, CJA 2003 s.224A(1)(a) and (b). Those aged 18-20 receive a sentence of custody for life; those aged 21+ receive a sentence of life imprisonment.

### Who is liable?

A person:

(a)  aged 18+;
(b)  convicted of an offence listed in Sch.15B, committed on or after 3 December 2012;
(c)  who, but for s.224A would receive a custodial sentence of 10 years or more (disregarding any extension period under s.226A); and
(d)  who at the time the offence was committed, had previously been convicted of a Sch.15B offence for which a *"relevant sentence"* had been imposed, CJA 2003 s.224A(1); (3) and (4).

A *"relevant sentence"* is one which (disregarding any reduction for time spent on bail or in custody pre-sentence);

(i)    is a life sentence where the offender was not eligible for release during the first five years of the sentence;
(ii)   is an extended sentence where the custodial period was 10 years or more;
(iii)  is any other sentence of imprisonment or detention for determinate period of 10 years or more, CJA 2003 s.224A(5)-(10).

### Exception

The court must impose a life sentence unless the court is of the opinion that there are particular circumstances which:

(a)  relate to the offence, to the previous offence, or to the offender; and
(b)  would make it unjust to do so in all the circumstances, CJA 2003 s.224A(2).

*Note: The term "unjust" is the same term used in the minimum sentence provisions under the PCC(S)A 2000 and the case law in respect of those provisions may assist.*

### Dangerousness

There is no requirement that the offender be found to be dangerous under the 2003 Act. Therefore the fact that an offender is not dangerous is not something that, of itself, would make it unjust to pass a life sentence under s.224A. Additionally, there is no requirement to consider whether the *"seriousness"* threshold has been passed for the purposes of CJA 2003 s.225(2)(b), *AG's Ref. (No. 27 of 2013) (Burinskas)* [2014] EWCA Crim 334; [2014] 2 Cr.App.R. (S.) 45.

**The correct approach**    The court should approach a relevant case in the following manner:

(i)     consider the question of dangerousness. If the offender is not dangerous and s.224A does not apply, a determinate sentence should be passed. If the offender is not dangerous and the conditions in s.224A are satisfied then a life sentence must be imposed;

(ii)    if the offender is dangerous, consider whether the seriousness of the offence and offences associated with it justify a life sentence;

(iii)   if a life sentence is justified then the judge must pass a life sentence in accordance with s.225. If s.224A also applies, the judge should record that fact in open court;

(iv)    if a life sentence is not justified, then the sentencing judge should consider whether s.224A applies. If it does, then a life sentence must be imposed; and

(v)     if s.224A does not apply the judge should then consider the provisions of s.226A. Before passing an extended sentence the judge should consider a determinate sentence, *AG's Ref. (No. 27 of 2013) (Burinskas)* [2014] EWCA Crim 334; [2014] 2 Cr.App.R. (S.) 45.

# BINDING OVER

## JUSTICES OF THE PEACE ACT 1968 s.1(7)

*References: Current Sentencing Practice B4; Archbold 5A-346*

### To Come Up for Judgment

A person who has been convicted of an offence may be bound over to come up for judgment when called, on such conditions as the court may specify.

The order is not available in the magistrates' court, *Ayu* [1958] 43 Cr.App.R. 31.

If the Crown Court is considering binding over an individual to come up for judgment, the court should specify any conditions with which the individual is to comply in the meantime and not specify that the individual is to be of good behaviour, *CPD 2015* [2015] EWCA Crim 1567 Sentencing J.17. The Crown Court should, if the individual is unrepresented, explain the consequences of a breach of the binding over order in these circumstances, *CPD 2015* [2015] EWCA Crim 1567 Sentencing J.18.

### To Keep the Peace

**Availability**    A person *"who or whose case"* is before the Crown Court or a magistrates' court may be bound over to keep the peace and to be of good behaviour, whether or not he has been charged with or convicted of an offence, JPA 1968 s.1(7).

A complainant may be bound over, *Sheldon v Bromfield Justices* [1964] 2 All ER 131.

A witness who has not given evidence is not liable to be bound over, *Swindon Crown Court ex parte Singh* [1983] 5 Cr.App.R. (S.) 422.

An acquitted defendant may be bound over, however such orders should be rare, *Middlesex Crown Court ex part Khan* (1996) 161 JP 240.

A person who has not been charged with an offence should not be bound over without being given the opportunity to make representations before being bound over, *Sheldon v Bromfield Justices* [1964] 2 All ER 131.

An order can be made at any time during the proceedings, *Aubrey-Fletcher ex part Thompson* [1969] 53 Cr.App.R. 380.

The power can be exercised by the magistrates' court and the Crown Court, JPA 1968 s.1(7) and *DPP v Speede* [1998] 2 Cr.App.R. 108.

### Considerations

**Test to apply**    Before imposing a binding over order, the court must be satisfied so that it is sure that a breach of the peace involving violence, or an imminent threat of violence, has occurred or that there is a real risk of violence in the future. Such violence may be perpetrated by the individual who will be subject to the order or by a third party as a natural consequence of the individual's conduct, *CPD 2015* [2015] EWCA Crim 1567 Sentencing J.2.

**Burden of proof**   The court should be satisfied so that it is sure of the matters complained of before a binding over order may be imposed. Where the procedure has been commenced on complaint, the burden of proof rests on the complainant. In all other circumstances, the burden of proof rests upon the prosecution, *CPD 2015* [2015] EWCA Crim 1567 Sentencing J.18.

**Evidence**   Sections 51 to 57 of the Magistrates' Courts Act 1980 set out the jurisdiction of the magistrates' court to hear an application made on complaint and the procedure which is to be followed. This includes a requirement under s.53 to hear evidence and the parties, before making any order. This practice should be applied to all cases in the magistrates' court and the Crown Court where the court is considering imposing a binding over order. The court should give the individual who would be subject to the order and the prosecutor the opportunity to make representations, both as to the making of the order and as to its terms. The court should also hear any admissible evidence the parties wish to call and which has not already been heard in the proceedings. Particularly careful consideration may be required where the individual who would be subject to the order is a witness in the proceedings, *CPD 2015* [2015] EWCA Crim 1567 Sentencing J.5.

**Giving reasons**   The court must indicate the reasons why it is minded to bind the individual over so that he or his representatives may make submissions, *South Molton Justices ex parte Anderson* (1990) 90 Cr.App.R. 158.

**Making the Order**

**Recognisance**   The court must be satisfied on the merits of the case that an order for binding over is appropriate and should announce that decision before considering the amount of the recognisance. If unrepresented, the individual who is made subject to the binding over order should be told he has a right of appeal from the decision, *CPD 2015* [2015] EWCA Crim 1567 Sentencing J.10.

When fixing the amount of recognisance, courts should have regard to the individual's financial resources and should hear representations from the individual or his legal representatives regarding finances, *CPD 2015* [2015] EWCA Crim 1567 Sentencing J.11.

A recognisance is made in the form of a bond giving rise to a civil debt on breach of the order, *CPD 2015* [2015] EWCA Crim 1567 Sentencing J.12.

**Contents of the order**   In light of the judgment in *Hashman and Harrup v United Kingdom* (2000) 30 EHRR 241, [2000] Crim. L.R. 185, courts should no longer bind an individual over *"to be of good behaviour"*. Rather than binding an individual over to *"keep the peace"* in general terms, the court should identify the specific conduct or activity from which the individual must refrain, *CPD 2015* [2015] EWCA Crim 1567 Sentencing J.3.

When making an order binding an individual over to refrain from specified types of conduct or activities, the details of that conduct or those activities should be specified by the court in a written order, served on all relevant parties. The court should state its reasons for the making of the order, its length and the amount of the recognisance. The length of the order should be proportionate to the harm sought to be avoided and should not generally exceed 12 months, *CPD 2015* [2015] EWCA Crim 1567 Sentencing J.4.

There is no power to include conditions in a bind over to keep the peace, *Ayu* [1958] 43 Cr.App.R. 31.

## Refusal to be Bound Over

If there is any possibility that an individual will refuse to enter a recognizance, the court should consider whether there are any appropriate alternatives to a binding over order (for example, continuing with a prosecution). Where there are no appropriate alternatives and the individual continues to refuse to enter into the recognisance, the court may commit the individual to custody. In the magistrates' courts, the power to do so will derive from s.1(7) of the Justices of the Peace Act 1968 or, more rarely, from s.115(3) of the Magistrates' Courts Act 1980, and the court should state which power it is acting under; in the Crown Court, this is a common law power, *CPD 2015* [2015] EWCA Crim 1567 Sentencing J.13.

A person who refuses to be bound over may be committed to prison. A person under 18 may consent to be bound over, but may not be committed to custody if he refuses to be bound over, PCC(S)A 2000 ss.60(1)(b) and 108.

## Breach

Where a person who has been bound over to keep the peace and be of good behaviour fails to comply with the terms of the binding over, he is liable to be ordered to pay the amount in which he has been bound over, but cannot be sentenced to custody. However they can be committed to prison for non-payment.

**Burden of proof**   Where there is an allegation of breach of a binding over order, the court should be satisfied on the balance of probabilities that the defendant is in breach before making any order for forfeiture of a recognisance. The burden of proof shall rest on the prosecution, *CPD 2015* [2015] EWCA Crim 1567 Sentencing J.9.

# COMMITTAL FOR SENTENCE

## PCC(S)A 2000 ss.3–7

*References: Current Sentencing Practice H2-100; Archbold 5A-204*

### Adult offenders (section 3)

Where an offender aged 18 or over is convicted on summary trial of an offence triable either way, he may be committed to the Crown Court for sentence, either in custody or on bail, if the court by which he is convicted is of the opinion that the offence or the combination of the offence and one or more offences associated with it was so serious that the Crown Court should, in the court's opinion, have the power to deal with him in any way in which it could deal with him if he had been convicted on indictment.

(This provision does not apply to offences where the section is excluded by reference to the value of the property involved.)

A person committed for sentence under this provision may be dealt with by the Crown Court in any way in which the Crown Court could deal with them had they just been convicted of the offence on the indictment. Where an offender crosses a relevant age threshold between committal and the appearance at the Crown Court, the relevant date for determining the offender's age is the date of conviction, *Robson* [2007] 1 Cr.App.R. (S.) 54.

### "Dangerous" adult offenders (section 3A)

Where an offender aged 18 or over is convicted on a summary trial of an either-way offence which is a specified offence for the purposes of the Criminal Justice Act 2003 Sch.15 and it appears to the court that the criteria for the imposition of an extended sentence under the Criminal Justice Act 2003 s.226A are met, the court must commit the offender either in custody or on bail to the Crown Court for sentence.

In reaching any decision or their taking any steps under this section, the court shall not be bound by any indication of sentence given in respect of the offence under the Magistrates' Courts Act 1980 s.20, and nothing the court does under this section may be challenged or be the subject of any appeal in any court on the ground that it is not consistent with an indication of sentence.

A person committed for sentence under this provision may be dealt with by the Crown Court in any way in which the Crown Court could deal with him if he had just been convicted of the offence on the indictment.

Where an offender crosses a relevant age threshold between committal and the appearance at the Crown Court, the relevant date for determining the offender's age is the date of conviction, *Robson* [2007] 1 Cr.App.R. (S.) 54.

### Adult offenders: Related offences (section 4)

If a magistrates' court has sent an offender aged 18 or over for trial for some offences, but has to deal with the offender for other either-way offences in relation to which he has indicated an intention to plead guilty, the magistrates' court may commit the defendant to the Crown Court for sentence for those offences, provided that they are offences which could be included in the same indictment as the first offences.

The offender may be committed for sentence even though the court is not satisfied that greater punishment should be inflicted for those offences than the magistrates' court has power to inflict.

If the offender has indicated an intention to plead guilty to certain offences, but the magistrates' court has not yet determined whether to send the offender to the Crown Court for trial in respect of related offences, the magistrates' court must adjourn the proceedings in relation to the offences in respect of which the offender has indicated an intention to plead guilty, and if it sends the offender to the Crown Court for trial for the related offence or offences, it may then commit him for sentence.

If the magistrates' court commits an offender under this provision, it should state whether it has power also to commit the offender under the PCC(S)A 2000 s.3.

If the offender is convicted of the offences for which he has been sent for trial, or if the magistrates' court on committing him for sentence has stated that it has power to commit him for sentence for the other offences under the PCC(S)A 2000 s.3, the Crown Court may impose any sentence for the offences for which he has been committed for sentence which it would have power to impose if the offender had just been convicted on indictment.

If the defendant is not convicted of those offences for which he has been sent for trial, and the magistrates' court has not stated that it had power to commit him under the PCC(S)A 2000 s.3, the Crown Court must deal with the offender for the offences for which he has been committed for sentence in a manner in which the magistrates' court could deal with him if it had just convicted him.

This procedure should not be used unless the defendant has been sent for trial for related offences. A defendant who has been convicted by a magistrates' court after indicating an intention to plead guilty in other circumstances should be committed under s.3.

### Young offenders: Summary trial of certain serious offences (section 3B)

Where on the summary trial of an offence mentioned in PCC(S)A 2000 s.91(1) a person aged under 18 is convicted of the offence and the court is of the opinion that the offence or the combination of the offence and one or more offences associated with it was such that the Crown Court should in the court's opinion have power to deal with the offender as if the provisions of s.91 applied, the court may commit him in custody or on bail to the Crown Court for sentence. Under s.3B, the youth court was not making a once and for all decision at the point of allocation and, accordingly, taking the prosecution case at its highest was no longer necessary and whether there was a *"real prospect"* of a sentence in excess of the youth court powers required a different emphasis. In most cases, it would generally be after conviction when the assessment could and should be made. The observations in *Southampton Youth Court* [2004] EWHC 2912 (Admin); [2005] 2 Cr.App.R. (S.) 30 that a Crown Court trial for a youth *"should be reserved for the most serious cases"* remained entirely apposite, *South Tyneside Youth Court and B* [2015] EWHC 1455 (Admin); [2015] 2 Cr.App.R. (S.) 59.

In considering the associated offence it is submitted that the magistrates' court is not limited to the consideration of offences in respect of which the sentencing court would have power to impose a term of detention under the PCC(S)A 2000 s.91(1).

A person committed for sentence under this provision may be dealt with by the Crown Court in any way in which the Crown Court could deal with them had they just been convicted of the offence on the indictment.

### Young Offenders: Dangerousness provisions (section 3C)

A defendant under 18 who has been convicted by a magistrates' court of a specified offence must be committed to the Crown Court if the court considers that the criteria for the imposition of an extended sentence the imposition of an extended sentence of detention would be met.

Where a young defendant is committed for sentence under this provision the Crown Court may deal with the offender in any way in which it could deal with him if he had just been convicted of the offence on indictment before the court.

The Crown Court is not bound to deal with the defendant under the Criminal Justice Act 2003 s.226B. If it considers that there is a significant risk of serious harm to the public caused by further specified offences committed by him, it may impose an extended sentence. If it does not so consider, the Crown Court may impose any other sentence which is open to the court for an offender of the defendant's age.

The age of the defendant for the purpose of determining the sentencing powers of the Crown Court is his age on the date on which he was convicted. If a defendant is convicted by a magistrates' court at the age of 17 and is committed for sentence, but attains the age of 18 before he appears before the Crown Court, the Crown Court must deal with him as a 17-year-old. Whatever the word *"just"* in s.5A(1) of the PCC(S)A 2000 added, it was not to be taken to have the effect of deeming the date of conviction to be the date of appearance before the Crown Court, *Robson* [2007] 1 Cr.App.R.(S.) 54.

Additionally, in the case of an offender who has attained the age of 18 during the course of proceedings, the court may deal with the offender and make any order it could have made if the offender had not attained that age, s.29 CYPA 1963.

### Young offenders: Related offences (section 4A)

If a magistrates' court has sent an offender aged under 18 for trial for some offences, but has to deal with the offender for other related offences in respect of which the sentencing court would have power to impose a term of detention under the PCC(S)A 2000 s.91(1), in respect of which he has indicated that he would plead guilty if the offence were to proceed to trial, the court may commit him in custody or on bail to the Crown Court for sentence.

This procedure does not apply to offences in respect of which the sentencing court would not have power to impose a term of detention under the PCC(S) A 2000 s.91(1).

The offender may be committed for sentence even though the court is not satisfied that greater punishment should be inflicted for those offences than the magistrates' court has power to inflict.

If the offender has indicated an intention to plead guilty to certain offences, but the magistrates' court has not yet determined whether to send the offender to the Crown Court for trial in respect of related offences, the magistrates' court must adjourn the proceedings in relation to the offences in respect of which the offender has indicated an intention to plead guilty, and if it sends the offender to the Crown Court for trial for the related offence or offences, it may then commit him for sentence.

If the magistrates' court commits an offender under this provision, it should state whether it has power also to commit the offender under the PCC(S)A 2000 ss.3B or 3C.

If the offender is convicted of the offences for which he has been sent for trial, or if the magistrates' court on committing him for sentence has stated that it has power to commit him for sentence for the other offences under the PCC(S)A 2000 ss.3B or 3C, the Crown Court may impose any sentence for the offences for which he has been committed for sentence which it would have power to impose if the offender had just been convicted on indictment.

If the defendant is not convicted of those offences for which he has been sent for trial, and the magistrates' court has not stated that it had power to commit him under the PCC(S)A 2000 ss.3B or 3C, the Crown Court must deal with the offender for the offences for which he has been committed for sentence in a manner in which the magistrates' court could deal with him if it had just convicted him.

This procedure should not be used unless the defendant has been sent for trial for related offences. A defendant who has been convicted by a magistrates' court after indicating an intention to plead guilty in other circumstances should be committed under ss.3B or 3C in relation to the offences to which those sections apply.

**Subsidiary offences (section 6)**

Where an offender is committed for sentence under:

(a)  ss.3, 3A, 3B, 3C, 4 or 4A of the Vagrancy Act 1824;
(b)  s.13(5) of PCC(S)A 2000 (person conditionally discharged convicted of further offence); or
(c)  para.11(2) of Sch.12 of CJA 2003 (person convicted of offence during operational period of suspended sentence),

the magistrates' court may commit the offender for other offences for which he could not be committed under the principal provision. The offence must be: a) punishable with imprisonment, b) punishable with disqualification from driving under ss.34, 35 or 36 of the Road Traffic Offenders Act 1988, or c) be a suspended sentence in respect of which a magistrates' court has power to deal with the offender.

The power may be exercised in conjunction with other powers of committal. The section does not apply in the case of an offender subject to a community order made under the Criminal Justice Act 2003 who is committed to the Crown Court under the Criminal Justice Act 2003 Sch.8, para.22, following his conviction by a magistrates' court of an offence while a community order made by the Crown Court is in force.

Where an offender is committed under s.6, the Crown Court must observe all limits which would apply to a magistrates' court passing sentence for those offences, both in relation to the maximum term of imprisonment which the magistrates' court may pass for the individual offences, and the limitations on the aggregate maximum term of imprisonment which the magistrates' court may impose for all the offences. See **MAGISTRATES' COURTS' POWERS— CUSTODIAL SENTENCE**, p.195.

### Defective committals

Where an offender is committed to the Crown Court for sentence, and it is alleged that the committal is unlawful for want of jurisdiction or otherwise, the normal remedy is by way of judicial review. The Crown Court may decline to pass sentence only if the committal is obviously bad on its face.

A procedural failure does not necessarily render a committal invalid. The court will, inter alia, have to ask itself whether the intention of the legislature was that any act done following that procedural failure should be invalid. If the answer to that question was no, then the court should go on to consider the interests of justice generally, and most particularly whether there was a real possibility that either the prosecution or defence might suffer prejudice on account of the procedural failure, *Ashton* [2006] EWCA Crim 794; [2006] 2 Cr.App.R. (S.) 15. See also *Burke* [2017] EWCA Crim 848.

A circuit judge and a High Court judge may reconstitute the court in order to exercise the powers of a district judge. There is the same power at the Court of Appeal, *Buisson* [2011] EWCA Crim 1841.

The Crown Court has no power to remit the case to the magistrates' court where it appears that the defendant is not guilty of the offence for which he had been committed, but it may allow him to withdraw or change his plea and then remit the case to the magistrates' court, see *Isleworth Crown Court ex part Buda* [2000] 1 Cr.App.R. (S.) 538.

# COMMUNITY ORDERS

## CJA 2003 s.177 ET SEQ.

*References: Current Sentencing Practice B1; Archbold 5A-494*

### Availability

**Power**   Where a person aged 18+ is convicted of an offence committed on or after 4 April 2005, subject to the restrictions set out below, the court may make a community order imposing one or more requirements (see below), CJA 2003 s.177(1) and SI 2005/950.

**Test to apply**   A court may not impose a community sentence unless it is of the opinion that:

(a)   the offence or the combination of the offence and one or more offences associated with the offence are "*serious enough to warrant such a sentence*";

(b)   the particular requirements or combination of requirements are "*the most suitable for the offender*"; and

(c)   the restrictions on liberty imposed by the order are "*commensurate with the seriousness of the offence*" or the combination of offences for which the sentence is imposed, CJA 2003 s.148(1) and (2).

The fact that the offence is serious enough to warrant a community order or the proposed requirements are commensurate with the seriousness of the offence or the combination of offences for which the order would be imposed, does not mean that the court is required to make a community order or to impose those restrictions, CJA 2003 s.148(5).

**No power to make community order**   A community order is *not* available in respect of an offence for which:

(a)   the sentence is fixed by law; or

(b)   a custodial sentence must be imposed under:
   (i)   s.51A(2) of the Firearms Act 1968 (minimum sentence for certain firearms offences);

(c)   ss.110(2) or 111(2) of the PCC(S)A 2000 (minimum sentence for third domestic burglary or drug trafficking offence);

(d)   s.29(4) or (6) of the Violent Crime Reduction Act 2006 (minimum sentence for offence of using someone to mind a weapon);

(e)   s.224A of the Criminal Justice Act 2003 (automatic life sentence); or

(f)   s.225(2) or 226(2) of the Criminal Justice Act 2003 (requirement to impose sentence of imprisonment for life or detention for life);

(g)   ss.1(2B) or 1A(5) of the Prevention of Crime Act 1953 (minimum sentence for certain offences involving offensive weapons); or

(h)   ss.139(6B), 139A(5B) or 139AA(7) of the CJA 1988 (minimum sentence for certain offences involving article with blade or point or offensive weapon), CJA 2003 s.150(1) and (2).

**Offence must carry imprisonment**   A community order may not be made in respect of an offence which is not punishable with imprisonment, CJA 2003 s.150A(1)(a).

## Making the Order

**Punitive element**   The order *must* include at least one requirement imposed for the purpose of punishment, or impose a fine for the offence in respect of which the community order is made, or both, CJA 2003 s.177(2A). That obligation does not apply where the court is of the view that there are exceptional circumstances which relate to the offender which would make it unjust to impose a requirement for the purposes of punishment and/or a fine, CJA 2003 s.177(2B).

**Maximum length**   A community order must specify a date, not more than three years after the date of the order, by which all the requirements must have been complied with, CJA 2003 s.177(5).

Where the court imposes two or more requirements, it may specify a date by which each of those requirements must be completed, the last of which must be the end date of the order, CJA 2003 s.177(5A).

The order itself cannot exist other than as a vehicle through which a particular requirement was performed. Therefore, where a single requirement is time-limited, e.g. unpaid work, 12 months, the order cannot extend beyond 12 months in absence of another requirement with a longer permissible maximum period, *Khan* [2015] EWCA Crim 835.

**Discount for time on remand**   Where a court makes a community order in respect of an offender who has previously been remanded in custody, it may have regard to any period during which the offender has been remanded in custody in connection with the offence for which the order is made, or any offence founded on the same facts or evidence, in determining the restrictions on liberty to be imposed on the offender. The court has a discretion; there is no obligation to make any allowance in the terms of the order for time spent in custody on remand, CJA 2003 s.149.

See *Pereira-Lee* [2016] EWCA Crim 1705; [2017] 1 Cr.App.R. (S.) 17 as an example of the issues.

**Local justice area**   A community order must specify the local justice area in which the offender resides or will reside, CJA 2003 s.216.

**Copies of the order**   These must be given to the offender, and to an officer of a local probation board or (in the case of an offender under 18) either an officer of a local probation board or a member of a youth offending team, and to others concerned with the operation of the order, CJA 2003 s.219.

**Breach**   The Crown Court may include in the order a direction that any breach of the order is to be dealt with by a magistrates' court. If no such direction is made, any breach will be dealt with by the Crown Court, CJA 2003 Sch.8 paras.5-8.

## Requirements

There is no restriction on the requirements which may be combined in the same community order, but the court must consider whether the requirements are compatible with each other, CJA 2003 s.177(6).

The requirements of a community order shall, as far as is practicable, avoid any conflict with the offender's religious beliefs or the requirements of any other community order to which he may be subject, and any interference with the times at which he normally works, or attends school or an educational establishment, CJA 2003 s.217.

**Activity requirements (CJA 2003 s.201)**  (repealed by ORA 2014 on 1 February 2015. See the 2015 edition for details.

**Alcohol abstinence and monitoring requirements (CJA 2003 s.212A)**  This section is in force in relation to the Humber, Lincolnshire and North Yorkshire local justice areas from 1 May 2017 to 30 April 2019 (see SI 2017/525 and SI 2017/573.) The pilot which was in force in nine London justice areas (see SI 2017/225) expired on 1 April 2018 and was not extended. There are transitional arrangements in place to ensure existing orders with such requirements continue.

An alcohol abstinence and monitoring requirement is a requirement that subject to such exceptions as are specified, the offender must abstain from consuming alcohol throughout a specified period, or must not consume alcohol during a specified period so that the level of alcohol in the offender's body does not exceed a specified amount, CJA 2003 s.212A(1)(a).

The specified period must not exceed 120 days, CJA 2003 s.212A(2).

An alcohol abstinence and monitoring requirement may not be made unless:

(i)     the consumption of alcohol is an element of the offence for which the order is to be imposed, or of an associated offence;
(ii)    the court is satisfied that the offender is not dependent on alcohol;
(iii)   the order does not include an alcohol treatment requirement; and
(iv)    the court has been informed that arrangements for monitoring the requirement are available, CJA 2003 s.212A(8)–(12).

If the requirement is that the offender must not consume alcohol during a specified period so that the level of alcohol in the offender's body does not exceed a specified amount, the amount specified must be the amount prescribed by the Secretary of State, CJA 2003 s.212A(4).

The offender must submit to monitoring in accordance with arrangements specified by the Secretary of State, CJA 2003 s.212A(1)(b). An alcohol abstinence and monitoring requirement may not be made unless such arrangements are in force, CJA 2003 s.212A(6).

**Alcohol treatment requirements (CJA 2013 s.212)**  An alcohol treatment requirement is a requirement that the offender must submit during a period specified in the order to treatment with a view to the reduction or elimination of the offender's dependency on alcohol, CJA 2003 s.212(1).

An alcohol treatment requirement may be made if the court is satisfied that the offender:

(i)     is dependent on alcohol; and
(ii)    that his dependency is such as requires, and may be susceptible to, treatment; and
(iii)   that arrangements have been or can be made for the treatment intended to be specified in the order (including arrangements for the reception of the offender where he is to be required to submit to treatment as a resident), CJA 2003 s.212(2).

The court may not include or make an alcohol treatment requirement unless the offender expresses his willingness to comply with the requirement, CJA 2003 s.212(3).

The treatment required by the alcohol treatment requirement must be:

(i)     treatment as a resident in such institution or place as may be specified in the order;
(ii)    treatment as a non-resident in such institution or place at such intervals as may be specified in the order; or
(iii)   treatment by or under the direction of a qualified person specified in the order, CJA 2003 s.212(5).

The court may not make an alcohol treatment requirement unless it is satisfied that arrangements have been made for the proposed treatment, including arrangements for the offender's reception where he is required to submit to treatment as a resident, CJA 2003 s.212(2)(c).

Where the court imposes an activity requirement, it may also impose an electronic monitoring requirement (see **Electronic Monitoring Requirements** p.62), CJA 2003 s.177(4).

**Attendance centre requirements (CJA 2003 s.215)**   An attendance centre requirement may be made in respect of an offender under 25, CJA 2003 s.177(1)(l). It requires the offender to attend an attendance centre for a number of hours specified in the order, CJA 2003 s.214(1).

The order must be for a total of not less than 12 hours and not more than 36 hours, CJA 2003 s.214(2).

The court must not make an attendance centre requirement unless it is satisfied that the attendance centre to be specified is reasonably accessible to the person concerned, having regard to the means of access available to him, and any other circumstances, CJA 2003 s.214(3).

The offender must not be required to attend at an attendance centre on more than one occasion on any one day, or for more than three hours on any occasion, CJA 2003 s.214(6).

A court may not include an attendance centre requirement in a relevant order in respect of an offender unless the court has been notified by the Secretary of State that an attendance centre is available for persons of his description, CJA 2003 s.218(3).

Where the court imposes an activity requirement, it may also impose an electronic monitoring requirement (see **Electronic Monitoring Requirements**, p.62), CJA 2003 s.177(4).

**Curfew requirements (CJA 2003 s.204)**   A curfew requirement requires the offender to remain, for periods specified in the requirement, at a place specified in the order, CJA 2003 s.204(1).

The periods specified must be not less than two hours and not more than 16 hours (12 hours if the offence was committed before 3 December 2012) in any day, CJA 2003 s.204(2).

The requirement may specify different places or different periods for different days.

All the specified periods must fall within the period of twelve months (six months if the offence was committed before 3 December 2012) beginning with the day on which the order is made, CJA 2003 s.204(3).

Before making a curfew requirement, the court must obtain and consider information about the place to be specified in the order and the attitude of persons likely to be affected by the enforced presence there of the offender, CJA 2003 s.204(6).

The court must impose an electronic monitoring requirement unless a person whose cooperation is necessary does not consent, or the court has not been notified that arrangements for electronic monitoring are available, or in the particular circumstances of the case the court considers it inappropriate to do so (see **Electronic Monitoring Requirements**, p.62), CJA 2003 s.177(3).

**Drug rehabilitation requirements (CJA 2003 s.209)**   A drug rehabilitation requirement requires the offender to submit, during the treatment and testing period, to treatment by a specified person with a view to the reduction or elimination of the offender's dependency on or propensity to misuse drugs, CJA 2003 s.209(1)(a). The requirement must also require the offender to provide samples during the treatment and testing period at times and in circumstances determined by a responsible officer or person providing treatment, for the purpose of ascertaining whether he has any drug in his body during the treatment and testing period, CJA 2003 s.209(1)(b).

The treatment must be treatment as a resident in a specified institution or place, or treatment as a non-resident in a specified institution or place, CJA 2003 s.209(4). The nature of the treatment is not specified in the order, CJA 2003 s.209(4).

A drug rehabilitation requirement may be made only if the court is satisfied that:

(i)     the offender is dependent on or has a propensity to misuse drugs;
(ii)    his dependency or propensity is such as requires and may be susceptible to treatment;

(iii)  arrangements have been or can be made for the treatment intended to be specified in the order;

(iv)  the requirement has been recommended by an officer of a local probation board; and

(v)  the offender has expressed his willingness to comply with the requirement, CJA 2003 s.209(2).

A drug rehabilitation requirement may (and must if the treatment and testing period is more than 12 months) provide for the order to be reviewed periodically at intervals of not less than one month at a hearing held for the purpose by the court responsible for the order. The offender may be required to attend each review hearing (and must if the period is more than 12 months).

A drug rehabilitation requirement may (and must if the treatment and testing period is more than 12 months):

(a)  provide for the requirement to be reviewed periodically at intervals of not less than one month;

(b)  provide for each review of the requirement to be made at a hearing held for the purpose by the court responsible for the order (a "*review hearing*");

(c)  require the offender to attend each review hearing;

(d)  provide for a probation officer to produce a report in writing on the offender's progress under the requirement before each review; and

(e)  provide for each report to include the test results (under s.209(6)) and the views of the treatment provider as to the treatment and testing of the offender, CJA 2003 s.210(1).

At a review hearing the court, after considering the responsible officer's report, may amend any requirement or provision of the order, CJA 2003 s.211(1). The court may not amend the treatment or testing requirement unless the offender expresses his willingness to comply with the amended requirement, CJA 2003 s.211(2)(a).

If the offender fails to express his willingness to comply with the amended order, the court may revoke the order, and deal with him, for the offence in respect of which the order was made, in any manner in which it could deal with him if he had just been convicted by the court of the offence, CJA 2003 s.211(3). Partial compliance will be taken into account when dealing with the offender under s.211(3), CJA 2003 s.211(4). A custodial sentence may only be imposed where one was available for the original offence, CJA 2003 s.211(4).

If at a review hearing the court is of the opinion that the offender's progress under the order is satisfactory, the court may so amend the order as to provide for each subsequent review to be made by the court without a hearing, but this may be reversed, CJA 2003 s.211(6) and (7).

Where the court imposes an activity requirement, it may also impose an electronic monitoring requirement (see **Electronic Monitoring Requirements** below), CJA 2003 s.177(4).

**Electronic monitoring requirements (CJA 2003 s.215)**  An electronic monitoring requirement is a requirement for securing the electronic monitoring of the offender's compliance with other requirements imposed by the order, CJA 2003 s.215(1).

A court which makes a community order imposing an unpaid work requirement, an activity requirement, a programme requirement, a prohibited activity requirement, a residence requirement, a foreign travel prohibition requirement, a mental health treatment requirement, a drug rehabilitation requirement, an alcohol treatment requirement, a supervision requirement or an attendance centre requirement, the court *may* also impose an electronic monitoring requirement, CJA 2003 s.177(4).

Where the court makes a community order imposing a curfew requirement or an exclusion requirement, the court *must* also impose an electronic monitoring requirement, CJA 2003 s.177(3).

An electronic monitoring requirement may not be included without the consent of any person without whose co-operation monitoring cannot be secured, CJA 2003 s.215(2).

An electronic monitoring requirement must include provision for making a person of a specified description responsible for the monitoring, CJA 2003 s.215(3).

An electronic monitoring requirement may be made only if the court has been notified that electronic monitoring requirements are available in the relevant areas and is satisfied that necessary provision can be made under those arrangements, CJA 2003 s.218(4).

*Note: There is in force a pilot scheme extending the electronic monitoring requirement available under a community order or suspended sentence order. The pilot is in force from 13 March 2017 to 12 March 2019 in relation to north and east London. The effect is to extend the requirement from merely monitoring an offender's compliance with other requirements to enable the probation service to monitor an offender's location. See SI 2017/236 and 2018/357 for details of the London pilot.*

**Exclusion requirements (CJA 2003 s.205)** An exclusion requirement prohibits the offender from entering any place specified in the order, CJA 2003 s.205(1). The requirement cannot exceed two years (whatever the length of the community order), CJA 2003 s.205(2). The prohibition may operate continuously or only during specified periods and different places may be specified in the order for different periods or days, CJA 2003 s.205(3).

The court must impose an electronic monitoring requirement unless a person whose cooperation is necessary does not consent, or the court has not been notified that arrangements for electronic monitoring are available, or in the particular circumstances of the case the court considers it inappropriate to do so, CJA 2003 s.177(3).

**Foreign travel prohibition requirement (CJA 2003 s.206A)** (only available for offences committed on or after 3 December 2012).

A foreign travel prohibition requirement may prohibit the offender from travelling to any country or territory outside the British Islands specified in the order, to any country or territory outside the British Islands not specified in the order, or to any country or territory outside the British Islands, CJA 2003 s.206A(1).

The requirement may apply to the day or days specified in the order, or for a period specified in the order, CJA 2003 s.206A(1).

The period specified may not exceed twelve months beginning with the day on which the order is made, and the day or days specified may not fall outside the period of twelve months beginning with the day on which the order is made, CJA 2003 s.206A(2) and (3).

Where the court imposes an activity requirement, it may also impose an electronic monitoring requirement (see **Electronic Monitoring Requirements**, p.62), CJA 2003 s.177(4).

**Mental health treatment requirements (CJA 2003 s.207)**   A mental health treatment requirement is a requirement that the offender must submit, during a period or periods specified in the order, to treatment by or under the direction of a registered medical practitioner or a registered psychologist with a view to the improvement of the offender's mental condition, CJA 2003 s.207(1).

A court may not include a mental health treatment requirement in an order unless it is satisfied:

(a)   it is satisfied:
    (i)    that the mental condition of the offender is such as requires; and
    (ii)   is susceptible to treatment, but does not warrant his detention under a hospital order;
(b)   the offender has expressed his willingness to comply with the order; and
(c)   arrangements have been or can be made for the proposed treatment, including arrangements for the offender's reception as a resident patient, where treatment as a resident is proposed, CJA 2003 s.207(3).

The requirement relating to treatment may be for the whole period of the order, or for any part of the period of the order.

The treatment required by the order may be either treatment as a resident patient in an independent hospital or care home, or a hospital under the MHA 1983, other than a hospital where high-security services are provided, or treatment as a non-resident patient at such institution or place as may be specified in the order, or treatment by or under the direction of a medical practitioner or chartered psychologist specified in the order, CJA 2003 s.207(2).

The medical nature of the treatment is not specified in the order, CJA 2003 s.207(2).

Where the court imposes an activity requirement, it may also impose an electronic monitoring requirement (see **Electronic Monitoring Requirements**, p.62), CJA 2003 s.177(4).

**Programme requirements (CJA 2003 s.202)**   A programme requirement requires the offender to participate in an accredited programme specified in the order, at a place so specified, on a number of days specified in the order.

*"Programme"* means a systematic set of activities. Where the court imposes an

activity requirement, it may also impose an electronic monitoring requirement (see **Electronic Monitoring Requirements**, p.62), CJA 2003 s.177(4).

**Prohibited activity requirements (CJA 2003 s.203)**   A prohibited activity requirement requires the offender to refrain from participating in activities specified in the requirement on a day or days specified in the order or during a period specified in the requirement, CJA 2003 s.203(1). The primary purpose is not to punish but to prevent – or at least reduce – further offending, *J* [2008] EWCA Crim 2002.

A prohibited activity requirement may not be included in an order unless the court has consulted an officer of a local probation board, CJA 2003 s.203(2).

The prohibited activity requirements may include requirements relating to possessing, carrying or using firearms, CJA 2003 s.203(3).

Where the court imposes an activity requirement, it may also impose an electronic monitoring requirement (see **Electronic Monitoring Requirements** p.62), CJA 2003 s.177(4).

**Rehabilitation activity requirements**   (CJA 2003 s.200A) (in force 1 February 2015).

A *"rehabilitation activity requirement"*, is a requirement that, during the relevant period, the offender must comply with any instructions given by the responsible officer to attend appointments or participate in activities or both, CJA 2003 s.200A(1).

The activities in which offenders may be instructed to participate include activities forming an accredited programme (see s.202(2)) and activities whose purpose is reparative, such as restorative justice activities, CJA 2003 s.200A(7).

**Residence requirements (CJA 2003 s.206)**   A residence requirement is a requirement that, during a period specified in the relevant order, the offender must reside at a place specified in the order, CJA 2003 s.206(1).

Before making an order containing a residence requirement, the court must consider the home surroundings of the offender, CJA 2003 s.206(3).

The requirement may provide for the offender to reside at a place other than the place specified. A hostel or other institution may not be specified as the place of residence except on the recommendation of an officer of a local probation board, CJA 2003 s.206(2) and (4).

Where the court imposes an activity requirement, it may also impose an electronic monitoring requirement (see **Electronic Monitoring Requirements**, p.62), CJA 2003 s.177(4).

**Supervision requirements (CJA 2003 s.213)**      (repealed by ORA 2014 on 1 February 2015. See 2015 edition for details).

**Unpaid work requirements (CJA 2003 ss.199 and 200)**   An unpaid work requirement requires the offender to perform unpaid work for a number of hours, not less than 40 and not more than 300, specified in the order, CJA 2003 s.199(1).

An unpaid work requirement may not be made unless the court is satisfied that the offender is a suitable person to perform work under such a requirement, CJA 2003 s.199(3).

Where an offender is convicted of more than one offence, an unpaid work requirement may be made in respect of each offence, and may direct that the hours of work specified in any of the requirements should be concurrent with or in addition to the hours of work required by the other requirement, but the total number of hours which are not concurrent must not exceed the permissible maximum of 300, CJA 2003 s.199(5).

The work must normally be completed within 12 months, but the requirement remains in force until all the hours of work have been completed, CJA 2003 s.200(2) and (3).

It is not necessary for the offender to consent to the making of an unpaid work requirement, CJA 2003 s.199.

An unpaid work requirement is subject to the availability of local arrangements, CJA 2003 s.218(1).

Where the court imposes an activity requirement, it may also impose an electronic monitoring requirement (see **Electronic Monitoring Requirements**, p.62), CJA 2003 s.177(4).

**Offender's Obligations**

The offender must keep in touch with the responsible officer, CJA 2003 s.220. The offender must not change residence without permission given by the responsible officer, or a court, CJA 2003 s.220A(1).

# COMMUNITY ORDERS: BREACH OF

## CRIMINAL JUSTICE ACT 2003 SCH.8

*References: Current Sentencing Practice B2; Archbold 5A-1287*

There are two types of breach: (a) a failure to comply with a requirement of the order and (b) the commission of a further offence during the currency of the order.

### Failure to Comply with Requirement of Order: Magistrates' Court

**Powers**   Where it is proved to a magistrates' court that an offender subject to a community order has failed without reasonable excuse to comply with any of the requirements of the relevant order, the court must either:

  (a)   impose more onerous requirements than the original order;

  (aa)  impose a fine not exceeding £2,500 (if the failure to comply took place on or after 3 December 2012);

  (b)   if the order was made by a magistrates' court, deal with him, for the offence in respect of which the order was made, in any manner in which it could deal with him if he had just been convicted by the court of the offence;

  (c)   where:

      (i)    the community order was made by the magistrates' court;

      (ii)   the original offence was not punishable by imprisonment;

      (iii)  the offender is aged 18 or over; and

      (iv)  the offender has wilfully and persistently failed to comply with the terms of the order,

deal with him in respect of the original offence by imposing a sentence of imprisonment (or detention in young offender institution) for a term not exceeding six months, CJA 2003 Sch.8 para.9(1).

**Partial compliance**   In dealing with the offender, the court must take into account the extent to which the offender has complied with the requirements of the relevant order, CJA 2003 Sch.8 para 9(2).

However, there is a distinction to be drawn between requirements intended to be therapeutic in nature and those intended to be punitive in nature. In *Wolstenholme* [2016] EWCA Crim 638 the court found that making no reduction for partial compliance with a requirement the purpose of which was therapeutic rather than punitive was justified.

**Revoke order if re-sentencing**   If the magistrates' court deals with the offender for the offence, (i.e. re-sentences him) it must revoke the order, CJA 2003 Sch.8 para.9(5).

**Can commit to Crown Court** If the community order was made by the Crown Court, the magistrates' court may commit the offender to the Crown Court, as an alternative to (a)-(c) above, CJA 2003 Sch.8 para.9(6).

### Failure to Comply with Requirement of Order: Crown Court

**Powers** When the offender appears before the Crown Court, the breach of the order must be proved to the satisfaction of the Crown Court. If the breach is proved, the Crown Court must:

a) amend the terms of the order so as to impose more onerous requirements which the Crown Court could impose if it were then making the order;

(aa) impose a fine not exceeding £2,500 (where the failure to comply occurred after 3 December 2012);

(b) deal with him, for the offence in respect of which the order was made, in any way in which he could have been dealt with for that offence by the court which made the order;

(c) where:

   (i) the original offence was not an offence punishable by imprisonment;

   (ii) the offender is aged 18 or over; and

   (iii) the offender has wilfully and persistently failed to comply with the requirements of the order,

deal with him, in respect of the original offence, by imposing a sentence of imprisonment (or detention in a young offender institution) for a term not exceeding six months, CJA 2003 Sch.8 para.10(1).

**Partial compliance** In dealing with the offender, the court must take into account the extent to which the offender has complied with the requirements of the relevant order, CJA 2003 Sch.8 para.10(2).

**Revoke order if re-sentencing** If the court deals with the offender for the offence, it must revoke the order, CJA 2003 Sch.8 para.10(5).

### Conviction for Further Offence: Magistrates' Court

**Powers** If an offender in respect of whom a community order made by a magistrates' court is in force is convicted by magistrates' court, and the magistrates' court considers it in the interests of justice to do so, the magistrates' court may either:

(a) simply revoke the community order; or

(b) revoke the order and deal with the offender in any way in which he could have been dealt with by the court which made the order, CJA 2003 Sch.8 para.21.

**Commit to Crown Court** If an offender in respect of whom a community order made by the Crown Court is in force is convicted by magistrates' court, the magistrates' court may commit the offender to the Crown Court, CJA 2003 Sch.8 para.22.

## Conviction for Further Offence: Crown Court

**Powers**   If an offender who is subject to a community order (whether imposed by the Crown Court of magistrates' court) appears before the Crown Court having been:

(a)   committed by the magistrates' court following a conviction by the magistrates' court; or

(b)   convicted of an offence before the Crown Court while he is subject to a community order, and where the Crown Court considers it is in the interests of justice to do so, the Crown Court may either:

    (i)   revoke the order; or

    (ii)   revoke the order and deal with the order in any way in which he could have been dealt with by the court which made the order, CJA 2003 Sch.8 para.23.

The power to deal with the offender depends on his being convicted while the order is still in force; it does not arise where he is convicted after the order has expired of an offence committed while the order was current, CJA 2003 Sch.8 para.23(3).

## Defendant Crosses Age Threshold

The offender must be sentenced on the basis of his age when the original order was made, not on his age at the date of sentence, CJA 2003 Sch.8 paras.9 and 21 (magistrates' court) and paras.10 and 23 (Crown Court).

# COMPENSATION ORDERS

## PCC(S)A 2000 s.130

*References: Current Sentencing Practice C1-150; Archbold 5A-377*

### General

**Power**   A compensation order may be made in respect of any *personal injury, loss or damage* which results from an offence of which the offender is convicted or from any offence which is taken into consideration, PCC(S)A 2000 s.130(1)(a).

A compensation order may be made as the only sentence for an offence, or in addition to most other forms of sentence, PCC(S)A 2000 s.130(1)(a).

**No need for application**   A court may make an order of its own volition, PCC(S)A 2000 s.130(1).

**Reduction in sentence**   A compensation order does not allow a defendant to "*buy*" a shorter sentence, *Copley* [1979] 1 Cr.App.R. (S.) 55.

**Duty upon the court**   A court must consider making a compensation order in any case where it is empowered to do so, PCC(S)A 2000 s.130(2A).

**No profit from offence**   The offender may be ordered to pay compensation even though he has not profited from the offence and his available assets are not themselves the proceeds of crime, PCC(S)A 2000 s.130(1).

**State reasons for not making an order**   If the court has power to make a compensation order, but does not exercise the power, it must state its reasons for not doing so, PCC(S)A 2000 s.130(3).

**Magistrates' courts limit**   In relation to a person aged under 18 who has been convicted of an offence in the magistrates' court, the court may order a maximum of £5,000 in respect of any one offence. If compensation is ordered to be paid in respect of offences taken into consideration, the total amount of the compensation must not exceed the total amount which the court could order in respect of all the offences of which the offender has been convicted (that is, £5,000 multiplied by the number of offences of which he has been convicted), PCC(S)A 2000 s.131.

### The Loss/Injury

The court must be satisfied that the injury, loss or damage which has occurred, is attributable to the offence in respect of which the compensation order is made, PCC(S)A 2000 s.130(1), *Boardman* (1987) 9 Cr.App.R. (S) 74.

The amount of loss must be agreed or proved by evidence, not inference or guesswork, *Amey* [1982] 4 Cr.App.R. (S). 410.

The process of making a compensation order should be a very simple one. A

[71]

court should decline to make an order unless it is based on very simple proposi-
tions which have been agreed or are easy to resolve. Where the amount of loss or
damage is disputed, the sentencer may hear evidence on the matter but should
hesitate before undertaking any complicated investigation, *Kneeshaw* (1974) 58
Cr.App.R. 439, *Hyde v Emery* (1984) 6 Cr.App.R. (S.) 206.

A compensation order may be made in respect of a loss which is not itself action-
able, *Chappell* [1984] 6 Cr.App.R. (S.) 214.

A compensation order can only be made for loss or injury, not general
inconvenience, *Stapylton* [2012] EWCA Crim 728; [2013] 1 Cr.App.R. (S.) 12.

**Fixing the Amount**

A compensation order may if appropriate contain an element of interest, *Schofield*
[1978] 67 Cr.App.R. 282.

If the victim of an assault has provoked the assault by his own violent behaviour
towards the offender, the amount of the compensation order may be reduced,
*Flinton* [2007] EWCA Crim 2322; [2008] 1 Cr.App.R. (S.) 96 (p.575).

Where the court proposes to impose a fine and to make a compensation order,
but considers that the offender has insufficient means to pay both an appropriate fine
and appropriate compensation, the compensation order takes preference, see
PCC(S)A 2000 s.130(12).

The *Magistrates' Court Sentencing Guidelines* 2008 contains a table of sugges-
tion personal injury awards, at p.166. The table is based on the Criminal Injuries
Compensation Authority tariff.

**The Offender's Means**

**Duty to consider means**   In determining whether to make a compensation order,
or the amount of such an order, the court must have regard to the means of the offender so far as they appear or are known to the court, PCC(S)A 2000 s.130(11).
The court does not need to have a precise calculation but rather must take a broad
picture, *Howell* (1978) 66 Cr.App.R. 179.

**No prospect of payment in reasonable time**   It is wrong in principle to impose
a compensation order when there is no realistic possibility that the compensation
will be paid within a reasonable time, *Stapylton* [2012] EWCA Crim 728; [2013]
1 Cr.App.R. (S.) 12.

**Immediate payment not possible**   If the compensation cannot be paid out of
resources immediately available to the offender the court should determine the
amount that he can reasonably pay out of income and order payment by instalments.
The period of payment by instalments may extend to three years in appropriate
cases, *Magistrates' Court Sentencing Guidelines* 2008 p.167.

**Future income**   The fact that the offender has been sentenced to custody does not
necessarily mean that a compensation order is inappropriate, but a compensation
order should not be made on the basis that the compensation will be paid out of

future income unless the offender has clear prospects of employment on release from custody and the obligation to pay compensation will not be an encouragement to commit further offences, *TICs and Totality Guideline* 2012 p.16.

**Selling assets to satisfy the order**    If it is proposed to raise the necessary funds by selling assets, the court should satisfy itself that the assets do exist and should ensure that the assets have been valued by a competent person, before acting on the valuation, see *Chambers* [1981] 3 Cr.App.R. (S.) 318. There is no principle that a compensation order should not be made where the order would force the sale of the matrimonial home, however the judge should take into account such a consequence of making an order, see *Parkinson* [2015] EWCA Crim 1448; [2016] 1 Cr.App.R. (S.) 6.

**Particular Circumstances**

**Multiple offences**    If the offender has been convicted of more than one offence, a separate order should be made in respect of each offence. If more than one offender has been convicted, a separate order should be made against each offender. If more than one offender has been convicted, but not all of them have the means to pay compensation, it is permissible to make an order against one offender for the whole amount of the loss, damage or injury, *Grundy and Moorehouse* [1974] All. E.R. 292.

**Death**    Where a person has died as a result of an offence, a compensation order may be made for funeral expenses or bereavement in respect of death, except in the case of a death due to an accident arising out of the presence of a motor vehicle on a road, PCC(S)A 2000 s.130(1)(b).

A compensation order in respect of funeral expenses may be made for the benefit of anyone who incurred the expenses, PCC(S)A 2000 s.130(9). A compensation order in respect of bereavement may be made only for the benefit of a person for whose benefit a claim for damages for bereavement could be made under the Fatal Accidents Act 1976 s.1A. The amount of compensation in respect of bereavement must not exceed £12,980, PCC(S)A 2000 s.130(10).

**Road accidents**    If personal injury, loss or damage arises out of an accident caused by the presence of a motor vehicle on a road, a compensation order may be made only if either:

(a)    the damage can be treated as damage arising out of an offence under the Theft Act 1968 or the Fraud Act 2006 (this would include any damage to a vehicle which has been stolen or taken without consent, whoever has actually caused the damage, so long as the damage occurred while the vehicle was out of the owner's possession); or

(b)    the offender is uninsured in respect of the personal injury, loss or damage concerned and compensation is not payable under the Motor Insurer's Bureau Agreement, PCC(S)A 2000 s.130(6).

In practice the effect of this appears to be that a compensation order may not be made in respect of loss, damage or injury, unless the claimant was driving a vehicle which was itself not insured for the purposes of the Road Traffic Acts, or the claimant was a person who at the relevant time knew or ought to have known that the vehicle in which he was travelling had been stolen or unlawfully taken, or was not covered by insurance. In these cases the claimant is not covered by the MIB Agreement and the court may make a compensation order for the full amount of the loss, damage or personal injury. The court may also make a compensation order in favour of a claimant claiming by virtue of a right of subrogation.

**Confiscation orders**    If the court has made a confiscation order under CJA 1988 or the POCA 2002, the court should consider whether to make an order under CJA 1988 s.72(7) or the POCA 2002 s.13(6), which allows the court to direct that if the offender is unable to satisfy the compensation order because his means are inadequate, the deficiency shall then be made good from the proceeds of the confiscation order.

### Prison in Default

The court does not fix any term of imprisonment in default, but may allow time for payment or fix payment by instalments. If the amount of the compensation order exceeds £20,000, the Crown Court has power to enlarge the powers of the magistrates' court responsible for enforcing the order if it considers that the maximum default term of 12 months under MCA 1980 Sch.4 is inadequate, *Bunce* (1977) 66 Cr.App.R. 109.

The court should make an order that the maximum term of imprisonment in default should be a figure taken from the table below, PCC(S)A 2000 s.139:

| Amount not exceeding: | Maximum term: |
| --- | --- |
| £50,000 | 18 months |
| £100,000 | 24 months |
| £250,000 | 36 months |
| £1 million | 60 months |
| Over £1 million | 120 months |

# CONCURRENT AND CONSECUTIVE SENTENCES

*References: Current Sentencing Practice H3-2500; Archbold 5A-165*

## General

Consecutive sentences of imprisonment *should not* normally be passed in respect of offences which arise out of the same transaction or incident, but may be passed in such cases in exceptional circumstances.

Consecutive sentences should normally be passed in the following cases:

(a)  where a burglar used violence towards an occupant of premises who interrupted him;
(b)  where violence is used to resist arrest for the primary offence;
(c)  where an offender is convicted of an offence under the Firearms Act 1968 committed by having a firearm with him at the time of another offence;
(d)  where one offence is committed while the offender is on bail in connection with the other offence;
(e)  where a community order is revoked following the offender's conviction of a further offence;
(f)  where a suspended sentence is activated following the offender's conviction of a further offence;
(g)  where an offender is convicted of doing an act tending to pervert the course of justice in relation to the other offence;
(h)  where offences are of the same or similar kind but where the overall criminality will not be reflected by concurrent sentences, e.g. where there are multiple victims or where domestic or sexual abuse is committed against the same victim. However, where, e.g., injuries are caused to multiple victims by a single piece of dangerous driving, a concurrent sentence would normally be appropriate.

## Focus on the Total Sentence

In all cases, whether or not the sentences are passed on the same occasion or by the same sentencer, the court should have regard to the principle of totality and review the aggregate sentence to ensure that it is just and appropriate for the offender's behaviour, taken as a whole, *AG's Ref. (No.28 of 2013)* [2013] EWCA Crim 1190. Reference should be made to the *TICs and Totality Guideline*, 2012.

## Specific Sentences

**Life**  The Sentencing Council's *Totality Guideline* states that it is generally undesirable to order an indeterminate sentence to be served consecutively to any other determinate period of imprisonment. The guideline recommends that the court should instead order the sentence to run concurrently but can adjust the minimum term for the new offence to reflect half of any period still remaining to be served under the existing sentence (to take account of the early release provisions for determinate sentences). For an offender serving an indeterminate sentence in circumstances where the court wishes to impose another indeterminate sentence, the guideline states that where necessary the court can order an indeterminate sentence to run consecutively to an indeterminate sentence passed on an earlier occasion. In such circumstances, the second sentence will commence on the expiration of the minimum term of the original sentence and the offender will become eligible for a parole review after serving both minimum terms. The court should consider the length of the aggregate minimum terms that must be served before the offender will be eligible for consideration by the Parole Board. If this is not just and proportionate, the court can adjust the minimum term. Finally, in the case of an offender serving an indeterminate sentence in circumstances where the court wishes to impose a determinate sentence, the court can order the determinate sentence to run consecutively to the indeterminate sentence. The determinate sentence will commence on the expiry of the minimum term of the indeterminate sentence and the offender will become eligible for a parole review after serving half of the determinate sentence (see p.11 of the guideline and *Taylor* [2011] EWCA Crim 2236; [2012] 1 Cr.App.R. (S.) 75).

**Extended determinate sentences**

It is not lawful to make extended sentences partly concurrent and partly consecutive, see *Francis* [2014] EWCA Crim 631.

There is no objection to imposing an extended sentence consecutive to a determinate sentence (either on the same occasion, or in addition to an existing determinate sentence), *Brown* [2006] EWCA Crim 1996 and *Hibbert* [2015] EWCA Crim 507; [2015] 2 Cr.App.R. (S.) 15 (p.159).

However, the Court of Appeal has repeatedly stated that it is undesirable to impose a determinate sentence consecutive to an extended sentence (see e.g. *Brown* and *Prior* [2014] EWCA Crim 1290).

This issue was considered in *Ulhaqdad* [2017] EWCA Crim 1216, where the court established that the order in which a court imposed an extended sentence and a determinate sentence (where those sentences are made to run consecutively) created no practical difficulty for the prison service in relation to the calculation of sentences and release dates etc. However, having identified no practical or principled reason for the guidance given in *Brown*, the court in *Ulhaqdad* maintained the status quo. Therefore the position remains that where extended and determinate sentences are being imposed to run consecutively, the determinate sentence should be imposed first.

Two further points remain. First, that in *Prior*, the court suggested that an alternative approach was to increase the custodial term of the extended sentence and make the sentences run concurrently. Secondly, despite the guidance in *Brown*, there is nothing unlawful about imposing an extended sentence consecutive to a determinate sentence in an appropriate case, *Hibbert* [2015] EWCA Crim 507; [2015] 2 Cr.App.R. (S.) 15.

In *B* [2015] EWCA Crim 1295, the Court of Appeal imposed two consecutive extended sentences where the total extended licence period was 10 years, that being in excess of the statutory maximum of eight years, this being a sexual case.

A five-judge court in *Thompson* [2018] EWCA Crim 639; [2018] 2 Cr.App.R. (S.) 19 confirmed that this was lawful though noted that the circumstances in which it would be appropriate would be *"exceptional"*.

## Licence Revoked

A court must not order a term of imprisonment to commence on the expiration of any other sentence of imprisonment from which the offender has already been released and in respect of which his licence has been revoked, CJA 2003 s.265(1).

# CONDITIONAL DISCHARGE

## PCC(S)A 2000 s.12

*References: Current Sentencing Practice B5; Archbold 5A-367*

## General

**Power**   The court may grant a discharge for any offence other than murder or an offence in respect of which the court is obliged to pass a mandatory custodial sentence under the PCC(S)A 2000 ss.110 or 111, the Firearms Act 1968 s.51A, the CJA 2003 ss.224A, 225 or 226, the Prevention of Crime Act 1953 s.1A(5), the Violent Crime Reduction Act 2006 s.29 or the CJA 1988 s.139AA(7), PCC(S)A 2000 s.12(1).

**Test**   The court must be of the opinion, having regard to the circumstances including the nature of the offence and the character of the offender, that it is inexpedient to inflict punishment, PCC(S)A 2000 s.12(1).

**Maximum period**   The discharge may be for any period not exceeding three years. There is no minimum period, PCC(S)A 2000 s.12(1)(b).

**Security**   On making an order for conditional discharge, the court may, if it thinks it expedient for the purpose of the offender's reformation, allow any person who consents to do so to give security for the good behaviour of the offender, PCC(S)A 2000 s.12(6). When making such an order, the court should specify the type of conduct from which the offender is to refrain, *CPD* 2015 [2015] EWCA Crim 1567 Sentencing J.20.

**Consent**   It is not necessary for the offender to consent, PCC(S)A 2000 s.12(1).

## Combining Orders

The following orders may be made in conjunction with a discharge:

(i)     a CBO, ASBCPA 2014 s.22(6);
(ii)    a compensation order, PCC(S)A 2000 s.12(7);
(iii)   a confiscation order, *Varma* [2012] UKSC 42;
(iv)    an order for costs, PCC(S)A 2000 s.12(8);
(v)     a deprivation order, PCC(S)A 2000 s.12(7);
(vi)    an order imposing any disqualification, PCC(S)A 2000 s.12(7);
(vii)   a football banning order, FSA 1989 s.14A(4)(b);
(viii)  an order to pay prosecution costs, PCC(S)A 2000 s.12(8);
(ix)    a recommendation for deportation, PCC(S)A 2000 s.12(7);
(x)     a restitution order, PCC(S)A 2000 s.12(7);
(xi)    a serious crime prevention order, SCA 2007 s.36(5); and
(xii)   an unlawful profit order, PCC(S)A 2000 s.12(7).

When imposing a conditional discharge, the court may not also make a fine or a referral order, *Sanck* (1990) 12 Cr.App.R. (S.) 155, PCC(S)A 2000 s.19(1)-(4)(d).

## Commission of Further Offence During Discharge Period

The power to deal with an offender subject to a conditional discharge arises when he is convicted of an offence committed during the period of the discharge, whether or not the discharge is still effective when he appears before the court, PCC(S)A 2000 s.13(1).

**Jurisdiction**  If the conditional discharge was granted by the Crown Court, the offender may be dealt with only by the Crown Court. If the conditional discharge was granted by a magistrates' court, the offender may be dealt with either by the Crown Court or by a magistrates' court, PCC(S)A 2000 s.13(2).

A magistrates' court may commit the offender to the Crown Court to be dealt with in respect of the conditional discharge, and to be sentenced for the latest offence, PCC(S)A 2000 s.13(5) (see **COMMITTAL FOR SENTENCE**, p.51.)

**Sentenced by court which imposed the original order**  Where the offender is before the court for breach of a conditional discharge where the discharge was imposed by that court, the court may deal with the offender as if he had just been convicted of the offence, PCC(S)A 2000 s.13(6).

**Order imposed by magistrates' court**  If the conditional discharge was granted by a magistrates' court, the court may deal with the offender for the offence in respect of which the conditional discharge was granted in any way in which a magistrates' court could deal with him for the offences concerned if it had just convicted him of that offence. The Crown Court must observe the relevant limitations on the powers of the magistrates' court, in relation to maximum terms of imprisonment, aggregate terms of imprisonment, and financial penalties, PCC(S)A 2000 s.13(7) and (8).

**Two conditional discharges**  If the offender is subject to two conditional discharges, the court may impose separate sentences for each of the offences in respect of which the orders were made.

**Effect of re-sentence**  If the court imposes a custodial sentence for the latest offence it will normally be appropriate for the court to impose a sentence for the original offence, which will terminate the conditional discharge, but there may be exceptional cases where it will be appropriate to leave the conditional discharge in effect, PCC(S)A 2000 s.14(3).

**Maximum served for the offence**  Where the offender has already served the maximum sentence for the offence, it will in appropriate to impose a conditional discharge, *Lynch* [2007] EWCA Crim 2624.

**Age of offender**  The offender should be sentenced on the basis of his current age, not his age on the date of conviction, PCC(S)A 2000 s.13(6)-(8).

# CONFISCATION ORDER—PROCEEDS OF CRIME ACT 2002

PROCEEDS OF CRIME ACT 2002

*References: Current Sentencing Practice D1; Archbold 5B*

**Preliminary Matters**

**Applicability**   The 2002 Act applies where all offences were committed on or after 24 March 2003, SI 2003/333 para.3(1). Where an offence has been committed over a period of two or more days, or at some time during a period of two or more days, it is taken to have been committed on the earliest of those days.

**Conditions**

(1)   A confiscation order is available where the defendant has either been:
    (a)   convicted of an offence or offences in proceedings before the Crown Court; or
    (b)   committed to the Crown Court for sentence in respect of an offence or offences under, s.70 POCA 2002, s.6(2).
(2)   The court must proceed with a view to a confiscation order if it is asked to do so by the prosecutor, or if the court believes *"it is appropriate for it to do so"*.

**Absconded defendants**   If the defendant absconds after conviction, the Court may proceed under s.27. If the defendant absconds prior to conviction, the court may proceed under s.28, providing that a period of two years from the date the court believed he absconded has passed, see e.g. *Okedare* [2014] EWCA Crim 1173; [2014] 2 Cr.App.R. (S.) 68 (p.529).

**Postponement**   The court may proceed with the confiscation hearing before sentencing the defendant for the offence(s) or may postpone the confiscation proceedings for a specified period, POCA 2002 s.14(1). This period may be extended, but not beyond the permitted period, POCA 2002 s.14(2) and (3). The permitted period is two years from the date of conviction, POCA 2002 s.14(5), however that limit does not apply where there are exceptional circumstances, POCA 2002 s.14(3). A postponement or extension may be made on application by the defence or prosecution, or by the court of its own motion, POCA 2002 s.14(7).

If the court has postponed confiscation proceedings it may proceed to sentence the defendant (see **Sentencing the Defendant for the Offence** p.85).

**Civil proceedings**   If the court believes that any victim of the offence has initiated, or intends to initiate, civil proceedings against the defendant, it is not bound to institute confiscation proceedings, but may do so in its discretion, POCA 2002 s.6(6).

## (1) Criminal Lifestyle

If the Crown Court embarks on confiscation proceedings, it must first decide whether the defendant has a *"criminal lifestyle"*, POCA 2002 s.6(4)(a).

(1)  A person has a *"criminal lifestyle"* if either:
   (a)  he is convicted of one of the offences specified in POCA 2002 Sch.2; or
   (b)  the offence constitutes *"conduct forming part of a course of criminal activity"*; or
   (c)  if the offence was committed over a period of at least six months and the defendant has benefited from the conduct, POCA 2002 s.75(2).

   An offence constitutes part of a course of criminal conduct if either:
   (a)  the defendant has been convicted in the same proceedings of at least four offences, he has benefited from at least four offences, and his *"relevant benefit"* is at least £5,000; or
   (b)  the defendant has been convicted on at least two separate occasions during the period of six years ending with a day when the proceedings for the present offence were started and has benefited from the offences in respect of which he was convicted on both of those occasions, and the *"relevant benefit"* amounts to at least £5,000, POCA 2002 s.75(3) and (4).

The latest offence must have been committed on or after 24 March 2003, but it is not necessary that the two earlier offences should have been if the offender has a criminal lifestyle, see (2A) below; otherwise see (2B).

**(2A)  Offender has a criminal lifestyle**  If the court decides that the defendant has a *"criminal lifestyle"* it must decide whether he has benefited from his *"general criminal conduct"*, POCA 2002 s.6(4)(b).

*"General criminal conduct"* is *"all his criminal conduct"*, and it is immaterial whether the conduct occurred before or after the passing of the Act or whether property constituting a benefit from conduct was obtained before or after the passing of the Act, POCA 2002 s.76(2).

**Assumptions**  In making this decision, the Court *must* make any of the assumptions required by s.10 which apply, unless the assumption is *"shown to be incorrect"* or there would be a *"serious risk of injustice"* if the assumption were made, POCA 2002 s.10(1) and (6).

(1)  The first assumption is that any property transferred to the defendant within the period of six years ending on the day on which proceedings were started against the defendant was obtained by him as a result of his general criminal conduct.
(2)  The second assumption is that any property held by the defendant at any time after the date of conviction was obtained by him as a result of his general criminal conduct.
(3)  The third assumption is that any expenditure incurred by the defendant within a period of six years ending with the date on which the proceedings were started against him was met from property obtained by him as a result of his general criminal conduct.
(4)  The fourth assumption is that any property obtained or assumed to have been obtained by the defendant was free of any other interest in the property, POCA 2002 s.10(2)–(5).

**(2B)  Offender does not have a criminal lifestyle**  If the court decides that the defendant does not have a *"criminal lifestyle"*, the court must then decide whether the defendant has benefited from his *"particular criminal conduct"*, POCA 2002 s.6(4)(c).

*"Particular criminal conduct"* is *"all his criminal conduct"* which *"constitutes the offence or offences concerned"*, or *"constitutes the offences of which he was convicted in the same proceedings as those in which he was convicted of the offence or offences concerned"*, or *"constitutes offences which the court will be taking into consideration in deciding his sentence for the offence or offences concerned"*, POCA 2002 s.76(3).

Benefit arising from offences committed before 24 March 2003, and which are taken into consideration, must be disregarded.

**Standard of proof**  Any question arising in connection with whether the defendant has a criminal life style or whether he has benefited from his general or particular criminal conduct must be decided on a *"balance of probabilities"*, POCA 2002 s.6(7).

### Benefit Figure and Available Amount

The court must then determine the benefit derived, POCA 2002 s.8. The benefit is the total value of property or advantage gained, not the net profit after deductions for expenses etc., *May* [2008] UKHL 28; [2009] 1 Cr.App.R. (S.) 31.

The court must make an order for the amount which it has assessed to be the defendant's benefit, unless either:

(a)  it believes that a victim of the offence has started or intends to start civil proceedings against the defendant (in which case the amount of the order is such amount *"as the court believes is just"*, but the amount must not exceed the amount of the defendant's benefit; or
(b)  the defendant shows that the *"available amount"* is less than the benefit (in which case the amount of the confiscation order is either the *"available amount"* itself, or a nominal amount).

The *"available amount"* includes the total of the values of all *"free property"* held by the defendant at the time the confiscation order is made, and the total value of all *"tainted gifts"*, POCA 2002 s.83. See also POCA 2002 s.9.

### Procedure

The court will set a timetable for the key procedural steps.

**Prosecution**  If the Crown Court is proceeding with a view to a confiscation order on the application of the prosecutor, the prosecutor must give the Crown Court a statement of information, POCA 2002 s.16(1). If the Crown Court is proceeding with a view to confiscation on its own initiative, it may order the prosecutor to give such a statement, POCA 2002 s.16(2).

**Defence**  Where a statement of information has been given to the court and a copy served on the defendant, the Crown Court may order the defendant to indicate to what extent he accepts the allegations made in the statement, and in so far as he does not accept an allegation, "*to give particulars of any matters he proposes to rely on*", POCA 2002 s.17(1). If the defendant accepts any allegation, the Crown Court may treat that acceptance as conclusive, POCA 2002 s.17(2). If the defendant fails to comply with an order, he may be treated as accepting every allegation in the statement of information other than an allegation in respect of which he has complied with the requirement, or an allegation that he has benefited from his general or particular criminal conduct, POCA 2002 s.17(3). No acceptance of an allegation by the defendant is admissible in evidence in proceedings for an offence, POCA 2002 s.17(6).

The Crown Court may order the defendant to give it the "*information specified in the order*", POCA 2002 s.18(2). There is no restriction on the kind of information which may be specified. If the defendant fails "*without reasonable excuse*" to comply with an order, the court "*may draw such inference as it believes is appropriate*" from the failure, POCA 2002 s.18(4).

### Other Orders to be Made after Confiscation Order Imposed

When the Crown Court makes a confiscation order it must make the following orders:

### Enforcement receiver

(a) *Appoint receiver (ss.50–55)* The court may appoint an "*enforcement receiver*" on the application of the prosecutor.

(b) *Empower the receiver* The court must confer on the enforcement receiver the powers under s.51.

(c) *Transfer from management receiver to enforcement receiver (s.64)* Where a receiver has been appointed in connection with a restraint order, and the Crown Court makes a confiscation order and a receiver is appointed under s.50, the Crown Court must order the "*management receiver*" appointed in connection with the restraint order to transfer to the "*enforcement receiver*" appointed in connection with the confiscation order all property held by the first receiver by virtue of the exercise of his powers.

**Allow time for payment (s.11)**   If the defendant shows that he needs time to pay the order, the court may make an order allowing the payment to be made within a specified period which must not exceed six months from the day on which the confiscation order is made, POCA 2002 s.11(1)–(3).

If the defendant makes a further application to the Crown Court within the specified period and Court believes that there are "*exceptional circumstances*" it may make an order extending the period. The extended period must not extend beyond 12 months from the day on which the confiscation order was made, POCA 2002 s.11(4)–(6).

Although the second application must be made within the original six month specified period, the order extending the period may be made after the end of that period, but not after the end of the period of 12 months starting with the day on which the confiscation order was made, POCA 2002 s.11(6).

It is not open to the Crown Court to make an order allowing 12 months for payment on the defendant's initial application, even though the defendant shows that there are exceptional circumstances in which this would be appropriate. The defendant must make a further application within the six month period.

**Fix term of imprisonment in default (s.35)**    Sections 139(2) to (3) and (9) and 140(1) to (4) of the PCC(S)A 2000 apply as if the amount ordered to be paid were a fine imposed on the defendant by the court making the confiscation order (see **DEFAULT TERMS—CROWN COURT**, p.95). Where a court fixes a term under s.139(2) of the PCC(S)A 2000 in respect of an amount to be paid under a confiscation order, the maximum terms are those set out in the table below.

| Amount | Maximum term |
| --- | --- |
| £10,000 or less | 6 months |
| More than £10,000 but no more than £500,000 | 5 years |
| More than £500,000 but no more than £1million | 7 years |
| More than £1million | 14 years |

The prosecution cannot appeal against the making of a default order, *Mills* [2018] EWCA Crim 944; [2018] 2 Cr.App.R. (S.) 32.

### Sentencing the Defendant for the Offence (ss.13, 15, 71)

The defendant cannot claim that his sentence should be mitigated because a confiscation order has been made.

**Before sentencing**    The court must take account of the confiscation order before imposing:

(i)    a fine;
(ii)   an order involving payment by the defendant, other than a compensation order or an unlawful profit order;
(iii)  a deprivation order under PCC(S)A 2000; or
(iv)   a forfeiture order under MDA 1971; or
(v)    a forfeiture order under TA 2000, POCA 2002 s.13(2).

**Postponement**    If the court has postponed confiscation proceedings it may proceed to sentence the defendant, however during the postponement period, it *must not* impose:

(i)    a fine;
(ii)   a compensation order;
(iii)  an unlawful profit order;
(iv)   a deprivation order under PCC(S)A 2000; or
(v)    a forfeiture order under MDA 1971; or
(vi)   a forfeiture order under TA 2000, POCA 2002 s.15(2);
(vii)  the statutory surcharge.

It appears that the court may impose a slavery and trafficking reparation order, however, it is suggested that such is simply a missed consequential amendment and that when postponing confiscation proceedings, such an order should not be made prior to the imposition of the confiscation order.

Where the defendant has been sentenced and subsequently a confiscation order is made following a postponement, the sentence originally passed may be varied by the addition of:

(i)     a fine; or
(ii)    a compensation order; or
(iii)   an unlawful profit order; or
(iv)    a deprivation order under PCC(S)A 2000; or
(v)     a forfeiture order under MDA 1971; or
(vi)    a forfeiture order under TA 2000 within 28 days starting with the last day of the period of postponement. This does not necessarily mean the day on which the confiscation order is actually made, POCA 200 s.15(3)–(4).

**Compensation**   A court which has made a confiscation order may leave the confiscation order out of account in deciding whether to make a compensation order in favour of the victim of the offence and in deciding the amount of the order, POCA 2002 s.13(2). It is open to the Crown Court to make a confiscation order and a compensation order in respect of the same offence, even though this means that the defendant will be required to pay twice the amount involved in the offence, see *Copley* (1979) 1 Cr.App.R. (S.) 55 for a related decision.

**Sentencing powers**   If the defendant has been committed for sentence under s.70 for an either way offence, the powers of the Crown Court to deal with the offender for the offence depend on whether the magistrates' court at the time of committal stated in accordance with s.70(5) that it would have committed the defendant for sentence under the PCC(S)A 2000 s.3. If it did, the Crown Court must inquire into the circumstances of the case and may deal with the defendant in any way in which it could deal with him if he had just been convicted of the offence on indictment, POCA 2002 s.71(1) and (2).

If the magistrates' court did not make a statement under s.70(5) in respect of an either way offence, or the offence is not an either way offence, the Crown Court, having inquired into the circumstances of the case, may deal with the defendant in any way in which the magistrates' court could deal with him if it had just convicted him of the offence, POCA 2002 s.71(3).

### Enforcing the Default Term (ss.35–39)

All questions relating to serving the default term will be dealt with in the magistrates' court, in the same way as a fine, subject to the amendments made by s.35(3) to the normal procedure, POCA 2002 s.35.

# CRIMINAL BEHAVIOUR ORDERS

*References: Current Sentencing Practice C2-100, Archbold 5A-805*

**Availability**   The power to make a CBO is available where a person is convicted of an offence and where the court imposes a sentence or conditional discharge, ASBCPA 2014 s.22(1) and (6).

For offenders aged under 18 when the application is made, the prosecution must find out the views of the local youth offending team before applying, ASBCPA 2014 s.22(8).

**Test**   The court must be satisfied beyond reasonable doubt that:
(1)   the offender has engaged in behaviour that caused or was likely to cause harassment, alarm or distress to any person; and
(2)   making the order will help in preventing the offender from engaging in such behaviour, ASBCPA 2014 s.22(3) and (4).

*Note: This is a less stringent test than the test for imposing a post-conviction ASBO.*

Threshold Home Office Guidance (2017) stated that the CBO "*is intended for tackling the most serious and persistent offenders where their behaviour has brought them before a criminal court.*" Section 22 of the 2014 Act might on a literal construction be said to apply to a high proportion of cases in the criminal courts. It was not Parliament's intention that criminal behaviour orders should become a mere matter of box-ticking routine. As was said in *DPP v Bulmer*, such orders were not lightly to be imposed; the court should proceed with a proper degree of caution and circumspection; the order must be tailored to the specific circumstances of the person on whom it was to be imposed; and assessments of proportionality were intensively fact sensitive, *Khan (Kamran)* [2018] EWCA Crim 1472.

**Prosecution must apply**   An order may only be made on the application of the prosecution, ASBCPA 2014 s.22(7).

**Guidance**   *Relevance of ASBO caselaw* As with any order of a criminal court which has characteristics of an injunction, it is essential that the guidance set out in *Boness* [2005] EWCA Crim 2395; [2006] 1 Cr.App.R. (S.) 120 at paras 19-23 in relation to anti-social behaviour orders should be borne in mind, *Khan (Kamran)* [2018] EWCA Crim 1472.

*Explanation of the legislation* The court gave guidance as to the operation of the provisions in *DPP v Bulmer* [2015] EWHC 2323 (Admin); [2016] 1 Cr.App.R. (S.) 12.

## How Long May the Order Last/When Does it Take Effect?

**Effective date**   The order takes effect on the day it is made, save for where on the day an order is made the offender is subject to another criminal behaviour order. In such a circumstance, the new order may be made so as to take effect on the day on which the previous order ceases to have effect, ASBCPA 2014 s.25(1) and (2).

**Length: Aged 18+ when order made**   A fixed period of not less than two years, or for an indefinite period, ASBCPA 2014 s.25(4).

**Length: Aged under 18 when order made**   A fixed period of not less than one year and not more than three years, ASBCPA 2014 s.25(4).

### Making the order

**Findings of Fact**   The findings of fact giving rise to the making of the order must be recorded, *Khan*.

**Explaining the order**   The order must be explained to the offender. The exact terms of the order must be pronounced in open court and the written order must accurately reflect the order as pronounced. In the case of a foreign national, consideration should be given for the need for the order to be translated, *Khan (Kamran)* [2018] EWCA Crim 1472.

### Prohibitions and Requirements Forming Part of the Order

**Contents**   The order may, for the purpose of preventing the offender from engaging in such behaviour, (a) prohibit the offender from doing anything, or (b) require the offender to do anything, described in the order.

The order may specify periods for which particular prohibitions or requirements have effect, ASBCPA 2014 s.25(6).

**Must hear from supervising officer**   Before including a requirement, the court must receive evidence about its suitability and enforceability from the supervising officer, ASBCPA 2014 s.24(1) and (2).

**The terms of the order**   Prohibitions should be reasonable and proportionate; realistic and practical; and be in terms which make it easy to determine and prosecute a breach. Because an order must be precise and capable of being understood by the offender, a court should ask itself before making an order "*are the terms of this order clear so that the offender will know precisely what it is that he is prohibited from doing?*", *Khan (Kamran)* [2018] EWCA Crim 1472.

**Geographical prohibitions**   These should be clearly delineated (generally with the use of clearly marked maps, although there is no problem of definition in an order extending to Greater Manchester for example) and individuals whom the defendant is prohibited from contacting or associating with should be clearly identified, *Khan*. Prohibitions need not be related to the geographical area in which the behaviour giving rise to the order was conducted, *Browne-Morgan* [2016] EWCA Crim 1903; [2017] 1 Cr.App.R. (S.) 33.

**Interference with other elements of offender's life**   Prohibitions and requirements must avoid any interference with the times at which the offender normally works or attends an educational establishment and any conflict with the requirements of any other court order or injunction to which the offender may be subject, ASBCPA 2014 s.22(9).

Prohibitions interfering with the operation of the offender's business will not contravene the legislation in an appropriate case, *Janes* [2016] EWCA Crim 676; [2016] 2 Cr.App.R. (S.) 27.

**Obligations on the offender**   An offender must keep in touch with the person responsible for supervising compliance in relation to a requirement and notify the person of any change of address. These obligations have effect as requirements of the order, ASBCPA 2014 s.24(6).

### Review periods

A CBO is subject to review periods every 12 months, beginning on the day on which the order took effect, or the day on which it was varied or most recently varied, ASBCPA 2014 s.28(2).

**Content of review**   A review must consider:

(a)   the extent to which the offender has complied with the order;
(b)   the adequacy of any support available to the offender to help him or her comply with it;
(c)   any matters relevant to the question whether an application should be made for the order to be varied or discharged, ASBCPA 2014 s.28(3).

### Interim Orders

The court may make a criminal behaviour order that lasts until the final hearing of the application or until further order if the court thinks it just to do so, ASBCPA 2014 s.26(2).

There is no requirement to consult the local youth offending team, that the prosecution make an application, or that the order is in addition to a sentence or conditional discharge, ASBCPA 2014 s.26(3).

The court has the same powers whether or not the criminal behaviour order is an interim order.

### Variation and Discharge

**Power**   An order may be varied or discharged by the court which made it on the application of the offender, or the prosecution, ASBCPA 2014 s.27(1).

**Extent of power**   The power to vary an order includes power to include an additional prohibition or requirement in the order or to extend the period for which a prohibition or requirement has effect, ASBCPA 2014, s.27(4).

**Bar on future applications**   If an application by the offender is dismissed, the offender may make no further application without the consent of the court which made the order, or the agreement of the prosecution, ASBCPA 2014 s.27(2).

If an application by the prosecution is dismissed, the prosecution may make no further application without the consent of the court which made the order, or the agreement of the offender, ASBCPA 2014 s.27(3).

**Breach**

**Offence**   A person who, without reasonable excuse, (a) does anything prohibited or, (b) fails to do anything required by a criminal behaviour order, commits an offence, ASBCPA 2014 s.30(1).

**Maximum sentence**   Five years, ASBCPA 2014 s.30(2).

**Conditional discharge**   A court may not impose a conditional discharge for a breach of a CBO, ASBCPA 2014 s.30(3).

**Reporting restrictions**   YJCEA 1999 s.45 (power to restrict reporting of criminal proceedings involving persons under 18) applies to proceedings for a breach of a CBO, but CYPA 1933 s.49 does not apply, ASBCPA 2014 s.30(5).

# CUSTODIAL SENTENCES: GENERAL CRITERIA

CRIMINAL JUSTICE ACT 2003 ss.152, 153, 156

*References: Current Sentencing Practice A1; Archbold 5A-236, 5A-625*

## General Restriction on Imposing Custodial Sentence

A court must not pass a custodial sentence unless it is of the opinion that the offence or the combination of the offence and one or more offences associated with it was so serious that neither a fine alone nor a community sentence can be justified for the offence, save where the sentence is:

(a) fixed by law; or
(b) a mandatory or required minimum sentences under:
  (i) PCC(S)A 2000 ss.110 and 111;
  (ii) Firearms Act 1968 s.51A;
  (iii) Prevention of Crime Act 1953 s.1(2B) or s.1A(5);
  (iv) Violent Crime Reduction Act 2006 s.29(4) or (6);
  (v) Criminal Justice Act 1988 ss.139(6B), 139A(5B) and 139AA(7); or
  (vi) sentences of life imprisonment or detention under CJA 2003 ss.224A, 225 or 226, CJA 2003 s.152(1) and (2).

**Community order exception** A custodial sentence may be passed for an offence which is not "*so serious that neither a fine alone nor a community sentence can be justified*" if the offender refuses to express his willingness to comply with a proposed requirement of a community order which requires him to express his willingness to comply, CJA 2003 s.152(3)(a) (See **COMMUNITY ORDERS**, p.57).

## Length of Discretionary Custodial Sentences

Subject to a required minimum sentence under:

(a) Prevention of Crime Act 1953 ss.1(2B) and 1A(5);
(b) Firearms Act 1968 s.51A(2);
(c) Criminal Justice Act 1988 ss.139(6B), 139A(5B) and 139AA(7);
(d) Powers of Criminal Courts (Sentencing) Act 2000 ss.110(2) and 111(2);
(e) Criminal Justice Act 2003 ss.226A(4) and 226B(2);
(f) Violent Crime Reduction Act 2006 s.29(4) or (6), and save where a court imposes a sentence;
(g) under Criminal Justice Act 2003 s.224A, 225 or 226; or
(h) which is fixed by law;

a custodial sentence must be for the shortest term (not exceeding the permitted maximum) that in the opinion of the court is commensurate with the seriousness of the offence, or the combination of the offence and one or more offences associated with it, CJA 2003 s.153.

[91]

A magistrates' court may not impose a custodial sentence of less than five days, MCA 1980 s.132.

## Determining Seriousness

The court must take account of all available information about the circumstances of the offence when forming an opinion about the seriousness of the offence, for the purpose of deciding whether the offence is so serious that a custodial sentence is necessary and what is the shortest term which is commensurate with the seriousness of the offence, CJA 2003 s.156(1) and (2).

In considering the seriousness of any offence, the court must consider the offender's culpability in committing the offence and any harm which the offence caused, was intended to cause or might forseeably have caused, CJA 2003 s.143(1).

## Reports

**Offender aged 18+**   If a court proposes to impose a custodial sentence on an offender over the age of 18 on any ground other than the failure of an offender to express his willingness to comply with one of the orders mentioned in s.152(3) it must *"obtain and consider"* a pre-sentence report unless it is of the opinion *"that it is unnecessary"* to do so, CJA 2003 s.156(3).

**Offender aged under 18**   In the case of an offender under the age of 18, a pre-sentence report is mandatory before the court imposes a custodial sentence (other than on the basis of a failure to express willingness under s.152(3) save for where there exists a previous pre-sentence report, and the court has had regard to the information contained in that report, or, if there is more than one such report, the most recent report, CJA 2003 s.156(5).

**No report obtained**   If the sentencing court does not obtain a pre-sentence report, where such a report is required, the failure does not affect the validity of the sentence or order of the court, but any appellate court dealing with the case is placed under similar obligations, subject to the same exceptions, CJA 2003 s.156(6).

**Guidelines**   See also the Sentencing Council's *Imposition of Community and Custodial Sentences Definitive Guideline* (2017).

# CUSTODY FOR LIFE

## PCC(S)A 2000 ss.93, 94

*References: Current Sentencing Practice A2 and F2; Archbold 5A-725, 5A-1044*

### Mandatory life

Where a person aged under 21 is convicted of murder, he must be sentenced to custody for life unless he is liable to be detained during Her Majesty's pleasure (see **MURDER**, p.205), PCC(S)A 2000 ss.90 and 93.

### Discretionary life

Where a person aged 18-20 is convicted of an offence for which an offender aged 21+ would be liable to a sentence of imprisonment for life, the court may impose a sentence of custody for life (see **AUTOMATIC LIFE SENTENCE**, p.45 and **LIFE SENTENCE: "DISCRETIONARY"** p.191).

### Minimum term

A court which imposes a sentence of custody for life must fix a minimum term in accordance with the relevant provisions (see **MINIMUM TERM**, p.203 for minimum terms in non-murder cases, and **MURDER**, p.205 for the minimum term in murder cases. A whole life tariff is not available for those under the age of 21, CJA 2003 Sch.21 para.4.

# DEFAULT TERMS (CROWN COURT): FINES

## PCC(S)A 2000 s.139

*References: Current Sentencing Practice B3-1050; Archbold 5A-407*

If the Crown Court imposes a fine, the court must fix a term of imprisonment in default of payment of the fine, PCC(S)A 2000 s.139(2).

The following table shows the default terms applicable to fines and confiscation orders, PCC(S)A 2000 s.139(4).

| Fine | Term |
| --- | --- |
| Not exceeding £200 | 7 days |
| More than £200, not exceeding £500 | 14 days |
| More than £500, not exceeding £1,000 | 28 days |
| More than £1,000, not exceeding £2,500 | 45 days |
| More than £2,500, not exceeding £5,000 | 3 months |
| More than £5,000, not exceeding £10,000 | 6 months |
| More than £10,000, not exceeding £20,000 | 12 months |
| More than £20,000, not exceeding £50,000 | 18 months |
| More than £50,000, not exceeding £100,000 | 2 years |
| More than £100,000, not exceeding £250,000 | 3 years |
| More than £250,000, not exceeding £1 million | 5 years |
| Over £1 million | 10 years |

These terms are maximum terms for the sums in question; the court should exercise its discretion and fix an appropriate default term within the relevant maximum, PCC(S)A 2000 s.139(2) and (4).

## Compensation or costs orders

The Crown Court does not fix a default term when it makes a compensation order or orders the offender to pay the costs of the prosecution, but may enlarge the powers of the magistrates' court, see *Bunce* (1977) 66 Cr.App.R. 109.

# DEFERMENT OF SENTENCE

## PCC(S)A 2000 ss.1, 1ZA, 1A, 1B, 1C, 1D, AND 2

*References: Current Sentencing Practice B7; Archbold 5A-187*

### Making the Order

**Availability**   These provisions apply to all offences irrespective of the date on which the offence was committed.

**Power**   Either the magistrates' court or the Crown Court may defer passing sentence on an offender for the purpose of enabling the court to have regard to his conduct after conviction (including the making by him of reparation for the offence) or any change to his circumstances, PCC(S)A 2000 s.1(1).

**Test**   The power may be exercised only if:

(a)   the offender consents;
(b)   the offender undertakes to comply with any requirements as to his conduct during the period of deferment that the court considers it appropriate to impose; and

the court is satisfied that it is in the interests of justice to exercise the power, having regard to the nature of the offence and the characteristics of the offender, PCC(S)A 2000 s.1(3).

**Maximum period**   Sentence may be deferred for a period of not more than six months. A court cannot impose a second deferral, PCC(S)A 2000 s.1(4).

**Adding requirements**   The court is not obliged to impose requirements on deferring sentence, but it may do so, PCC(S)A 2000 s.1(3)(b) and *New Sentences: CJA 2003 Guideline*, para.1.2.8.

**Requirements**   The requirements which the court may require the offender to comply with during the period of deferment are not specified, but it is provided that the court may appoint an officer of a local probation board or other person to act as a supervisor, PCC(S)A 2000 s.1(5).

The statutory power is not limited to the requirements which may be imposed in connection with a community order.

The requirements that may be imposed under that paragraph include restorative justice requirements, PCC(S)A 2000 s.1ZA(1). A restorative justice requirement is a requirement to participate in an activity:

(a)   where the participants consist of, or include, the offender and one or more of the victims;
(b)   which aims to maximise the offender's awareness of the impact of the offending concerned on the victims; and

(c)   which gives an opportunity to a victim or victims to talk about, or by other means express experience of, the offending and its impact, PCC(S)A 2000 s.1ZA(2).

## After the Order is Made

**AG's reference**   An order deferring the passing of sentence is a sentence for the purposes of CJA 1988 s.36 and therefore can be referred, *AG's Ref. (No.22 of 1992)* (1993) 14 Cr.App.R. (S.) 435.

**Failure to comply**   If the offender fails to comply with the requirements imposed during the period of deferment, he may be brought before the court and dealt with before the end of the period of deferment, PCC(S)A 2000 s.1B(1).

**Convicted of an offence during period of deferment**   A court, which has deferred sentence may deal with the offender before the end of the period of deferment if he is convicted of an offence during the deferment period, PCC(S)A 2000 s.1C(1).

If the conviction for the later offence occurs in England and Wales, the court which sentences him for the later offence may deal with him for the offence or offences in respect of which sentence has been deferred, but a magistrates' court may not deal with an offender in respect of a sentence deferred by the Crown Court, and if the Crown Court deals with an offender in respect of a sentence deferred by a magistrates' court, the Crown Court may not pass a sentence which could not have been passed by a magistrates' court, PCC(S)A 2000 s.1C(3).

# DEPORTATION

IMMIGRATION ACT 1971 S.6 AND SCH.3 AND UK BORDERS ACT 2007 S.32

*References: Current Sentencing Practice C5; Archbold 5A-923, 5A-1114*

## Introduction

For the purposes of sentencing, there are two types of deportation; the *"automatic liability to deportation"* regime and the *"recommendation for deportation"* regime.

Other sentencing powers are not to be used to removed offenders from the UK, *R. (Dragoman) v Camberwell Green Magistrates' Court* [2012] EWHC 4105.

Notwithstanding the below, it is the Secretary of State's policy that no EU citizen be deported unless the term of imprisonment imposed is two years or more, *Kluxen* [2010] EWCA Crim 1081; [2011] 1 Cr.App.R. (S.) 39 (p.249).

## Automatic Liability to Deportation

**Duty to deport**    The Secretary of State must make a deportation order in respect of a foreign criminal. A foreign criminal means a person who:

(a)  is not a British citizen;
(b)  is convicted of an offence in the UK; and
(c)  satisfies one of the following conditions:
  (i)   is sentenced to a period of imprisonment of at least 12 months, or;
  (ii)  the offence is an offence specified by the Secretary of State under NIAA 2002 s.2(4)(a), and the person is sentenced to a period of imprisonment, UKBA 2007 s.32(1) and (5).

*Note: The second condition was not in force on 31 October 2018.*

**Do not rearrange sentences to avoid liability**    As a matter of principle it would not be right to reduce an otherwise appropriate sentence so as to avoid the provisions of the UK Borders Act 2007 because: (a) sentences are intended to be commensurate with the seriousness of the offence, (b) when passing sentence a judge is neither entitled nor obliged to reach a contrived result so as to avoid the operation of a statutory provision and (c) automatic deportation provisions are not a penalty included in the sentence, *Mintchev* [2011] EWCA Crim 499.

Note however, that in *Hakimzadeh* [2009] EWCA Crim 959; [2010] 1 Cr.App.R. (S.) 10 (p.49) where the defence suggested the sentences be rearranged to avoid the deportation provisions, relying upon the age of the offending and the fact that *"deportation was never in the judge's mind"*, the Court of Appeal acceded to the request.

**Definition of "12 months imprisonment"**    A *"period of imprisonment of at least 12 months"* does not include:

(a)   a suspended sentence (unless a court subsequently orders that the sentence or any part of it is to take effect);

(b)   a person who is sentenced to a period of at least 12 months only by virtue of being sentenced to consecutive sentences.

However, it does include a person sentenced to detention or to be detained in an institution other than a prison and any indeterminate period, provided it could last for more than 12 months, UKBA 2007 s.38(1).

**Exceptions**   There are a series of exceptions to the duty to make a deportation order. These include:

(a)   where the Secretary of State thinks that the foreign criminal was aged under 18 at the date of conviction;

(b)   where the deportation order would breach a person's Convention rights, or the UK's obligations under the Refugee Convention;

(c)   where the removal of the foreign criminal from the United Kingdom in pursuance of a deportation order would breach rights of the foreign criminal under the EU treaties;

(d)   where certain provisions of the EA 2003 apply;

(e)   where certain orders or directions under the MHA 1983 apply (including s.37, 45A, and 47), UKBA 2007 s.33.

The existence of an exception does not prevent the making of a deportation order, see UKBA 2007 s.33(7).

### Recommendations for Deportation

**No recommendation where automatic liability exists**   A court should not make a recommendation for deportation in the case of an offender who is liable to automatic deportation as no useful purpose would be served, *Kluxen* [2010] EWCA Crim 1081; [2011] 1 Cr.App.R. (S.) 39 (p.249).

**Availability**   A court may recommend for deportation an offender aged 17 on the day of conviction if he is not a British citizen and has been convicted of an offence punishable with imprisonment, IA 1971 s.3(6) and 6(1).

The offender is deemed to have attained the age of 17 at the date of his conviction if on considering any evidence he appears to have done so to the court, IA 1971 s.6(3)(a).

If any question arises as to whether any person is a British citizen, or is entitled to any exemption, the person claiming to be a British citizen or to be entitled to any exemption must prove that he is, IA 1971 s.3(8).

**Irish and Commonwealth citizens**   The principal classes of persons exempted from liability to deportation are Commonwealth citizens and citizens of the Republic of Ireland who:

(a)   had that status in 1973; and

(b)   were then ordinarily resident in the UK; and

(c)   had been ordinarily resident in the UK during the five years prior to the conviction, IA 1971 s.7(1).

**Principles**   The following principles are found in the cases:

(a)   The principal criterion for recommending deportation is the extent to which the offender will represent a potential detriment to the United Kingdom if he remains in the country, *Nazari* (1980) 71 Cr.App.R. 87;

(b)   The court is primarily concerned with his expected future behaviour, as evidenced by his offence and previous record, see e.g. *Benabbas* [2005] EWCA Crim 2113;

(c)   The court is not concerned with the political situation or conditions in the offender's home country, *Nazari* (1980) 71 Cr.App.R. 87;

(d)   The fact that the offender is living on social security benefit is not a relevant consideration, *Serry* (1980) 2 Cr.App.R. (S.) 336;

(e)   The fact that the offender is not lawfully in the United Kingdom is not a relevant consideration, except in cases where he has secured admission to the United Kingdom by fraudulent means, see e.g. *Benabbas* [2005] EWCA Crim 2113;

(f)   The court should not take into account the Convention Rights of the offender; the effect that a recommendation might have on innocent persons not before the Court; the provisions of Art.28 of Dir.2004/38; or the Immigration (European Economic Area) Regulations 2006 (SI 2006/1003), *Carmona* [2006] EWCA Crim 508; [2006] 2 Cr.App.R. (S.) 102 (p.662);

(g)   The courts have no desire to break up a family, and in making the decision as to whether or not a recommendation is appropriate, the court should consider the effect upon those not before the court, *Nazari* (1980) 71 Cr.App.R. 87. However, that statement is not to be interpreted literally and the court will uphold a recommendation in an appropriate case, *Carmona* [2006] EWCA Crim 508; [2006] 2 Cr.App.R. (S.) 102 (p.662);

(h)   The making of a recommendation does not justify a reduction in sentence, as the recommendation is not part of the punishment of the offender, *Carmona* [2006] EWCA Crim 508; [2006] 2 Cr.App.R. (S.) 102 (p.662).

**Recommendations will now be rare**   A court should not normally make a recommendation in respect of an offender unless at least one of his offences justifies a sentence of twelve months' imprisonment or detention, *Kluxen* [2010] EWCA Crim 1081; [2011] 1 Cr.App.R. (S.) 39 (p.249).

**Full inquiry**   The court must not make a recommendation without a full inquiry into the relevant circumstances, *Nazari* (1980) 71 Cr.App.R. 87.

**Judge must warn counsel**   The judge should warn counsel if he or she is considering making recommendation for deportation so that the advocate can make submissions, *Carmona* [2006] EWCA Crim 508; [2006] 2 Cr.App.R. (S.) 102 (p.662).

**Duty to give reasons**   The court must give reasons for making a recommendation for deportation, if it does so, *Carmona* [2006] EWCA Crim 508; [2006] 2 Cr.App.R. (S.) 102.

**Procedural requirements**   The court may not recommend the offender for deportation unless he has been given seven days' notice in writing setting out the definition of a British citizen and explaining the exemptions from liability to be recommended for deportation. The court may adjourn to enable the required notice to be served, IA 1971 s.6(2).

Failure to comply with this requirement does not necessarily mean that any recommendation will be quashed on appeal, *Abdi* [2007] EWCA Crim 1913.

# DEPRIVATION ORDERS

## PCC(S)A 2000 s.143

*References: Current Sentencing Practice C3; Archbold 5A-440*

This section deals with orders under s.143 of the PCC(S)A 2000, for deprivation orders relating to drugs, terrorism, etc. see **FORFEITURE/DEPRIVATION ORDERS** p.165.

### Purpose

The order can serve a dual purpose; the removal from public circulation of an article which has been used to commit an offence, and the punishment of the offender, *Highbury Magistrates' Court ex part Di Matteo* (1991) 92 Cr.App.R. 263. Accordingly, the absence of such an order when one might have been imposed can constitute "*credit*" in the form of a reduction in sentence, *Price* [2015] EWCA Crim 318; [2015] 2 Cr.App.R. (S.) 8.

### Availability

The power may be used by the Crown Court or by a magistrates' court on conviction for any offence.

### Power

The court must be satisfied that either:

(a)  the property has been used for the purpose of committing or facilitating the commission of any offence; or
(b)  the property was intended by the offender to be used for the purpose of committing or facilitating the commission of any offence; or
(c)  that the offender has been convicted of unlawful possession of the property concerned; or
(d)  that an offence of unlawfully possessing the property concerned has been taken into consideration, PCC(S)A 2000 s.143(1) and (2).

### Property

The property must either:

(a)  have been lawfully seized from the offender; or
(b)  have been in his possession or control at the time when he was apprehended for the offence; or
(c)  have been in his possession or control at the time when a summons in respect of the offence was issued.

It is not necessary that the offence in relation to which the property has been used or was intended to be used should be the offence of which the offender has been convicted, PCC(S)A 2000 s.143(1)(a).

The power to make a deprivation order may not be used in relation to property taken from the offender, which has been used by another person to commit an offence.

Deprivation orders do not apply to land or buildings see, for example, *Khan* (1983) 76 Cr.App.R. 29.

Deprivation orders should be used in simple and uncomplicated circumstances; the order can only affect the rights of the defendant and where complicating features such as hire purchase or part-ownership are present, an order may be inappropriate, *Kearney* [2011] EWCA Crim 826; [2011] 2 Cr.App.R. (S.) 106.

### Facilitating the commission of an offence

This includes *"the taking of any steps after it has been committed for the purpose of disposing of any property to which it relates or of avoiding apprehension or detection"*, PCC(S)A 2000 s.143(8).

### Making the Order

**Proper investigation**   A deprivation order should not be made without a proper investigation of the grounds for making an order, *Pemberton* (1982) 4 Cr.App.R. (S.) 328. A court considering whether to make an order must normally have evidence of the value of the property concerned before making a deprivation order, see e.g. *Joyce* (1989) 11 Cr.App.R. (S.) 253.

A deprivation order should be considered as part of the total sentence, and the court should bear in mind that the overall penalty, including the deprivation order, should be commensurate with the offence.

The need for a proper enquiry was restated in *Jones (Rowan)* [2017] EWCA Crim 2192; [2018] 1 Cr.App.R. (S.) 35.

**Considerations**   In considering whether to make an order under this section in respect of any property, a court shall have regard to the value of the property; and to the likely financial and other effects on the offender of the making of the order (taken together with any other order that the court contemplates making), PCC(S) 2000 s.143(5).

In *De Jesus* [2015] EWCA Crim 1118; [2015] 2 Cr.App.R. (S.) 44, the court quashed a deprivation order in circumstances where the sentencing judge had failed to consider the total effect of the custodial sentence and deprivation order imposed upon the offender.

**Disparity**   Where a deprivation order is to be made against one of a number of offenders, who are all equally responsible, there may be unjustifiable disparity, *Burgess* [2001] 2 Cr.App.R. (S.) 2.

**Confiscation order**   Where a court has postponed confiscation proceedings and proceeds to sentence the offender before making the confiscation order, it must not make a deprivation order until the confiscation order has been made.

**No need for another sentence**   The power may be used in addition to any other sentence for the offence, or as the only sentence for the offence, PCC(S)A 2000 s.143(4).

## Vehicles

If a person commits an offence by driving, attempting to drive or being in charge of a vehicle, failing to provide a specimen for analysis or laboratory test or to give permission for such a test, or failing to stop and give information or report an accident:

(a) under the Road Traffic Act 1988 punishable with imprisonment;
(b) manslaughter; or
(c) wanton and furious driving (Offences against the Person Act 1861 s.35) the vehicle shall be regarded as used for the purpose of committing the offence and any offence of aiding the commission of the offence, PCC(S)A 2000 s.143(6) and (7).

# DETENTION AND TRAINING ORDERS

## PCC(S)A 2000 ss.100–107

*References: Current Sentencing Practice F2-3200; Archbold 5A-1002*

### General

**Availability**    A detention and training order may be made in the case of a child or young person (i.e. aged under 18) convicted of an offence punishable with imprisonment, PCC(S)A 2000 s.100(1).

A detention and training order is a custodial sentence and the criteria for the imposition of a custodial sentence must be satisfied. (See **CUSTODIAL SENTENCES: GENERAL CRITERIA** p.91.)

**Exceptions**    A DTO is available subject to PCC(S)A 2000 ss.90 and 91, CJA 2003 ss.226 (detention for life) and 226B (extended sentences for under 18s), PCA 1953 s.1A(5) (minimum sentence for offence of threatening with offensive weapon in public) and CJA 1988 s.139AA(7) (minimum sentence for offence of threatening with article with blade or point or offensive weapon).

### Age Restrictions

The order is available (as set out above) for offenders aged 15–17, PCC(S)A 2000 s.110(1)(a).

If the offender is under 15, in addition the court must be of the opinion that the offender is a *"persistent offender"*, PCC(S)A 2000 s.100(2)(a).

If the offender is under 12, in addition to being of the opinion that the offender is a persistent offender, the court must be of the opinion that only a custodial sentence would be adequate to protect the public from further offending by the offender and the offence must have been committed on or after the appointed day, PCC(S)A 2000 s.100(2)(b). No day had been appointed for this purpose by 31 October 2018 and so a DTO remains unavailable for those aged under 12.

### Length

**Maximum**    The maximum term of a detention and training order is two years, but it may not exceed the maximum term of imprisonment that the Crown Court could (in the case of an offender aged 21 or over) impose for the offence, PCC(S)A 2000 s.101(2).

A detention and training order must be for 4, 6, 8, 10, 12, 18 or 24 months. No other period may be specified, PCC(S)A 2000 s.101(1).

The powers of the youth court to impose detention and training orders are not restricted to those of a magistrates' court. Any period in excess of 24 months is automatically remitted.

**Time on remand/curfew** Time in custody on remand is not deducted automatically, PCC(S)A 2000 s.101(8).

In determining the length of a detention and training order, the court must take account of any period for which the offender has been remanded in custody or on bail subject to a qualifiying curfew condition in connection with the offence. This includes time spent in police detention and in local authority secure accommodation. The court must also make such allowance as is appropriate for a plea of guilty.

## The Effect of the Sentence

**Supervision under the order** At the half-way point of the sentence, the offender will be released from custody and the supervision period will begin. The supervision period ends at the expiry of the term of the order, PCC(S)A 2000 s.103(1).

**Additional supervision** Where the offender is aged 18 or over at the half-way point of the sentence, the term of the order is less than 12 months, and the offence for which the sentence was imposed was committed on or after 1 February 2015, there is an additional 12-month period of supervision, PCC(S)A 2000 s.106B.

**Combining sentences** If the offender is convicted of more than one offence, or is convicted of offences while he is subject to an existing detention and training order, the court may pass consecutive detention and training orders, so long as the aggregate of the orders to which the offender is subject does not exceed two years, PCC(S)A 2000 s.101(4).

A court cannot order that a DTO is to commence upon the expiration of the term of a DTO under which the supervision period has already commenced, PCC(S)A 200 s.101(6).

The court may impose consecutive detention and training orders which amount in aggregate to a term which would not be lawful as a single detention and training order, *Norris* [2001] 1 Cr.App.R. (S.) 116 (p.401). A detention and training order may be ordered to run consecutively to a term of detention under the PCC(S)A 2000 s.91 or an extended sentence of detention, PCC(S) A 2000 s.106A.

## Offence Committed after Release

If an offender who has been released from a detention and training order commits an offence punishable with imprisonment during the period between his release and the end of the term of the order, the court which sentences him for that offence may order him to be detained for the whole or any part of a period equivalent to the period which remained of the original order on the date the offence was committed, PCC(S)A 2000 s.105(1) and (2).

The period of detention must begin on the date when the order is made. Any sentence imposed for the new offence may run concurrently with the order for detention or consecutively to it, but the order for detention must not be ordered to run consecutively to any other sentence, PCC(S)A 2000 s.105(3).

Where a court makes a further detention and training order in respect of an offender who has been sentenced to a detention and training order from which he has been released, the length of the original detention and training order is disregarded for the purposes of the two year aggregate limit, PCC(S) A 2000 s.105(3). It is uncertain whether a period of renewed detention counts against the aggregate for this purpose.

## Breach of Supervision Requirement

If an offender fails to comply with a supervision requirement, he may be brought before the appropriate youth court who may order him:

(a) to be detained for a period not exceeding the remainder of the order or three months, whichever is the less;

(b) to be subject to supervision for a period not exceeding the remainder of the order or three months, whichever is the less, or;

(c) a fine not exceeding level 3 on the standard scale, PCC(S)A 2000 s.104(3) and (3A).

Where such an order is made in the case of a person who has attained the age of 18, the order has effect to require the person to be detained in prison for the period specified by the court, PCC(S)A 2000 s.104(4A).

# DETENTION IN A YOUNG OFFENDER INSTITUTION

## PCC(S)A 2000 s.96

*References: Current Sentencing Practice; F2-2050; Archbold 5A-643*

*Note: the sentence of detention in a young offender institution is abolished by the Criminal Justice and Court Services Act 2000 s.61 with effect from a day to be appointed. The minimum age for imprisonment is reduced by the same Act to 18 (see Sch.7, para.180). That provision had not been brought into force on 31 October 2018. References in the Criminal Justice Act 2003 to sentences of imprisonment are for the most part to be read as references to imprisonment or detention in a young offender institution.*

### Availability

A sentence of detention in a young offender institution may be passed on an offender aged 18 and under 21 on the day of conviction, PCC(S)A 2000 s.96(1).

The sentence is a custodial sentence and the general requirements for custodial sentences apply. (See **CUSTODIAL SENTENCES: GENERAL CRITERIA**, p.91.)

### Length

The minimum term of a sentence of detention in a young offender institution is 21 days, PCC(S)A 2000 s.97(2).

The maximum term is the maximum term of imprisonment available to the court for the offence, PCC(S)A 2000 s.97(1).

The sentence takes effect in the same way as a sentence of imprisonment, and the court has the power to impose consecutive sentences in the same manner, PCC(S)A 200 s.97(4).

### Suspended sentences

A sentence of detention in a young offender institution passed for an offence committed on or after 4 April 2005, may be subject to a suspended sentence order, CJA 2003 s.189(1). (See **SUSPENDED SENTENCE ORDERS**, p.291.)

# DETENTION IN DEFAULT OR FOR CONTEMPT

## PCC(S)A 2000 s.108

*References: Current Sentencing Practice B4-2050; Archbold 5A-418*

### Availability

In any case where a court would have power to commit a person aged at least 18 and under 21 to prison in default of payment of a fine or other sum of money, or for contempt, or any kindred offence, the court may commit the person to be detained for a term not exceeding the appropriate term of imprisonment, see PCC(A)A 2000 s.108.

The court may not commit a person to be detained unless it is of the opinion that no other method of dealing with him is appropriate, and in forming that opinion the court must take into account all such information about the default or contempt as is available to it and may take into account any information about the person which is before it, PCC(S)A 2000 s.108(3).

### Magistrates' Courts

If a magistrates' court commits a person to be detained, it must state in open court the reason for its opinion that no other method of dealing with him is appropriate and cause that reason to be specified in the warrant of commitment, PCC(S)A 2000 s.108(4).

# DETENTION UNDER SECTION 91

## PCC(S)A 2000 s.91

*References: Current Sentencing Practice F2-1100 and F2-2600; Archbold 5A-1020*

### Availability

The power to impose detention under s.91 applies where a person aged under 18 is convicted on indictment of:

(1) an offence punishable in the case of a person aged 21 or over with imprisonment for 14 years or more, not being an offence the sentence for which is fixed by law;

(2) an offence under ss.3, 13, 25 or 26 of the Sexual Offences Act 2003;

(3) an offence:
    (a) under s.5(1)(a), (ab), (aba), (ac), (ad), (ae), (af) or (c) or s.5(1A) of the Firearms Act 1968;
    (b) committed on/after 22 January 2004;
    (c) committed at a time when he was aged 16 or over; and
    (d) where the court is of the opinion mentioned in s.51A(2)of that Act (exceptional circumstances which justify its not imposing required custodial sentence).

(4) an offence:
    (a) under the Firearms Act 1968 that is listed in s.51A(1A)(b) (e) or (f) of that Act which was committed in respect of a firearm or ammunition specified in s.5(1)(a), (ab), (aba), (ac), (ad), (ae), (af) or (c) or s.5(1A)(a) of that Act;
    (b) was committed on/after 6 April 2007;
    (c) which was committed at a time when he was aged 16 or over; and
    (d) where the court is of the opinion mentioned in s.51A(2) of the Firearms Act 1968 (exceptional circumstances which justify its not imposing required custodial sentence).

(5) an offence:
    (a) under s.28 of the Violent Crime Reduction Act 2006 (using someone to mind a weapon);
    (b) committed at a time when he was aged 16 or over and the dangerous weapon in respect of which the offence was committed was a firearm mentioned in s.5(1)(a) to (af) or (c) or s.5(1A)(a) of the 1968 Act; and
    (c) where the court is of the opinion mentioned in s.29(6) of that Act (exceptional circumstances which justify not imposing the minimum sentence).

See PCC(S)A 2000 s.91(1)-(1C).

The power may be exercised only where the offender is convicted on indictment, PCC(S)A 2000 s.91(1).

**Test**   The power may be exercised only if the court is of the opinion that neither a youth rehabilitation order nor a detention and training order is suitable, PCC(S)A 2000 s.91(3).

A detention and training order is a custodial sentence and the criteria for the imposition of a custodial sentence must be satisfied. (See **CUSTODIAL SENTENCES: GENERAL CRITERIA** p.91.)

**Detention and training order not available**   Cases involving offenders under 15 for whom a detention and training order is not available will only rarely attract a period of detention under s.91; the more rarely if the offender is under 12. The usual sentence will be a non-custodial disposal, *R. (W) v Thetford Youth Justices* [2002] EWHC 1252 (Admin); [2003] 1 Cr.App.R. (S.) 67.

**Making the Order**

**Maximum length**

Where the power is available, the court may sentence the offender to be detained for such period not exceeding the maximum term of imprisonment for the offence as the court specifies, PCC(S)A 2000 s.91(3). A sentence of detention for life may be passed in an appropriate case, see CJA 2003 s.226(2).

**Minimum length**

There is no statutory minimum period. A sentence of detention for less than two years may be passed in appropriate circumstances, *R. (W) v Southampton Youth Court* [2002] EWCA Civ 1649; [2003] 1 Cr.App.R. (S.) 87. Such an occurrence is likely to be rare, however, *R. (D) v Manchester Youth Court* [2001] EWHC 869 (Admin); [2002] 1 Cr.App.R. (S.) 135.

**Multiple offences**

Where the offender is to be sentenced for a number of associated offences, the court may pass a single sentence of detention which is commensurate with the seriousness of all the associated offences (including those for which detention under s.91 is not available) and impose no separate penalty for the other offences, provided that the other offences do not attract mandatory sentences, *Mills* [1998] 2 Cr.App.R. (S.) 128.

**Release**

An offender sentenced to detention under PCC(S)A 2000 s.91 is subject to the same provisions relating to early release as one sentenced to imprisonment, namely at the half-way point. Where the sentence is less than 12 months, there will be a minimum period of three months supervision immediately following release, CJA 2003 s.256B.

# DISPARITY OF SENTENCE

*References: Archbold 5A-83*

## General

As a general rule, when two or more offenders are convicted of the same of-fence, and their individual responsibility is the same, and there is no relevant dif-ference in their personal circumstances, they should receive the same sentence. Where one offender has the benefit of personal mitigation which is not available to other offenders, the other offenders should not be given the benefit of that mitigation.

Where there is an unjustified disparity in the sentences passed on two offend-ers, the Court of Appeal may reduce the more severe sentence if the disparity is so substantial as to create the appearance of injustice, see *Fawcett* (1983) 5 Cr.App.R. (S.) 158.

Disparity arguments will not be entertained where the alleged disparity is based on other cases in the Crown Court, separate to that of the defendant, *Large* (1981) 3 Cr.App.R. (S.) 80.

When considering disparity arguments, it is dangerous for a court to draw infer-ences from the sentences imposed on counts that were not the "*lead*" count, *Planken* [2017] EWCA Crim 1807; [2018] 1 Cr.App.R. (S.) 25.

## Test

The correct consideration is not whether the appellant feels aggrieved but whether the public, viewing the various sentences, would perceive that the appel-lant had suffered an injustice, *Lowe* (1989) *The Times* 14 November 1989.

## The proper approach to sentencing multiple defendants

Where an offender has already been sentenced by one judge, another judge who on a later occasion has to deal with his accomplice should pass the sentence on the accomplice which he considers appropriate, without regard to the sentence passed on the other offender, *Broadbridge* (1983) 5 Cr.App.R. (S.) 269.

A difference in sex is not in itself a reason for discriminating between offend-ers, *Okuya* (1984) 6 Cr.App.R. (S.) 253.

## No objectionable disparity

There is no disparity if a difference in sentence reflects a difference in the respective:

(a)  responsibilities of the offenders;
(b)  ages of the offenders, *Turner*, unreported, 4 October 1976;

(c) previous convictions, *Walsh* (1980) 2 Cr.App.R. (S.) 224;

(d) the existence of personal mitigating factors peculiar to one of them, *AG's Ref. (Nos. 62, 63 and 64 of 1995) (O'Halloren)* [1996] 2 Cr.App.R. (S.) 223.

There is no disparity where one offender has received an appropriate sentence and his co-defendant has received a lesser sentence as a result of statutory restrictions which apply only to him, or where an accomplice has been sentenced in a foreign jurisdiction where sentencing laws and practices are different from those of England and Wales, *Harper* (1995) 16 Cr.App.R. (S.) 639 and see *Lillie* (1995) 16 Cr.App.R. (S.) 534.

There is no disparity if one offender who is likely to respond favourably to a community order is dealt with by means of a community order and the other offender is not, *Devaney* [2001] EWCA Crim 1997; [2002] 1 Cr.App.R. (S.) 109.

The fact that one defendant received a lenient sentence is no reason to reduce a proper sentence on another; there is no objectionable disparity where an appropriate sentence has been imposed, *Martin* [2012] EWCA Crim 1908, *Saliuka* [2014] EWCA Crim 1907.

## Circumstances capable of amounting to objectionable disparity

There may be objectionable disparity if one offender receives a more severe sentence than a co- defendant, and there are no relevant differences in their responsibility or personal mitigation, *Church* (1985) 7 Cr.App.R. (S.) 370:

(a) where two offenders receive the same sentence, despite a difference in their responsibility or personal mitigation, *Goodacre* [1996] 1 Cr.App.R. (S.) 424; or

(b) where the difference in their sentences is either too large or too small to reflect the difference in their responsibility or personal mitigation see, for example, *Tilley* (1983) 5 Cr.App.R. (S.) 235.

# DISQUALIFICATION FROM BEING THE DIRECTOR OF A COMPANY

COMPANY DIRECTORS DISQUALIFICATION ACT 1986 s.2

*References: Current Sentencing Practice C2-5825; Archbold 5A-831*

### Power to Order/Test to Apply

**Indictable offences**    The court may make a disqualification order where a person is convicted of an indictable offence (whether on indictment or summarily) in connection with the promotion, formation, management, liquidation or striking off of a company with the receivership of a company's property or with his being an administrative receiver of a company, CDDA 1986 s.2(1).

**Summary offences**    Where a person is convicted of a summary offence, in consequence of a contravention of, or failure to comply with, any provision of the companies legislation requiring a return, account or other document to be filed with, delivered or sent, or notice of any matter to be given, to the registrar of companies (whether the contravention or failure is on the person's own part or on the part of any company) and during the five years ending with the date of the conviction, the person has had made against him, or has been convicted of, in total not less than three default orders and offences as specified above, the court may make a disqualification order, CDDA 1986 s.5(1)–(3).

The offence concerned may relate to the internal management of the company, or the general conduct of its business, *Georgiou* (1988) 10 Cr.App.R. (S.) 137.

It is not necessary in a criminal case for the court to consider the tests of fitness required for the purposes of an order under s.6 of the Act, see *Young* (1990) 12 Cr.App.R. (S.) 262.

### Making the Order

The period of a disqualification order is determined by the court in the exercise of its discretion. The maximum term is 15 years (where the order is made by a magistrates' court, five years). There is no minimum period, CDDA 1986 s.2(3).

If the offender is already subject to a disqualification order, any new order will run concurrently with the existing order, CDDA 1986 s.1(3).

The court should inform counsel of its intentions and invite him to mitigate on the question before making an order of disqualification.

### Effect of the Order

A person subject to an order shall not:

(a)   be a director of a company;
(b)   act as receiver of a company's property; or

(c)  in any way, whether directly or indirectly, be concerned or take part in the promotion, formation or management of a company unless (in each case) he has the leave of the court; and

(d)  he shall not act as an insolvency practitioner, CDDA 1986 s.1(1).

# DISQUALIFICATION FROM DRIVING—DISCRETIONARY (GENERAL POWER)

## PCC(S)A 2000 ss.146 and 147

*References: Current Sentencing Practice; C4-100; Archbold 5A-465*

### The Two Types of Discretionary Qualification

There are two *"general powers"*; one which enables the court to disqualify an offender convicted of any offence, and one which requires the court to be of the opinion that a vehicle was used for the purposes of crime.

### "Any Offence"

**Availability** The power to disqualify may be used by the Crown Court or a magistrates' court.

**Power** Any court may disqualify an offender from driving on conviction for any offence, either in addition to any other sentence or instead of any other sentence.

It is not necessary that the offence should be connected in any way with the use of a motor vehicle, PCC(S)A 2000 s.146(1).

**Required sentences** If the sentence for the offence is fixed by law, or the court is required to impose a mandatory custodial sentence, the court may impose a disqualification in addition to the sentence, PCC(S)A 2000 s.146(2).

**Those without a driving licence** The power may be used in respect of an offender who does not hold a driving licence, PCC(S)A 2000 s.146(4)(a).

### "Used for the Purposes of Crime"

**Availability** The power is available in two sets of circumstances

(1) Where a person:
    (a) is convicted in the Crown Court of an offence punishable on indictment with imprisonment for a term of two years or more; or
    (b) having been convicted by a magistrates' court of such an offence, is committed under PCC(S)A 2000 s.3 to the Crown Court for sentence, PCC(S)A 2000 s.147(1).

In such a case where the Crown Court is satisfied that a motor vehicle was used (by the person convicted or by anyone else) for the purpose of committing, or facilitating the commission of, the offence in question, the court may order the person convicted to be disqualified, for such period as the court thinks fit, for holding or obtaining a driving licence, PCC(S)A 2000 s.147(3).

The only type of conspiracy which a defendant can be disqualified under

[121]

s.147(3) on conviction for is one in which the vehicle was used directly in the formation of the conspiracy itself. The mere fact that vehicles were used in acts performed in furtherance of a conspiracy is not sufficient to engage the powers in s.147 as was made clear in *Riley* (1984) 5 Cr.App.R. (S.) 335, *Gorry* [2018] EWCA Crim 1867.

(2) Where a person is convicted by or before any court of common assault or of any other offence involving an assault (including an offence of aiding, abetting, counselling or procuring, or inciting to the commission of, an offence), PCC(S)A 2000 s.147(2).

Where the court is satisfied that the assault was committed by driving a motor vehicle, the court may order the person convicted to be disqualified, for such period as the court thinks fit, for holding or obtaining a driving licence, PCC(S)A 2000 s.147(4).

**General**

**Two or more offences involving discretionary disqualification**   As orders of disqualification take effect immediately, it is generally desirable for the court to impose a single disqualification order that reflects the overall criminality of the offending behaviour, *TICs and Totality Guideline* 2012, p.15.

**Extension of disqualification where custodial sentence also imposed**   Where the court imposes a custodial sentence and a driving disqualification, the order under s.146 or 147 must provide for the person to be disqualified for the appropriate extension period, in addition to the discretionary disqualification period, PCC(S)A 2000 s.147A.

The extension does not apply to a suspended sentence order. The period for a determinate custodial sentence is one half of the custodial term. There are other periods specified in s.147A for other sentencing orders.

In *Needham* [2016] EWCA Crim 455 the court offered guidance on the effect and operation of the sister provisions (ss.35A and B, RTOA 1988), including providing a checklist to follow in such cases. That guidance and checklist applies to ss.147A and B. The checklist can be seen at **DISQUALIFICATION FROM DRIVING—DISCRETIONARY (ROAD TRAFFIC)**, p.123.

**Warn the defence**   If the court proposes to disqualify, the offender's advocate should be warned of the possibility of disqualification, see *Doherty* [2011] EWCA Crim 1591; [2012] 1 Cr.App.R. (S.) 48.

# DISQUALIFICATION FROM DRIVING—DISCRETIONARY (ROAD TRAFFIC)

ROAD TRAFFIC OFFENDERS ACT 1988 s.34

*References: Current Sentencing Practice C4-1000; Archbold 32-249*

## Availability

Where a person is convicted of an offence involving discretionary disqualification, and either:

(a)  the penalty points to be taken into account on that occasion number fewer than 12; or

(b)  the offence is not one involving obligatory endorsement, the court may order him to be disqualified for such period as the court thinks fit, RTOA 1988 s.34(2).

## Offences

See RTOA 1988 Sch.2 for the list of offences carrying discretionary disqualification. As a general rule, offences which are endorsable are also liable to discretionary disqualification.

The following offences are subject to discretionary disqualification but not endorsement:

(a)  stealing or attempting to steal a motor vehicle;

(b)  taking a motor vehicle without consent, or being carried;

(c)  going equipped to steal a motor vehicle, RTOA 1988 Sch.2 Part.II para.1.

## Discretion

There is no obligation to disqualify.

## Penalty points

If the court does disqualify, the court does not award penalty points, *Kent* (1983) 5 Cr.App.R. (S.) 171 and *Usaceva* [2015] EWCA Crim 166; [2015] 2 Cr.App.R. (S.) 7 (p.90).

In some cases in which the court is considering discretionary disqualification, the offender may already have sufficient penalty points on his or her licence that he or she would be liable to a "*totting up*" disqualification if further points were imposed. In these circumstances, the court should impose penalty points rather than discretionary disqualification so that the minimum totting up disqualification period applies, *Magistrates' Court Sentencing Guidelines* 2008, p.185.

## Length

If an offender is convicted of any of these offences, the court may order the offender to be disqualified for such period as it thinks fit. There is no maximum or minimum period, RTOA 1988 s.34(2).

## Extension of disqualification where custodial sentence also imposed

Where the court imposes a custodial sentence and a driving disqualification, the order under s.34 or 35 must provide for the person to be disqualified for the appropriate extension period, in addition to the discretionary disqualification period, RTOA 1988 s.35A.

The extension does not apply to a suspended sentence order. The period for a determinate custodial sentence is one half of the custodial term. There are other periods specified in s.35A for other sentencing orders.

## Checklist

The court in *Needham* [2016] EWCA Crim 455; [2016] 2 Cr.App.R. (S.) 26 suggested the following checklist be used in such cases:

*Step 1* – does the court intend to impose a *"discretionary"* disqualification under s.34 or s.35 for any offence?

> *Yes* – go to Step 2

*Step 2* – does the court intend to impose a custodial term for that *same* offence?

> *Yes* – s.35A applies and the court must impose an extension period (see s.35A s.35A(4)(h) for that *same* offence and consider Step 3).

> *No* – does not apply to all - go on to consider s.35A does not apply at all – go on to consider s.35B and Step 4.

*Step 3* – does the court intend to impose a custodial term for *another* offence (which is longer or consecutive) or is the defendant already serving a custodial sentence?

> *Yes* – then consider what increase (*"uplift"*) in the period of *"discretionary"* disqualification is required to comply with s.35B(2) and (3) – in accordance with s.35B(4), ignore any custodial term imposed for an offence involving disqualification under s.35A

*Discretionary period + extension period + uplift = total period of disqualification*

> *No* – no need to consider s.35B at all.

*Discretionary period + extension period = total period of disqualification*

*Step 4* – does the court intend to impose a custodial term for *another* offence or is the defendant already serving a custodial sentence?

*Yes* – then consider what increase ("*uplift*") in the period of "*discretionary disqualification*" is required to comply with s.35B(2) and (3).

*Discretionary period + uplift = total period of disqualification*

See *Needham* [2016] EWCA Crim 455; [2016] 2 Cr.App.R. (S.) 26 for further guidance.

### Two or more offences involving discretionary disqualification

As orders of disqualification take effect immediately, it is generally desirable for the court to impose a single disqualification order that reflects the overall criminality of the offending behaviour, *TICs and Totality Guideline* 2012, p.15.

### Warn the defence

If the court proposes to disqualify, the offender's advocate should be warned of the possibility of disqualification, see *Doherty* [2011] EWCA Crim 1591; [2012] 1 Cr.App.R. (S.) 48.

ROAD TRAFFIC OFFENDERS ACT 1988 s.34

*References: Current Sentencing Practice C4-1000; Archbold 32-249*

## General

**Obligation to disqualify** Where a person is convicted of an offence involving obligatory disqualification, the court must order him to be disqualified, RTOA 1988 s.34(1).

**Special reasons exception** The obligation to disqualify exists unless the court for special reasons thinks fit to order him to be disqualified for a shorter period or not to order him to be disqualified, RTOA 1988 s.34(1). See below for more details.

**Length** The disqualification period must be for such period not less than twelve months as the court thinks fit, RTOA 1988 s.34(1).

**Extension of disqualification where custodial sentence also imposed** The disqualification period must be for such period not less than twelve months as the court thinks fit, RTOA 1988 s.34(1).

Where the court imposes a custodial sentence and a driving disqualification, the order under s.34 or 35 must provide for the person to be disqualified for the appropriate extension period, in addition to the discretionary disqualification period, RTOA 1988 s.35A.

The extension does not apply to a suspended sentence order. The period for a determinate custodial sentence is one half of the custodial term. There are other periods specified in s.35A for other sentencing orders.

In *Needham* [2016] EWCA Crim 455; [2016] 2 Cr.App.R. (S.) 26 the court offered guidance on the effect and operation of ss.35A and B, including providing a checklist to follow in such cases. The checklist can be seen at **DISQUALIFICATION FROM DRIVING—DISCRETIONARY (ROAD TRAFFIC)** p.123.

**Penalty points** If the court disqualifies the defendant, it does not award penalty points, RTOA 1988 s.44(1).

## Offences Carrying Obligatory Disqualification

The following offences are subject to obligatory disqualification:

### Six months

(a) using vehicle in a dangerous condition within three years of a previous conviction for same offence;

### One year

(b) causing death by careless or inconsiderate driving;

(c) causing death by driving while unlicensed, disqualified or uninsured;
(d) dangerous driving;
(e) driving or attempting to drive while unfit (three years for repeat offenders);
(f) driving or attempting to drive with excess alcohol (three years for repeat offenders);
(g) driving with concentration of specified drug above limit;
(h) failing to provide a specimen for analysis (driving or attempting to drive) (three years for repeat offenders);
(i) failing to allow a specimen to be subject to a laboratory test (three years for repeat offenders);
(j) racing or speed trials;

**Two years**

(k) causing death by dangerous driving;
(l) causing death by careless driving while under the influence of drink or drugs (three years for repeat offenders);
(m) causing serious injury by dangerous driving;
(n) manslaughter;
(o) causing death by driving: disqualified drivers;
(p) causing serious injury by driving: disqualified drivers.

RTOA 1988 s.34(4)(a) and Sch 2.

Where the defendant has been twice disqualified for 56 days or more in the three years before the commission of the present offence the minimum is two years, RTOA 1988 s.34(4)(b).

Where the defendant has been convicted of an excess alcohol or failure to provide a specimen offence and has been convicted of such an offence within the last 10 years the minimum is three years, RTOA 1988 34(3).

**Special Reasons**

**Burden and standard of proof**   The existence of special reasons must be established by the defendant by calling evidence on the relevant matter, unless the prosecution are willing to admit the existence of the facts which are alleged to constitute special reasons. The defendant must establish the relevant facts on the balance of probabilities, *Pugsley v Hunter* 1973 W.L.R. 578.

**Test**   A special reason must be a mitigating or extenuating circumstance:

(a) not amounting in law to a defence to the charge, but
(b) directly connected with the commission of the offence, and
(c) one which the court ought properly to take into consideration when imposing punishment, *Whittall v Kirby* [1947] K.B. 194.

Matters related to the effect of disqualification on the offender (e.g. personal hardship), or his employer or clients or patients, cannot constitute special reasons for this purpose, see e.g. *Steel* [1968] Crim L.R. 450.

**What amounts to a special reason?**

The following matters have been held to be *capable* of amounting to special reasons in excess alcohol cases:

(a)  the fact that the defendant consumed alcohol in the expectation that he would not be required to drive again that day, but was required to drive as a result of a sudden emergency see, for example, *Jacobs v Reed* [1974] RTR 81;

(b)  the fact that the defendant's consumption of excess alcohol was due to the act of another person who had laced his drink, or caused him to drink stronger liquor than he thought he was drinking, see e.g. *DPP v O'Connor* (1992) 13 Cr.App.R. (S.) 188;

(c)  the fact that the defendant has driven an extremely short distance in circumstances where there was no risk to other road users, see e.g. *Reay v Young* [1949] 1 All E.R. 1102.

Each of these matters may amount to a special reason in narrowly defined circumstances.

The following matters have been held *not to be capable* of amounting to special reasons:

(a)  the fact that the defendant's alcohol level is only just over the relevant limit, *Delroy-Hall v Tadman* [1969] 1 All E.R. 25;

(b)  the fact that the defendant's capacity to drive was not affected, *Brown v Dyerson* [1968] 3 All E.R. 39;

(c)  the fact the defendant's peculiar metabolism caused him to retain the alcohol in his body for longer than the normal period, *Kinsella v DPP* [2002] EWCA Crim 545;

(d)  the fact that no other road user was endangered by the defendant's driving, *Reay v Young* [1949] 1 All E.R. 1102;

(e)  the fact that the defendant had lost or destroyed part of his sample, see *Harding v Oliver* [1973] RTR 497, but see *Anderson* [1972] RTR 113 for a contrary decision;

(f)  the fact that the defendant had taken a test earlier on the same day which proved negative, *DPP v White* [1988] RTR 267;

(g)  the fact that the defendant had consumed the alcohol the day before he was tested and assumed that he had slept it off overnight, *DPP v O'Meara* (1988) 10 Cr.App.R. (S.) 56.

**Discretion**    If the court finds that special reasons exist, it is not obliged to disqualify the defendant, but may do so in the exercise of its discretion.

**Warn defence counsel**    Before disqualifying, where disqualification is discretionary, the court should inform counsel of its intention and invite submissions on the question of disqualification, see *Doherty* [2011] EWCA Crim 1591; [2012] 1 Cr.App.R. (S.) 48, p.282.

**Special reasons and penalty points**    If the court finds that special reasons exist and does not disqualify, the court must award penalty points (within the range of 3 to 11) and follow the penalty points procedure. (See **DISQUALIFICATION FROM DRIVING—PENALTY POINTS**, p.131).

## Extended Driving Test

Where the offender is convicted of and offence of:

(i)     manslaughter (where the defendant caused the death by driving a vehicle);
(ii)    causing death by dangerous driving (s.1 RTA 1988);
(iii)   causing serious injury by dangerous driving (s.1A RTA 1988);
(iv)    dangerous driving (s.2 RTA 1988);
(v)     causing death by driving (disqualified drivers) (s.3ZC RTA 1988);
(vi)    causing serious injury by driving: disqualified drivers) (s.3ZD RTA 1988), and the court has disqualified the offender under s.34 RTOA 1988, the court must impose an order for an extended driving test, RTOA 1988 s.36(1) and (2).

If the defendant is convicted of any other offence involving obligatory endorsement the court may impose an order for an extended driving test, RTOA 1988 s.36(4).

Where a person is disqualified until he passes the extended driving test — (a) any earlier order under this section shall cease to have effect, and (b) a court shall not make a further order under this section while he is so disqualified, RTOA 1988 s.36(7).

# DISQUALIFICATION FROM DRIVING—PENALTY POINTS (ENDORSEMENT AND TOTTING UP)

ROAD TRAFFIC OFFENDERS ACT 1988 s.28

*References: Current Sentencing Practice C4-4950; Archbold 32-236*

## Endorsement

**Applicability** If the offender is convicted of an offence subject to obligatory endorsement, the court must determine the number of penalty points which are to be attributed to the offence from the table below, see Road Traffic Offenders Act 1988 s.28(1).

If the table shows a range of points, the court must determine a number within that range, RTOA 1988 s.28(1).

(For offences not shown below, see Road Traffic Offenders Act 1988 Sch.2.)

| Offence | Penalty |
|---|:---:|
| Speeding | 3-6 |
| Careless driving | 3-9 |
| Being in charge of vehicle when unfit to drive | 10 |
| Being in charge of vehicle with excess alcohol level | 10 |
| Failing to provide breath specimen | 4 |
| Failing to provide specimen when disqualification not obligatory | 10 |
| Leaving vehicle in dangerous position | 3 |
| Failing to comply with directions or signs | 3 |
| Using vehicle in dangerous condition | 3 |
| Driving without licence | 3 |
| Driving with uncorrected eyesight | 3 |
| Driving while disqualified | 6 |
| Using vehicle without insurance | 6-8 |
| Failing to stop after accident | 5-10 |
| Failing to give information as to driver | 6 |

**Multiple offences** If the offender has committed more than one offence on the same occasion, the court must normally determine points only for the offence carrying the highest number of points, unless the court decides to determine points for other offences, RTOA 1988 s.28(4) and (5).

The court must add to these penalty points any other points on the offender's licence, except (a) points for offences committed more than three years before the date of the commission of the offences for which points have just been awarded and

[131]

(b) points awarded before a disqualification imposed on the basis of penalty points, RTOA 1988 s.29(2).

## Disqualification as a "Totter"

If the total number of points is 12 or more, the defendant must be disqualified, unless there are grounds for mitigating the normal consequences of conviction, RTOA 1988 s.35(1) and (1A).

**Mitigating the normal consequences of conviction**   The defendant must establish the mitigating grounds, normally by calling evidence, *Owen v Jones* [1988] RTR 102.

The following matters *"may not"* constitute grounds for mitigating the normal consequences of conviction:

- (a)   circumstances alleged to make the offence or any of the offences not a serious one;
- (b)   hardship, other than exceptional hardship;
- (c)   any circumstances which have been taken into account as mitigating grounds within the last three years, RTOA 1988 s.35(4).

The fact that the offender has been sentenced to custody on this occasion *"may"* constitute a mitigating ground in an appropriate case, *Thomas* (1983) 5 Cr.App.R. (S.) 354.

If the court finds that there are mitigating grounds, the court may either disqualify for a shorter period than would otherwise be required, or refrain from disqualifying at all, RTOA 1988 s.35(1).

If the court does not disqualify, it should order the licence to be endorsed with the appropriate penalty points unless there are special reasons for not doing so, RTOA 1988 s.44(1) and (2).

**No mitigating circumstances found**   If the defendant does not establish mitigating grounds, the court must disqualify him for at least the relevant minimum period; there is no maximum period, RTOA 1988 s.35(2).

The normal minimum period is six months. If there are previous disqualifications to be taken into account, the minimum period of disqualification may be 12 months or two years. The court may order the offender to take an extended driving test, RTOA 1988 s.36(4).

## Extension of Disqualification where Custodial Sentence also Imposed

Where the court imposes a custodial sentence and a driving disqualification, the order under s.34 or 35 must provide for the person to be disqualified for the appropriate extension period, in addition to the discretionary disqualification period, RTOA 1988 s.35A.

The extension does not apply to a suspended sentence order. The period for a determinate custodial sentence is one half of the custodial term. There are other periods specified in s.35A for other sentencing orders.

In *Needham* [2016] EWCA Crim 455; [2016] 2 Cr.App.R (S.) 26. the court offered guidance on the effect and operation of ss.35A and B, including providing a checklist to follow in such cases. The checklist can be seen at **DISQUALIFICATION FROM DRIVING—DISCRETIONARY (ROAD TRAFFIC)**, p.123.

## Extended driving test

Where the offender is convicted of and offence of:

(i)     manslaughter (where the defendant caused the death by driving a vehicle);
(ii)    causing death by dangerous driving (s.1 RTA 1988);
(iii)   causing serious injury by dangerous driving (s.1A RTA 1988);
(iv)    dangerous driving (s.2 RTA 1988);
(v)     causing death by driving (disqualified drivers) (s.3ZC RTA 1988);
(vi)    causing serious injury by driving: disqualified drivers) (s.3ZD RTA 1988), and the court has disqualified the offender under s.34 RTOA 1988, the court must impose an order for an extended driving test, RTOA 1988 s.36(1) and (2).

If the defendant is convicted of any other offence involving obligatory endorsement the court may impose an order for an extended driving test, RTOA 1988 s.36(4).

Where a person is disqualified until he passes the extended driving test— (a) any earlier order under this section shall cease to have effect, and (b) a court shall not make a further order under this section while he is so disqualified, RTOA 1988 s.36(7).

# EARLY RELEASE FROM DETERMINATE CUSTODIAL SENTENCES— CRIMINAL JUSTICE ACT 2003

CRIMINAL JUSTICE ACT 2003 ss.243A–264

*References: Current Sentencing Practice A8; Archbold 5A-1250*

## General

**Applicability**   These provisions apply to all prisoners sentenced on or after 3 December 2012, irrespective of the date on which the offence for which they were sentenced was committed.

## Unconditional Release

**Applicability**   Unconditional release applies to:

(a)   a prisoner serving a sentence of a term of one day;
(b)   a prisoner serving a term of less than 12 months who is aged under 18 on the last day of the requisite custodial period; or
(c)   a prisoner serving sentence of less than 12 months imposed before 1 February 2015, CJA 2003 s.243A.

Offenders entitled to unconditional release must be released after serving one half of the sentence. There is no licence period, CJA 2003 s.243A.

**Concurrent/consecutive sentences**   Where more than one sentence is imposed and the aggregate terms are less than 12 months, release will be unconditional, CJA 2003 s.264 (3A).

## Release on Licence

**Applicability**   Prisoners who are not serving sentences under CJA 2003 ss.226A, 226B, 227, 228, or 236A, or who are not entitled to unconditional release must be released on licence after serving half of the sentence imposed by the court (the "*requisite custodial period*") and will remain on licence until the end of the whole term of the sentence, CJA 2003 ss.244 and 249(1).

**Licence conditions**   Where a fixed term prisoner serving a sentence of 12 months or more is released on licence, the licence must include the standard conditions prescribed by the Secretary of State and such other conditions as may be specified. It may also include conditions relating to drug testing or electronic monitoring, CJA 2003 s.250(4).

**Recommending licence conditions**   When a court passes a sentence of imprisonment or detention in a young offender institution for 12 months or more (but not a sentence of detention under CJA 2003 s.226B or PCC(S)A 2000 s.91) it may "*recommend any particular conditions which in its view should be included in any licence granted to the offender*", CJA 2003 s.238.

[135]

The recommendation is not binding on the Secretary of State and does not form part of the sentence *"for any purpose"*, CJA 2003 s.238(2) and (3). It is therefore not subject to appeal. The recommendation will be considered by the Secretary of State when the offender is released at the half way point in the sentence, or if he is released on licence at any other stage—under the home detention curfew scheme, or on compassionate grounds.

**Supervision**

**Young offenders**    Those who a) are aged under 18 on the last day of the requisite custodial period (the half-way stage of the total sentence) serving a sentence of s.91 detention of a period of less than 12 months, or b) are serving a sentence of detention under ss.91 or 96 of less than 12 months for an offence committed prior to 1 February 2015, are subject to a supervision period beginning on their release and ending three months later, CJA 2003 s.256B.

**Young offenders: Breach**    If it is proved to the satisfaction of the court that the offender has failed to comply with requirements under s.256B(6), the court may:

(a)    order the offender to be detained, in prison or such youth detention accommodation as the Secretary of State may determine, for such period, not exceeding 30 days, as the court may specify; or

(b)    order the offender to pay a fine not exceeding level 3 on the standard scale, CJA 2003 s.256C(4).

**Adults**    Those who are serving sentences of more than one day but less than two years who a) are 18 or over on the last day of the requisite custodial period, b) are not serving sentences under ss.226A, 226B, or s.236A or c) are not serving sentences for an offence committed before 1 February 2015, are subject to supervision beginning on the expiry of the sentence and ending 12 months later, CJA 2003 s.256AA.

**Adults: Breach**    If it is proved to the satisfaction of the court that the person has failed without reasonable excuse to comply with a supervision requirement imposed under s.256AA, the court may:

(a)    order the person to be committed to prison for a period not exceeding 14 days;

(b)    order the person to pay a fine not exceeding level 3 on the standard scale; or

(c)    make a *"supervision default order"* imposing on the person:
    (i)    an unpaid work requirement (as defined by CJA 2003 s.199); or
    (ii)    a curfew requirement (as defined by CJA 2003 s.204), CJA 2003 s.256AC(4).

Under a supervision default order:

(a)    an unpaid work requirement may be for 20–60 hours;

(b)    a curfew order may be for 2–16 hours per day and must require the person to remain at the specified place or places on at least 20 days, CJA 2003 Sch.19A para.3(4).

## Home Detention Curfew (HDC)

**Eligibility**   Prisoners serving determinate custodial sentences where:

a) the requisite custodial period (i.e. half of the total sentence) is at least six weeks; and
b) the prisoner has served both:
   (i) at least four weeks of that period; and
   (ii) at least one half of that period.

The effect is that HDC only applies to prisoners whose sentences are at least 12 weeks, CJA 2003 246(1) and (2).

**The effect**   Where the conditions are met, a prisoner may be released up to 135 days before the date on which he would be otherwise be entitled to be released (the half way point in his sentence), CJA 2003 s.246(1)(a).

**Exclusions**   The home detention curfew scheme does not apply to:

(a) offenders sentenced to four years' imprisonment or more;
(b) extended sentences of imprisonment or detention (under ss.226A, 227 or 228); or
(c) those subject to the notification requirements under SOA 2003 Pt.2;
(d) those subject to a hospital order, hospital direction or transfer direction;
(e) prisoners whose sentence was imposed in a case where they failed to comply with a curfew requirement of a community order;
(f) prisoners liable to removal from the UK;
(g) certain prisoners who have been recalled or returned to prison;
(h) cases where due to time spent in custody prior to sentence, the interval between the date of sentence and the expiration of the requisite custodial period is less than 14 days, CJA 2003 s.246(4).

PSI 43/2012 sets out at Annex B a list of offences for which prisoners will be deemed to be unsuitable for HDC. It will then be for the prisoner to show that there are exceptional circumstances in order to be considered for release. Such offences include manslaughter, possession of an offensive weapon and racially or religiously aggravated offences under CDA1998 ss.29 to 32.

**Release**   An offender serving a sentence of 12 months or more who is released under this scheme must be subject to the standard licence conditions and to a curfew condition; he may also be subject to other conditions of a kind prescribed by the Secretary of State, CJA 2003 s.250(4). The licence remains for the duration of the sentence, CJA 2003 s.249.

The curfew condition remains in force until the day on which the offender would otherwise be entitled to be released from custody, CJA 2003 s.253(3). It must require that the offender remains at a specified place for periods of not less than nine hours each day, and must provide for electronic monitoring of his whereabouts during the specified periods, CJA 2003 s.253(1) and (2).

## Recall

**Licence recall**   The Secretary of State may revoke the licence of a person who has been released on licence and recall him to custody. No particular conditions must be specified before this power is exercised, CJA 2003 s.254(1).

On his return to custody, the prisoner must be informed of the reason for his recall and may make representations about his recall, CJA 2003 s.254(2).

Prisoners who are not serving extended sentences will qualify for automatic release after 28 days from the date of return to custody if the Secretary of State is satisfied that the person will not present a risk of serious harm to members of the public if released at the end of that period, CJA 2003 s.255A(4).

The case must be referred to the Parole Board, CJA 2003 ss.255B(4) and 255C(4)(a). If the Board does not recommend his immediate release, the Board must either fix a date for his release or fix a date for the next review of his case. The review must take place not later than one year after the decision to fix the date has been made, CJA 2003 s.256. If the prisoner is not recommended for release at a later review, he will remain in custody until the end of the sentence.

**HDC recall**   A person released on home detention curfew may have his licence revoked if he fails to comply with any condition of his licence, or if his whereabouts can no longer be monitored electronically, CJA 2003 s.255(1).

He must be informed of the reasons for the revocation and may make representations about the revocation to the Secretary of State, but he does not have the right to ask for his case to be reviewed by the Parole Board, CJA 2003 s.255(2).

If the Secretary of State does not reverse his/her decision to revoke the licence, the prisoner will remain in custody until the date on which he would otherwise have been released.

### Concurrent and Consecutive Sentences

Where an offender is sentenced to terms of imprisonment which are wholly or partly concurrent, the offender does not become eligible for or entitled to be released from any of the sentences before the date on which he would be eligible for or entitled to be released from each of the other sentences, CJA 2003 s.263.

Where an offender is sentenced to consecutive terms the aggregate of which is 12 months or more, whether they are imposed on the same occasion or different occasions, he is not entitled to be released until he has served half of the aggregate term, and will remain on licence until the end of the aggregate term, CJA 2003 s.264(3). Where the aggregate terms are less than 12 months, the release is unconditional, CJA 2003 s.264(3A).

**See CONCURRENT AND CONSECUTIVE SENTENCES**, p.75.

# EXCLUSION ORDERS (LICENSED PREMISES)

LICENSED PREMISES (EXCLUSION OF CERTAIN PERSONS) ACT 1980

*References: Current Sentencing Practice C2-6900; Archbold 5A-1326*

Note: The Licensed Premises (Exclusion of Certain Persons) Act 1980 is repealed by the Violent Crime Reduction Act 2006, Sch.5. That repeal was not in force on 31 October 2018.

**Availability**    If the offender has been convicted of an offence committed on licensed premises in the course of which he made resort to violence, the court may make an exclusion order, LP(ECP)A 1980 s.1(1).

**Effect**    The order prohibits the offender from entering the licensed premises specified in the order without the express consent of the licensee or his servant or agent.

The order may be made in respect of any licensed premises, whether or not the offender has committed an offence in those premises, but all the premises to which the order applies must be specified in the order.

**Length**    The court must fix the term of the order. The minimum term is three months; the maximum term is two years, LP(ECP)A 1980 s.1(3).

**Combining sentences**    An exclusion order may be made in addition to any other form of sentence or order including a discharge. An exclusion order may not be made as the only sentence of order for the offence, LP(ECP)A 1980 s.1(2).

# EXTENDED DETERMINATE SENTENCES

CRIMINAL JUSTICE ACT 2003 ss.226A AND 226B

*References: Current Sentencing Practice A3 and F2-1300; Archbold 5A-698, 5A-1029*

## Defendants Aged 18+ at Conviction

**Availability**    A court may impose an extended sentence where:

(1)  the defendant is convicted of a specified offence (i.e. one listed in CJA 2003 Sch.15, see Part 3); or, where the offence was abolished before 4 April 2005, the offence would have constituted a specified offence if committed on the day of conviction, CJA 2003 ss.226A(1) and (4);

(2)  the court considers that there is a significant risk of serious harm occasioned by the commission by the defendant of further specified offences, CJA 2003 ss.226A(1), see **Assessing dangerousness** p.143.

(3)  the court is not required by CJA 2003 ss.224A or 225(2) to impose a sentence of imprisonment for life;

(4)  Condition A or B is met:
     Condition A: at the time the offence was committed, the defendant had been convicted of a CJA 2003 Sch.15B offence (see Part 3), CJA 2003 s.226A(2);
     Condition B: if the court were to impose an extended sentence, the period it would specify as the custodial portion of the sentence would be at least four years, CJA 2003 s.226A(3).

**Composition of the sentence**    An extended sentence is comprised of the aggregate length of the custodial portion and the extended licence portion of the sentence, CJA 2003 s.226A(5).

**Length of custodial portion**    The appropriate custodial term is the term of imprisonment that would, apart from s.226B, be imposed in compliance with s.153(2), CJA 2003 s.226B(4).

**Extended licence**    The extension period must:

(a)  be for a period of at least one year, CJA 2003 s.226A(7A);

(b)  be a period of such length as the court considers necessary for the purpose of protecting members of the public from serious harm occasioned by the commission by the offender of further specified offences, CJA 2003 s.226A(7); and

(c)  must not exceed five years in the case of a violent offence and eight years in the case of a sexual offence, CJA 2003 s.226A(8).

An extended licence period is different in kind from a determinate sentence. It is not tied to the seriousness of the offending; its purpose is protective. Like all sentences, it should not be longer than necessary for the relevant purpose. It should be just and proportionate, and not such as to crush the defendant, *Phillips* [2018]

EWCA Crim 2008.

**Maximum sentence**   The term of an extended sentence of imprisonment must not exceed the term that, at the time the offence was committed, was the maximum term permitted for the offence, CJA 2003 s.226A(9).

**Those aged 18–20**   References to *"imprisonment"* include detention in YOI and custody for life where appropriate, CJA 2003 s.226A(12).

### Defendants aged under 18 at conviction

**Availability**   A court may impose an extended sentence where:

(1)   the defendant is convicted of a specified offence (i.e. one listed in CJA 2003 Sch.15, see Pt.3), or, where the offence was abolished before 4 April 2005, the offence would have constituted a specified offence if committed on the day of conviction, CJA 2003 s.226B(1)(a) and (8);

(2)   the court considers that there is a significant risk of serious harm occasioned by the commission by the defendant of further specified offences, CJA 2003 s.226B(1)(b); See **Assessing dangerousness** below.

(3)   the court is not required by CJA 2003 s.226 to impose a sentence of detention for life under s.91, CJA 2003 s.226B(1)(c).

(4)   if the court were to impose an extended sentence, the period it would specify as the custodial portion of the sentence would be at least four years, CJA 2003 s.226B(1)(d).

**Composition of the sentence**   An extended sentence is comprised of the aggregate length of the custodial portion and the extended licence portion of the sentence, CJA 2003 s.226A(3).

**Length of custodial portion**   The appropriate custodial term is the term of imprisonment that would be imposed in compliance with s.153(2), CJA 2003 s.226B(4).

**Not available where s.91 not available**   The combination of s.226B(1), (3) and (4) means that where a sentence of detention under s.91 is not available, an extended sentence is not available (by virtue of the maximum period of a DTO being 24 months, thereby falling short of satisfying the four-year requirement).

**Extended licence**   The extension period must:

(a)   be for a period of at least one year, CJA 2003 s.226B(5A);

(b)   be a period of such length as the court considers necessary for the purpose of protecting members of the public from serious harm occasioned by the commission by the offender of further specified offences, CJA 2003 s.226B(5); and

(c)   must not exceed five years in the case of a violent offence and eight years in the case of a sexual offence, CJA 2003 s.226B(6).

**Maximum sentence**   The total term of an extended sentence of detention must not exceed the term that, at the time the offence was committed, was the maximum term of imprisonment permitted for the offence in the case of a person aged 21 or over, CJA 2003 s.226B(7).

## Assessing Dangerousness

The following apply when the court is considering whether or not there is a *"significant risk of serious harm"*.

**Must take into account**    The court must take into account all such information as is available to it about the nature and circumstances of the offence, CJA 2003 s.229(2)(a).

**May take into account**    The court may take into account:

(a) all such information as is available about the nature and circumstances of any other offences of which the offender has been convicted by a court anywhere in the world;

(b) any information which is before it about any pattern of behaviour of which any of the offences of which the offender has been convicted forms part; and

(c) any information about the offender which is before it, CJA 2003 s.229(2)(aa)–(c).

**Serious harm**    *"Serious harm"* means death or personal injury, whether physical or psychological, CJA 2003 s.224(3).

**Risk**    The risk does not have to be based on the instant offence, *Green* [2007] EWCA Crim 2172; [2008] 1 Cr.App.R. (S.) 97 (p.579). The absence of previous offences causing serious harm requiring an extended sentence does not preclude the finding of dangerousness, *Powell* [2015] EWCA Crim 2200; [2016] 1 Cr.App.R. (S.) 49.

## Determining the Appropriate Sentence

A finding of dangerousness does not automatically lead to the imposition of an extended sentence (in circumstances where the seriousness is not such that a life sentence is required). The court has a discretion as to whether an extended sentence is necessary, *Bourke* [2017] EWCA Crim 2150; [2018] 1 Cr.App.R. (S.) 41. A determinate sentence may provide adequate public protection alongside, e.g. sexual notification, an SHPO and the barring provisions. This will be a fact-specific decision.

## Determining the Length of the Sentence

**Custody**    Where the condition that the custodial term be at least four years applies, it is permissible to consider the totality of the offending and to aggregate the offending to satisfy the four-year requirement. It is not permissible to impose consecutive sentences to reach the four-year limit, see *Pinnell* [2010] EWCA Crim 2848; [2011] 2 Cr.App.R. (S.) 30, p.168.

The length of sentence must be for the shortest period commensurate with the seriousness of the offence(s), in compliance with the requirement in CJA 2003 s.153(2).

The custodial period must be adjusted for totality in the same way as determinate sentences would be, *Totality Guideline*, p.10.

**Extended licence**    The extension period is such as the court considers necessary for the purpose of protecting members of the public from serious harm caused by the offender committing further specified offences, *Cornelius* [2002] EWCA Crim 138. The length of the extension period is a matter of judicial judgement and the Court of Appeal will only interfere where it could be demonstrated that the judge had erred in deciding what factors should be taken into account when exercising his/her judgement or where the judge had reached a wholly unreasonable conclusion as to the necessary term, *ARD* [2017] EWCA Crim 1882; [2018] 1 Cr.App.R. (S.) 23.

As the extension period is measured by the need for protection, it does not require adjustment for totality, *Totality Guideline*, p.10.

**Consecutive Sentences**

In appropriate circumstances, consecutive extended sentences may be imposed, see e.g. *Watkins* [2014] EWCA Crim 1677; [2015] 1 Cr.App.R. (S.) 6. However in such circumstances, the explanation of the sentences (and their effect) is likely to be complex, and care should be taken in determining the true position.

In *B* [2015] EWCA Crim 1295; [2015] 2 Cr.App.R. (S.) 78, the court substituted consecutive extended sentences, aggregating the licence periods resulting in a total 10-year extended licence. In *Thompson* [2018] EWCA Crim 639; [2018] 2 Cr.App.R (S.) 19, a five-judge court confirmed that it was permissible to impose consecutive sentences so as to take the total extended licence period beyond the five or eight year limits provided by the Act. The court commented that it would be permissible only in exceptional circumstances, however.

It is not permissible to make the sentences partly concurrent and partly consecutive, *Francis* [2014] EWCA Crim 631; *DJ* [2015] EWCA Crim 563.

There is no objection to imposing an extended sentence consecutive to a determinate sentence (either on the same occasion, or in addition to an existing determinate sentence), *Brown* [2006] EWCA Crim 1996 and *Hibbert* [2015] EWCA Crim 507; [2015] 2 Cr.App.R. (S.) 15. However, the Court of Appeal has repeatedly stated that it is undesirable to impose a determinate sentence consecutive to an extended sentence (see e.g. *Brown* and *Prior* [2014] EWCA Crim 1290). This issue was considered in *Ulhaqdad* [2017] EWCA Crim 1216, where the court established that the order in which a court imposed an extended sentence and a determinate sentence (where those sentences are made to run consecutively) created no practical difficulty for the prison service in relation to the calculation of sentences and release dates etc. However, having identified no practical or principled reason for the guidance given in *Brown*, the court in *Ulhaqdad* maintained the status quo. Therefore the position remains that where extended and determinate sentences are being imposed to run consecutively, the determinate sentence should be imposed first. Two further points remain. First, that in *Prior*, the court suggested that an alternative approach was to increase the custodial term of the extended sentence and make the sentences run concurrently. Secondly, despite the guidance in *Brown*, there is nothing unlawful about imposing an extended sentence consecutive to a determinate sentence in an appropriate case, *Hibbert* [2015] EWCA Crim 507; [2015] 2 Cr.App.R. (S.) 15. However, it is submitted that the operation of the release provisions renders either approach permissible.

## Giving Reasons

The usual duty to give reasons for, and explain, the sentence in accordance with the CJA 2003 s.174 applies, *Lang* [2005] EWCA Crim 2864; [2006] 2 Cr.App.R. (S.) 3.

## Release

**Sentence imposed on or after 13 April 2015** At the 2/3 point of the custodial portion of the sentence, defendants will be referred to the Parole Board for consideration for release, CJA 2003 s.246A(3) and (4)(a).

If the first application is unsuccessful, there must be another referral after two years. The test for the Parole Board is whether or not it is satisfied that it is no longer necessary for the protection of the public that the defendant should be confined, CJA 2003 s.246A(4)(b) and (6).

Release is automatic at the expiry of the custodial portion of the sentence, CJA 2003 s.246A(7).

The defendant is then on licence for the aggregate of the remaining custodial portion (if there is one) and the extended licence period.

**Sentence imposed 3 December 2012–12 April 2015** For sentences imposed prior to 13 April 2015, the previous release regime applies: Where the sentence was imposed in relation to a Sch.15B offence or the custodial term is 10 years or more, release is at the discretion of the Parole Board at the 2/3 point of the custodial portion of the sentence, as set out above. All others will be automatically released at the 2/3 point of the custodial portion of the sentence, CJA 2003 s.246A(2).

# EXTRADITED OFFENDERS

CRIMINAL JUSTICE ACT 2003 s.243

*References: Current Sentencing Practice A7; Archbold 5A-635*

## Availability

A fixed term prisoner is an extradited prisoner if he has been sentenced after having been extradited to the United Kingdom and without having been first restored or had an opportunity of leaving the United Kingdom, and he was kept in custody while he was awaiting his extradition for any period, CJA 2003 s.243(1).

## Duty to specify number of days in custody

The court by which an extradited prisoner is sentenced must specify in open court the number of days for which he was kept in custody while awaiting extradition. These days count as time served as part of the sentence, CJA 2003 s.243(2).

Section 240ZA applies to days specified under subs.2 as if they were days for which the prisoner was remanded in custody in connection with the offence or a related offence, CJA 2003 s.243(2A).

Where a court omits to state that days spent in custody awaiting extradition are to be credited, there is no entitlement to have those days credited and the failure of the SoS to credit such days did not render the continuing detention unlawful, see *R. (Shields-McKinley) v Secretary of State for Justice and Lord Chancellor* [2017] EWHC 658 (Admin); [2017] 2 Cr.App.R. (S.) 17.

**Direction**   There exists a discretion to modify a sentence that was otherwise lawful, however cases in which that would be appropriate will be exceptional. That was because the rules laid down in the CJA 2003 for the according of credit against sentence for periods spent on remand or on qualifying bail were intended to lay down a comprehensive scheme governing the issue. Parliament has also made clear that time spent on remand in cases unrelated to the case under consideration should not, prima facie, warrant any adjustment to the sentence, *Prenga* [2018] EWCA Crim 2149; [2018] 4 W.L.R 59.

## No power to disallow days

The sentencing court has no power to disallow any days spent in custody prior to extradition.

Where a court omits to state that days spent in custody awaiting extradition are to be credited, there is no entitlement to have those days credited and the failure of the SoS to credit such days did not render the continuing detention unlawful, see *R. (Shields-McKinley) v Secretary of State for Justice and Lord Chancellor* [2017] EWHC 658 (Admin); [2017] 2 Cr.App.R. (S.) 17.

# FACTUAL BASIS FOR SENTENCING AND *NEWTON* HEARINGS

*References: Current Sentencing Practice H2-2250; Archbold 5A-258*

## Summary

The court provided a summary of the authorities in *Marsh*; *Cato* [2018] EWCA Crim [2018]; EWCA Crim 986; [2018] 2 Cr.App.R. (S.) 28.

## After a trial

**Interpreting the jury's verdict**   The correct approach by the judge, after a trial, to the determination of the factual basis on which to pass sentence was clear. If there was only one possible interpretation of a jury's verdict(s), the judge had to sentence on that basis. When there was more than one possible interpretation, the judge had to make up his or her own mind, to the criminal standard, as to the factual basis on which to pass sentence. If there was more than one possible interpretation, and the judge was not sure of any of them, (in accordance with basic fairness) they were obliged to pass sentence on the basis of the interpretation (whether in whole or in relevant part) most favourable to the defendant, *King* [2017] EWCA Crim 128; [2017] 2 Cr.App.R. (S.) 6.

## Guilty pleas

**Basis should be written**   If the prosecution does accept the defendant's basis of plea, it must be reduced to writing, be signed by advocates for both sides, and made available to the judge prior to the prosecution's opening, *CPD 2015* [2015] EWCA Crim 1567 Sentencing B.8(c).

**General**   If the prosecution does accept the defendant's basis of plea, it must be reduced to writing, be signed by advocates for both sides, and made available to the judge prior to the prosecution's opening, *CPD 2015* [2015] EWCA Crim 1567 Sentencing B.8(c).

The purpose of a *Newton* hearing is to determine factual issues which are relevant to the sentence and which have not been resolved by the offender's plea of guilty to the charges in the indictment. It is not a substitute for a jury trial.

The same procedure applies in the magistrates' court as it does in the Crown Court, *Telford Justices ex p. Darlington* (1988) 87 Cr.App.R. 194.

**Defence duty to inform prosecution of dispute of facts**   If the defendant intends to plead guilty to a charge on a basis of facts that differs significantly from that on which the prosecution will rely, the defendant's representatives must inform the prosecution and where the plea is entered, the judge must be informed of the basis of the plea, *Underwood* [2004] EWCA Crim 2256.

**Prosecution lack evidence to dispute basis of plea**   Where the prosecution lack the evidence positively to dispute the defendant's account, for example, where the defendant asserts a matter outside the knowledge of the prosecution, the prosecution should not automatically agree to the basis of plea. In such a case, the prosecution should test the defendant's evidence and submissions by requesting a *Newton* hearing, *CPD 2015* [2015] EWCA Crim 1567 Sentencing B.8(e).

**Basis is subject to judicial approval**    The judge is not bound to accept a plea offered by a defendant on a particular basis, even though the prosecution have agreed to accept the plea on that basis, *CPD 2015* [2015] EWCA Crim 1567 Sentencing B.9.

### When a hearing is appropriate: Pleas

(a)  the defendant offers a plea on a basis which is not acceptable to the prosecution;
(b)  the issue cannot be resolved by amending the indictment;
(c)  there is a substantial dispute of facts, the judge must either hear evidence and determine the issue of fact, or sentence on the basis put forward by the defendant, *Newton* (1982) 4 Cr.App.R. (S.) 388.

Where a *Newton* hearing is ordered, the defendant is not entitled to withdraw his plea and counsel for the prosecution must present the evidence to the court, *Beswick* [1996] 1 Cr.App.R. (S.) 343.

**The hearing**    Such a hearing is limited to the determination of matters which are consistent with the terms of the counts in the indictment to which the defendant has pleaded guilty. It is not open to the prosecution to allege that the defendant is guilty of more offences than are charged in the indictment or taken into consideration, or that the offence committed was more serious than the offence charged in the indictment, *Druce* (1993) 14 Cr.App.R. (S.) 691.

The hearing is conducted in the form of a trial without a jury. Evidence is adduced and witnesses are examined in the normal way. The judge should not intervene in the examination of witnesses, *McGrath* (1983) 5 Cr.App.R. (S.) 460.

The judge should direct himself that the prosecution must establish their version of the facts to the criminal standard of proof, *Underwood* [2004] EWCA Crim 2256.

It is not necessary for the judge to hear evidence if the matter in issue is not relevant to sentence, or the defendant's story can be considered wholly false or manifestly implausible, or where the matters put forward by the defendant relate to personal mitigation only, *CPD 2015* [2015] EWCA Crim 1567 Sentencing B10.

In circumstances where an offender's version of events is rejected at a *Newton* hearing or special reasons hearing, the reduction which would have been available at the stage of proceedings the plea was indicated should normally be halved. Where witnesses are called during such a hearing, it may be appropriate further to decrease the reduction, *Reduction in Sentence for a Guilty Pleas Guideline* (2017), para.F2.

# FEMALE GENITAL MUTILATION PROTECTION ORDERS

FEMALE GENITAL MUTILATION ACT 2003 SCH.2

*References: Current Sentencing Practice C2-6675*

## Making the Order

**Power**   The court before which there are criminal proceedings in England and Wales for a genital mutilation offence may make an FGM protection order (without an application being made to it) if:

(a)   the court considers that an FGM protection order should be made to protect a girl (whether or not the victim of the offence in relation to the criminal proceedings); and
(b)   a person who would be a respondent to any proceedings for an FGM protection order is a defendant in the criminal proceedings, FGMA 2003 Sch.2 para.3.

*"Genital mutilation offence"* means an offence under FGMA 2003 ss.1, 2 or 3, FGMA 2003 Sch.2 para.17(1).

**Contents of the order**   An FGM protection order may contain:

(a)   such prohibitions, restrictions or requirements, and
(b)   such other terms, as the court considers appropriate for the purposes of the order, FGMA 2003 Sch.2 para.1(3).

The terms of an FGM protection order may, in particular, relate to:

(a)   conduct outside England and Wales as well as (or instead of) conduct within England and Wales;
(b)   respondents who are, or may become, involved in other respects as well as (or instead of) respondents who commit or attempt to commit, or may commit or attempt to commit, a genital mutilation offence against a girl;
(c)   other persons who are, or may become, involved in other respects as well as respondents of any kind, FGMA 2003 Sch.2 para.1(4).

## Variation

**Power to vary on application**   The court may vary or discharge an FGM protection order on an application by:

(a)   the prosecution or the defendant;
(b)   the girl being protected by the order; or
(c)   any person affected by the order, FGMA 2003 Sch.2 para.6(1).

**Power to vary of own motion**   The court may vary or discharge a *"criminal"* FGM protection order even though no application has been made to the court, FGMA 2003 Sch.2 para.6(3).

[151]

### Breach

**Offence** A person who without reasonable excuse does anything that the person is prohibited from doing by an FGM protection order is guilty of an offence, FGMA 2003 Sch.2 para.4(1).

Where an individual is convicted of an offence, the conduct forming the basis of the conviction is not punishable as a contempt of court, FGMA 2003 Sch.2 para.4(3).

**Penalty** The maximum penalty for breaching an order is five years' imprisonment, FGMA 2003 Sch.2 para.4(5).

# FINANCIAL CIRCUMSTANCES ORDERS

## CRIMINAL JUSTICE ACT 2003 s.162

*References: Current Sentencing Practice B3-700; Archbold 5A-245*

### Availability

Where an individual has been convicted of an offence, the court may, before sentencing, make a financial circumstances order, CJA 2003 s.162(1).

A court may make a financial circumstances order irrespective of the kind of sentence that it has in mind.

### Effect

The order requires a person to give to the court, within such period as may be specified in the order, such a statement of his financial circumstances as the court may require, CJA 2003 s.162(3).

### Court notified of plea

A financial circumstances order may also be made by a magistrates' court which has been notified that an individual desires to plead guilty without appearing before the court, or by a court considering whether to make an order against the parent or guardian of a child or young person who has been convicted of an offence, CJA 2003 s.162(2).

### Offences

Failure to comply with a financial circumstances order, or making a false statement in response to a financial circumstances order, is a summary offence, CJA 2003 s.162(4) and (5).

# FINANCIAL REPORTING ORDERS

## SERIOUS ORGANISED CRIME AND POLICE ACT 2005 s.76

**Repeal**    The power to make a financial reporting order was repealed by the Serious Crime Act 2015 s.50, in force 3 May 2015, SI 2015/820. The Act consolidated financial reporting orders into the serious crime prevention order. The repeal does not apply in relation to a financial reporting order made before 3 May 2015. See **SERIOUS CRIME PREVENTION ORDERS**, p.273.

# FINES

## CRIMINAL JUSTICE ACT 2003 s.163

*References: Current Sentencing Practice B3; Archbold 5A-407*

### Crown Court

**Availability**   The Crown Court may impose a fine in lieu of, or in addition to, any other form of sentence, except a discharge, for any offence other than murder, CJA 2003 s.163.

Where a person is convicted on indictment of any offence, other than an offence for which the sentence is fixed by law or falls to be imposed under PCC(S)A 2000 ss.110(2) or 111(2) or under CJA 2003 ss.224A, 225 or 226, the court, if not precluded from sentencing an offender by its exercise of some other power may impose a fine instead of or in addition to dealing with him in any other way in which the court has power to deal with him, subject however to any enactment requiring the offender to be dealt with in a particular way, CJA 2003 s.163.

*Note: This is likely to be construed as also including the various prescribed sentence provisions under the PCA 1953, CJA 1988 and VCRA 2006.*

**Amount of fine**   There is no maximum level of fine in the Crown Court, CLA 1977 s.32(1). The amount of the fine must reflect the seriousness of the offence, CJA 2003 s.164(2).

**Inquire into offender's circumstances**   Before fixing the amount, the court must inquire into the offender's financial circumstances, CJA 2003 s.164(2).

The court may make a financial circumstances order. (See **FINANCIAL CIRCUMSTANCES ORDERS**, p.153.)

**Corporate offenders**   In the case of a corporation, the court is not obliged to inquire into the means of the offender but must take them into account as far as they are known. See *Thames Water Ltd.* [2015] EWCA Crim 960; [2015] 2 Cr.App.R. (S.) 63 for guidance.

**Time for payment/Payment by instalments**   Where the Crown Court imposes a fine it may allow time for payment and direct payment by instalments. Time for payment must be allowed unless the offender appears to have sufficient means to pay the fine immediately, or is unlikely to remain long enough at a fixed address to allow the fine to be enforced, or is simultaneously sentenced to, or is already serving, a custodial sentence, PCC(S)A 2000 s.139(1).

**Prison in default**   The court *must* fix a term of imprisonment to be served in default of payment. (See **DEFAULT TERMS—CROWN COURT**, p.95.) The default term is fixed in relation to the whole amount of the fine, not to individual instalments, PCC(S)A 2000 s.139(2).

## Magistrates' Court

**The standard scale**   For offences committed on or after 12 March 2015, the standard scale is to be read as follows:

> Level 1 £200
> Level 2 £500
> Level 3 £1,000
> Level 4 £2,500
> Level 5 Unlimited
> CJA 1982 s.37(2) and LASPOA 2012 s.85(1).

For offences committed between 1 October 1992 and 12 March 2015, the scale is as above save for the fact that Level 5 carries a £5,000 maximum; the other amounts remain the same.

**Exceptions**   There are a number of offences for which the removal of the limit on a Level 5 fine is disapplied, see SI 2015/664 rr.2 and 3 and Schs.1 and 3.

**Young offenders**   The maximum fine which a magistrates' court may impose on an offender under 14 is £250, and on a person aged 14 to 17 is £1,000, PCC(S)A 2000 s.135. The age of offender is that at conviction.

**Time for payment/Payment by instalments**   A magistrates' court may allow time for payment and direct payment by instalments. Time for payment must be allowed unless the offender appears to have sufficient means to pay the fine immediately, or is unlikely to remain long enough at a fixed address to allow the fine to be enforced, or is simultaneously sentenced to, or is already serving, a custodial sentence, MCA 1980 s.75(1).

**Prison in default**   A magistrates' court does not fix a term to be served in default on the occasion when a fine is imposed, unless the offender appears to have insufficient means to pay the fine immediately, or is unlikely to remain long enough at a fixed address to allow the fine to be enforced, or is simultaneously sentenced to, or is already serving, a custodial sentence.

The default terms for fines imposed by magistrates' courts are the same as for the Crown Court (see **DEFAULT TERMS—CROWN COURT**, p.95) except that the maximum default term which may be fixed is 12 months.

# FOOTBALL BANNING ORDERS (POST-CONVICTION)

FOOTBALL SPECTATORS ACT 1989 s.14A

*References: Current Sentencing Practice C2-3475; Archbold 5A-839*

## General

**Purpose**  The order is not designed as a punishment (although it will have that effect), it is designed as a preventive measure, *Doyle* [2013] EWCA Crim 995, [2013] 1 Cr.App.R. (S.) 36.

**Effect**  A banning order prohibits the offender from attending a regulated football match in England and Wales, and requires him to report when required to a police station when football matches are being played outside England and Wales. A banning order may include other requirements. The order must require the offender to surrender his passport in connection with matches played outside England and Wales, FSA 1989 s.14(4).

## Making the Order

A banning order may be made only in addition to any other form of sentence or in addition to a conditional discharge, FSA 1989 s.14(4)(a).

**Test to apply**  There are two conditions which must be met:

(a)  The individual has been convicted of a *relevant offence* (see below); and
(b)  the court is satisfied that there are reasonable grounds to believe that a banning order would help to prevent violence or disorder at or in connection with any regulated football matches, FSA 1989 s.14A(1) and (2).

In such a case, the court must make a banning order, FSA 1989 s.14A(2).

**State reasons where order not made**  If the court is not so satisfied, it *must* state that fact in open court and give its reasons, FSA 1989 s.14A(3).

**Length of the order**  If the offender receives an immediate custodial sentence, the banning order must be for at least six years and not more than 10 years. In all other cases, the banning order must be for at least three years and not more than five years.

**Limiting the order to specific teams**  It is not permissible to make an order restricted to certain football teams, see *Commissioner of Police of the Metropolis v Thorpe* [2015] EWHC 3339 (Admin); [2016] 1 Cr.App.R. (S.) 46.

## Relevant offences

The following offences are relevant offences:

(a)  any offence under the Football Spectators Act 1989 ss.14J(1), 19(6), 20(10) or; 21C(2);

(b) any offence under ss.2 or 2A of the Sporting Events (Control of Alcohol, etc.) Act 1985 (alcohol, containers and fireworks) committed by the accused at any regulated football match or while entering or trying to enter the ground;

(c) any offence under s.4A or s.5 of the Public Order Act 1986 (harassment, alarm or distress) or any provision of Pt III of that Act (racial hatred) committed at any premises while the accused was at, or was entering or leaving or trying to enter or leave, the premises;

(d) any offence involving the use or threat of violence by the accused towards another person committed during a period relevant to a regulated football match at any premises while the accused was at, or was entering or leaving or trying to enter or leave, the premises;

(e) any offence involving the use or threat of violence towards property committed during a period relevant to a regulated football match at any premises while the accused was at, or was entering or leaving or trying to enter or leave, the premises;

(f) any offence involving the use, carrying or possession of an offensive weapon or a firearm committed during a period relevant to a regulated football match at any premises while the accused was at, or was entering or leaving or trying to enter or leave, the premises;

(g) any offence under s.12 of the Licensing Act 1872 (persons found drunk in public places, etc.) of being found drunk in a highway or other public place committed while the accused was on a journey to or from a regulated football match applies in respect of which the court makes a declaration of relevance;

(h) any offence under s.91(1) of the Criminal Justice Act 1967 (disorderly behaviour while drunk in a public place) committed in a highway or other public place while the accused was on a journey to or from a regulated football match in respect of which the court makes a declaration of relevance;

(j) any offence under s.1 of the Sporting Events (Control of Alcohol, etc.) Act 1985 (alcohol on coaches or trains to or from sporting events) committed while the accused was on a journey to or from a regulated football match in respect of which the court makes a declaration of relevance;

(k) any offence under s.4A or s.5 of the Public Order Act 1986 (harassment, alarm or distress) or any provision of Pt III of that Act (racial hatred) committed while the accused was on a journey to or from a regulated football match in respect of which the court makes a declaration of relevance;

(l) any offence under ss.4 or 5 of the Road Traffic Act 1988 (driving, etc. when under the influence of drink or drugs or with an alcohol concentration above the prescribed limit) committed while the accused was on a journey to or from a regulated football match in respects of which the court makes a declaration of relevance;

(m) any offence involving the use or threat of violence by the accused towards another person committed while one or each of them was on a journey to or from a regulated football match in respect of which the court makes a declaration of relevance;

(n) any offence involving the use or threat of violence towards property committed while the accused was on a journey to or from a regulated football match in respect of which the court makes a declaration of relevance;

(o) any offence involving the use, carrying or possession of an offensive weapon or a firearm committed while the accused was on a journey to or from a regulated football match in respect of which the court makes a declaration of relevance;

(p) any offence under the Football (Offences) Act 1991;

(q) any other offence under s.4A or s.5 of the Public Order Act 1986 (harassment, alarm or distress) or any provision of Pt III of that Act (racial hatred) which does not fall within (c) or (k) above was committed during a period relevant to a regulated football match in respect of which the court makes a declaration that the offence related to that match or to that match and any other football match which took place during that period;

(r) any other offence involving the use or threat of violence by the accused towards another person which does not fall within (d) or (m) above was committed during a period relevant to a regulated football match in respect of which the court makes a declaration that the offence related to that match or to that match and any other football match which took place during that period;

(s) any other offence involving the use or threat of violence towards property which does not fall within (e) or (n) above was committed during a period relevant to a regulated football match in respect of which the court makes a declaration that the offence related to that match or to that match and any other football match which took place during that period;

(t) any other offence involving the use, carrying or possession of an offensive weapon which does not fall within (f) or (o) above was committed during a period relevant to a regulated football match in respect of which the court makes a declaration that the offence related to that match or to that match and any other football match which took place during that period;

(u) any offence under s.166 of the Criminal Justice and Public Order Act 1994 (sale of tickets by unauthorised persons) which relates to tickets for a football match.

**"Period relevant"**   The period relevant to a football match is the period beginning 24 hours before the start of the match, or the advertised start, and ending 24 hours after the end of the match. If the match does not take place, the period is the period beginning 24 hours before the time at which it was advertised to start, and ending 24 hours after that time.

**"Regulated football match"**   A regulated football match is an association football match in which one or both of the participating teams represents a club which is for the time being a member (whether a full or associate member) of the Football League, the Football Association Premier League or the Football Conference, or represents a club from outside England and Wales, or represents a country or territory; and which is either played at a sports ground which is designated by order under s.1(1) of the Safety of Sports Grounds Act 1975, or registered with the Football League or the Football Association Premier League as the home ground of a club which is a member of the Football League or the Football Association Premier League at the time the match is played; or is played in the Football Association Cup (other than in a preliminary or qualifying round), FSA 1989 s.14(2) and SI 2004/2409 art.3(3).

## Declarations of Relevance

**Definition**   A declaration by a court that an offence related to football matches, or that it related to one or more particular football matches, FSA 1989 s.23(5).

**Notice must be served**   The court may not make a declaration of relevance unless the prosecutor gave notice to the defendant five days before the first day of the trial that it was proposed to show that the offence related to football matches, unless the offender consents to waive the requirement or the court is satisfied that the interests of justice do not require more notice to be given, FSA 1989 s.23(1) and (2).

**Failure to make a declaration**   The failure to make a declaration of relevance does not render a football banning order invalid, *DPP v Beaumont* [2008] EWHC 523 (Admin); [2008] 2 Cr.App.R. (S.) 98, p.549.

**Declarations serve no purpose**   There appears to be no purpose in a declaration of relevance in the present state of the legislation, *Boggild* [2011] EWCA Crim 1928; [2012] 1 Cr.App.R. (S.) 81, (*obiter*).

*Note: A football banning order may only be made in respect of a relevant offence. There are two routes to satisfying that criterion, first, that the offence is deemed to automatically "relate" to football matches and second, an offence for which may or may not relate to a football match, for which it is necessary to make a determination. The purpose therefore appears to be safeguard against the imposition of orders in cases where the offence coincidentally occurred during a period relevant to a football match. However, an offence which coincidentally occurred during a period relevant to a football match would presumably fail the "reasonable grounds" test in FSA 1989 s.14A(1) and (2) and so the declaration appears to be without purpose as noted in Boggild.*

## Notice Requirements

An order must require the person subject to the order to report initially at a police station specified in the order within the period of five days beginning with the day on which the order is made, FSA 1989 s.14E(2).

An order must require the person subject to the order to give notification of:

(a)   a change of any of his names;
(b)   the first use by him after the making of the order of a name for himself that was not disclosed by him at the time of the making of the order;
(c)   a change of his home address;
(d)   his acquisition of a temporary address;
(e)   a change of his temporary address or his ceasing to have one;
(f)   his becoming aware of the loss of his passport;
(g)   receipt by him of a new passport;
(h)   an appeal made by him in relation to the order;
(i)   an application made by him under s.14H(2) for termination of the order;
(j)   an appeal made by him under s.23(3) against the making of a declaration

of relevance in respect of an offence of which he has been convicted, FSA 1989 s.14E(3).

## Appeals

A defendant may appeal against the making of a declaration of relevance, FSA 1989 s.23(3). The prosecution may appeal against the failure of a court to make a banning order, FSA 1989 s.14A(5A).

## Termination or Variation

An application to terminate the order may be made once the period of two thirds of the length of the of the order has expired, FSA 1989 s.14H(1). Upon an application by the person subject to the order, the person who applied for the order or the prosecutor in relation to the order may be varied so as to impose, omit or replace or omit any requirements, FSA 1989 s.14G(2).

## Breach

A failure to comply with a requirement of a football banning order constitutes an offence to which a maximum sentence of six months' imprisonment and/or a level 5 fine applies, FSA 1989 s.14J.

# FORFEITURE/DEPRIVATION ORDERS

*References: Current Sentencing Practice C3; Archbold 5A-440*

This section includes orders in relation to:

(1) drugs; (2) terrorism offences; (3) offensive weapons; (4) crossbows; (5) knives; (6) forgery and counterfeiting; (7) written material (racial hatred); (8) immigration offences; and (9) trafficking offences. For the general power to deprive an offender of property etc., see p.165 below.

## (1) Misuse of Drugs Act 1971 s.27

**Availability** The offender must be convicted of a drug trafficking offence (as defined in the Proceeds of Crime Act 2002 Sch.2) or an offence under the Misuse of Drugs Act 1971, MDA 1971 s.27(1).

**Test** The court may order forfeiture of anything shown to the satisfaction of the court to relate to the offence, MDA 1971 s.27(1). The offender may give evidence to show that the property is not related to the offence, *Churcher* (1986) 8 Cr.App.R. (S.) 94.

**Property** The court may not order forfeiture of intangible property or land or buildings, see e.g. *Cuthbertson* (1980) 2 Cr.App.R. (S.) 214. Property may not be forfeited on the grounds that it is the proceeds of offences of which the offender has not been convicted, or is intended to be used to facilitate the commission of future offences, *Ribeyre* (1982) 4 Cr.App.R. (S.) 165.

**Others claiming to own the property** If anyone claims to be the owner of the property or otherwise interested in it, he must be given the chance to show cause why the forfeiture order should not be made, MDA 1971 s.27(2).

**Effect** The court may order the property concerned to be destroyed, or dealt with in such manner as the court may order, MDA 1971 s.27(1).

**Confiscation** Where a court has postponed confiscation proceedings and proceeds to sentence the offender before making the confiscation order, it must not make a forfeiture order until the confiscation order has been made, POCA 2002 s.15(2)(b).

**Direct money paid to charity** When ordering money to be forfeited under this section, the court may direct that the sum is to be paid to a specific charity. The charity must be registered with the Charity Commission and have indicated its willingness to receive the monies. The judge must have no substantive connection with the charity awarded the monies so as to avoid the appearance of a conflict of interest, Guidance on forfeiture of monies to specific charities, *Senior Presiding Judge, 10 June 2015*.

## (2)  Terrorist Offences

### Powers

**TA 2000 ss.15(1) or (2) or 16**  The court may order the forfeiture of any money or other property which, at the time of the offence, the person had in their possession or under their control and which had been used for the purposes of terrorism, or they intended should be used, or had reasonable cause to suspect might be used, for those purposes, TA 2000 s.23(2).

**TA 2000 s.15(3)**  The court may order the forfeiture of any money or other property which, at the time of the offence, the person had in their possession or under their control and which had been used for the purposes of terrorism, or which, at that time, they knew or had reasonable cause to suspect would or might be used for those purposes, TA 2000 s.23(3).

**TA 2000 ss.17 or 18**  The court may order the forfeiture of any money or other property which, at the time of the offence, the person had in their possession or under their control and which had been used for the purposes of terrorism, or was, at that time, intended by them to be used for those purposes, TA 2000 s.23(4).

**TA 2000 s.17**  The court may order the forfeiture of the money or other property to which the arrangement in question related, and which had been used for the purposes of terrorism, or at the time of the offence, the person knew or had reasonable cause to suspect would or might be used for those purposes, TA 2000 s.23(5).

**TA 2000 s.18**  The court may order the forfeiture of the money or other property to which the arrangement in question related, TA 2000 s.23(6).

**TA 2000 ss.15 to 18**  The court may order the forfeiture of any money or other property which wholly or partly, and directly or indirectly, is received by any person as a payment or other reward in connection with the commission of the offence, TA 2000 s.23(7).

**TA 2000, TA 2006 and other offences**  Where a person is convicted of an offence under:

   (a)   Terrorism Act 2000 ss.54, 57, 58 or 58A, 59, 60 or 61;
   (b)   Terrorism Act 2006 ss.2, 5, 6, 9, 10, or 11;
   (c)   an offence that is specified in Sch.2 to the Counter-Terrorism Act 2008 as to which the court dealing with the offence has determined that the offence has a terrorist connection;
   (d)   any ancillary offence related to these offences.

The court may order the forfeiture of any money or other property which was, at the time of the offence, in the possession or control of the person convicted and had been used for the purposes of terrorism, was intended by that person to be used for the purposes of terrorism, or the court believes that it will be used for the purposes of terrorism unless forfeited, TA 2000 s.23A.

**Others claiming to own the property**  Before making a forfeiture order, the court must give an opportunity to be heard to any person, other than the convicted person, who claims to be the owner or otherwise interested in anything which can be forfeited. The court must have regard to the value of the property, and the likely financial and other effects on the convicted person of the making of the order (taken together with any other order that the court contemplates making), TA 2000 s.23B(1) and (2).

**Compensating for loss etc.**    Where a court makes a forfeiture order in a case where the offender has been convicted of an offence that has resulted in a person suffering personal injury, loss or damage, or any such offence is taken into consideration by the court in determining sentence, the court may also order that an amount not exceeding a sum specified by the court is to be paid to that person out of the proceeds of the forfeiture. The court may make, and only if it is satisfied that but for the inadequacy of the offender's means it would have made a compensation under which the offender would have been required to pay compensation of an amount not less than the specified amount, TA 2000 Sch.4 para.4A.

**Additional powers**    Before making an order under the following provisions, the court must give an opportunity to be heard to any person, other than the convicted person, who claims to be the owner or otherwise interested in anything which can be forfeited. The court may also make such other provision as appears to it to be necessary for giving effect to the forfeiture, including, in particular, provision relating to the retention, handling, disposal or destruction of what is forfeited, see TA 2000 s.120A(2) and TA 2006 ss.7(2) and 11A(3).

**TA 2000 s.54**    The court may order the forfeiture of anything that the court considers to have been in the possession of the person for purposes connected with the offence, TA 2000 s.120A(1).

**TA 2000 s.57**    The court may order the forfeiture of any article that is the subject matter of the offence, TA 2000 s.120A(1).

**TA 2000 s.58**    The court may order the forfeiture of any document or record containing information of the kind mentioned in subs.(1)(a) of that section, TA 2000 s.120A(1).

**TA 2000 s.58A**    The court may order the forfeiture of any document or record containing information of the kind mentioned in subs.(1)(a) of that section, TA 2000 s.120A(1).

**TA 2006 s.6**    The court may order the forfeiture of anything the court considers to have been in the person's possession for purposes connected with the offence, TA 2006 s.7(1).

**TA 2006 s.9 or s.10**    The court may order the forfeiture of any radioactive device or radioactive material, or any nuclear facility, made or used in committing the offence, TA 2006 s.11A(1).

**TA 2006 s.11**    The court may order the forfeiture of any radioactive device or radioactive material, or any nuclear facility, which is the subject of a demand under subs.(1) of that section, or a threat falling within subs.(3) of that section, TA 2006 s.11A(2).

### (3)  Offensive Weapons

**Power**   Where a person is convicted of an offence under PCA 1953 s.1(1), the court may make an order for the forfeiture or disposal of any weapon in respect of which the offence was committed, PCA 1953 s.1(2).

### (4)  Crossbows Act 1987

**Power**   The court by which a person is convicted of an offence under the Crossbows Act 1987 may make such order as it thinks fit as to the forfeiture or disposal of any crossbow or part of a crossbow in respect of which the offence was committed, CA 1987 s.6(3).

### (5)  Knives Act 1997

**Knives**   If a person is convicted of an offence under s.1 (unlawful marketing of knives) in relation to a knife of a particular description, the court may make an order for forfeiture in respect of any knives of that description:

(a)  seized under a warrant issued under s.5; or

(b)  in the offender's possession or under his control at the relevant time, KA 1997 s.6(1).

**Publications**   If a person is convicted of an offence under s.2 (publications) in relation to particular material, the court may make an order for forfeiture in respect of any publications consisting of or containing that material which:

(a)  have been seized under a warrant issued under s.5; or

(b)  were in the offender's possession or under his control at the relevant time, KA 1997 s.6(2).

**Duty to consider value etc.**   The court must consider the value of the item/material and the effect it will have upon the offender, KA 1997 s.6(4).

**Recovery order**   The court may make an order in for the delivery of the forfeited item/material upon an application by an individual who claims to be the owner and is not the offender from whom it was forfeited, KA 1997 s.7(3).

### (6)  Forgery and Counterfeiting Act 1981

**Forgery etc. offences**   The court by or before which a person is convicted of an offence under FCA 1981 Pt.1 may order any object shown to the satisfaction of the court to relate to the offence to be forfeited and either destroyed or dealt with in such other manner as the court may order, FCA 1981 s.7(3).

The court shall not order any object to be forfeited under where a person claiming to be the owner of or otherwise interested in it applies to be heard by the court, unless an opportunity has been given to him to show cause why the order should not be made, FCA 1981 s.7(4).

**Counterfeiting etc. offences**   The court by or before which a person is convicted of an offence under FCA 1981 Pt.2 may order any thing shown to the satisfaction of the court to relate to the offence to be forfeited and either destroyed or dealt with in such other manner as the court may order, FCA 1981 s.24(3).

The court shall not order any thing to be forfeited where a person claiming to be the owner of or otherwise interested in it applies to be heard by the court, unless an opportunity has been given to him to show cause why the order should not be made, FCA 1981 s.24(4).

The powers conferred on the court by s.24(3) and (4) include the power to direct that any object shall be passed to an authority with power to issue notes or coins or to any person authorised by such an authority to receive the object, FCA 1981 s.24(5).

### (7)   Written Material (Racial Hatred)

**Powers**   A court by or before which a person is convicted of:

(a)   an offence under s.18 (use of words or behaviour or display of written material); or

(b)   an offence under s.19 (publishing or distributing written material); 21 (distributing, showing or playing a recording) or 23 (possession of racially inflammatory material), shall order to be forfeited any written material or recording produced to the court and shown to its satisfaction to be written material or a recording to which the offence relates, POA 1986 s.25(1).

A court by or before which a person is convicted of:

(a)   an offence under s.29B (use of words or behaviour or display of written material) relating to the display of written material; or

(b)   an offence under s.29C (publishing or distributing written material), 29E (distributing, showing or playing a recording) or 29G (possession of inflammatory material), shall order to be forfeited any written material or recording produced to the court and shown to its satisfaction to be written material or a recording to which the offence relates, POA 1986 s.29I(1).

The order is suspended until the time limit for applying to appeal has expired, POA 1986 ss.25(2) and 29I(2).

### (8)   Immigration Offences

**Power**   The court may order the forfeiture of a vehicle, ship or aircraft used or intended to be used in connection with the offence if the convicted person:

(a)   owned the vehicle, ship or aircraft at the time the offence was committed;

(b)   was at that time a director, secretary or manager of a company which owned the vehicle, ship or aircraft;

(c)   was at that time in possession of the vehicle, ship or aircraft under a hire-purchase agreement;

(d)   was at that time a director, secretary or manager of a company which was in possession of the vehicle under a hire-purchase agreement;

(e)   was at that time a charterer of the ship or aircraft;

(f)   was driving the vehicle, ship or aircraft in the course of the commission of the offence; or

(g)   committed the offence while acting as captain of the ship or aircraft, IA 1971 s.25C(2) and (3).

**Limitations**   There are certain limitations on forfeiture which arise depending on the link between the individual and the ship, vehicle or aircraft being forfeited, IA 1971 s.25C(4)–(6).

**Representations**    Where a person who claims to have an interest in a vehicle, ship or aircraft applies to a court to make representations on the question of forfeiture, the court may not make an order under this section in respect of the ship, aircraft or vehicle unless the person has been given an opportunity to make representations, IA 1971 s.25C(8).

### (9)  Trafficking Offences

**Power**    Where an individual is convicted of an offence under MSA 2015 s.2 (trafficking), the court has the power to make a forfeiture order, MSA 2015 s.11(1).

**Land vehicles**    The court may order the forfeiture of a land vehicle used or intended to be used in connection with the offence if the convicted person:

(a)  owned the vehicle at the time the offence was committed,

(b)  was at that time a director, secretary or manager of a company which owned the vehicle,

(c)  was at that time in possession of the vehicle under a hire-purchase agreement,

(d)  was at that time a director, secretary or manager of a company which was in possession of the vehicle under a hire-purchase agreement, or

(e)  was driving the vehicle in the course of the commission of the offence, MSA 2015 s11(2).

**Ships or aircraft**    The court may order the forfeiture of a ship or aircraft used or intended to be used in connection with the offence if the convicted person—

(a)  owned the ship or aircraft at the time the offence was committed,

(b)  was at that time a director, secretary or manager of a company which owned the ship or aircraft,

(c)  was at that time in possession of the ship or aircraft under a hire purchase agreement,

(d)  was at that time a director, secretary or manager of a company which was in possession of the ship or aircraft under a hire-purchase agreement,

(e)  was at that time a charterer of the ship or aircraft, or

(f)  committed the offence while acting as captain of the ship or aircraft, MSA 2015 s.11(3).

*Note: There are limited exceptions in the case of ships and aircraft. See MSA 2015 s.11(4) and (5).*

**Third party interest**    Where a person who claims to have an interest in a land vehicle, ship or aircraft applies to a court to make representations about its forfeiture, the court may not order its forfeiture without giving the person an opportunity to make representations, MSA 2015 s.11(6).

# *GOODYEAR* INDICATIONS (ADVANCE INDICATION OF SENTENCE)

*Goodyear* [2015] EWCA Crim 1567; [2006] 1 Cr.App.R. (S.) 6

*References: Current Sentencing Practice H2-1850; Archbold 5A-111*

## Objective

The objective of the *Goodyear* guidelines is to safeguard against the creation or appearance of judicial pressure on a defendant, and allow the defendant to make a more informed decision whether or not to plead guilty, *Goodyear* at [53] and CPD Sentencing C.2.

## Availability

Prior to pleading guilty, it is open to a defendant in the Crown Court to request from the judge an indication of the maximum sentence that would be imposed if a guilty plea were to be tendered at that stage in the proceedings, CPD Sentencing C.1.

An indication should not be sought while there is any uncertainty about an acceptable plea or the factual basis of sentencing. An indication should not be sought on a basis of hypothetical facts. Where appropriate, there must be an agreed, written basis of plea. Unless there is, the judge should refuse to give an indication: otherwise he may become inappropriately involved in negotiations about the acceptance of pleas, and any agreed basis of plea, *Goodyear* at [62].

A *Goodyear* indication is not available in the magistrates' court and magistrates should confine themselves to the statutory arrangements in CJA 2003 Sch.3, *Goodyear* at [78].

The judge should only give a *Goodyear* indication if one is requested by the defendant, although the judge can, in an appropriate case, remind the defence advocate of the defendant's entitlement to seek an advance indication of sentence, *Goodyear* at [55]–[56] and CPD Sentencing C.2.

Whether or not the judge has given an appropriate reminder, the defendant's advocate should not seek an indication without written authority, signed by his or her client, that the client wishes to seek an indication, *Goodyear* at [64].

A judge should not give an indication of sentence in advance of a *Newton* hearing, not only because the judge would find it hard to predict what basis he or she would be sentencing upon, but because it will not be known to what extent the amount of credit for pleading guilty will need to be reduced, *Martin* [2014] 2 Cr.App.R (S) 21 at [11].

## Judge entitled to refuse or defer the application

In whatever circumstances an advance indication of sentence is sought, the judge retains an unfettered discretion to refuse to give one, *Goodyear* at [57]. Just as the judge may refuse to give an indication, he or may reserve their position until such time as they feel able to give one, for example, until a pre-sentence report is available, *Goodyear* at [58].

The judge may or may not give reasons. In many cases involving an outright refusal, the judge would probably conclude that it would be inappropriate to give reasons. If the judge has in mind to defer an indication, the probability is that the reasons would be explained and further indicate the circumstances in which, and when, they would be prepared to respond to a request for a sentence indication, *Goodyear* at [59].

If at any stage the judge refuses to give an indication (as opposed to deferring it) it remains open to the defendant to seek a further indication at a later stage. However once the judge has refused to give an indication, he should not normally initiate the process, except, where it arises, to indicate that the circumstances had changed sufficiently for him to be prepared to consider a renewed application for an indication, *Goodyear* at [60].

**Giving the indication**

Any advance indication of sentence to be given by the judge should normally be confined to the maximum sentence if a plea of guilty were tendered at the stage at which the indication is sought, *Goodyear* at [54].

The hearing should normally take place in open court, with a full recording of the entire proceedings, and both sides represented, in the defendant's presence, *Goodyear* at [75]. Reporting restrictions should normally be imposed, CPD Sentencing C.8.

**Effect of the indication**

Once an indication has been given, it is binding and remains binding on the judge who has given it, and it also binds any other judge who becomes responsible for the case. In principle, the judge who has given an indication should, where possible, deal with the case immediately, and if that is not possible, any subsequent hearings should be listed before him, *Goodyear* at [61].

The indication is binding save in exceptional circumstances, such as arose in *Newman* [2010] EWCA Crim 1566, [2011] 1 Cr.App.R. (S.) 68 in which the judge gave an indicated but subsequently stated he had been wrong to do so and that the indication was wholly inadequate, CPD Sentencing C.6.

Revisions to *Goodyear* indications should be very much the exception, and can only be made in a manner which is fair to the defendant: in other words, where the matter can be revised without the defendant sustaining any prejudice other than mere disappointment, *Newman* at [18].

The right of the Attorney General to refer a sentence to the Court of Appeal on the ground that it is unduly lenient is not affected by the giving of an advance indication of sentence. The defendant's entitlement to apply for leave to appeal against sentence if, for example, insufficient allowance has been made for matters of genuine mitigation, is similarly unaffected, *Goodyear* at [71]–[72].

If the defendant does not plead guilty, the indication will not thereafter bind the court, CPD Sentencing C.6.

In *Davies* [2015] EWCA Crim 930; [2015] 2 Cr.App.R. (S.) 57, where a *Goodyear* indication had been given after which the defendant had pleaded guilty, but where the defendant had subsequently absconded, the court held that the judge was not entitled to depart from the indication.

### Advocates' duties

The defendant's advocate is responsible for ensuring that the defendant fully appreciates that:

(a)   he should not plead guilty unless he is guilty;
(b)   any sentence indication given by the judge remains subject to the entitlement of the Attorney General (where it arises) to refer an unduly lenient sentence to the Court of Appeal;
(c)   any indication given by the judge reflects the situation at the time when it is given, and that if a "*guilty plea*" is not tendered in the light of that indication the indication ceases to have effect;
(d)   any indication which may be given relates only to the matters about which an indication is sought, *Goodyear* at [65].

The prosecution advocate is responsible for the following:

(a)   if there is no final agreement about the plea to the indictment, or the basis of plea, and the defence nevertheless proceeds to seek an indication, which the judge appears minded to give, prosecuting counsel should remind him of the guidance given in *Goodyear*, that normally speaking an indication of sentence should not be given until the basis of the plea has been agreed, or the judge has concluded that he can properly deal with the case without the need for a *Newton* hearing;
(b)   if an indication is sought, the prosecution should normally enquire whether the judge is in possession of or has had access to all the evidence relied on by the prosecution, including any impact statement from the victim of the crime, as well as any information of relevant previous convictions recorded against the defendant;
(c)   if the process has been properly followed, it should not normally be necessary for counsel for the prosecution, before the judge gives any indication, to do more than, first, draw the judge's attention to any minimum or mandatory statutory sentencing requirements, and where he would be expected to offer the judge assistance with relevant guideline cases, or the views of the Sentencing Council, to invite the judge to allow him to do so, and second, where it applies, to remind the judge that the position of the Attorney General to refer any eventual sentencing decision as unduly lenient is not affected;
(d)   in any event, counsel should not say anything which may create the impres-

sion that the sentence indication has the support or approval of the Crown, *Goodyear* at [70].

## Complex cases

Judges are most unlikely to be able to give an indication of sentence in complicated or difficult cases unless issues between the prosecution and defence have been addressed and resolved. In such cases, no less than seven days' notice of an intention to seek an indication should be given to the prosecution and to the court. If an application is made without notice when it should have been given, the judge may conclude that any inevitable adjournment should have been avoided and that the discount for pleading guilty should be reduced accordingly, *Goodyear* at [74].

## Dangerousness

If the offence is a specified offence such that the defendant might be liable to an assessment of "*dangerousness*" in accordance with the CJA 2003 it is unlikely that the necessary material for such an assessment will be available. The court can still proceed to give an indication of sentence, but should state clearly the limitations of the indication that can be given, CPD Sentencing C.7.

There is scope, additionally, for a judge to give what might be termed a qualified *Goodyear* indication, depending on the ultimate conclusion as to dangerousness, and applicable only if a determinate sentence was ultimately imposed, see *Newman* at [16].

## Subsequent trials

The fact that notice has been given, and any reference to a request for a sentence indication, or the circumstances in which it was sought, would be inadmissible in any subsequent trial, *Goodyear* at [76].

# GUARDIANSHIP ORDERS

## MENTAL HEALTH ACT 1983 s.37

*References: Current Sentencing Practice E1; Archbold 5A-1188*

### Availability

The court may make a guardianship order provided that the offender is 16 or older, MHA 1983 s.37(2).

### Test

(1) The court is satisfied on the written or oral evidence of two medical practitioners that the offender is suffering from mental disorder and the court is satisfied that the mental disorder from which he is suffering is of a nature or degree which warrants his reception into guardianship, MHA 1983 s.37(2).

Evidence may not be received by telephone, *Clark* [2015] EWCA Crim 2192; [2016] 1 Cr.App.R. (S.) 52.

(2) The court must be of the opinion, having regard to all the circumstances, including the nature of the offence and the character and antecedents of the offender that the most suitable method of disposing of the case is by means of a guardianship order, MHA 1983 s.37(2).

(3) A guardianship order may not be made unless the court is satisfied that the local authority or other person concerned is willing to receive the offender into guardianship, MHA 1983 s.37(6).

### Contents of the order

The order must specify the form or forms of mental disorder from which the offender is suffering. At least two practitioners must agree that the offender is suffering from the same form of mental disorder.

### Combining sentences

The court may not impose a sentence of imprisonment, impose a fine or make a community order but may make such other forms of order as may be appropriate, MHA 1983 s.37(8).

# GUILTY PLEA, DISCOUNT FOR

SENTENCING COUNCIL REDUCTION IN SENTENCE FOR GUILTY PLEA (2017) AND
CRIMINAL JUSTICE ACT 2003 s.144

*References: Current Sentencing Practice H3-100; Archbold 5A-130*

## General

As a general rule a court which imposes a custodial sentence should reduce the length of the sentence to recognise the fact that the offender has pleaded guilty and the stage at which the plea was entered. The extent of the reduction is a matter for the discretion of the court, CJA 2003 s.144(1).

A court which passes a custodial sentence following a plea of guilty should always indicate that it has taken the plea into account.

## Application

The new guideline applies to cases in which the first appearance was on or after 1 June 2017, *Guideline* p.4.

## General approach

Stage 1    Determine the appropriate sentence for the offence(s) in accordance with any offence specific sentencing guideline;

Stage 2    Determine the level of reduction for a guilty plea in accordance with this guideline;

Stage 3    State the amount of that reduction;

Stage 4    Apply the reduction to the approproiate sentence;

Stage 5    Follow any further steps in the offence specific guideline to determine the final sentence *Guideline* p.5.

## Indications

An indication of the type envisaged by the guideline must make a clear acceptance of guilt; an indication of a consideration of pleading guilty will be insufficient, *Reid* [2017] EWCA Crim 1523; [2018] 1 Cr.App.R. (S.) 8.

## Giving lying evidence in aid of co-defendant

As a general rule, credit for a guilty plea should not be reduced on account of the offender having given lying evidence in support of a co-defendant at their trial, *Wilson* [2018] EWCA Crim 449.

## Determining the reduction

The maximum level of discount is one-third.

**Plea indicated at first stage of proceedings**    Plea indicated at first stage of proceedings Where a guilty plea is indicated at the first stage of proceedings a reduction of one-third should be made (subject to the exceptions in section F of the guideline). The first stage will normally be the first hearing at which a plea or indication of plea is sought and recorded by the court.

**Plea indicated after first stage of proceedings**     Plea indicated after first stage of proceedings After the first stage of the proceedings the maximum level of reduction is one-quarter (subject to the exceptions in section F of the guideline). The reduction should be decreased from one-quarter to a maximum of one-tenth on the first day of trial having regard to the time when the guilty plea is first indicated to the court relative to the progress of the case and the trial date (subject to the exceptions in section F of the guideline).

The reduction should normally be decreased further, even to zero, if the guilty plea is entered during the course of the trial.

For the purposes of the guideline a trial will be deemed to have started when pre-recorded cross-examination has begun, *Guideline* p.5.

Page 6 of the guideline deals with the application of the reduction, in particular in relation to imposing another type of sentence or keeping a case in the magistrates' court rather than committing for sentence.

Page 7 of the guideline deals with exceptions to the general approach, including where further advice may have been necessary or where there has been a *Newton* hearing.

**Dangerousness**

While there are legitimate reasons for departing from the general approach of applying the stated reductions listed in the sentencing guidelines, doing so to keep the sentence within the four-year minimum so as to enable the imposition of an extended sentence is not one of them, *Nsumbu* [2017] EWCA Crim 1046; [2017] 2 Cr.App.R. (S.) 51.

**Minimum sentences**

In the case of an offender aged 18 or over convicted of an offence the sentence for which falls to be imposed under:

(a)   PCA 1953 ss.1(2B) or 1A(6)(a) (offensive weapons offences);
(b)   PCC(S)A 2000 s.110(2) (third Class A drug trafficking offence);
(c)   PCC(S)A 2000 s.111(2) (third domestic burglary offence);
(d)   CJA 1988 ss.139(6B), 139A(5B) or 139AA(7) (bladed article or offensive weapon offences),

the discount for a guilty plea may only have the effect of reducing the period to not less than 80% of that specified, CJA 2003 s.144(2) and (3).

Where a young offender aged 16 or 17 pleads guilty to an offence under PCA 1953 s.1(2B) or 1A(5), or CJA 1988 ss.139(6B), 139A(5B) or 139AA(7), the court may impose any sentence it considers appropriate and is not limited to the minimum four-month DTO specified in the legislation, CJA 2003 s.144(4).

# HOSPITAL AND LIMITATION DIRECTION (HYBRID ORDERS)

## MENTAL HEALTH ACT 1983 ss.45A, 45B

*References: Current Sentencing Practice E1; Archbold 5A-1210*

### General

A *"hybrid order"* is an order which combines a hospital order (with restriction) and a sentence of imprisonment. The offender is sentenced to custody but removed to hospital for treatment.

### Availability

A direction under s.45A is not available for those under 21 at conviction, *Fort* [2013] EWCA Crim 2332; [2014] 2 Cr.App.R.(S.) 24.

### Order in which the court should approach the issue

In a case where the medical evidence suggests that D is suffering from a mental disorder, that the offending is wholly or in significant part attributable to that disorder, and that treatment is available, and where the court considers that a hospital order with or without restrictions may be appropriate, it must address the issues in the following order:

(i)    can the mental disorder can be appropriately dealt with by a hospital and limitation direction, under the terms of s.45A?

(ii)    if it can, and if D was aged 21 at the time of conviction, it should make such a direction under s.45A;

(iii)    if not, consider whether the medical evidence fulfils the requirements for a hospital order under s.37(2)(a), and (where applicable) for a restriction order under s.41, and consider whether such an order is the *"most suitable method of disposing of the case"* under s.37(2)(b);

(iv)    the wording of s.37(2)(b) requires a court, when deciding on suitability, to have regard to *"other available methods of dealing with"* D. Relevant to this is the power to transfer an offender from prison to hospital for treatment, under s.47;

(v)    if the court determines that a hospital order is the most suitable method of dealing with D, the order should normally be made without considering an interim order under s.38 unless there is clear evidence that such an order is needed, *Vowles* [2015] EWCA Crim 45; [2015] 2 Cr.App.R. (S.) 6.

*Vowles* was further considered in *Edwards* [2018] EWCA Crim 595; [2018] 4 W.L.R. 64 in which the court noted that a level of misunderstanding of the guidance offered in *Vowles* had arisen as to the order in which a sentencing judge should approach the making of a s.37 or a s.45A order and the precedence allegedly given in *Vowles* to a s.45A order. The court stated that the position was clear that s.45A and the judgment in *Vowles* did not provide a *"default"* setting of imprisonment; that the sentencing judge should first consider if a hospital order may be appropriate under s.37(2)(a); if so, before making such an order, the court had to consider all the powers at its disposal including a s.45A order; therefore consideration of a s.45A order must come before the making of a hospital order because a disposal under s.45A includes a penal element and the court must have "*sound reasons*" for departing from the usual course of imposing a sentence with a penal element.

## Test

A court which passes a sentence of imprisonment for an offence other than murder on an offender may make a hospital and limitation direction, if the court is satisfied on the evidence of two medical practitioners (one of whom must give evidence orally) that:

(a) the offender is suffering from a mental disorder;
(b) the disorder is of a nature or degree which makes it appropriate for him to be detained in a hospital for medical treatment; or
(c) appropriate medical treatment is available for him MHA 1983 s.45A(1), (2) and (4).

The hospital must be specified in the direction, and the court must be satisfied that the offender will be admitted to the hospital within 28 days of the making of the order, MHA 1983 s.45A(5).

## Oral evidence

Evidence may not be received by telephone, *Clark* [2015] EWCA Crim 2192; [2016] 1 Cr.App.R. (S.) 52.

## Effect

The order must direct that the offender (a) be removed to a hospital, and (b) be subject to the restrictions set out in MHA 1983 s.41, s.45A(3).

An offender subject to a hospital and limitation direction will be treated as if he had been sentenced to imprisonment and transferred to hospital by order of the Secretary of State, MHA 1983 s.45B.

If the offender ceases to be in need of treatment before the expiration of the sentence, he will be liable to be returned to prison. If he is still in hospital when the period during which he is liable to be detained under the sentence expires, he will be liable to be detained in hospital as an unrestricted patient.

## Combining sentences

A hospital and limitation direction may be made in conjunction with a determinate sentence of imprisonment, a longer than commensurate sentence of imprisonment, a discretionary sentence of life imprisonment or an automatic sentence of life imprisonment. It may not be made in conjunction with a mandatory life sentence imposed for murder, MHA 1983 s.45A(1).

## Release

The First-tier Tribunal (Mental Health) decides when the offender should be released when an order is made under ss.37/41. However, for s.45A orders the release regime differs depending on whether an offender is serving a determinate or indeterminate sentence of imprisonment, *Edwards*.

If combined with a determinate sentence, where the patient's health improves so that the responsible clinician or the tribunal notifies the Secretary of State that treatment in hospital under the MHA is no longer required, the SoS will generally remit the patient to prison under s.50(1) of the MHA to serve the rest of his sentence. On arrival in prison, the s.45A order would cease to have effect and the offender would be released from prison in the usual way. If there has been no improvement at the automatic release date (in respect of the custodial sentence), the limitation direction aspect of s.45A falls away and the patient remains in hospital but is treated as though they are subject to an unrestricted hospital order. Discharge is then a matter for the clinicians, *Edwards*.

If combined with an indeterminate sentence and where patient's health improves such that the responsible clinician or the tribunal notifies the SoS that treatment in hospital under the MHA is no longer required, the SoS will generally remit the patient to prison under s.50(1) of the MHA. On arrival in prison, the s.45A order would cease to have effect and release would be considered by the Parole Board in the usual way. Where the patient has served the entirety of the minimum term and the tribunal subsequently notified the SoS that the patient is ready for conditional discharge, the SoS could notify the tribunal that he should be so discharged (s.74(2)). In that case, the offender would be subject to mental health supervision and recall in the usual way. However, the SoS would, in practice, refer the offender to the Parole Board, *Edwards*.

# HOSPITAL ORDERS

## MENTAL HEALTH ACT 1983 s.37

*References: Current Sentencing Practice E1; Archbold 5A-1188*

### Availability

Where a person has been convicted of an offence punishable by imprisonment which is not one where the sentence is fixed by law, MHA 1983 s.37(1).

The statute refers to orders in respect of those aged 14+ but there appears no restriction for those aged 10–14.

### Order in which the court should approach the issue

In a case where the medical evidence suggests that D is suffering from a mental disorder, that the offending is wholly or in significant part attributable to that disorder, and that treatment is available, and where the court considers that a hospital order with or without restrictions may be appropriate, it must address the issues in the following order:

(i)    can the mental disorder can be appropriately dealt with by a hospital and limitation direction, under the terms of s.45A;

(ii)   if it can, and if D was aged 21 at the time of conviction, it should make such a direction under s.45A;

(iii)  if not, consider whether the medical evidence fulfils the requirements for a hospital order under s.37(2)(a), and (where applicable) for a restriction order under s.41, and consider whether such an order is the "*most suitable method of disposing of the case*" under s.37(2)(b);

(iv)   the wording of s.37(2)(b) requires a court, when deciding on suitability, to have regard to "*other available methods of dealing with*" D. Relevant to this is the power to transfer an offender from prison to hospital for treatment, under s.47;

(v)    if the court determines that a hospital order is the most suitable method of dealing with D, the order should normally be made without considering an interim order under s.38 unless there is clear evidence that such an order is needed, *Vowles* [2015] EWCA Crim 45; [2015] 2 Cr.App.R. (S.) 6.

*Vowles* was further considered in *Edwards* [2018] EWCA Crim 595 in which the court noted that a level of misunderstanding of the guidance offered in *Vowles* had arisen as to the order in which a sentencing judge should approach the making of a s.37 or a s.45A order and the precedence allegedly given in *Vowles* to a s.45A order. The court stated that the position was clear that s.45A and the judgment in *Vowles* did not provide a "*default*" setting of imprisonment; that the sentencing judge should first consider if a hospital order may be appropriate under s.37(2)(a); if so, before making such an order, the court had to consider all the powers at its disposal including a s.45A order; therefore consideration of a s.45A order must come before the making of a hospital order because a disposal under s.45A includes a penal element and the court must have "*sound reasons*" for departing from the usual course of imposing a sentence with a penal element.

**Test**

(1) The court may make a hospital order provided that it is satisfied on the written or oral evidence of two medical practitioners that the offender is suffering from mental disorder and the court is satisfied that the mental disorder from which he is suffering is of a nature or degree which makes it appropriate for him to be detained in a hospital for medical treatment, MHA 1983 s.37(1) and (2).

(2) The court must be of the opinion, having regard to all the circumstances including the nature of the offence and the character and antecedents of the offender, and to the other means of dealing with him that the most suitable means of dealing with the case is by means of a hospital order, MHA 1983 s.37(2).

(3) A hospital order may not be made unless the court is satisfied that arrangements have been made for his admission to a hospital within 28 days of the making of the order, MHA 1983 s.37(4).

**Oral evidence**

Evidence may not be received by telephone, *Clark* [2015] EWCA Crim 2192; [2016] 1 Cr.App.R. (S.) 52.

**Discretion**

There is a discretion whether to make an order, *Nafei* [2004] EWCA Crim 3238; [2005] 2 Cr.App.R. (S.) 24 (p.127).

**Requesting information**

The court may request any regional health authority to furnish such information as the authority has or can reasonably obtain with respect to hospitals in its region or elsewhere at which arrangements could be made for the admission of the offender, MHA 1983 s.39(1).

**Contents of the order**

The order must specify the hospital to which the offender is to be admitted and the form or forms of mental disorder from which the offender is suffering, MHA 1983 s.37(1).

**Minimum sentences**

A hospital order may be made despite the fact that the offender would otherwise qualify for a required minimum sentence under FA1968 s.51A, a prescribed custodial sentence under PCC(S)A 2000 ss.110 or 111, PCA 1953 ss.1(2B) or 1A(5), VCRA 2006 s.29, CJA 1988 ss.139(6B), 139A(5B) or 139AA(7), or CJA 2003 ss.224A, 225 or 226, MHA 1983 s.37(1A).

**Hospital order made in absence of offender**

A court may make a hospital order in the case of an offender subject to an interim hospital order in the absence of the offender, provided that he is represented by a legal representative and his legal representative is given the opportunity to be heard, MHA 1983 s.38(2).

# HOSPITAL ORDERS: INTERIM

## MENTAL HEALTH ACT 1983 s.38

*References: Current Sentencing Practice E1; Archbold 5A-1221*

### Availability

An order may be made where a person is convicted of an offence punishable with imprisonment which is not one fixed by law, MHA 1983 s.38(1). The statute refers to orders in respect of those aged 14+ and there appears no restriction for those aged 10–14.

**Order in which the issues should be considered**   See this section in **HOSPITAL ORDERS** p.183.

### Test

The court may make an interim hospital order provided that it is satisfied on the written or oral evidence of two medical practitioners that the offender is suffering from mental disorder and there is reason to suppose that the mental disorder from which he is suffering is such that it may be appropriate for a hospital order to be made in his case, MHA 1983 s.38(1).

An interim hospital order may be made only if a hospital place is available.

One of the practitioners on whose evidence the order is based must be employed at the hospital to be specified in the order, MHA 1983 s.38(3).

An order may not be made unless the court is satisfied that arrangements have been made for the offender's admission to the hospital specified within 28 days of the making of the order, MHA 1983 s.38(4).

### Oral evidence

Evidence may not be received by telephone, *Clark* [2015] EWCA Crim 2192; [2016] 1 Cr.App.R. (S.) 52.

### Directions

The court must give directions for the conveyance of the offender and his detention in a place of safety pending his admission to hospital, MHA 1983 s.38(4).

### Length

An interim hospital order may be made for any period not exceeding 12 weeks in the first instance, MHA 1983 s.38(5).

### Renewing an order

The order may be renewed for further periods of 28 days at a time, if the court is satisfied that the continuation of the order is warranted. The order may not continue for more than 12 months in all, MHA 1983 s.38(5).

An interim hospital order may be renewed in the absence of the offender provided that he is represented by a legal representative and his legal representative is given the opportunity to be heard. At the conclusion of the interim order the offender must be sentenced or dealt with by means of a hospital order or otherwise, MHA 1983 s.38(6).

### Duty to terminate the order

The order must be terminated if the court makes a hospital order or decides after considering the evidence of the responsible medical officer to deal with the case in some other way, MHA 1983 s.38(5)(a).

### Hospital order made in absence of offender

A court may make a hospital order in the case of an offender subject to an interim hospital order in the absence of the offender, provided that he is represented by a legal representative and his legal representative is given the opportunity to be heard, MHA 1983 s.38(2).

# LEGAL REPRESENTATION, REQUIREMENT FOR

## PCC(S)A 2000 s.83

*References: Current Sentencing Practice H1-100; Archbold 5A-313*

A court must not impose the following sentences on those who are not represented:

(a) a sentence of imprisonment passed on a person who has not previously been sentenced to a sentence of imprisonment in the UK (for this purpose, a previous committal for contempt or in default, a suspended sentence, a sentence of detention in a young offender institution or detention under CYPA 1933 ss.53(2) and(3) or under PCC(S)A 2000 s.91, does not count);

(b) a sentence of detention under PCC(S)A 2000 s.91 irrespective of previous sentences;

(c) a sentence of detention at HM's Pleasure, irrespective of previous sentences;

(d) a sentence of custody for life, irrespective of previous sentences;

(e) a detention and training order, irrespective of previous sentences;

(f) a sentence of detention in a young offender institution, irrespective of previous sentences;

(g) a youth rehabilitation order containing either a local authority residence requirement or a fostering requirement.

*Note: It appears that, in error, s.226B was omitted from this section. It is therefore suggested that the section should be read as though it was included, PCC(S)A 2000 s.83(1), (2,) (5) and (6).*

### Exception

A court must not pass such a sentence on a person who is not legally represented unless he has applied for legal representation and his application has been refused on the ground that his means are adequate, or he has refused or failed to apply for legal representation after being told of his right to do so, PCC(S)A 2000 s.83(3).

### Meaning of "legal representation"

A person is legally represented only if he has the assistance of counsel or a solicitor at some time after he has been found guilty and before he has been sentenced. It is not sufficient that the offender was represented at the trial, or when he pleaded guilty, PCC(S) A 2000 s.83(4).

An offender who has dismissed his representatives after having advice between conviction and sentence may be sentenced while unrepresented, but the court must first withdraw any legal representation order.

### Effect of breach

A sentence passed in breach of these requirements is unlawful, but the Court of Appeal on an appeal against such a sentence may substitute a lawful sentence, *McGinlay* (1975) 62 Cr.App.R. 156.

# LIFE SENTENCE ("DISCRETIONARY")

CRIMINAL JUSTICE ACT 2003 ss.225–229

*References: Current Sentencing Practice A2 and F2-750; Archbold 5A-732, 5A-1036*

## General

**Types of life sentence**   There are four types of life sentence:

(a)  where the dangerousness provisions apply, CJA 2003 ss.225 and 226;
(b)  discretionary life (the inherent jurisdiction of the court to impose a life sentence);
(c)  "*automatic life*" under CJA 2003 s.224A; and
(d)  mandatory life (murder).

For (c) and (d), see the **AUTOMATIC LIFE SENTENCE** and **MURDER** sections on pages 45 and 205.

**Life licence**   An offender sentenced to life imprisonment (or custody for life) will remain on licence for the rest of his life.

## CJA 2003 ss.225-226 (Dangerousness Provisions Apply)

**Aged 18 or over at conviction**   The court must impose a life sentence where:

(1)  the defendant is convicted of a serious offence (committed on or after 4 April 2005);
(2)  the court considers that there is a significant risk of serious harm occasioned by the commission by the defendant of further specified offences;
(3)  the offence is one in respect of which the offender would apart from s.225 be liable to imprisonment for life; and
(4)  the court considers that the seriousness of the offence, or of the offence and one or more offences associated with it, is such as to justify the imposition of a sentence of imprisonment for life, CJA 2003 s.225(1) and (2).

In the case of a person aged 18–20 at conviction, the court must impose a sentence of custody for life, CJA 2003 s.225(2).

A "*serious offence*" is one that is:

(a)  listed in CJA 2003 Sch.15 (see p.329);
(b)  apart from CJA 2003 s.224A, is punishable in the case of a person aged 18 + with imprisonment for life or imprisonment for a determinate sentence of 10 years or more, CJA 2003 s.224(2).

**Aged under 18 at conviction**   The court must impose a life sentence where:

(1)  the defendant is convicted of a serious offence (committed on or after 4 April 2005);

[191]

(2) the court considers that there is a significant risk of serious harm occasioned by the commission by the defendant of further specified offences;

(3) the offence is one in respect of which the defendant would apart from this section be liable to detention for life under PCC(S)A 2000 s.91; and

(4) the court considers that the seriousness of the offence, or of the offence and one or more offences associated with it, is such as to justify the imposition of a sentence of detention for life under s.91, CJA 2003 s.226(1) and (2).

A *"serious offence"* is one that is:

(a) listed in CJA 2003 Sch.15 (see p.329);

(b) apart from CJA 2003 s.224A, is punishable in the case of a person aged 18+ with imprisonment for life or imprisonment for a determinate sentence of 10 years or more, CJA 2003 s.224(2).

**Does the seriousness of the offence justify a life sentence?**   The question as to whether or not the seriousness of the offence, or of the offence and one or more offences associated with it, was such as to justify a life sentence required consideration of:

(i)   the seriousness of the offence itself, on its own or with other offences associated with it in accordance with the provisions of s.143(1), which was always a matter for the judgment of the court;

(ii)   the defendant's previous convictions in accordance with s.143(2);

(iii)   the level of danger to the public posed by the defendant and whether or not there was a reliable estimate of the length of time he would remain a danger; and

(iv)   the available alternative sentences, *AG's Ref. (No. 27 of 2013) (Burinskas)* [2014] EWCA Crim 334; [2014] 2 Cr.App.R. (S.) 45.

**Assessing dangerousness**   The following apply when the court is considering whether or not there is a *"significant risk of serious harm"*.

The court *must* take into account *all* such information as is available to it about the nature and circumstances of the offence, CJA 2003 s.229(2)(a).

The court *may* take into account:

(a) all such information as is available about the nature and circumstances of any other offences of which the offender has been convicted by a court anywhere in the world;

(b) any information which is before it about any pattern of behaviour of which any of the offences of which the offender has been convicted forms part; and

(c) any information about the offender which is before it, CJA 2003 s.229(2)(aa)–(c).

*"Serious harm"* means death or personal injury, whether physical or psychological, CJA 2003 s.224(3).

**Risk**   The risk does not have to be based on the instant offence, *Green* [2007] EWCA Crim 2172; [2008] 1 Cr.App.R. (S.) 97.

The absence of previous offences causing serious harm requiring an extended sentence does not preclude the finding of dangerousness, *Powell* [2015] EWCA Crim 2200; [2016] 1 Cr.App.R. (S.) 49.

In *Neville* [2015] EWCA Crim 1874; [2016] 1 Cr.App.R. (S.) 38, the court held that a finding of dangerousness founded on unpredictability demonstrated by a long absence of serious offending prior to the instant offence was permissible.

### The correct approach

(i)    consider the question of dangerousness. If the offender is not dangerous and s.224A does not apply, a determinate sentence should be passed. If the offender is not dangerous and the conditions in s.224A are satisfied then a life sentence must be imposed;

(ii)    if the offender is dangerous, consider whether the seriousness of the offence and offences associated with it justify a life sentence;

(iii)    if a life sentence is justified then the judge must pass a life sentence in accordance with s.225. If s.224A also applies, the judge should record that fact in open court;

(iv)    if a life sentence is not justified, then the sentencing judge should consider whether s.224A applies. If it does then a life sentence must be imposed; and

(v)    if s.224A does not apply the judge should then consider the provisions of s.226A. Before passing an extended sentence the judge should consider a determinate sentence, *AG's Ref. (No. 27 of 2013) (Burinskas)* [2014] EWCA Crim 334; [2014] 2 Cr.App.R. (S.) 45.

### Setting the minimum term

A court which imposes a sentence of imprisonment (or custody) for life must fix a minimum term in accordance with PCC(S)A 2000 s.82A. The offender is not entitled to be released until he has served the minimum term. For details on setting the minimum term, see **MINIMUM TERM** p.203.

### Discretionary Life (Inherent Jurisdiction of the Court)

**Availability**   Where:

(a)   the offence was committed prior to 4 April 2005; or

(b)   the offence is not a "*serious offence*", the court has an inherent jurisdiction to impose a life sentence.

Such instances are likely to be rare, *Saunders* [2013] EWCA Crim 1027; [2014] 1 Cr.App.R. (S.) 45.

**Test**   It will be necessary to consider whether the criteria established in the case law for a discretionary sentence of life imprisonment are satisfied, see e.g. *Chapman* [2000] 1 Cr.App.R. (S.) 377.

**Example**   Some of these offences may involve a significant risk of serious harm to the public, but are not included within the list of "*specified*" offences in the dangerousness provisions in the 2003 Act. One obvious example is the offender who commits repeated offences of very serious drug supplying which justifies the imposition of the life sentence. In circumstances like these the court is not obliged to impose the sentence in accordance with s.225(2), but its discretion to do so is unaffected, *Saunders* [2013] EWCA Crim 1027; [2014] 1 Cr.App.R. (S.) 45 at [11].

MAGISTRATES' COURTS ACT 1980 SS.132 AND 133, PCC(S)A 2000 S.78

*References: Current Sentencing Practice A1-600; Archbold 5A-628*

*Note: Substantial amendments to the provisions summarised below are made by the Criminal Justice Act 2003. The amendments were not generally in force on 31 October 2018.*

**Applicability**   The following limitations apply to sentences of imprisonment and detention in a young offender institution.They do not apply to detention and training orders.

**Minimum term**   A magistrates' court shall not impose imprisonment for fewer than five days, MCA 1980 s.132.

### Summary offences

The maximum for any one offence is six months, or the maximum provided for the offence in question, if that is fewer, PCC(S)A 2000 s.78(1).

The maximum aggregate term for more than one summary offence is six months, MCA 1980 s.133(1).

### Either-way offences

The maximum term for any one offence is six months, PCC(S)A 2000 s.78(1), MCA 1980 s.32(1).

The maximum aggregate term for more than one either-way offence is 12 months, MCA 1980 s.133(2).

**Suspended sentence activation**   The restrictions on aggregate terms do not include activation of suspended sentences, *Chamberlain* (1992) 13 Cr.App.R. (S.) 525.

**Default terms**   The restrictions do not apply to default terms fixed in respect of fines imposed on the same occasion as a custodial sentence is imposed, but they do apply where an offender is sentenced to a custodial sentence and committed in default on the same occasion, PCC(S)A 2000 s.78(4).

### Crown Court

The restrictions must be observed by the Crown Court when dealing with an offender in respect of the following matters:

(a) an offence for which he has been committed for sentence under PCC(S)A 2000 s.6;

(b) an offence in respect of which the offender has been committed which a view to a restriction order under MHA 1983 s.43 and in respect of whom the Crown Court does not make a hospital order;

(c) an offence in respect of which a magistrates' court has made a community order which the Crown Court has revoked;

(d) an offence for which the Crown Court has power to deal with the offender under CJA 1988 s.40;

(e) an offence in respect of which the offender has appealed against his conviction or sentence;

(f) an offence for which the offender is sentenced under PCC(S)A 2000 s.4(5).

# MAXIMUM SENTENCE

*References: Archbold 5A-560*

**General rule**   The maximum sentence for an offence should normally be reserved for the most serious examples of that offence which are likely to be encountered in practice.

**Particular circumstances**   The maximum sentence for an offence should normally be reserved for the most serious examples of that offence which are likely to be encountered in practice.

The maximum sentence should not normally be imposed for:

(a)   an attempt to commit an offence, *Robson*, unreported 6 May 1974; or

(b)   where there is substantial mitigation, *Thompson* (1980) 2 Cr.App.R. (S.) 244.

**Consecutive sentences**   Consecutive maximum sentences may be properly imposed provided that each individual offence is one of the most serious examples of the type of offence, and the sentences are properly made consecutive, *Hunter* (1979) 1 Cr.App.R. (S.) 7. (See **CONCURRENT AND CONSECUTIVE SENTENCES**, p.75.)

**Change in maximum sentence**   Where the maximum sentence for an offence is increased, the new maximum sentence will apply only to offences committed after the increase has taken effect. Where an offender has been convicted of an offence committed on a date unknown between two dates, and the maximum sentence has been increased between those two dates, the lower maximum sentence applies, see *Penrith Justices ex parte Hay* (1979) 1 Cr.App.R. (S.) 265. See also *Hobbs* [2002] EWCA Crim 387; [2002] 2 Cr.App.R. (S.) 93 in relation to conspiracies.

Where the offender has been convicted of an offence of a general nature, but the facts fall within the scope of a more narrowly defined offence for which a lower maximum sentence has been provided, the court should have regard to the lower maximum sentence, but is not necessarily bound by it, *Bright* [2008] EWCA Crim 462; [2008] 2 Cr.App.R. (S.) 102. *Bright* was endorsed in *Bridger,* [2018] EWCA Crim 1678.

# MEDICAL REPORTS/MEDICAL TREATMENT

## CRIMINAL JUSTICE ACT 2003 s.157

*References: Current Sentencing Practice: H2-7650; Archbold 5A-242*

### Reports on Mentally Disordered Defendants Prior to Sentencing

**Duty to obtain report**   In any case where the offender is or appears to be mentally disordered, the court must obtain and consider a medical report before passing a custodial sentence other than one fixed by law, CJA 2003 s.157(1). But the duty does not apply if, in the circumstances of the case, the court is of the opinion that it is unnecessary to obtain a medical report, CJA 2003 s.157(2).

**Failure to comply with duty**   No custodial sentence is invalid if it is imposed in breach of that duty, CJA 2003 s.157(4).

**Appeals**   However, any court on appeal against sentence must obtain a medical report if none was obtained by the court below, and must consider any such report obtained by it or by that court, CJA 2003 s.157(4).

**"Mentally disordered"**   *"Mentally disordered"*, in relation to any person, means suffering from a mental disorder within the meaning of the MHA 1983, CJA 2003 s.157(5).

**Procedure rules**   Where, for sentencing purposes, the court requires a medical report or where the court is considering making a guardianship or hospital order, the court must:

(a)     identify each issue in respect of which the court requires expert medical opinion and the legislation applicable;

(b)     specify the nature of the expertise likely to be required for giving such opinion;

(c)     identify each party or participant by whom a commission for such opinion must be prepared, who may be—

(i)      a party (or party's representative) acting on that party's own behalf,

(ii)     a party (or party's representative) acting on behalf of the court, or

(iii)    the court officer acting on behalf of the court;

(d)     where there are available to the court arrangements with the National Health Service under which an assessment of a defendant's mental health may be prepared, give such directions as are needed under those arrangements for obtaining the expert report or reports required;

(e)     where no such arrangements are available to the court, or they will not be used, give directions for the commissioning of an expert report or expert reports, including—

(i)      such directions as can be made about supplying the expert or experts with the defendant's medical records,

(ii)     directions about the other information, about the defendant and about the offence or offences alleged to have been committed by the defendant,

[199]

which is to be supplied to each expert, and (iii) directions about the arrangements that will apply for the payment of each expert;

(iii) directions about the arrangements that will apply for the payment of each expert;

(f) set a timetable providing for—

(i) the date by which a commission is to be delivered to each expert,

(ii) the date by which any failure to accept a commission is to be reported to the court,

(iii) the date or dates by which progress in the preparation of a report or reports is to be reviewed by the court officer, and

(iv) the date by which each report commissioned is to be received by the court; and

(g) identify the person (each person, if more than one) to whom a copy of a report is to be supplied, and by whom, Crim PR 2015 r.28.8.

## Power to Adjourn for Medical Report

**Magistrates' Court**   If, on the trial by a magistrates' court of an offence punishable on summary conviction with imprisonment, the court:

(a) is satisfied that the accused did the act or made the omission charged, but

(b) is of the opinion that an inquiry ought to be made into his physical or mental condition before the method of dealing with him is determined, the court shall adjourn the case to enable a medical examination and report to be made, and shall remand him, PCC(S)A 2000 s.11(1).

The maximum period for adjourning a case under s.11(1) is three weeks if the accused is remanded in custody, or four weeks if the accused is remanded on bail, PCC(S)A 2000 s.11(2).

## Power to Remand to Hospital for Medical Report

**Crown Court/Magistrates' Court**   The Crown Court or a magistrates' court may remand an accused person (convicted of an offence in the Crown Court, or convicted of an imprisonable offence in the magistrates' court) to a hospital specified by the court for a report on his mental condition, MHA 1983 s.35(1) and (2).

**Test to apply**   The power to remand for a medical report is only exercisable if:

(a) the court is satisfied, on the written or oral evidence of a registered medical practitioner, that there is reason to suspect that the accused person is suffering from mental disorder; and

(b) the court is of the opinion that it would be impracticable for a report on his mental condition to be made if he were remanded on bail; but those powers shall not be exercised by the Crown Court in respect of a person who has been convicted of murder, MHA 1983 s.35(3).

**Length of remand to hospital**   An accused person shall not be remanded or further remanded under s.35 for more than 28 days at a time or for more than 12 weeks in all; and the court may at any time terminate the remand if it appears to the court that it is appropriate to do so, MHA 1983 s.35(7).

## Power to Remand to Hospital for Treatment

**Availability**   The power (see below) applies to someone who at any time before sentence is in custody in the course of a trial before that court for such an offence, MHA 1983 s.36(2). It is also exercisable pre-trial.

**Power**   The Crown Court may, instead of remanding an accused person in custody, remand him to a hospital specified by the court if satisfied, on the written or oral evidence of two registered medical practitioners, that:

(a)   he is suffering from mental disorder of a nature or degree which makes it appropriate for him to be detained in a hospital for medical treatment; and
(b)   appropriate medical treatment is available for him, MHA 1983 s.36(1).

**Test to apply**   The court shall not remand an accused person under s.36 to a hospital unless it is satisfied, on the written or oral evidence of the approved clinician who would have overall responsibility for his case or of some other person representing the managers of the hospital, that arrangements have been made for his admission to that hospital and for his admission to it within the period of seven days beginning with the date of the remand, MHA 1983 s.36(3).

**Directions for conveyance to hospital**   Where the court is satisfied that the test to apply is satisfied, it may, pending his admission, give directions for his conveyance to and detention in a place of safety, MHA 1983 s.36(3).

**Length of remand to hospital**   An accused person shall not be remanded or further remanded under s.35 for more than 28 days at a time or for more than 12 weeks in all; and the court may at any time terminate the remand if it appears to the court that it is appropriate to do so, MHA 1983 s.36(6).

# MINIMUM TERM (NON-MURDER CASES)

## PCC(S)A s.82A

*References: Current Sentencing Practice A2-650 and A2-2050; Archbold 5A-714*

### General

**Applicability**   These provisions apply where the court passes any of the following sentences:

(a)   a life sentence whether or not under CJA 2003 s.225;
(b)   an automatic life sentence under CJA 2003 s.224A;
(c)   a sentence of custody for life (otherwise than on conviction for murder);
(d)   a sentence of detention under the PCC(S)A 2000 s.91, for life.

This section does not apply where the court passes a mandatory life sentence on a person convicted of murder.

**Specify the minimum term**   In addition to passing the sentence, the court must normally specify the minimum period during which the offender will be required to remain in prison before becoming eligible for consideration by the Parole Board with a view to release, PCC(S)A 2000 s.82A(2).

However, where the offence was committed when the offender was aged 21 or over and the court considers that because of the seriousness of the offence, the court may specific that the early release provisions under s.82A(2) should not apply, PCC(S)A 2000 s.82A(4).

### How to Determine the Length

**General**   The period is calculated by deciding what determinate term of imprisonment would have been appropriate if a sentence of life imprisonment had not been passed (the notional determinate sentence) and then specifying a period equal to between one-half and one-third of that term. Normally, the period should be equal to one-half of the term.

In certain exceptional cases the period may be more than one-half of the notional determinate sentence. For commentary as to the circumstances when such an increase may be appropriate and the potential problems in identifying the appropriate term, see *Rossi* [2015] Crim. L.R. 294.

**Guilty plea**   In fixing the specified period, the court should give appropriate credit for a guilty plea, PCC(S)A 2000 s.82A(3)(b).

**More than one offence**   If the offender has been convicted of more than one offence, the period should reflect the gravity of all of the offences of which he has been convicted, including those for which a sentence of life imprisonment is not passed, *Lundberg* (1995) 16 Cr.App.R. (S.) 948 and CJA 2003 s.225(2)(b).

**Discount for time on remand/subject to curfew**   If the offender has spent time in custody on remand, or awaiting extradition, the sentencer should deduct an appropriate amount of time from the minimum term. The time deducted should not exceed the actual period spent in custody on remand. If the offender has been on bail subject to a qualifying curfew, the court should deduct half the number of days spent on bail subject to curfew, if the Criminal Justice Act s.240A would have applied to those days, PCC(S)A 2000 s.82A(3)(b).

## Combining Sentences

**Consecutive indeterminate sentences**   It is generally undesirable to order an indeterminate sentence to be served consecutively to any other period of imprisonment on the basis that indeterminate sentences should start on their imposition. However, where necessary the court can order an indeterminate sentence to run consecutively to an indeterminate sentence passed on an earlier occasion. The second sentence will commence on the expiration of the minimum term of the original sentence and the offender will become eligible for a parole review after serving both minimum terms, *Totality Guideline*, p.11.

**Determinate sentence consecutive to indeterminate sentence**   The court can order a determinate sentence to run consecutively to an indeterminate sentence. The determinate sentence will commence on the expiry of the minimum term of the indeterminate sentence and the offender will become eligible for a parole review after serving half of the determinate sentence, *Totality Guideline*, p.11.

# MURDER

## CRIMINAL JUSTICE ACT 2003 s.269

*References: Current Sentencing Practice II; Archbold 5A-741*

**Mandatory Sentences**

**Aged 21 + at conviction** A person convicted of murder who is aged 21 on the date of conviction must be sentenced to imprisonment for life, M(ADP)A 1965 s.1. This is unless he was under 18 on the date when the offence was committed (see below).

**Aged 18–20 at conviction** A person convicted of murder who is aged under 21 and over 18 on the date of conviction, must be sentenced to custody for life, unless he was under 18 on the date when the offence was committed, PCC(S)A 2000 s.93.

**Aged under 18 at date of offence** A person convicted of murder who was under 18 on the date when the offence was committed must be sentenced to be detained during Her Majesty's Pleasure, irrespective of his age on the date of conviction, PCC(S)A 2000 s.90.

**Minimum Term**

**Early release or whole life order** In all cases, a court which imposes a mandatory life sentence on a person convicted of murder must order that the early release provisions shall apply to him after he has served a part of the sentence specified by the court, unless the offender is over 21 and the seriousness of the offence or offences concerned is such that a "*whole life order*" must be made, CJA 2003 s.269(2) and (4).

**Selecting a starting point** In deciding what part of the life sentence to specify, the court must have regard to the general principles set out in the CJA 2003 Sch.21, and any guidelines relating to offences in general which are relevant to the case and are not incompatible with the provisions of Sch.21, CJA 2003 s.269(5).

**Adjusting the starting point** Having identified an appropriate starting point in accordance with Sch.21, the court must take into account any aggravating or mitigating factors, to the extent that it has not allowed for them in its choice of starting point, and specify a minimum term which it considers appropriate to the seriousness of the offence or offences concerned. The minimum term may be of any length (whatever the starting point).

**Guilty plea** Whereas a court should consider the fact that an offender has pleaded guilty to murder when deciding whether it is appropriate to order a whole life term, where a court determines that there should be a whole life minimum term, there will be no reduction for a guilty plea.

In other circumstances:

- the court will weigh carefully the overall length of the minimum term taking into account other reductions for which the offender may be eligible so as to avoid a combination leading to an inappropriately short sentence;
- where it is appropriate to reduce the minimum term having regard to a plea of guilty, the reduction will not exceed one-sixth and will never exceed five years;
- the maximum reduction of one-sixth or five years (whichever is less) should only be given when a guilty plea has been indicated at the first stage of the proceedings. Lesser reductions should be given for guilty pleas after that point, with a maximum of one-twentieth being given for a guilty plea on the day of trial. The exceptions at F1 and F2 of the guideline apply to murder cases, *Reduction in Sentence for a Guilty Plea* (2017) p.8.

**Time on remand/qualifying curfew**   The court should deduct from the minimum term a number of days equal to the number of days spent in custody on remand, unless the days would not have counted as remand days if the sentence had been a determinate sentence. If the offender has been on bail subject to a qualifying curfew, the court should deduct half the number of days spent on bail subject to curfew, if the Criminal Justice Act s.240A would have applied to those days, CJA 2003 s.269(3).

**Transitional cases**   In the case of a person sentenced to custody for life or imprisonment for life for an offence committed before 18 December 2003, the minimum term must not be greater than the term which under the practice followed by the Secretary of State before December 2002, the Secretary of State would have been likely to have specified, CJA 2003 Sch.22.

**Duty to explain sentence**

On passing sentence, the court must state in open court, in ordinary language, its reasons for deciding on the order made, and in particular must state which of the starting points in Sch.21 it has chosen and its reasons for doing so, and why it has departed from that starting point, CJA 2003 s.270(1) and (2).

# OFFENDERS OF PARTICULAR CONCERN

CRIMINAL JUSTICE ACT 2003 s.236A AND SCH.18A

*References: Current Sentencing Practice A4; Archbold 5A-646*

## Making the Order

**Applicability**   Section 236A applies where:

(a) a person is convicted of an offence (committed before or after the commencement date) listed in CJA 2003 Sch.18A, see p.341;
(b) the person was aged 18 or over when the offence was committed, and
(c) the court does not impose one of the following for the offence (and any offences associated with it):
   (i) a sentence of imprisonment for life, or
   (ii) an extended sentence under s.226A, CJA 2003 s.236A(1).

**The sentence**   If the court imposes a sentence of imprisonment for the offence (and any offences associated with it), the term of the sentence must be equal to the aggregate of:

(a) the appropriate custodial term; and
(b) a further period of 1 year for which the offender is to be subject to a licence, CJA 2003 s.236A(2).

The *"appropriate custodial term"* is the term that, in the opinion of the court, ensures that the sentence is appropriate, CJA 2003 s.236A(3).

It appears that the provision requires the court to first decide on a term of imprisonment (including its length) and then apply s.236A. This therefore suggests that one must subtract one year from the custodial term to accommodate the licence. That would of course be an odd result (and in contrast with the process for extended sentences) however that appears to the be effect of the statute.

**Suspended sentences**   Courts should not suspend a sentence under s.236A. Ordinarily the court will be considering an immediate custodial sentence: in the unusual event that the court might have considered suspending the sentence, it should consider making a community order instead, *LF and DS* [2016] EWCA Crim 561; [2016] 2 Cr.App.R. (S.) 30.

**Maximum sentence**   The term of a sentence of imprisonment imposed under this section for an offence must not exceed the term that, at the time the offence was committed, was the maximum term permitted for the offence, CJA 2003 s.236A(4).

This includes the *"further period of 1 year"*.

**Those under 21**   The order operates as if the reference to *"imprisonment"* was to detention in a young offender institution, CJA 2003 s.236A(8).

**Consecutive sentences**   There is in principle no reason why a court should not be permitted to impose consecutive section 236A sentences if it considers it appropriate, *LF and DS* [2016] EWCA Crim 561; [2016] 2 Cr.App.R. (S.) 30.

Licence periods are cumulative as it is not possible to impose a partly concurrent, partly consecutive sentence. Accordingly, judges imposing consecutive s.236A sentences should think carefully about structuring the sentences so as to avoid disproportionately long licence periods.

**Drafting indictments** It would clearly be helpful if those settling indictments were able to assist in recognition of s.236A cases by drafting counts which take account of threshold ages of alleged victims or defendants, or by identifying if a relevant penetration occurred, see *LF and DS* [2016] EWCA Crim 561; [2016] 2 Cr.App.R. (S.) 30.

**Release**

**Referral to the Parole Board** The Secretary of State must refer the offender to the Parole Board at the expiration of the relevant custodial period; for orders under s.236A, that occurs at the half-way point of the custodial term, CJA 2003 s.244A(2) and (6).

Where there has been such a referral and the Parole Board has declined to release the offender, the Secretary of State need not refer the offender to the Parole Board again until the second anniversary of the previous referral, CJA 2003 s.236A(2)(b).

**Test for release** The offender will be released by the Parole Board when it is satisfied that it is not necessary for the protection of the public that the offender should be confined, CJA 2003 s.236A(4)(b).

# OFFENCES TAKEN INTO CONSIDERATION

TICs Guideline, Sentencing Council

*References: Current Sentencing Practice H2-9400; Archbold 5A-77*

**General**

Where an offender admits an offence with which he has not been charged and asks the court to take it into consideration, the court may take account of that offence when passing sentence for the offence of which the offender has been convicted.

When sentencing an offender who requests offences to be taken into consideration (TICs), courts should pass a total sentence which reflects all the offending behaviour. The sentence must be just and proportionate and must not exceed the statutory maximum for the conviction offence.

**Discretion**

The court has discretion as to whether or not to take TICs into account. In exercising its discretion the court should take into account that TICs are capable of reflecting the offender's overall criminality. The court is likely to consider that the fact that the offender has assisted the police (particularly if the offences would not otherwise have been detected) and avoided the need for further proceedings demonstrates a genuine determination by the offender to "*wipe the slate clean*".

Where the offender has been sentenced on an earlier occasion and, having expressed a desire to have a "*clean slate*", had failed to ask for an offence to be taken into consideration for which the offender later fell to be sentenced, no reduction will follow. It is incumbent on defendants to volunteer this information at the relevant time and to ensure that the police listed it as one of the TICs; otherwise, the defendant ran a risk, *Murray* [2018] EWCA Crim 1252; [2018] 2 Cr.App.R. (S.) 41.

**Circumstances in which TICs are generally undesirable**

- where the TIC is likely to attract a greater sentence than the conviction offence;
- where it is in the public interest that the TIC should be the subject of a separate charge;
- where the offender would avoid a prohibition, ancillary order or similar consequence which it would have been desirable to impose on conviction. For example where the TIC attracts mandatory disqualification or endorsement and the offence(s) for which the defendant is to be sentenced do not;
- where the TIC constitutes a breach of an earlier sentence;
- where the TIC is a specified offence for the purposes of s.224 of the CJA 2003, but the conviction offence is non-specified; or
- where the TIC is not founded on the same facts or evidence or part of a series of offences of the same or similar character (unless the court is satisfied that it is in the interests of justice to do so), *TICs Guideline*, p.3.

Additionally, an offence should not normally be taken into consideration if the court would not have power to deal with the offender for the offence, or if the offence would result in a mandatory sentence.

## Effect of TICs

An offence which has been taken into consideration is an "*associated offence*" for the purposes of the PCC(S)A 2000. and the CJA 2003, see ss.161 and 305 respectively.

A TIC does not amount to a conviction, *Howard* (1991) 92 Cr.App.R. 223.

## Procedure

A court should generally only take offences into consideration if the following procedural provisions have been satisfied:

- the police or prosecuting authorities have prepared a schedule of offences (TIC schedule) that they consider suitable to be taken into consideration. The TIC schedule should set out the nature of each offence, the date of the offence(s), relevant detail about the offence(s) (including, for example, monetary values of items) and any other brief details that the court should be aware of;
- a copy of the TIC schedule must be provided to the defendant and his representative (if he has one) before the sentence hearing. The defendant should sign the TIC schedule to provisionally admit the offences;
- at the sentence hearing, the court should ask the defendant in open court whether he admits each of the offences on the TIC schedule and whether he wishes to have them taken into consideration;
- if there is any doubt about the admission of a particular offence, it should not be accepted as a TIC. Special care should be taken with vulnerable and/or unrepresented defendants;
- if the defendant is committed to the Crown Court for sentence, this procedure must take place again at the Crown Court even if the defendant has agreed to the schedule in the magistrates' court, *TICs Guideline*, p.3.

**Specimen counts**   Where an offender admits that the offences to which he has pleaded guilty are specimen offences representing a larger number of offences which are not separately identified, those other offences are not "*offences taken into consideration*".

## Determining sentence

The sentence imposed on an offender should, in most circumstances, be increased to reflect the fact that other offences have been taken into consideration. The court should:

- (a) determine the sentencing starting point for the conviction offence, referring to the relevant definitive sentencing guidelines. No regard should be had to the presence of TICs at this stage.
- (b) consider whether there are any aggravating or mitigating factors that justify an upward or downward adjustment from the starting point. The presence

of TICs should generally be treated as an aggravating feature that justifies an upward adjustment from the starting point. Where there is a large number of TICs, it may be appropriate to move outside the category range, although this must be considered in the context of the case and subject to the principle of totality. The court is limited to the statutory maximum for the conviction offence.

(c) continue through the sentencing process including:

- consider whether the frank admission of a number of offences is an indication of a defendant's remorse or determination and/or demonstration of steps taken to address addiction or offending behaviour;
- any reduction for a guilty plea should be applied to the overall sentence;
- the principle of totality;
- when considering ancillary orders these can be considered in relation to any or all of the TICs, specifically: compensation orders (PCC(S)A 2000 s.130(1) and (5)) – in the magistrate's court the total compensation cannot exceed the limit for the conviction offence;
- restitution orders (PCC(S)A 2000 s.148), *TICs Guideline*, p.4.

# PARENTING ORDERS

CRIME AND DISORDER ACT 1998 s.8

*References: Current Sentencing Practice F4; Archbold 5A-1059*

**General**

**Effect**   A parenting order is an order which requires the parent:

(a) to comply with such requirements as are specified in the order; and
(b) to attend such counselling or guidance programme as may be specified in directions given by the responsible officer, CDA 1998 s.8(4).

**Consent**   The consent of the parent or guardian is not required.

**Length**   The order may not last for more than 12 months. The counselling or guidance may not exceed a concurrent period of three months, CDA 1998 s.8(4).

**Duty to obtain report**   Before making a parenting order:

(a) where the child or young person is aged under 16 and is made subject to a criminal behaviour order or a sexual harm prevention order, or is convicted of an offence; or
(b) where a person is convicted of an offence under the EA 1996 ss.443 or 444 and the person to whom the offence related is aged under 16, a court shall obtain and consider information about the person's family circumstances and the likely effect of the order on those circumstances, CDA 1998 s.9(2).

**Discretionary Order**

**Availability**   An order is available where, in any court proceedings:

(a) a criminal behaviour order, or a sexual harm prevention order is made in respect of a child or young person;
(b) a child or young person is convicted of an offence; or
(c) a person is convicted of an offence under EA 1996 s.443 (failure to comply with school attendance order) or s.444 (failure to secure regular attendance at school of registered pupil), and the relevant condition is satisfied, CDA 1998 s.8(1) and (2).

**The "relevant condition"**   The parenting order would be desirable in the interests of preventing:

(a) in the case of a CBO or SHPO, any repetition of the kind of behaviour which led to the order being made;
(b) in the case of the child having been convicted of an offence, the commission of any further offence by the child or young person;
(c) in the case of a person being convicted under EA 1996 ss.443 or 444, the commission of any further offence under EA 1996 ss.443 or 444, CDA 1998 s.8(6).

**Arrangements must be in place**    A court shall not make a parenting order unless it has been notified by the Secretary of State that arrangements for implementing such orders are available in the are in which it appears to the court that the parent resides or will reside and the notice has not been withdrawn, CDA 1998 s.8(3).

## Mandatory Order

**Applicability**    Where a person under the age of 16 is:

  (a)  convicted of an offence;
  (b)  made the subject of a criminal behaviour order, the court, if it is satisfied
        that the relevant condition is fulfilled, shall make a parenting order, CDA
        1998 s.9(1) and (1B).

There is no duty to make an order where the court makes a referral order in respect of the offence, CDA 1998 s.9(1A). However, the court may make both a referral order and a parenting order after considering a report from an appropriate officer.

**The "relevant condition"**    The parenting order would be desirable in the interests of preventing the commission of any further offence by the child or young person, CDA 1998 s.8(6).

**Duty to give reasons when not making an order**    If the court is not satisfied that the relevant condition is met, it shall state in open court that it is not and why it is not, CDA 1998 s.9(1).

**Arrangements must be in place**    A court shall not make a parenting order unless it has been notified by the Secretary of State that arrangements for implementing such orders are available in the are in which it appears to the court that the parent resides or will reside and the notice has not been withdrawn, CDA 1998 s.8(3).

## After the Order is Made

**Duty to explain the order etc.**    The court must explain the effect of the order, the consequences that may follow a failure to comply with the requirements of the order, and the power of the court to review the order, CDA 1998 s.9(3).

# PARENTS AND GUARDIANS

## PCC(S)A 2000 ss.136–138, 150

*References: Current Sentencing Practice F4; Archbold 5A-965, 5A-1057*

This section contains information on:

(a) fines/financial orders paid by parent/guardian;
(b) financial circumstances orders; and
(c) bind overs of parent/guardian.

### Fine/compensation/costs/surcharge to be paid by parent/guardian

**Under 16s**   Where a person under 16 is found guilty of an offence, and the court considers that the matter should be dealt with by means of a fine, costs or compensation order, the court *must* order the fine, costs or compensation order to be paid by the offender's parent or guardian, unless the parent or guardian cannot be found or it would be unreasonable to make an order for payment, PCC(S)A 2000 s.137(1).

Where a court would otherwise order a child or young person to pay the statutory surcharge, the court must order that the surcharge be paid by the parent or guardian of the child or young person instead of by the child or young person himself, unless the court is satisfied, unless the parent or guardian cannot be found or it would be unreasonable to make an order for payment, PCC(S)A 2000 s.137(1A).

**Those aged 16–18**   Where a person over 16 but under 18 is found guilty of an offence, and the court considers that the matter should be dealt with by means of a fine, costs or compensation order, the court may order the fine, costs or compensation order to be paid by the offender's parent or guardian, unless the parent or guardian cannot be found or it would be unreasonable to make an order for payment, PCC(S)A 2000 s.137(1) and (3).

Where a court would otherwise order a child or young person to pay the statutory surcharge, the court may order that the surcharge be paid by the parent or guardian of the child or young person instead of by the child or young person himself, unless the court is satisfied, unless the parent or guardian cannot be found or it would be unreasonable to make an order for payment, PCC(S)A 2000 s.137(1A) and (3).

**The parent or guardian must be given the opportunity to be heard**   The parent or guardian must be given the opportunity to be heard before the order is made, unless they have been required to attend and have failed to do so, PCC(S)A 2000 s.137(4).

**Means**   In considering the means of the offender for the purpose of such an order, the court should consider the means of the parent or guardian, rather than the means of the offender, PCC(S)A 2000 s.138(1). There is no requirement to consider the means of a local authority, PCC(S)A 2000 s.138(2).

**Adverse findings forming the basis of an order**   A court should not make an order against a parent or guardian on the basis that the offender has been neglected unless there is evidence of such neglect. The court should not base a finding adverse to a parent or guardian on information disclosed by the parent or guardian for the purposes of a pre-sentence report, *Lenihan v West Yorks. Metropolitan Police* (1981) 3 Cr.App.R. (S.) 42.

**Offender in local authority care**   Where the offender is in the care of a local authority, or living in local authority accommodation, and the local authority has parental responsibility, the court may make an order against the local authority, PCC(S)A 2000 s.137(8).

An order should not be made against a local authority unless the local authority has failed to do everything that it reasonably could have done to protect the public from the offender, and there is a causative link between the failure and the offence, *D (A Minor) v DPP* (1995) 16 Cr.App.R. (S.) 1040.

Where the offender is living in local authority accommodation on a voluntary basis, it will normally be unreasonable to make an order against the parent or guardian.

**Appeals**   A parent or guardian may appeal to the Crown Court against an order under s.137(1) made by a magistrates' court, PCC(S)A 2000 s.137(6). A parent or guardian may appeal to the Court of Appeal against an order under s.137(1) made by the Crown Court, as if he had been convicted on indictment and the order were a sentence passed on his conviction, PCC(S)A 2000 s.137(7).

**Financial circumstances order**

Before making an order under s.137 (power to order parent or guardian to pay fine/costs/compensation/surcharge) against the parent or guardian of an individual who has been convicted of an offence, the court may make a financial circumstances order with respect to the parent or (as the case may be) guardian, PCC(S)A 2000 s.136(1). See **FINANCIAL CIRCUMSTANCES ORDERS**, p.153 for more details.

**Bind Over of Parent/Guardian**

**Powers**   The court has the power to:
  (a)  with the consent of the offender's parent or guardian, to order the parent or guardian to enter into a recognizance to take proper care of him and exercise proper control over him;
  (b)  if the parent or guardian refuses consent and the court considers the refusal unreasonable, to order the parent or guardian to pay a fine not exceeding £1,000; and
  (c)  where the court has imposed a youth rehabilitation order upon the offender, it may include in the recognizance a provision that the offender's parent or guardian ensure that the offender complies with the requirements of that sentence, PCC(S)A 2000 s.150(1).

**Test**   Where an offender under the age of 18 is found guilty of an offence, the court may (and if the offender is under 16, *must*) bind over the parent or guardian, if it is satisfied that this would be desirable in the interests of preventing further offences by the offender, PCC(S)A 2000 s.150(2).

**Duty to explain where order not made**   If the court fails to exercise this power, it must state in open court that it is not satisfied that this would be desirable in the interests of preventing further offences by the offender, PCC(S)A 2000 s.150(1).

**Recognisance**   The recognisance may be in an amount not exceeding £1,000, PCC(S)A 2000 s.150(3).

**Length of the order**   The bind over may not be for a period exceeding three years, or until the offender's 18th birthday, whichever is the shorter, PCC(S)A 2000 s.150(4).

**Fixing the amount**   Before fixing the amount of the recognisance, the court must take into account the means of the parent or guardian, so far as they appear or are known, PCC(S)A 2000 s.150(7).

**Appeals**   A parent or guardian may appeal to the Crown Court against an order under s.150 made by a magistrates' court, PCC(S)A 2000 s.150(8). A parent or guardian may appeal to the Court of Appeal against an order under s.150 made by the Crown Court, as if he had been convicted on indictment and the order were a sentence passed on his conviction, PCC(S)A 2000 s.150(9). (See also **PARENTING ORDERS**, p.213.)

# PRESCRIBED CUSTODIAL SENTENCES—BLADED ARTICLES/ OFFENSIVE WEAPONS

CRIMINAL JUSTICE ACT 1988 SS.139, 139AA AND 139A, PREVENTION OF CRIME ACT 1953 SS.1 AND 1A

*References: Current Sentencing Practice A5; Archbold 5A-688*

Generally there are two circumstances in which a prescribed sentence falls to be imposed; these are (1) for the commission of a trigger offence and (2) for the commission of a trigger offence where the offender has a previous relevant conviction.

## (1)  Prescribed Sentence

**Offences to which it applies**  The prescribed sentences apply to the following offences:

  (a)  PCA 1953 s.1A (threatening with an offensive weapon in a public place); and
  (b)  CJA 1988 s.139AA (offence of threatening with article with blade or point or offensive weapon).

**Circumstances in which the prescribed sentence applies**  Where an offender aged 16 or over is convicted of an offence listed above, the court must impose a) in the case of a person aged 18 or over at conviction, a custodial sentence of at least six months, or b) in the case of a person aged 16 or 17 at conviction, a detention and training order of at least four months, CJA 1988 s.139AA(7) and (8) and PCA 1953 s.1A(5) and (6).

**Unjust to impose the prescribed sentence**  The prescribed sentence does not apply where the court is of the opinion that there are particular circumstances which relate to the offence, to the previous offence or to the offender, and would make it unjust to do so in all the circumstances, CJA 1988 s.139AA(7) and PCA 1953 s.1A(5).

**Guilty plea discount**  If the defendant has pleaded guilty the court may pass a sentence which is not less than 80% of the prescribed sentence, CJA 2003 s.144(2) and (3).

The restriction on the guilty plea discount does not apply to those aged 16 or 17 sentenced under CJA 1988 s.139A(5A) or PCA 1953 s.1A(5), CJA 2003 s.144(4) and (5).

If the court finds that there are particular circumstances which would make it unjust to impose the prescribed custodial sentence, the discount for the plea of guilty is not limited to 20% of the sentence which would have been appropriate following a contested trial.

[219]

## (2) Prescribed Sentence for Repeat Offenders

**Offences to which it applies**   The prescribed sentences apply to the following offences:

(a)   PCA 1953 s.1 (possession of an offensive weapon);
(b)   CJA 1988 s.139 (possession of bladed article); and
(c)   CJA 1988 s.139A (having bladed article or offensive weapon on school premises).

**Circumstances in which the prescribed sentence applies**   Where the instant offence was committed on or after 17 July 2015, and when the offence was committed, the person was aged 16 or over and had a conviction for a *"relevant offence"*, the court must impose a) in the case of a person aged 18 or over at conviction, a custodial sentence of at least six months, or b) in the case of a person aged 16 or 17 at conviction, a detention and training order of at least four months, CJA 1988 s.139A(6A)–(6C), 139A(5A)–(5C) and PCA 1953 s.1(2A) and (2C).

**Unjust to impose the prescribed sentence**   The prescribed sentence does not apply where the court is of the opinion that there are particular circumstances which relate to the offence, to the previous offence or to the offender, and would make it unjust to do so in all the circumstances, CJA 1988 ss.139(5B), 139A(5B) and PCA 1953 s.1(2B).

**Relevant offence**   A *"relevant offence"* is a conviction for an offence under:

(i)    PCA 1953 ss.1 or 1A; or
(ii)   CJA 1988 ss.139, 139A; or 139AA, whenever committed, CJA 1988 s.139AZA and PCA 1953 s.1ZA.

**Guilty plea discount**   If the defendant has pleaded guilty the court may pass a sentence which is not less than 80% of the prescribed sentence), CJA 2003 s.144(2) and (3).

The restriction on the guilty plea discount does not apply to those aged 16 or 17 sentenced under CJA 1988 ss.139(6B), 139A(5B) and 139AA(7) or PCA 1953 s.1(2B) and 1A(5), CJA 2003 s.144(4) and (5).

If the court finds that there are particular circumstances which would make it unjust to impose the prescribed custodial sentence, the discount for the plea of guilty is not limited to 20% of the sentence which would have been appropriate following a contested trial.

# PRESCRIBED CUSTODIAL SENTENCE—DOMESTIC BURGLARY

## PCC(S)A 2000 s.111

*References: Current Sentencing Practice A5; Archbold 5A-670*

### Applicability

A court which sentences an offender for a domestic burglary must impose a sentence of at least three years' imprisonment or detention in a young offender institution if:

(a) the burglary was committed on or after 1 December 1999;
(b) at the time when the burglary was committed the offender was 18 or over;
(c) at the time when the burglary was committed the offender had been convicted of two other domestic burglaries;
(d) each of the earlier domestic burglaries was committed on or after 1 December 1999;
(e) the offender had been convicted of the first domestic burglary before he committed the second, and was convicted of the second before he committed the third, PCC(S)A 2000 s.111(1).

### Aged 18

The offender must have been 18 or over at the time of the third burglary, but it is not necessary that he should have been 18 at the time of either of the earlier burglaries, PCC(S)A 2000 s.111(1)(b).

### Domestic burglary

A domestic burglary is a burglary that is committed in respect of a building or part of a building which is a dwelling. A burglary may not be treated as a domestic burglary for this purpose unless the fact that it was committed in respect of a dwelling is alleged in the indictment or information.

A houseboat is a *"building or part of a building"* for the purposes of s.111, see *Coleman* [2013] EWCA Crim 544; [2013] 2 Cr.App.R. (S.) 79.

As to whether an uninhabited domestic property is a *"dwelling"* for the purposes of the Act, see *Hudson v CPS* [2017] EWHC 841 (Admin).

### Attempts

Attempted burglaries do not count for the purposes of s.111, *McGuire* [2003] 2 Cr.App.R. (S.) 39.

### Convictions

A conviction which has been followed by a conditional or absolute discharge does not count for these purposes. A conviction by a magistrates' court does count.

A finding of guilt by a youth court does count. A conviction in any part of the United Kingdom other than England and Wales or any EEC Member State for an offence committed on or after 15 April 2010, which would amount to domestic burglary if done in England and Wales counts for this purpose.

### "Unjust" to impose prescribed sentence

The court is not obliged to impose a sentence of three years if there are particular circumstances which relate to any of the offences and which would make it unjust to do so in all the circumstances, PCC(S)A 2000 s.111(2).

Where the court does not impose the prescribed sentence, it must state in open court what the circumstances are.

If the court finds that there are particular circumstances which would make it unjust to impose the prescribed custodial sentence, the discount for the plea of guilty is not limited to 20% of the sentence which would have been appropriate following a contested trial.

### Interaction with sentencing guidelines

Consideration should first be made to the sentencing guidelines in order to determine the appropriate sentence and only then should the minimum sentence provision be consulted to ensure that the sentence complies with the statute, *Silvera* [2013] EWCA Crim 1764.

### Guilty plea reduction

If the offender has pleaded guilty, the court may pass a sentence which is not less than 80% of three years (876 days, slightly less than two years and five months), CJA 2003 s.144(2) and (3).

### Mentally disordered defendants

If the offender qualifies for a hospital order under MHA 1983, the court may make a hospital order, CJA 2003 s.166(1)(b) and MHA 1983 s.37(1A)(b).

### Triable on indictment only

A burglary committed in circumstances in which the obligation to pass a minimum sentence applies is triable only on indictment, PCC(S)A 2000 s.111(4).

# PRESCRIBED CUSTODIAL SENTENCE—DRUG TRAFFICKING

## PCC(S)A 2000 s.110

*References: Current Sentencing Practice A5; Archbold 5A-653*

### Applicability

A court which sentences an offender for a Class A drug trafficking offence must pass a sentence of at least seven years' imprisonment or detention in a young offender institution, if:

(a) the offence was committed on or after 1 October 1997;
(b) the offender was 18 or over when he committed the offence;
(c) he has been convicted on at least two separate previous occasions of a Class A drug trafficking offence, PCC(S)A 2000 s.110(1) and (6).

It is not necessary that the two earlier offences should have been committed after 1 October 1997.

### Drug trafficking offences

The following offences are *"drug trafficking offences"*:

(i) producing, supplying or possessing with intent to supply controlled drugs, MDA 1971 ss.4(2); 4(3) and 5(3). (N.B. simple possession is not included);
(ii) permitting certain activities relating to controlled drugs, MDA 1971 s.8;
(iii) assisting in or inducing the commission outside the United Kingdom of an offence punishable under a corresponding law, MDA 1971 s.20;
(iv) improper importation, exportation, or fraudulently evading the rohibition or restriction on importation or exportation of controlled substances whose importation or exportation is prohibited by MDA 1971, CEMA 1979 ss.50(2), 68(2) or 170;
(v) manufacturing or supplying a scheduled substance, knowing or suspecting that it is to be used in the production of a controlled drug, CJ(IC)A 1990 s.12;
(vi) having possession of a controlled drug on a ship, or being concerned in carrying or concealing a controlled drug on a ship, knowing it is intended to be unlawfully imported or has been exported, CJ(IC)A 1990 s.19;
(vii) inciting, attempting or conspiring to commit any of these offences or aiding, abetting, counselling or procuring the commission of any of them, PCC(S)A 2000 s.111(5).

### Previous convictions

A conviction which has been followed by a conditional or absolute discharge does not count for these purposes. A conviction which has been followed by a probation order made before 1 October 1992 does not count.

A conviction by a magistrates' court does count. A finding of guilt by a youth court does count. A conviction in any part of the United Kingdom at any time, or in any EEC Member State for an offence committed on or after 15 April 2010, which would amount to a class A drug trafficking offence if done in the United Kingdom counts for this purpose, PCC(S)A 2000 s.110(2A).

## Unjust to impose prescribed sentence

The court need not pass a sentence of seven years if there are *"particular circumstances"* which would make it *"unjust to do so"*. If the court does not impose a sentence of seven years, the circumstances which make the sentence unjust must be stated in open court, PCC(S)A 2000 s.110(2). This is a fact-specific decision and there is little by way of guidance from the Court of Appeal.

## Interaction with sentencing guidelines

Consideration should first be made to the sentencing guidelines in order to determine the appropriate sentence and only then should the minimum sentence provision be consulted to ensure that the sentence complies with the statute, *Silvera* [2013] EWCA Crim 1764. *Silvera* was decided in relation to the minimum sentence under s.111 of the PCC(S)A 2000. The court in *AG's Ref (Marland)* [2018] EWCA Crim 1770 suggested that the guidelines should be used to check whether or not the required minimum sentence would be disproportionate and unjust, however it is suggested that this should not be followed and *Silvera* remains the appropriate approach.

## Guilty plea discount

If the defendant has pleaded guilty the court may pass a sentence which is not less than 80% of the seven years (2,045 days, slightly less than five years and eight months), CJA 2003 s.144(2) and (3).

If the court finds that there are particular circumstances which would make it unjust to impose the prescribed custodial sentence, the discount for the plea of guilty is not limited to 20% of the sentence which would have been appropriate following a contested trial.

## Mentally ordered defendants

If the offender qualifies for a hospital order under MHA 1983, the court may make a hospital order, CJA 2003 s.166(1)(b) and MHA 1983 s.37(1A)(b).

## Mode of trial

A drug trafficking offence committed in circumstances in which the obligation to pass a minimum sentence applies is triable only on indictment, PCC(S)A 2000 s.110(4).

# PRESCRIBED CUSTODIAL SENTENCES—PROHIBITED WEAPONS

FIREARMS ACT 1968 S.51A, VIOLENT CRIME REDUCTION ACT 2006 S.29

*References: Current Sentencing Practice A5; Archbold 5A-655*

## General

This section includes information on prescribed sentences under the firearms Act 1968 and the Violent Crime Reduction Act 2006.

The proper approach to sentencing in a minimum sentence firearms case is to determine the length of the sentence by reference to the relevant principles and authorities and then to consider whether that provisional sentence infringes the prescribed minimum, *Boyle* [2018] EWCA Crim 2035.

## Offences Under the Firearms Act 1968

**Applicability**   Offences:

(a)   under:
   (i)   the FA 1968 s.5(1)(a), (ab), (aba), (ac), (ad), (ae), (af) or (c), committed on or after 22 January 2004;
   (ii)   the FA 1968 s.5(1A)(a), committed on or after 22 January 2004; or
   (iii)   the following sections of the FA 1968 where the firearm is a prohibited weapon to which s.51A applies, if the offence was committed on or after 6 April 2007:
      (1)   s.16 (possession of a firearm with intent);
      (2)   s.16A (possession of a firearm with intent to cause fear);
      (3)   s.17 (possession or use of a firearm to resist arrest or when arrested for a Scheduled offence);
      (4)   s.18 (carrying a firearm with intent to commit an offence);
      (5)   s.19 (carrying a firearm in a public place); or
      (6)   s.20 (trespassing in a building with a firearm), where,
(b)   the offence was committed when the defendant was aged 16 or over, FA 1968 s.51A(1).

**Exceptional circumstances**   A court dealing with an offender for an offence to which the Firearms Act 1968 s.51A applies must impose the required minimum sentence *"unless the court is of the opinion that there are exceptional circumstances relating to the offence or to the offender which justify its not doing so"*, FA 1968 s.51A(2).

**Guilty plea discount**   The court may not allow a discount for a plea of guilty if the effect of doing so would be to reduce the length of the sentence below the required minimum term.

**Length of the prescribed sentence**   For those aged 18 and over at the date of the offence, five years' imprisonment/detention in YOI, for those aged 16 or over but under 18 at the time of the offence, three years' detention under s.91, FA 1968 s.51A(4) and (5).

## Offences Under the Violent Crime Reduction Act 2006

**Applicability**  The prescribed sentence applies to offences under the VCRA 2006 s.28 (using someone to mind a weapon), where:

(a) the defendant was aged 16 or over at the time of the offence; and
(b) the dangerous weapon in respect of which the offence was committed was a firearm mentioned in the FA 1968 ss.5(1)(a) to (af) or (c), or 5(1A)(a), VCRA 2006 s.29(4) and (6).

**Length of the prescribed sentence**  For those aged 18 or over at conviction, the prescribed term is five years' imprisonment/detention in YOI, VCRA 2006 s.29(4).

For those aged 16 or 17 at conviction, the prescribed term is three years' detention under s.91, VCRA 2006 s.29(6).

**Exceptional circumstances**  Where the court is considering the seriousness of s.28 offence, and at the time of the offence the offender was aged 18 or over and the person used to look after, hide or transport the weapon was not, the court must treat the fact that that person was under the age of 18 at that time as an aggravating factor, and must state in open court that the offence was so aggravated, VCRA 2006 s.29(11) and (12).

**Guilty plea discount**  The court may not allow a discount for a plea of guilty if the effect of doing so would be to reduce the length of the sentence below the required minimum term.

# PRE-SENTENCE REPORTS

## CRIMINAL JUSTICE ACT 2003 s.159

*References: Current Sentencing Practice H2-8450; Archbold 5A-234*

### General

A pre-sentence report is a report made by probation officer or other appropriate officer to assist the court in determining the most suitable method of dealing with the offender, CJA 2003 s.158(1).

### Written reports

A pre-sentence report need not be in writing, unless it is required before a court passes a custodial sentence on an offender under the age of 18 or is required to be in writing by rules made by the Secretary of State, CJA 2003 s.158(1A) and (1B).

### Duty to obtain report

A court must obtain and consider a pre-sentence report before:

(a) in the case of a custodial sentence, forming any such opinion as is mentioned in:
   (i) CJA 2003 s.152(2) (offence so serious that a fine/community sentence cannot be justified);
   (ii) CJA 2003 s.153(2) (custodial sentence must be for shortest term commensurate with seriousness of offence);
   (iii) CJA 2003 ss.225(1)(b) or 226(1)(b) (*"dangerousness test"*: life sentence);
   (iv) CJA 2003 ss.226A(1)(b) or 226B(1)(b) (*"dangerousness test"*: extended determinate sentence); or
(b) in the case of a community sentence, forming any such opinion as mentioned in:
   (i) CJA 2003 s.148(1) or (2)(b) (offence serious enough to warrant community order/restrictions on liberty under order commensurate with the seriousness of offence); or
   (ii) CJIA 2008 s.1(4)(b) or (c) (additional test for imposing YRO with intensive supervision and surveillance or fostering); or
   (iii) any opinion as to the suitability for the offender of the particular requirement or requirements to be imposed by a community order or youth rehabilitation order, CJA 2003 s.156(3).

However that duty does not apply if, in the circumstances of the case, the court is of the opinion that it is unnecessary to obtain a pre-sentence report, CJA 2003 s.156(4).

## Under 18s

The court must not come to the conclusion that a report is unnecessary in the case of an offender aged under 18 unless there exists a previous pre-sentence report obtained in respect of the offender, and the court has had regard to the information contained in that report, or, if there is more than one such report, the most recent report, CJA 2003 s.156(5).

It will usually be appropriate to order a report and in some of these cases a recent report may well be sufficient where:

(a)   the defendant is 17 and under;
(b)   the defendant is under 21 and is a first-time offender/has not served a prison sentence;
(c)   the defendant falls to be assessed for *"dangerousness"*
(d)   there is a realistic alternative to a custodial sentence (check the Sentencing Guidelines), Guidance, referred to in *Townsend* [2018] EWCA Crim 875; [2018] 2 Cr.App.R. (S.) 30.

## Failure to get report

A failure to get a report does not invalidate a custodial sentence or community sentence, however on appeal against sentence, the same requirements apply to the Court of Appeal, unless the court is of the opinion that the court below was justified in forming an opinion that it was unnecessary to obtain a pre-sentence report, or that, although the court below was not justified in forming that opinion, in the circumstances of the case at the time it is before the court, it is unnecessary to obtain a presentence report, CJA 2003 s.156(6) and (7).

The same requirement applies to the Court of Appeal in relation to those under 18 (see **Under 18s** above).

## Disclosure

The pre-sentence report must be disclosed to the offender or his representative, and to the prosecutor, if the prosecutor is a Crown Prosecutor, or represents the CPS, the Customs and Excise, the DSS, the Inland Revenue or the Serious Fraud Office. If the prosecutor is not of such a description (such as a local authority or private prosecutor), a copy of the report need not be given to the prosecutor if the court considers that it would be inappropriate for him to be given one, CJA 2003 s.159(1), (2) and (4).

If the offender is under 18, the court must give a copy of the report to any parent or guardian of the offender who is present in court, even though a copy has been given to the offender or his counsel or solicitor. If the disclosure to the offender or any parent or guardian of the information contained in the report would be likely to create a risk of significant harm to the offender, a complete copy of the report need not be given to the offender or his parents or guardians, but a full copy of the report must be given to the offender's counsel or solicitor, CJA 2003 s.159(1)–(3).

## Contents

It is important to remember that it was the role of the litigator and the advocate to put together the necessary mitigation by gathering all of the relevant information.

It was not the role of the Probation Service to do that work. Statements of what a defendant said about their background carry no more weight because they are contained in a pre-sentence report than if they were put forward by an advocate, *Townsend* [2018] EWCA Crim 875 [2018] 2 Cr.App.R. (S.) 30.

# PREVIOUS CONVICTIONS

## CRIMINAL JUSTICE ACT 2003 s.143

*References: Current Sentencing Practice A1-300; Archbold 5A-2*

*Note this section applies irrespective of the date on which the offence was committed.*

### Duty to treat as aggravating factor

If the offender has one or more previous convictions, the court must treat each previous conviction as an aggravating factor if (in the case of that conviction) the court considers that it can reasonably be treated as an aggravating factor, having regard to the nature of the offence to which the conviction relates and its relevance to the current offence, and the time that has elapsed since the conviction, CJA 2003 s.143(2).

### What is a previous conviction?

*"Previous conviction"* does not include convictions which are deemed not to be convictions by provisions dealing with discharges and probation orders. Under the PCC(S)A 2000 s.14(1), a conviction which results in a discharge is deemed not to be a conviction, subject to the qualifications set out in subss.(2) and (3). A conviction before 1 October, 1992 which led to a probation order is also deemed not to have been a conviction (see the PCC(S)A 2000 s.13). *"Previous conviction"* includes convictions by a court in an EEC Member State for an offence which would be an offence under the law of any part of the United Kingdom, and a previous conviction for a service offence.

A court is not required to treat convictions by a court outside the United Kingdom or Member States as aggravating factors, but may take them into account and treat them as aggravating factors if it considers it appropriate to do so, CJA 2003 s.143(5).

Previous convictions are those for which the conviction was obtained prior to the commission of *Darrigan* [2017] EWCA Crim 169; [2017] 1 Cr.App.R. (S.) 50.

# PROSECUTION COSTS

## PROSECUTION OF OFFENCES ACT 1985 s.18

*References: Current Sentencing Practice C1-5700; Archbold 6-22*

### General

**Power**  Where:

(a)  any person is convicted of an offence before a magistrates' court;
(b)  the Crown Court dismisses an appeal against such a conviction or against the sentence imposed on that conviction; or
(c)  any person is convicted of an offence before the Crown Court;

the court may make such order as to the costs to be paid by the accused to the prosecutor as it considers just and reasonable, POA 1985 s.18(1).

**No order where financial order does not exceed £5**  Where any person is convicted of an offence before a magistrates' court and:

(a)  the court orders payment of any sum as a fine, penalty, forfeiture or compensation; and
(b)  the sum so ordered to be paid does not exceed £5.

The court shall not order the accused to pay any costs under this section unless in the particular circumstances of the case it considers it right to do so, POA 1985 s.18(4).

**Guilty plea**  The fact that an offender has pleaded guilty is a material factor in considering whether to order him to pay the costs of the prosecution, but it does not necessarily mean that an order is inappropriate, *Matthews* (1979) 1 Cr.App.R. (S.) 346.

**Either way offences**  An offender should not be ordered to pay costs simply because he has refused to consent to summary trial, *Hayden* (1975) 60 Cr.App.R. 304.

### Making the Order

**Means**  An offender should not be ordered to pay costs unless the court is satisfied that he has the means to pay the costs ordered, or will have the means within a reasonable time, *Ahmed* [1997] 2 Cr.App.R. (S.) 8.

**Combining costs order with custody**  An offender who is sentenced to custody should not be ordered to pay costs unless he has the means to pay immediately, or good prospects of employment on release, *Gaston* (1970) 55 Cr.App.R. 88.

**Consider overall effect of financial penalties**  The fact that the amount of costs is greater than the amount of a fine imposed for the offence is not necessarily a ground for objecting to the order, but the court should consider the overall effect

[233]

of any combination of financial penalties, see *Glenister*, unreported, 28 November 1975.

## Imprisonment in Default

The court does not fix any term of imprisonment in default, but may allow time for payment or fix payment by instalments, *Bunce* (1977) 66 Cr.App.R. 109.

If the amount of the order exceeds £20,000, the Crown Court has the power to enlarge the powers of the magistrates' court responsible for enforcing the order if it considers that the maximum default term of 12 months is inadequate, PCC(S)A 2000 s.139.

The court should make an order that the maximum term of imprisonment in default should be a figure taken from the following table:

| Amount not exceeding | Maximum term |
| --- | --- |
| £50,000 | 18 months |
| £100,000 | 24 months |
| £250,000 | 36 months |
| £1 million | 60 months |
| Over £1 million | 120 months |

# PSYCHOACTIVE SUBSTANCES: PROHIBITION ORDERS

PSYCHOACTIVE SUBSTANCES ACT 2016 ss.17–22

*References: Current Sentencing Practice C2-7075; Archbold 27-131*

## General

*"Prohibition order"* means an order prohibiting the person against whom it is made from carrying on any prohibited activity or a prohibited activity of a description specified in the order, PSA 2016 s.17(1).

*"Prohibited activity"* means any of the following activities:

(a) producing a psychoactive substance that is likely to be consumed by individuals for its psychoactive effects;
(b) supplying such a substance;
(c) offering to supply such a substance;
(d) importing such a substance;
(e) exporting such a substance;
(f) assisting or encouraging the carrying on of a prohibited activity listed in any of paragraphs (a) to (e), PSA 2016 s.12(1).

But this is subject to the list of exceptions to offences, see PSA 2016 s.11.

The sections of the PSA 2016 pertinent to prohibition orders were commenced on 26 May 2016 (see SI 2016/553) with no transitional provisions.

## Availability of the Order

**Availability**   The order is available where the court is dealing with a person who has been convicted of a relevant offence, PSA 2016 s.19(1).

A *"relevant offence"* means:

(a) an offence under any of ss.4 to 8 of the PSA 2016;
(b) an offence of attempting or conspiring to commit an offence under any of ss.4 to 8;
(c) an offence under Pt.2 of the Serious Crime Act 2007 in relation to an offence under any of ss.4 to 8;
(d) an offence of inciting a person to commit an offence under any of ss.4 to 8;
(e) an offence of aiding, abetting, counselling or procuring the commission of an offence under any of ss.4 to 8, PSA 2016 s.19(5).

A prohibition order may not be made except:

(a) in addition to a sentence imposed in respect of the offence concerned, or

[235]

(b)  in addition to an order discharging the person conditionally, PSA 2016 s.19(2).

**Test to apply**  The court may only make the order if it considers it necessary and proportionate for the purpose of preventing the person from carrying on any prohibited activity, PSA 2016 s.19(1).

**Effect of Making Prohibition Order on Existing Prohibition Notice**  If a court makes a prohibition order under this section, any prohibition notice that has previously been given to the person against whom the order is made is to be treated as having been withdrawn, PSA 2016 s.19(3).

### Extent and contents of the order

**Nature**  The order may make prohibitions, restrictions or requirements, PSA 2016 s.22(1).

**Test for prohibitions etc.**  The order may only include prohibitions, restrictions or requirement which the court considers to be appropriate, PSA 2016 s.22(1).

**Mandatory prohibition**  Every order will include a prohibition on carrying on any prohibited activity or a prohibited activity of a description specified in the order, PSA 2016 s.17(1) and 22(1).

### Sample prohibitions

(a)  prohibitions or restrictions on, or requirements in relation to, the person's business dealings (including the conduct of the person's business over the internet);
(b)  a requirement to hand over for disposal an item belonging to the person that the court is satisfied:
    i)  is a psychoactive substance; or
    ii)  has been, or is likely to be, used in the carrying on of a prohibited activity.
(c)  a prohibition on access to premises owned, occupied, leased, controlled or operated by the person for a specified period not exceeding three months (an "*access prohibition*"), PSA 2016 s.22(3), (4) and (6).

A person (other than a mortgagee not in possession) "*owns*" premises in England and Wales or Northern Ireland if:

(a)  the person is entitled to dispose of the fee simple in the premises, whether in possession or reversion; or
(b)  the person holds or is entitled to the rents and profits of the premises under a lease that (when granted) was for a term of not less than three years, PSA 2016 ss.14(6) and 22(11).

**Items handed over for disposal**  Such items may not be disposed of:

(a)  before the end of the period within which an appeal may be made against the imposition of the requirement (ignoring any power to appeal out of time); or
(b)  if such an appeal is made, before it is determined or otherwise dealt with, PSA 2016 s.22(5).

**Access prohibitions**    An access prohibition may:

(a)  prohibit access by all persons, or by all persons except those specified, or by all persons except those of a specified description;

(b)  prohibit access at all times, or at all times except those specified;

(c)  prohibit access in all circumstances, or in all circumstances except those specified;

(d)  be made in respect of the whole or any part of the premises;

(e)  include provision about access to a part of the building or structure of which the premises form part, PSA 2016 s.22(8) and (9).

*"Specified"* means specified in the prohibition order, PSA 2016 s.22(10).

## Variation

**On application**    The court may vary or discharge a prohibition order or a premises order on the application of:

(a)  the person who applied for the order (if any);

(b)  the person against whom the order was made; or

(c)  any other person who is significantly adversely affected by the order, PSA 2016 s.28(1).

The court may vary or discharge the order on the application of:

(a)  in the case of an order made in England and Wales, the chief officer of police for a police area or the chief constable of the British Transport Police Force;

(b)  in the case of an order made in England and Wales or Northern Ireland, the Director General of the National Crime Agency;

(c)  in the case of an order made in England and Wales or Northern Ireland, the Secretary of State by whom general customs functions are exercisable, PSA 2016 s.28(2).

Where the order imposed an access condition and an application for the variation of the order is made by the person who applied for the order, or by a chief constable, the director of the NCA or the Secretary of State (see s.28(2)), before the expiry of the period for which the access prohibition has effect, the court may extend or further extend the access condition so long as it does not have effect for a period exceeding six months, PSA 2016 s.28(3)-(5).

**On conviction**    Where a court is dealing with a person who has been convicted of:

(a)  a relevant offence and against whom a prohibition order has previously been made; or

(b)  an offence under s.26 of failing to comply with a prohibition order, the court may vary the order, PSA 2016 s.29(1) and (2).

An order may not be varied except:

(a)  in addition to a sentence imposed in respect of the offence concerned; or

(b)   in addition to an order discharging the person conditionally or, in Scotland, discharging the person absolutely, PSA 2016 s.29(4).

## Appeals

**Against orders**   A person against whom a prohibition order is made on conviction for a relevant offence may appeal against the making of the order as if it were a sentence passed on the person for the offence referred to in s.19(1) (to the extent it would not otherwise be so appealable), PSA 2016 s.30(5).

**Against variations of orders made on conviction**   A person against whom a prohibition order has been made may appeal against a variation of the order made on conviction as if the varied order were a sentence passed on the person for the offence referred to in s.29(1) (to the extent it would not otherwise be so appealable), PSA 2016 s.31(7).

**Against variations of orders made on application**   A person against whom the order was made, or a person significantly affected by the order may appeal against the decision in relation to the variation/discharge of the order, PSA 2016 s.31(2).

A decision made by a youth court or magistrates' court may be appealed to the Crown Court; a decision made by the Crown Court may be appealed to the Court of Appeal, PSA 2016 s.31(1). The appeal must be made within 28 days from the date of the decision, PSA 2016 s.31(4).

On an appeal the court hearing the appeal may (to the extent it would not otherwise have power to do so) make such orders as may be necessary to give effect to its determination of the appeal, and may also make such incidental or consequential orders as appear to it to be just, PSA 2016 s.31(5).

## Breach of a Prohibition Order/Access Condition

**Prohibition order: Offence**   A person against whom a prohibition order or a premises order is made commits an offence by failing to comply with the order, PSA 2016 s.26(1).

**Prohibition order: Penalty**   The maximum term of imprisonment upon summary conviction is 12 months (subject to the limit on magistrates' court sentencing powers), PSA 2016 s.26(2).

**Prohibition order: Defence**   A person does not commit an offence if:
(a)   they took all reasonable steps to comply with the order; or
(b)   there is some other reasonable excuse for the failure to comply, PSA 2016 s.26(3).

**Access condition: Offences**   A person, other than the person against whom the order was made, who without reasonable excuse remains on or enters premises in contravention of the access prohibition commits an offence, PSA 2016 s.27(2).

A person who without reasonable excuse obstructs an authorised person acting in relation to enforcement of an access condition (see s.23) commits an offence, PSA 2016 s.27(3).

**Access condition: Penalty**   A person guilty of an access condition offence may, on summary conviction, be sentenced to imprisonment not exceeding 51 weeks (subject to the limit on magistrates' court sentencing powers) or a fine or both, PSA 2016 s.27(4).

# PURPOSES OF SENTENCING—ADULTS

CRIMINAL JUSTICE ACT 2003 s.142

*References: Current Sentencing Practice H1-450; Archbold 5A-14*

A court dealing with an offender aged 18 or over must have regard to the following purposes of sentencing:

(a) the punishment of offenders;
(b) the reduction of crime (including its reduction by deterrence);
(c) the reform and rehabilitation of offenders;
(d) the protection of the public; and
(e) the making of reparation by offenders to persons affected by their offences, CJA 2003 s.142(1).

## Exceptions

The provision does not apply to:

(a) an offender who is aged under 18 at the time of conviction;
(b) an offence the sentence for which is fixed by law;
(c) to an offence the sentence for which falls to be imposed under:
  (i) PCA 1953 ss.1(2B) or 1A(5) (minimum sentence for certain offences involving offensive weapons);
  (ii) FA 1968 s.51A(2) (minimum sentence for certain firearms offences);
  (iii) CJA 1988 s.139(6B), 139A(5B) or 139AA(7) (minimum sentence for certain offences involving article with blade or point or offensive weapon);
  (iv) PCC(S)A 2000 ss.110 or 111 (minimum sentence for certain drug trafficking and burglary offences);
  (v) CJA 2003 s.224A (life sentence for second listed offence for certain dangerous offenders);
  (vi) CJA 2003 ss.225(2) or 226(2) (imprisonment or detention for life for certain dangerous offenders);
  (vii) VCRA 2006 s.29(4) or (6) (minimum sentence in certain cases of using someone to mind a weapon); or
  (viii) in relation to the making of a hospital order (with or without a restriction order), an interim hospital order, a hospital direction or a limitation direction under the MHA 1983, CJA 2003 s.142(2) and (2AA).

# PURPOSES OF SENTENCING—YOUNG OFFENDERS

*References: Current Sentencing Practice F1; Archbold 5A-946*

## General aim

It is the principal aim of the youth justice system to prevent offending by children and young persons, and in addition to any other duty to which they are subject, it shall be the duty of all persons and bodies carrying out functions in relation to the youth justice system to have regard to that aim, CDA 1998 s.37(1).

## Duty to have regard to welfare

Every court in dealing with a child or young person who is brought before it, either as an offender or otherwise, shall have regard to the welfare of the child or young person and shall in a proper case take steps for removing him from undesirable surroundings, and for securing that proper provision is made for his education and training, CYPA 1933 s.4(1).

## Purposes of sentencing (not in force)

A court dealing with an offender aged under 18 must have regard to the prevention of offending (or reoffending) by persons aged under 18, the welfare of the offender, and the following purposes of sentencing:

(a) the punishment of offenders;
(b) the reform and rehabilitation of offenders;
(c) the protection of the public; and
(d) the making of reparation by offenders to persons affected by their offences, CJA 2003 s.142A(1) and (3).

The provision contains similar exclusions to those listed in the corresponding adult provision (see the previous page), CJA 2003 s.142A(4).

This provision was not in force on 31 October 2018.

# RACIALLY OR RELIGIOUSLY AGGRAVATED OFFENCES

CRIMINAL JUSTICE ACT 2003 s.145

*References: Current Sentencing Practice H3-4500; Archbold 5A-45*

## Applicability

Section 145 (duty to treat racially or religiously aggravated offences as aggravating factor) applies where the court is considering the seriousness of an offence other than one committed under CDA 1998 ss.29-31, CJA 2003 s.145(1).

## Definitions

A crime is racially or religiously aggravated if at the time of committing the offence, or immediately before or after doing so, the offender demonstrates towards the victim of the offence hostility based on the victim's membership (or presumed membership) of a racial or religious group or the offence is motivated (wholly or partly) by hostility towards members of a racial or religious group based on their membership of that group, CDA 1998 s.28(1).

A *"racial group"* means a group of persons defined by reference to race, colour, nationality (including citizenship) or ethnic or national origins, CDA 1998 s.28(4).

A *"religious group"* is a group of persons defined by reference to religious belief or lack of religious belief, CDA 1998 s.28(5).

## Duty to treat as aggravating factor

If the offence was racially or religiously aggravated, the court must treat that fact as an aggravating factor and must state in open court that the offence was so aggravated, CJA 2003 s.145(2).

## Discretion for certain offences

If an offender is convicted of a racially or religiously aggravated offence under CDA 1998 ss.29, 30, 31 or 32, the court may in its discretion treat the racial or religious aggravation as an aggravating factor, but it is not bound to do so by s.145. The court is not bound to make the statement required by s.145(2)(b), see CJA 2003 s.145(1).

## Offences not charged under ss.29-32

If the offender is convicted of an offence which could have been charged as a racially or religiously aggravated offence under CDA 1998 ss.29 to 32 (such as unlawful wounding or assault occasioning actual bodily harm), but he has not been charged with the racially or religiously aggravated offence, or he has been acquitted of the racially or religiously aggravated offence, generally it is not permissible to treat the offence as racially or religiously aggravated for the purposes of s.145.

[245]

## Approach

The decision in *Kelly* [2001] EWCA Crim 170; [2001] 2 Cr.App.R. (S.) 73 supported a two-stage approach to sentencing racially aggravated offences: first, a consideration of what the sentence should be absent the aggravation; and, secondly, a consideration of what, and by how much, the sentence should be increased to reflect this. That approach appeared to be more readily applicable in cases where there was a distinct offence, such as an assault, even without the racial element. In the instant case, the very essence of the offence was the racial nature of the remark, *Gargan* [2017] EWCA Crim 780; [2018] 1 Cr.App.R. (S.) 6.

# REASONS FOR SENTENCE

## CRIMINAL JUSTICE ACT 2003 s.174

*References: Current Sentencing Practice H3-8100; Archbold 5A-176*

### General Rule

The court must state in all cases, in open court, in ordinary language and in general terms, its reasons for deciding on the sentence imposed, CJA 2003 s.174(2).

It is not permissible to impose sentence and decline to give reasons orally and open court on the basis that written reasons will be provided at a later date, see *Billington* [2017] EWCA Crim 618; [2017] 4 W.L.R. 114.

### All Cases

**Sentencing guidelines**  The court must identify any definitive sentencing guidelines relevant to the offender's case and:

- (a) explain how the court discharged any duty imposed on it by s.125 of the CJA 2009 (duty to follow guidelines unless satisfied it would be contrary to the interests of justice to do so);
- (b) where the court was satisfied it would be contrary to the interests of justice to follow the guidelines, state why, CJA 2003 s.174(6).

**Guilty plea**  If the court has reduced the sentence as a result of taking into account the offender's guilty plea, state the fact that it has done so, CJA 2003 s.174(7).

**Effect of sentence**  The court must explain to the offender in ordinary language:

- (a) the effect of the sentence;
- (b) the effects of non-compliance with any order that the offender is required to comply with and that forms part of the sentence;
- (c) any power of the court to vary or review any order that forms part of the sentence; and
- (d) the effects of failure to pay a fine, if the sentence consists of or includes a fine, CJA 2003 s.174(3).

If the sentencing judge gives an inaccurate explanation of the effect of sentence, the inaccuracy of the explanation does not provide a ground of appeal against sentence.

In the case of a *custodial sentence*, s.174 appears to require an explanation of the relevant provisions governing release and licence, which will vary according to the nature of the sentence imposed (life imprisonment, extended sentence, fixed-term sentence).

In the case of a *community order*, the court must explain the requirements of the order, the effects of non-compliance, and the power of the court on application to vary the order.

In the case of a *fine* (but not a compensation order or confiscation order), the court must explain the effect of the order and the effect of failure to pay the fine.

**Statutory aggravating factors**   In all cases, if the offence is racially or religiously aggravated, the court must state that that has been treated as an aggravating factor; if the offence has been aggravated by reference to the victim's sexual orientation, disability, or transgender identity, state that that the offence has been committed in such circumstances, CJA 2003 ss.145 and 146.

### Those Aged Under 18

**Custodial sentence**   If the court passes a custodial sentence on an offender under 18, the court must in addition state that it is of the opinion that the offence or the combination of the offence and one or more offences associated with it was so serious that neither a fine nor a community sentence can be justified for the offence, CJA 2003 s.174(8).

**Enhanced YRO**   If the court makes a youth rehabilitation order with intensive supervision and surveillance or fostering, state that the court is of the opinion that the offence, or the combination of the offence and one or more offences associated with it, was so serious that, but for the power to make a youth rehabilitation order with intensive supervision and surveillance or fostering, a custodial sentence would be appropriate, and if the offender was aged under 15 at the time of conviction, the court is of the opinion that the offender is a persistent offender; if the offender is under 12, the court must state that a custodial sentence would be appropriate if he had been aged 12, CJA 2003 s.174(8).

### Special Cases

Where the court decides:

(a)   not to follow a relevant sentencing guideline;
(b)   not to make, where it could:
    (i)   a reparation order (unless it passes a custodial or community sentence);
    (ii)   a compensation order; or
    (iii)   a travel restriction order;
(c)   not to order, where it could:
    (i)   that a suspended sentence of imprisonment is to take effect;
    (ii)   the endorsement of the defendant's driving record; or
    (iii)   the defendant's disqualification from driving, for the usual minimum period or at all;
(d)   to pass a lesser sentence than it otherwise would have passed because the defendant has assisted, or has agreed to assist, an investigator or prosecutor in relation to an offence, the court must explain why it has so decided, CPR 2015 r.28.1.

**Informants**   Where the court decides to pass a lesser sentence than it otherwise would have passed because the defendant has assisted, or has agreed to assist, an investigator or prosecutor in relation to an offence, the court must arrange for such an explanation to be given to the defendant and to the prosecutor in writing, if the court thinks that it would not be in the public interest to explain in public, CPR 2015 r.28.1(3).

**Non-compliance with sentencing orders**   In the case of some orders (such as criminal behaviour orders, football banning orders, sexual harm prevention orders, disqualification from driving, etc.), the court must explain the effect of the order, the effect of non-compliance with the order, and any power of the court to vary the order. See the individual legislation for details.

# REFERRAL ORDERS

## PCC(S)A 2000 ss.16-32

*References: Current Sentencing Practice F3-1300; Archbold 5A-960*

### General

**Mandatory order**   Where a defendant under the age of 18 appears for sentence before a youth court or magistrates' court for an offence punishable with imprisonment the court *must* make a referral order if:

(a)   none of the offences is one for which the sentence is fixed by law;

(b)   the court is not proposing to impose a custodial sentence or make a hospital order, or to grant a conditional or absolute discharge;

(c)   the defendant has pleaded guilty to all the offences for which he is to be sentenced;

(d)   the defendant has never been convicted by a court in the UK of any other offence;

(e)   the offender has never been convicted by or before a court in another Member State of any offence, PCC(S)A 2000 ss.16(1) and (2) and 17(1).

**Discretionary order**   The court *may* make a referral order if the offender pleaded guilty to the offence, or to at least one of those offences for which he is being dealt with, whether or not he has previously been found guilty of an offence, PCC(S)A 2000 s.16(3) and 17(2).

### Making the Order

**Contents**   A referral order must specify the youth offending team responsible for implementing the order, require the offender to attend meetings of the panel established by the team, and specify the period during which the contract is to have effect, PCC(S)A 2000 s.18(1).

**Length of the order**   The order must be not less than three months and not more than 12 months, PCC(S)A 2000 s.18(1).

**Duty to explain order and effect of breach**   The court must explain the effect of the order and the consequences of non-compliance or breach, PCC(S)A 2000 s.18(3).

**Parental orders (to attend meetings)**   The court may order the offender's parent or a representative of the local authority to attend meetings of the panel, PCC(S)A 2000 s.20.

### Duties of the Offender

The offender must attend meetings of the panel and reach an agreement on a programme of behaviour aimed at preventing re-offending by the offender. The agreement takes effect as a *"youth offender contract"*, PCC(S)A 2000 s.18(1)(b).

If the offender does not agree with the panel within a reasonable time, or fails to sign the contract, or fails to comply with the contract, or if there is a change in the offender's circumstances, the panel may refer the offender back to the court, PCC(S)A 2000 ss.25 and 26.

## Combining Sentences

**Prohibited orders**   Where the court makes a referral order, the court must not:

(a)   impose a youth rehabilitation order, PCC(S)A 2000 s.19(1)–(4)(a);

(b)   impose a fine, PCC(S)A 2000 s.19(1)–(4);

(c)   grant a conditional discharge, PCC(S)A 2000 s.19(1)–(4)(d);

(d)   impose a reparation order, PCC(S)A 2000 s.19(1)–(4)(c) and 73(4)(b);

(e)   bind the offender over to keep the peace, PCC(S)A 2000 s.19(1) and (5)(a), or;

(f)   order the offender's parents or guardians to be bound over for that offence, PCC(S)A 2000 s.19(1) and (5)(b).

Where the mandatory referral order conditions are satisfied, the court may not make an order deferring sentence, PCC(S)A 2000 s.19(7). However, the court may remand for mental health reports or commit to Crown Court for a restriction order (MHA 1983 ss.35, 38, 43 or 44), remit the offender to another court, PCC(S)A 2000 s.8, or adjourn for inquiries, MCA 1980 s.10(3).

**Permitted orders**   It appears that the court may impose:

(a)   a compensation order under PCC(S)A 2000 s.130;

(b)   a deprivation order under PCC(S)A 2000 s.143;

(c)   a disqualification order under RTOA 1988 ss.34 or 35 or PCC(S)A ss.146 or 147;

(d)   a parenting order after considering a report from an appropriate officer, CDA 1998 s.9(1) and (1A).

### Referrals back to court for breach etc.

The offender may be referred back to the court by the panel:

(a)   if it considers there is no prospect of agreement being reached, PCC(S) A 2000 s.25(2);

(b)   where the offender fails to sign the youth offender contract, PCC(S)A 2000 s.25(3);

(c)   where the offender fails to attend a meeting, PCC(S)A 2000 s.25(4);

(d)   by the panel where the offender has breached the youth offender contract, having discussed the breach with the offender, PCC(S)A 2000 s.26(4);

(e)   if, at a progress meeting, thee contract is varied and agreed, but the offender does not sign the contract, PCC(S)A 2000 s.26(8);

(f)   at the request of the offender, where the panel consider this is or soon will be a change in circumstances, PCC(S)A 2000 s.26(10);

(g)   at the final meeting where the panel conclude that the contract has not been satisfactorily completed, PCC(S)A 2000 s.27(4);

(h)   where it considers that, due to circumstances that have arisen since the making of the order, it is in the interests of justice that the order be revoked (this includes good behaviour by the offender), PCC(S)A 2000 s.27A.

**Re-sentencing powers**  If the offender is referred back to the court, and the court is satisfied that the panel was entitled to make any finding of fact that it did make, and that the panel reasonably exercised its discretion, the court has several options:

(a)  it may revoke the order and deal with the offender in any manner in which the court which made the order could have dealt with him, PCC(S)A 2000 Sch.1 para.5(4) and (5);

(b)  it may extend the period for which the contract has effect, by a maximum of three months and so that the total period does not exceed 12 months, PCC(S)A 2000 Sch.1 para.9ZD;

(c)  extended the period (so that the total period does not exceed 12 months) or impose a fine of not exceeding £2,500, PCC(S)A 2000 Sch.1 para.6A.

The court which deals with the offender, must have regard to the circumstances of his referral back to the court, and the extent to which he has complied with the contract if one has been made. The court may decline to revoke the referral order, or may declare that the referral order is discharged, PCC(S)A 2000 Sch.1 para.5(5)(b).

**Commission of offence during referral period**  If the offender is convicted of an offence committed after the referral order was made, the court may:

(a)  revoke the referral order and deal with the offender in any manner in which the court which made the order, could have dealt with him, PCC(S)A 2000 Sch.1 para.14;

(b)  extend the compliance period if it is satisfied that there are exceptional circumstances which indicate that extending his compliance period is likely to help prevent further re-offending by him. The compliance period must not be extended so as to exceed a total period of 12 months, PCC(S)A 2000 Sch.1 para.10.

# REMITTING A JUVENILE

## PCC(S)A 2000 ss.8–10

*References: Current Sentencing Practice H2-1650; Archbold 5A-228*

Where a child or young person is found guilty before the Crown Court of an offence other than homicide, the Crown Court must remit the offender to the youth court, unless it is satisfied that it would be undesirable to do so, PCC(S)A 2000 s.8(1) and (2).

It will be undesirable to remit if the judge who presided over the trial will be better informed as to the facts and circumstances, or if there would be a risk of disparity if defendants were sentenced by different courts, or if there would be delay, duplication of proceedings or unnecessary expense, see for example, *Lewis* (1984) 6 Cr.App.R. (S.) 44.

Where a child or young person is found guilty before a magistrates' court which is not a youth court, the magistrates' court must remit the offender to a youth court unless it proposes to deal with the offender by means of a discharge, a fine, or an order binding over his parents or guardians to take proper care and exercise proper control, or where the mandatory referral conditions for a referral order apply (see **REFERRAL ORDERS**, p.251), PCC(S)A 2000 s.8(2) and (6)–(8).

# REPARATION ORDERS

## PCC(S)A 2000 S.73 AND 74

*References: Archbold 5A-955*

### General

**Outline of the order**   A reparation order is an order requiring an offender to make reparation for the offence otherwise than by the payment of compensation, PCC(S)A 2000 s.73(3).

**Length of the order**   The reparation must be made within three months of the making of the order, PCC(S)A 2000 s.74(8).

### Making the Order

**Availability**   A reparation order may be made against an offender under 18, PCC(S)A 2000 s.73(1).

The order may not be made without the consent of the person or persons to whom reparation is to be made, PCC(S)A 2000 s.74(1).

The consent of the offender is not required.

**Need for a probation report**   The court must obtain and consider a probation report as to the type of work that is suitable for the offender and the attitude of the victim or victims to the requirements proposed to be included in the order, PCC(S)A 2000 s.73(5).

**Contents of the order**   Reparation may me ordered to be made to either a person or persons specified in the order, or the community at large, PCC(S) A 2000 s.73(1).

The order may not require the offender to work for more than 24 hours in aggregate, PCC(S)A 2000 s.74(1).

The requirements of the order must be commensurate with the seriousness of the offence, and be compatible with religious beliefs and work/educational commitments, PCC(S)A 2000 s.74(2) and (3).

**Duty to give reasons when not making an order**   Where the court does not make, when it could, a reparation order, it must explain why it has so decided, PCC(S)A 2000 s.73(8).

### Combining Sentences

A court may not make a reparation order in respect of the offender if it proposes to impose:

(a)   a custodial sentence, PCC(S)A 2000 s.73(4)(a);

(b)   a youth rehabilitation order, PCC(S)A 2000 s.73(4)(b);

(c)   a referral order, PCC(S)A 2000 s.19(1)–(4)(c).

A court may not make a reparation order in respect of the offender at a time when a youth rehabilitation order is in force in respect of him unless it revokes the youth rehabilitation order, PCC(S)A 2000 s.73(4A).

# RESTITUTION ORDER

## PCC(S)A 2000 s.148 AND 149

*References: Current Sentencing Practice C1-8000; Archbold 5A-457*

### Availability

The court has power to make a restitution order if goods have been stolen and the offender has been convicted of any offence with reference to the theft (whether or not stealing is the gist of the offence). The power also exists where the offender is convicted of another offence but asks for such an offence to be taken into consideration, PCC(S)A 2000 s.148(1).

### Test to apply

The court may not make a restitution order unless all the relevant facts are admitted or appear from the evidence given at the trial and the witness statements or depositions. The court may not embark on its own investigations with a view to making a restitution order, PCC(S)A 2000 s.148(5).

### Powers under the order

The court may:

(a) order the offender to restore the stolen goods to any person entitled to recover them from him;
(b) on application from a person entitled to recover any goods directly or indirectly representing stolen goods (i.e. the proceeds of disposal or realisation in whole or in part), the court may order those goods to be delivered or transferred to the applicant;
(c) the court may order a sum not exceeding the value of the stolen goods shall be paid out of any money of the person convicted which was taken out of his possession on his apprehension, to any person who, if the goods were in the possession of the person convicted, would be entitled to recover from him, PCC(S)A 2000 s.148(2).

*"Stolen"* for this purpose includes obtained by deception or blackmail, or by fraud contrary to the Fraud Act 2006.

### Consequential victims

If any third party has possession of the stolen goods, the court may order him to restore them to the person entitled to recover them. If the third party has bought the goods in good faith from the person convicted, or lent money to him on the security of them, the court may order payment to that person of a sum not exceeding the purchase price of the goods, or the amount of the loan, out of money taken out of the possession of the offender on his apprehension, PCC(S)A 2000 s.148(4).

[259]

## Breach

Failure to comply with a restitution order is a contempt of court; the statute does not make any order provision dealing with failure to comply.

# RESTRAINING ORDERS

Protection from Harrassment Act 1997 ss.5, 5A

*References: Current Sentencing Practice C2-2850; Archbold 19-357b*

## Post-Conviction Orders

**Availability**   Where a court is sentencing an offender for any offence of which he has been convicted, irrespective of the date on which the offence was committed, the court may make a restraining order, PHA 1997 s.5(1).

A person who is unfit to plead but has been found to have done the act alleged may not be made subject to a restraining order; such a finding is neither a conviction nor an acquittal, *Chinegwundoh* [2015] EWCA Crim 109; [2015] 1 Cr.App.R. (S.) 61.

**Contents of the order**   The order may prohibit the defendant from doing anything described in the order, PHA 1997 s.5(1). This can include, for instance, a requirement to notify the police of entry into a particular county 48 hours prior to doing so, *Conlon* [2017] EWCA Crim 2450; [2018] 1 Cr.App.R. (S.) 38.

**Test to apply**   The order may only be made for the purpose of protecting the victim of the offence, or any other person mentioned in the order, from conduct which amounts to harassment, or will cause fear of violence, PHA 1997 s.5(2). This means that there must be an identifiable victim.

Harassing a person includes alarming the person or causing the person distress, PHA 1997 s.7(2).

*"Conduct"* includes speech, PHA 1997 s.7(4).

**Evidence**   Both the prosecution and the defence may lead, as further evidence, any evidence that would be admissible in proceedings for an injunction under s.3 of the Act, PHA 1997 s.5(3A).

**Length of the order**   The order may be for a specified period or until further order, PHA 1997 s.5(3).

**Wording of the order**   As with all other behaviour/preventive orders, the wording of the order must be specific, clear, and capable of being understood.

**Varying or discharging the order**   The prosecutor, the defendant or any other person mentioned in the order may apply to the court which made the order for it to be varied or discharged by a further order. Any person mentioned in the order is entitled to be heard on the hearing of an application to vary or discharge the order, PHA 1997 s.5(4).

[261]

Any person mentioned in the order is entitled to be heard on the hearing of an application to vary the order, PHA 1997 s.5(4A).

## Orders made following an Acquittal

**Availability**    A court may make a restraining order following an acquittal, PHA 1997 s.5A(1).

A person who is unfit to plead but has been found to have done the act alleged may not be made subject to a restraining order; such a finding is neither a conviction nor an acquittal, *Chinegwundoh* [2015] EWCA Crim 109; [2015] 1 Cr.App.R. (S.) 61.

**Test to apply**    An order may be made where the court considers it necessary to protect a person from harassment by the defendant, PHA 1997 s.5A(1).

It is necessary to find that the defendant is likely to pursue a course of conduct which amounts to harassment within the meaning of s.1 of the PHA 1997. Pursuit of a course of conduct requires intention, *Smith* [2012] EWCA Crim 2566; [2013] 2 Cr.App.R. (S.) 28.

Harassing a person includes alarming the person or causing the person distress, PHA 1997 s.7(2).

*"Conduct"* includes speech, PHA 1997 s.7(4).

A *"course of conduct"* must involve at least two occasions in relation to a single person, and at least once each, in relation two or more persons, PHA 1997 s.7(3).

**Evidence**    Both the prosecution and the defence may lead, as further evidence, any evidence that would be admissible in proceedings for an injunction under s.3 of the Act, PHA 1997 ss.5(3A) and 5A(2).

**Length of the order**    The order may be for a specified period or until further order, PHA 1997 ss.5(3) and 5A(2).

**Wording of the order**    As with all other behaviour/preventive orders, the wording of the order must be specific, clear, and capable of being understood.

**Varying or discharging the order**    The prosecutor, the defendant or any other person mentioned in the order may apply to the court which made the order for it to be varied or discharged by a further order. Any person mentioned in the order is entitled to be heard on the hearing of an application to vary or discharge the order, PHA 1997 ss.5(4) and 5A(2).

Any person mentioned in the order is entitled to be heard on the hearing of an application to vary the order, PHA 1997 ss.5(4A) and 5A(2).

**Appeals**    Where the Court of Appeal quashes a conviction, it may remit the case to the Crown Court to consider whether to make a restraining order, PHA 1997 s.5A(3).

Where the Crown Court allows an appeal against a conviction in the magistrates' court, the Crown Court may make a restraining order, PHA 1997 s.5A(4).

A person made subject to a restraining order on acquittal has the same right of appeal as if he had been convicted of an offence and the order had been made under s.5, PHA 1997 s.5A(5).

## Breach

A breach of an order under s.5 or 5A is punishable with imprisonment not exceeding five years, or a fine or both, PHA 1997 s.5(5) and (6) and 5A(2).

There is a defence if the act of doing something prohibited under the order was done with a reasonable excuse, PHA 1997 s.5(5).

## European Protection Orders (SI 2014/3300)

The order enables magistrates' courts and, in certain circumstances, the Crown Court the power to make a European protection order ("EPO"). An EPO may impose prohibitions or restrictions upon an individual and may be made after an application by an individual who is "*protected*" by a court order in England and Wales (most likely to be a restraining order) and who resides or is going to reside in another member state. The EPO requests that the relevant member state recognises the protection order.

The SI also makes provision for the recognition of an EPO made in another member state, which involves a magistrates' court imposing a restraining order under s.5 of the Protection from Harassment Act 1997 which replicates the provisions contained in the EPO as closely as possible (see reg.13).

# RESTRICTION ORDERS (MENTAL HEALTH ACT 1983)

MENTAL HEALTH ACT 1983 s.41

*References: Current Sentencing Practice E1; Archbold 5A-1200*

## Availability

A restriction order may be made only in conjunction with a hospital order, MHA 1983 s.41(1). (See **HOSPITAL ORDER**, p.183.)

## Oral evidence

A restriction order may be made only if at least one of the medical practitioners whose evidence has been taken into account has given evidence orally before the court, MHA 1983 s.41(2). Evidence may not be received by telephone, *Clark* [2015] EWCA Crim 2192; [2016] 1 Cr.App.R. (S.) 52.

## Test to apply

The Crown Court may make a restriction order if it makes a hospital order in respect of the offender and it appears to the court, having regard to the nature of the offence, the antecedents of the offender and the risk of his committing further offences if set at large, that is necessary for the protection of the public from serious harm to do so, MHA 1983 s.41(1).

In deciding whether to make a restriction order, the court is concerned with the seriousness of the harm which will result if the offender reoffends, rather than with the risk of reoffending.

The seriousness of the offence committed by the offender is not necessarily important for this purpose. An offender convicted of a relatively minor offence may properly be subjected to a restriction order if he suffers from a mental disorder and is dangerous. An offender convicted of a serious offence should not be subjected to a restriction order unless he is likely to commit further offences which will involve a risk of serious harm to the public.

It is not necessary that the offender should be dangerous to the public as a whole; it is sufficient if he is dangerous to a particular section of the public, or to a particular person.

The harm to which the public would be exposed if the offender were at large need not necessarily be personal injury.

It is the responsibility of the court, and not that of the medical witnesses, to determine whether a restriction order is appropriate.

# RETRIAL

## CRIMINAL APPEAL ACT 1968 SCH.2 PARA.2

### General

Where a person is convicted after a retrial ordered by the Court of Appeal (Criminal Division) under the CAA 1968 s.7, the court may pass in respect of the offence any sentence authorised by law, not being a sentence of greater severity than that passed on the original conviction, CAA 1968 Sch.2 para.2(1).

The court may pass any sentence passed in respect of that offence on the original conviction notwithstanding that, on the date of the conviction on retrial, the offender has ceased to be of an age at which such a sentence could otherwise be passed, CAA 1968 Sch.2 para.2(2).

### Approach

When sentencing after a retrial, the correct approach is to assess the offender's culpability on the basis of the evidence in the retrial and in accordance with the sentencing guidelines. The earlier trial and sentence should not be considered at that stage. The only relevance of the previous sentence was that the sentence imposed on the retrial could not be more severe than the first, *Bett* [2017] EWCA Crim 1909; [2018] 1 Cr.App.R. (S.) 29.

### Start date of sentence

If the offender is sentenced to imprisonment or other detention, the sentence begins to run from the time when a similar sentence passed at the original trial would have begun to run, CAA 1968 Sch.2 para.2(3).

### Calculating time to be served

In computing the term of the sentence or the period for which the offender may be detained, any time before his conviction on retrial which would have been disregarded in computing that term or period if the sentence had been passed at the original trial and the original conviction had not been quashed, and any time during which he was released on bail under s.8(2) of the CAA 1968, is disregarded, CAA 1968 Sch.2 para.2(3).

### Credit for time on remand

The judge should make appropriate orders in respect of any time spent on bail subject to a qualifying curfew condition, in relation to any sentence imposed on conviction on retrial as if they had been imposed on the original conviction, CAA 1968 Sch.2 para.2(4).

These provisions do not appear to apply to a *venire de novo* ordered by the Court of Appeal.

[267]

# SENTENCING GUIDELINES

CORONERS AND JUSTICE ACT 2009 s.125

*References: Current Sentencing Practice H5; Archbold 5A-19*

## General

**Draft Guidelines**   A court should not have regard to draft guidelines issued by the Council as a preliminary stage in the process of consultation, *Abbas* [2008] EWCA Crim 1897. Such draft guidance is of interest as part of the background which judges may wish to bear in mind, but the proposals do not constitute guidance and do not provide any justifiable basis for interfering with a sentencing decision in which the judge had applied the existing guidance of the court, *Valentas* [2010] EWCA Crim 200; [2010] 2 Cr.App.R. (S.) 73. This point was re-stated in *Connelly* [2017] EWCA Crim 1569; [2018] 1 Cr.App.R. (S.) 19.

**Guidelines not in force at date of sentence**   Where guidelines are expressly stated to apply from a certain date, they could not be said to affect sentencing practice prior to that date, *Boakye* [2012] EWCA Crim 838; [2013] 1 Cr.App.R. (S.) 2. In *Hodgkins* [2016] EWCA Crim 360; [2016] 1 Cr.App.R. (S.) 14, the court applied *Boakye* and stated that it was unhelpful to refer to the Theft guideline which was not in force at the date of the offender's sentencing hearing.

**Guideline in force after date of offence**   Where the offence is committed pre-publication, but the guideline is in force by the time of the sentencing hearing, the guideline is applied, *Bao* [2007] EWCA Crim 2781; [2008] 2 Cr.App.R. (S.) 10.

**Guideline published after offence committed**   Where a definitive guideline is published after an offence is committed, but before the offender is sentenced, there is no breach of art.7 of the European Convention on Human Rights if the sentencing judge takes the guideline into account.

**No guideline for specific offence**   When a case concerns an offence for which there is no guideline, the judge may well consider an analogous guideline, *Lewis* [2012] EWCA Crim 1071; [2013] 1 Cr.App.R. (S.) 23.

**Applying current guidelines to historic offences**   As a general rule, sentencing for historic offences is governed by current sentencing practice, *Bell* [2015] EWCA Crim 1426; [2016] 1 Cr.App.R. (S.) 16. However, caution should be exercised in applying current guidelines for modern equivalent offences to historic offences, *AG's Ref (No.75 of 2015) (L)* [2015] EWCA Crim 2116; [2016] 1 Cr.App.R. (S.) 61.

Reference should also be made to the decision in *Forbes* [2016] EWCA Crim 1388; [2017] 1 W.L.R. 53 in which the LCJ gave guidance as to the sentencing of historical offences.

**Making findings of fact**   When assessing roles (particularly under the drug offences guidelines) judges are encouraged to focus on the factors set out in detail in the guidelines and to make factual findings which clearly indicate how those factors apply in the particular case before them, *Martin* [2018] EWCA Crim 1569.

### Offence Committed on/after 6 April 2010

**Duty to follow**    Where the offence was committed on or after 6 April 2010 and a guideline applies, the court must, in sentencing an offender or exercising any other function relating to the sentencing of offenders, follow any sentencing guidelines which are relevant to the offender's case, unless the court is satisfied that it would be contrary to the interests of justice to do so, CJA 2009 s.125(1).

**Applies to all guidelines**    For this purpose, "*guidelines*" include definitive guidelines published by the Sentencing Guidelines Council which were in effect on 5 April 2010 and guidelines issued by the Sentencing Council under s.121 of the CJA 2009, SI 2010/816 art.7(1).

**Extent of the duty**    The duty to follow any sentencing guidelines which are relevant to the offender's case includes, in all cases:

(a)   a duty to impose on the offender, in accordance with the offence-specific guidelines, a sentence which is within the offence range, CJA 2009 s.125(3)(a);

(b)   where the offence-specific guidelines describe categories of case, a duty to decide which of the categories most resembles the offender's case in order to identify the sentencing starting point in the offence range, CJA 2009 s.125(3)(b).

However, there is no duty to impose a sentence which is within the category range, where the guideline specifies a category range, CJA 2009 s.125(3).

The duty to identify the category range does not apply if the court is of the opinion that, for the purpose of identifying the sentence within the offence range which is the appropriate starting point, none of the categories sufficiently resembles the offender's case, CJA 2009 s.125(4).

**Reductions in sentence**    The duty to pass a sentence within the offence range is subject to the reduction in sentences for:

(a)   guilty pleas;

(b)   ss.73 and 74 of the SOCPA 2005 (reduction or review of sentence in respect of assistance by defendants);

(c)   any other rule of law by virtue of which an offender may receive a discounted sentence in consequence of assistance given (or offered to be given) by the offender to the prosecutor or investigator of an offence; and

(d)   any rule of law as to the totality of sentences, CJA 2009 s.125(5).

**Other statutory duties**    The duty to follow the guidelines is subject to statutory provisions:

(a)   restricting the imposition of community sentences;

(b)   restricting the imposition of discretionary custodial sentences;

(c)   requiring that a custodial sentence must be for shortest term commensurate with seriousness of offence; and

(d)   requiring that a fine must reflect seriousness of offence, CJA 2009 s.125(6).

The duty to follow the guidelines is also subject to:

a)   the duty to have regard to the Criminal Justice Act 2003 Sch.21, in fixing the minimum term to be served by a person convicted of murder; and

b)   statutory provisions fixing minimum sentences to be served for certain offences under the Firearms Act 1968 or the Violent Crime Reduction Act 2006, or for repeated drug trafficking and burglary offences under the PCC(S)A 2000.

**Mentally disordered defendants**   The duty to follow the guideline does not restrict any power which enables a court to deal with a mentally disordered offender in the manner it considers to be most appropriate in all the circumstances, CJA 2009 s.125(7).

**Extended sentences**   The duty to impose a sentence within the offence range does not restrict the power of the court to impose an extended sentence. The duty to follow the guidelines does apply where the court is determining the notional determinate sentence for the purpose of determining the appropriate custodial term of an extended sentence.

**Giving reasons**   In giving reasons for the sentence imposed, the court must identify any definitive sentencing guidelines relevant to the offender's case and explain how the court discharged any duty imposed on it by s.125 of the CJA 2009, and where the court did not follow any such guidelines because it was of the opinion that it would be contrary to the interests of justice to do so, state why it was of that opinion, CJA 2003 s.174(6).

### Offence Committed Before 6 April 2010

**Duty to have regard**   If the offence was committed before 6 April 2010, and the Sentencing Guidelines Council or Sentencing Council has issued a *"definitive guideline"*, the court must *"have regard to"* any definitive guidelines which are relevant to the case, CJA 2009 s.136 and Sch.22 para.27 and SI 2010/886 as amended by SI 2011/722.

**Departing from guidelines**   The court has a discretion to depart from a guideline in any case where it considers it to be appropriate or just to do so, provided that the court can give reasons for the departure.

If the court decides that the appropriate sentence in a particular case is not one which is indicated by a relevant definitive guideline, the court must state its reasons for deciding that the appropriate sentence is of a different kind or outside the range of sentences indicated by the guideline. Where the court imposes a sentence which is consistent with a *"definitive guideline"*, the general duty imposed by CJA 2003 s.174(1)(a) to state the reasons for deciding on the sentence passed appears to include by implication a duty to refer to the guideline to which the court has had regard.

# SERIOUS CRIME PREVENTION ORDERS

Serious Crime Prevention Order Act 2007 ss.1–43

*References: Current Sentencing Practice C2-4325; Archbold 5A-862*

## Availability

**General**   An SCPO is available:

(a)   for an offence committed on or after 6 April 2008;
(b)   for an offence committed before 6 April 2008, where the conviction and sentence occur after that date.

However, an SCPO is not available where the conviction occurs before 6 April 2008 but where the sentence is imposed after that date, SCA 2007 Sch.13 para.2.

An order may be made only in addition to the sentence is respect of the offence concerned, or in addition to a conditional discharge or absolute discharge, SCA 2007 s.19(7).

A serious crime prevention order may be made against an individual, a body corporate, a partnership or an unincorporated association, SCA 2007 s.5.

**Offences**   An SCPO is available for a *"serious offence"*, that is one specified in SCA 2007 Sch.1 (see p.353).

Additionally, the court may treat any offence as if it were a specified offence if it considers the offence to be *"sufficiently serious"* to be treated as if it were a specified offence, SCA 2007 s.2(2)(b).

## The Hearing

**Application**   A serious crime prevention order may be made only on an application by the Director of Public Prosecutions, the Director of Revenue and Customs prosecutions, or the Director of the Serious Fraud Office, SCA 2007 s.8.

**Right of others to be heard**   The Crown Court must give an opportunity to a person other than the offender to make representations, if that person applies to do so, if it considers that the making of a serious crime prevention order would be likely to have a significant adverse effect on that person, SCA 2007 s.9(4).

**Nature of the proceedings**   Proceedings in the Crown Court in relation to serious crime prevention orders are civil proceedings and the standard of proof to be applied is the civil standard of proof. The court is not restricted to considering evidence that would have been admissible in the criminal proceedings in which the person concerned was convicted and may adjourn any proceedings in relation to a serious crime prevention order even after sentencing the person concerned.

**Extent of the order**   A serious crime prevention order is binding on a person only if he is present or represented at the proceedings at which the order is made, or a notice setting out the terms of the order has been served on him, SCA 2007 s.9(4).

## Making the Order

**Power**   The Crown Court may make a serious crime prevention order where person aged 18 or over is convicted of a "*serious offence*" or has been convicted of a "*serious offence*" by a magistrates court and committed to the Crown Court to be dealt with for the offence, SCA 2007 s.19(1).

**Test to apply**   The court may make an order where it has reasonable grounds to believe that the order would protect the public by preventing, restricting or disrupting involvement by the person in serious crime in England and Wales, SCA 2007 s.19(2).

## Contents of the Order

**Prohibitions and requirements**   The order may contain such prohibitions, restrictions or requirements as the court considers appropriate for protecting the public by preventing, restricting or disrupting involvement by the person concerned in serious crime, SCA 2007 s.19(5).

Examples of prohibitions, restrictions or requirements that may be imposed on individuals include prohibitions or restrictions on, or requirements in relation to:

(a)   an individual's financial, property or business dealings or holdings;
(b)   an individual's working arrangements;
(c)   the means by which an individual communicates or associates with others, or the persons with whom he communicates or associates;
(d)   the premises to which an individual has access;
(e)   the use of any premises or item by an individual;
(f)   an individual's travel (whether within the UK, between the UK and other places or otherwise), SCA 2007 s.5(3).

**Financial Reporting Orders**   These were repealed in 2015 and consolidated into the SCPO.

**Must specify start-date**   A serious crime prevention order must specify when it is to come into force and when it is to cease to be in force, SCA 2007 s.16(1).

**Length of the order**   An order may not be in force for more than five years beginning with the date on which it comes into force. Different provisions of the order may come into force or cease to be in force on different dates, SCA 2007 s.16(2) and (3).

## Effect of an Order

A serious crime prevention order may not require a person to answer questions or provide information orally or to answer any privileged question, or provide any privileged information or documents. An order may not require a person to produce any excluded material (Police and Criminal Evidence Act 1984 s.11). An order may not require a person to produce information or documents in respect of which he owes an obligation of confidence by virtue of carrying on a banking business unless the person to whom the obligation of confidence is owed consents to the disclosure or production or the order contains a requirement to disclose information or produce documents of this kind. An order may not require a person to answer any question, provide any information or produce any document if the disclosure concerned is prohibited under any other enactment, SCA 2007 s.11-14.

## Varying Orders

**Upon conviction**   Where a person, subject to an SCPO:

(a)   has been convicted by or before a magistrates' court of having committed a serious offence in England and Wales and has been committed to the Crown Court to be dealt with; or

(b)   has been convicted by or before the Crown Court of having committed a serious offence in England and Wales, the Crown Court may vary the order if the court has reasonable grounds to believe that the terms of the order as varied would protect the public by preventing, restricting or disrupting involvement by the person in serious crime in England and Wales, in addition to dealing with the person in relation to the offence, SCA 2007 s.20(1) and (2).

A variation on conviction may only be made in addition to a sentence or imposition of a discharge, SCA 2007 s.20(6).

**Upon breach**   Where a person:

(a)   has been convicted by or before a magistrates' court of having committed an offence under SCA 2007 s.25 in relation to an SCPO and has been committed to the Crown Court to be dealt with; or

(b)   has been convicted by or before the Crown Court of having committed an offence under s.25 in relation to an SCPO, the court may, in addition to imposing a sentence or a discharge in respect of the breach, vary or replace the order if it has reasonable grounds to believe that the terms of the order as varied, or the new order, would protect the public by preventing, restricting or disrupting involvement by the person in serious crime in England and Wales. SCA 2007 s.21(1) and (2).

The Crown Court may vary a serious crime prevention order which has been made by the High Court, SCA 2007 s.22(1).

## Extending Orders Where Person Charged with Serious Offence/Breach

Where a person is charged with a serious offence or an offence of breaching an SCPO, the authority may apply to the court to vary the order until:

(a)   following the conviction for the offence, the order is varied or a new order imposed;

(b)   the person is acquitted;

(c)   the charge is withdrawn; or

(d)   the proceedings are discontinued, SCA 2007 s.22E(4).

## Appeals

**Right to appeal**  A person who is subject to a serious crime prevention order, or an authority who has applied for an order, may appeal to the Court of Appeal in relation to a decision in relation to a serious crime prevention order. A person who has been given the opportunity to make representations in respect of an order may also appeal to the Court of Appeal, SCA 2007 s.24.

# SEXUAL HARM PREVENTION ORDERS

SEXUAL OFFENCES ACT 2003 ss.103A–103K

*References: Current Sentencing Practice C2-1250; Archbold 20-313*

### General

Note that by contrast to the SOPO regime, the SHPO regime employs a lower test for imposition and defines a child as a person under 18, not under 16; see *Parsons*; *Morgan* [2017] EWCA Crim 2163; [2018] 1 Cr.App. R. (S.) 43 for details.

**Availability**  A court may make an order where it deals with the defendant in respect of:

(a) an offence listed in SOA 2003 Sch.3 or 5;
(b) a finding that the defendant is not guilty of an offence listed in Sch.3 or 5 by reason of insanity; or
(c) a finding that the defendant is under a disability and has done the act charged against the him in respect of an offence listed in Sch.3 or 5, SOA 2003 s.103A(1) and (2).

Schedule 3 is to be read as though any condition subject to which an offence is so listed that relates:

(a) to the way in which the defendant is dealt with in respect of an offence so listed or a relevant finding (as defined by s.132(9)); or
(b) to the age of any person, is omitted, SOA 2003 s.103B(9).

**Test**  The court must be satisfied that the order is necessary for the purpose of:

(i) protecting the public or any particular members of the public from sexual harm from the defendant; or
(ii) protecting children or vulnerable adults generally, or any particular children or vulnerable adults, from sexual harm from the defendant outside the UK, SOA 2003 s.103A(2)(b).

**Defendant subject to earlier order**  Where a court makes a sexual harm prevention order in relation to a person who is already subject to such an order, the earlier order ceases to have effect, SOA 2003 s.103C(6).

### Contents of the Order

**Prohibitions**  A sexual harm prevention order prohibits the defendant from doing anything described in the order, SOA 2003 s.103C(1). Any conflict between the SHPO and condition upon release on licence should be avoided, *McLellan*; *Bingley* [2017] EWCA Crim 1464; [2018] 1 Cr.App.R. (S.) 18. Nor should there be a conflict with the notification regime, *Sokolowski* [2017] EWCA Crim 1903; [2018] 1 Cr.App.R. (S.) 30.

As to the contents of prohibitions, including issues concerning blanket bans on internet useage, age, risk management software, cloud storage and encryption, see *Parsons*; *Morgan* [2017] EWCA Crim 2163; [2018] 1 Cr.App.R. (S.) 43.

Orders should not be "*rubber-stamped*" Prohibitions should be proportionate and necessary in the individual case. It is insufficient for the prosecution to assert that the prohibitions are necessary on a "*safety first*" approach, *Sokolowski* [2017] EWCA Crim 1903; [2018] 1 Cr.App.R. (S.) 30.

**Length of prohibitions**   The order may specify that some of its prohibitions have effect until further order and some for a fixed period. Different periods for different prohibitions may be specified, SOA 2003 s.103C(3).

**Test for prohibitions**   Prohibitions must be necessary for the purpose of:

- (a)   protecting the public or any particular members of the public from sexual harm from the defendant; or
- (b)   protecting children or vulnerable adults generally, or any particular children or vulnerable adults, from sexual harm from the defendant outside the UK, SOA 2003 s.103C(4).

**Length of the order:**   A prohibition may have effect:

- (a)   for a fixed period of at least five years; or
- (b)   until further order, SOA 2003 s.103C(2).

**Foreign travel prohibition**   A prohibition on foreign travel contained in an order must be for a fixed period of not more than five years, SOA 2003 s.103D(1). A prohibition on foreign travel is one that prohibits travel to any country outside the UK, to any country outside the UK as specified or other than specified. Where an order prohibits travel to any country outside the UK, the order must also require the defendant to surrender all his passports, SOA 2003 s.103D(1)–(4).

**Variations, Renewals and Discharges**

**Who may apply**   (a) the defendant, (b) the chief officer of police for the area in which the defendant resides, or (c) a chief officer of police who believes that the defendant is in, or is intending to come to that officer's police area, may apply to a court to vary, discharge or renew an order, SOA 2003 s.103E(1) and (2).

**Renewing or varying an order**   An order may be renewed or varied so as to impose additional prohibitions on the defendant only if it is necessary to do so for the purpose of:

- (a)   protecting the public or any particular members of the public from sexual harm from the defendant; or
- (b)   protecting children or vulnerable adults generally, or any particular children or vulnerable adults, from sexual harm from the defendant outside the UK.

Any renewed or varied order may contain only such prohibitions as are necessary for this purpose, SOA 2003 s.103E(5).

**Discharging an order**   The court must not discharge an order before the end of five years beginning with the day on which the order was made, without the consent of the defendant and:

(a) where the application is made by a chief officer of police, that chief officer; or

(b) in any other case, the chief officer of police for the area in which the defendant resides, SOA 2003 s.103E(7).

## Interim Orders

An interim order is not available in post-conviction cases, SOA 2003 s.103F.

## Notification Requirements

**Subject to notification requirements**   Where a sexual harm prevention order is made in respect of a defendant who was subject to notification requirements under SOA 2003 immediately before the making of the order, and the defendant would cease to be subject to those notification requirements while the order has effect, the defendant remains subject to the notification requirements, SOA 2003 ss.80(2) and 103G(1).

**Length of SHPO**   As to the existence of any correlation between the length of the notification requirements that applied automatically on conviction and the length of any SHPO imposed:

(i)   there is no requirement of principle that the duration of an SHPO should not exceed the duration of the applicable notification requirements;

(ii)   as with any sentence, an SHPO should not be made for longer than was necessary;

(iii)   an SHPO should not be made for an indefinite period (rather than a fixed period) unless the court was satisfied of the need to do so. An indefinite SHPO should not be made without careful consideration or as a default option. Ordinarily, as a matter of good practice, a court should explain, however briefly, the justification for making an indefinite SHPO, although there were cases where that justification would be obvious; and

(iv)   all concerned should be alert to the fact that the effect of an SHPO of longer duration than the statutory notification requirements had the effect of extending the operation of those notification requirements; an indefinite SHPO would result in indefinite notification requirements. Notification requirements had practical, consequences for those subject to them and inadvertent extension was to be avoided, *McLellan*; *Bingley* [2017] EWCA Crim 1464; [2018] 1 Cr.App.R. (S.) 18.

**Not subject to notification requirements**   Where a sexual harm prevention order is made in respect of a defendant who was not subject to notification requirements under SOA 2003 immediately before the making of the order, the order causes the defendant to become subject to the notification requirements under SOA 2003 from the making of the order until the order (as renewed from time to time) ceases to have effect, SOA 2003 ss.80(2) and 103G(2).

## Appeals

**Against the making of an order**   A defendant may appeal against the making of an order "*as if the order were a sentence*", SOA 2003 s.103H(1).

**Against the variation etc. of an order**  A defendant may appeal against the variation, renewal or discharge, or the refusal to make such an order:

(a)  where the application for such an order was made to the Crown Court, to the Court of Appeal; and

(b)  in any other case, to the Crown Court, SOA 2003 s.103H(3).

## Breach

**Offence**  A person who, without reasonable excuse, does anything prohibited by a sexual harm prevention order, commits an offence. This includes a requirement to surrender all passports where a foreign travel prohibition prohibiting travel to any country outside the UK is included in an order, SOA 2003 s.103I(1) and (2).

**Maximum sentence**  Five years' imprisonment, SOA 2003 s.103I(3).

**Can't impose conditional discharge**  Where someone is sentenced for breaching their SHPO, the court may not impose a conditional discharge, SOA 2003 s.103I(4).

# SEXUAL OFFENDERS—NOTIFICATION REQUIREMENTS

SEXUAL OFFENCES ACT 2003 s.80

*References: Current Sentencing Practice H4-2000; Archbold 20-281*

## General

**Nature of the obligation**    Notification is not part of a sentence, *Longworth* [2006] UKHL 1; [2006] 2 Cr.App.R. (S.) 62 (p.401). It can therefore not be appealed.

**Applicability**    A person is subject to the notification requirements of the SOA 2003 if:

(a)  he is convicted of an offence listed in Sch.3;
(b)  he is found not guilty of such an offence by reason of insanity;
(c)  he is found to be under a disability and to have done the act charged against him in respect of such an offence; or
(d)  he is cautioned in respect of such an offence, SOA 2003 s.80(1).

**The Periods of Notification: the periods during which the offender is liable to the notification requirements are as follows:**

| | |
|---|---|
| A person who, in respect of the offence, is or has been sentenced to imprisonment for life or for a term of 30 months or more | An indefinite period beginning with the relevant date |
| A person who, in respect of the offence or finding, is or has been admitted to a hospital subject to a restriction order | An indefinite period beginning with that date |
| A person who, in respect of the offence, is or has been sentenced to imprisonment for a term of more than 6 months but less than 30 months | 10 years beginning with that date |
| A person who, in respect of the offence, is or has been sentenced to imprisonment for a term of 6 months or less | 7 years beginning with that date |
| A person who, in respect of the offence or finding, is or has been admitted to a hospital without being subject to a restriction order | 7 years beginning with that date |
| A person who has been cautioned | 2 years beginning with that date |
| A person in whose case an order for conditional discharge is made in respect of the offence | The period of conditional discharge |
| A person of any other description | 5 years beginning with the relevant date |

**Those under 18**   Where a person is *under 18* on the relevant date, the determinate periods are one half of those specified as fixed length periods, SOA 2003 s.82(1) and (2).

Where an offender under 18 is convicted of an offence within the scope of Sch.3 and sentenced in a manner which results in an obligation to notify, the court may direct that obligation shall be treated as an obligation of the parent, SOA 2003 s.89(1).

**Suspended sentence order**   The length of the notification period is determined by the length of the period of imprisonment (or detention) that is subject to the suspended sentence order, CJA 2003 s.189(6).

**Detention and training orders**   If an offender under 18 is sentenced to a detention and training order, the relevant period for the purpose of determining his liability to the notification requirements is the custodial part of the order (normally half of the term of the order). A person sentenced to a detention and training order where the total order is more than 12 months is liable to the requirements for a period of five years; if the total order is for any period not exceeding 12 months, the period of liability is three and a half years, SOA 2003 s.131.

**Community orders**   Where a community order with an unpaid work requirement is imposed (which states that the unpaid work must be completed within 12 months), notwithstanding the fact that the offender may complete the unpaid work sooner, notification requirements will apply as the order was made for 12 months, *Davison* [2008] EWCA Crim 2795; [2009] 2 Cr.App.R. (S.) 13.

**Absolute discharge**   An absolute discharge does not attract notification requirements. However in such cases the offender is required to comply with the notification requirements from the date of conviction to the date of the imposition of the absolute discharge, *Home Office Guidance on Part 2 of the Sexual Offences Act 2003* (November 2016) p.11.

**Sexual Harm Prevention Orders**   For the effect of an SHPO on existing notificaton requirements, see **Sexual Harm Prevention Orders** p.277.

**Start date**   Notification begins on the date of the conviction (or finding etc.), SOA 2003 s.82(1) and (6).

**Consecutive terms**   Where the offender is sentenced to terms which are wholly or partly consecutive, the table applies to the effective length of the aggregate terms, SOA 2003 s.82(3) and (4).

**Explaining the Order**

The only function of the court is to state that the offender has been convicted of a sexual offence to which the SOA 2003 applies, and to certify those facts.

This is not a mandatory obligation, and failure to make a statement does not affect the offender's liability under the Act. The court is not obliged to inform the offender of his liability, or of the period during which it will continue.

The obligation to notify imposed by the SOA 2003 is not a relevant consideration in determining the sentence for the offence.

## Reviews of Indefinite Notification Requirements

A person subject to indefinite notification requirements may apply for a review to the relevant chief officer of police with an appeal from that decision to the magistrates' court. No application may be made until after 15 years from the person's first notification (eight years for a person aged under 18), SI 2012/1883.

# SLAVERY AND TRAFFICKING REPARATION ORDERS

MODERN SLAVERY ACT 2015 s.8

*References: Current Sentencing Practice C2-6350; Archbold 19-452*

## General

**What is a slavery and trafficking reparation order?** A slavery and trafficking reparation order is an order requiring the person against whom it is made to pay compensation to the victim of a relevant offence for any harm resulting from that offence, MSA 2015 s.9(1).

## Availability

The court may make a slavery and trafficking reparation order against a person:

(1) if the person has been convicted of an offence under MSA 2015 ss.1, 2 or 4, and a confiscation order is made against the person in respect of the offence;

(2) if a confiscation order is made against a person by virtue of s.28 of the Proceeds of Crime Act 2002 (defendants who abscond during proceedings) and the person is later convicted of an offence under MSA 2015 ss.1, 2 or 4; or

(3) in addition to dealing with the person in any other way in respect of an offence under MSA 2015 ss.1, 2 or 4, MSA 2015 s.8(1)–(3).

The court *may not* make a slavery and trafficking reputation order in addition to a compensation order, MSA 2015 s.10(1).

The court *may* make a slavery and trafficking reparation order against the person even if the person has been sentenced for the offence before the confiscation order is made, MSA 2015 s.8(4).

## Duty to consider making an order in all cases

In any case in which the court has power to make a slavery and trafficking reparation order it must consider whether to make such an order (whether or not an application for such an order is made), and if it does not make an order, give reasons, MSA 2015 s.8(7).

## Making the Order

## Means

The court must consider the means of the individual when determining whether or not to make a slavery and trafficking reparation order, MSA 2015 s.8(5).

In determining the amount to be paid by the person under a slavery and trafficking reparation order the court must have regard to the person's means, MSA 2015 s.9(5).

If the court considers that it would be appropriate both to impose a fine and to make a slavery and trafficking reparation order, but the person has insufficient means to pay both an appropriate fine and appropriate compensation under such an order, the court must give preference to compensation (although it may impose a fine as well), MSA 2015 s.8(6).

### Determining the amount

The amount of the compensation is to be such amount as the court considers appropriate having regard to any evidence and to any representations made by or on behalf of the person or the prosecutor, but the amount of the compensation payable under the slavery and trafficking reparation order (or if more than one order is made in the same proceedings, the total amount of the compensation payable under those orders) must not exceed the amount the person is required to pay under the confiscation order, MSA 2015 s.9(3) and (4).

In determining the amount to be paid by the person under a slavery and trafficking reparation order the court must have regard to the person's means, MSA 2015 s.9(5).

### Variation and Appeals

**Appeals and reviews**   PCC(S)A 2000 ss.132 to 134 (appeals, review etc of compensation orders) apply to slavery and trafficking reparation orders, MSA 2015 s.10(3).

**Varying confiscation orders**   If the court varies a confiscation order so as to increase the amount required to be paid under that order, it may also vary any slavery and trafficking reparation order made by virtue of the confiscation order so as to increase the amount required to be paid under the slavery and trafficking reparation order, MSA 2015 s.10(4).

Where the order is made by virtue of the confiscation order and some or all of the amount required to be paid under it has not been paid and the court varies a confiscation order so as to reduce the amount required to be paid under that order, it may also vary any relevant slavery and trafficking reparation order so as to reduce the amount which remains to be paid under that order or discharge any relevant slavery and trafficking reparation order, MSA 2015 s.10(5) and (7).

**Discharging confiscation orders**   Where the order is made by virtue of the confiscation order and some or all of the amount required to be paid under it has not been paid and the court discharges a confiscation order, it may also discharge any relevant slavery and trafficking reparation order, MSA 2015 s.10(6) and (7).

**Court of Appeal**   If on an appeal the Court of Appeal:

(a)   quashes a confiscation order, it must also quash any slavery and trafficking reparation order made by virtue of the confiscation order;

(b)   varies a confiscation order, it may also vary any slavery and trafficking reparation order made by virtue of the confiscation order;

(c)   makes a confiscation order, it may make any slavery and trafficking reparation order that could have been made under s.8 above by virtue of the confiscation order, MSA 2015 s.10(8).

# STATUTORY SURCHARGE

## CRIMINAL JUSTICE ACT 2003 s.161A

*References: Current Sentencing Practice C1-8650; Archbold 5A-330*

### Offence(s) committed on or after 8 April 2016

These provisions do not apply where a court *"deals with an offender"* for more than one offence, at least one of which was committed before 8 April 2016, (SI 2016/389) art.3.

The court must make a surcharge in the appropriate amount. If the court imposes more than one form of sentence, the highest surcharge order applies, SI 2012/1696 arts.3(2)(b), 4(2)(b), 5(2)(b) and 6(2).

The court does not *"deal with an offender"* for the purposes of the duty to impose a surcharge where it imposes an absolute discharge or an order under the MHA 1983, CJA 2003 s.161A(4).

*Offences all committed by an offender aged under 18 (irrespective of age on date of conviction):*

| | |
|---|---|
| Conditional discharge | £15 |
| Fine | £20 |
| Youth rehabilitation order | £20 |
| Referral order | £20 |
| Community order | £20 |
| Suspended sentence | £30 |
| Custodial sentence | £30 |

*Offences all committed by an offender when aged over 18:*

| | |
|---|---|
| Conditional discharge | £20 |
| Fine | 10% of the value of the fine, rounded up or down to the nearest pound, which must be no less than £30 and no more than £170 |
| Community order | £85 |
| Suspended sentence, where the sentence of imprisonment or detention in a young offender institution is for a period of 6 months or less | £115 |
| Suspended sentence, where the sentence of imprisonment or detention in a young | £140 |

| | |
|---|---|
| offender institution is for a determinate period of more than 6 months | |
| A sentence of imprisonment or detention in a young offender institution for a determinate period of up to and including 6 months | £115 |
| A sentence of imprisonment or detention in a young offender institution for a determinate period of more than 6 months and up to and including 24 months | £140 |
| A sentence of imprisonment or detention in a young offender institution for a determinate period exceeding 24 months | £170 |
| A sentence of imprisonment or custody for life | £170 |

*Offences, some committed when an offender is under 18 and some when an offender is over 18, but all of which were committed on/after 8 April 2016:*

| | |
|---|---|
| Conditional discharge | £15 |
| Fine | £20 |
| Youth rehabilitation order | £20 |
| Referral order | £20 |
| Community order | £20 |
| Suspended sentence | £30 |
| Custodial sentence | £30 |

*Offences committed by a person who is not an individual:*

| | |
|---|---|
| Conditional discharge | £20 |
| Fine | 10% of the value of the fine, rounded up or down to the nearest pound, which must be no less than £30 and no more than £170 |

## Offence(s) committed between 1 September 2014 – 7 April 2016

These provisions do not apply where a court deals with an offender for more than one offence, at least one of which was committed before 1 September 2014 (SI 2014/2120) art.3.

The court must make a surcharge in the appropriate amount:

*Offences all committed by offender under the age of 18 (irrespective of age on date of conviction):*

| | |
|---|---|
| Conditional discharge | £10 |
| Fine | £15 |
| Youth rehabilitation order | £15 |
| Referral order | £15 |
| Community order | £15 |
| Suspended sentence | £20 |
| Custodial sentence | £20 |

*Offences all committed by an offender committing when over the age of 18:*

| | |
|---|---|
| Conditional discharge | £15 |
| Fine | 10% of the value of the fine, rounded up or down to the nearest pound, which must be no less than £20 and no more than £120 |
| Community order | £60 |
| Suspended sentence, where the sentence of imprisonment or detention in a young offender institution is for a period of 6 months or less | £80 |
| Suspended sentence, where the sentence of imprisonment or detention in a young offender institution is for a determinate period of more than 6 months | £100 |
| A sentence of imprisonment or detention in a young offender institution for a determinate period of up to and including 6 months | £80 |
| A sentence of imprisonment or detention in a young offender institution for a determinate period of more than months and up to and including 24 months | £100 |
| A sentence of imprisonment or detention in a young offender institution for a determinate period exceeding 24 months | £120 |
| A sentence of imprisonment or custody for life | £120 |

*Offences, some committed when an offender is under 18 and some when an offender is over 18:*

| | |
|---|---|
| Conditional discharge | £10 |
| Fine | £15 |

| Youth rehabilitation order | £15 |
| Referral order | £15 |
| Community order | £15 |
| Suspended sentence | £20 |
| Custodial sentence | £20 |

## Imposing other financial orders

Where a court dealing with an offender considers:

(a) that it would be appropriate to make one or more of a compensation order, an unlawful profit order and a slavery and trafficking reparation order; but

(b) that the offender has insufficient means to pay both the surcharge and appropriate amounts under such of those orders as it would be appropriate to make, the court must reduce the surcharge accordingly (if necessary to nil), CJA 2003 s.161A(3).

A court may reduce the amount of a fine if it finds that the offender has insufficient means to pay both the appropriate fine and the surcharge, CJA 2003 s.164(3) and (4).

## Re-sentencing

Where an offender is re-sentenced following the breach of a community order, it is not appropriate to make a second surcharge order, *George* [2015] EWCA Crim 1096; [2015] 2 Cr.App.R. (S.) 58. It is suggested that in such a case, the amount of the earlier order is amended according to the sentence imposed in respect of the breach, see [2015] Crim. L.R. 916 for more details.

## Enforcement

Surcharge orders are enforced in accordance with the Administration of Justice Act 1970 Sch.9. The Crown Court does not fix a default term when making a surcharge order.

# SUSPENDED SENTENCE ORDERS

CRIMINAL JUSTICE ACT 2003 ss.189–193

*References: Current Sentencing Practice A6; Archbold 5A-609*

## Availability

**Offence committed on/after 4 April 2005**   Suspended sentence orders are available for offences committed on or after 4 April 2005, SI 2005/950 para.2 and Sch.2 para.5.

**Aged 18+**   The defendant must be aged 18 at conviction, PCC(S)A 2000 s.89(1) and 96 and CJA 2003 s.189(1).

**Period of imprisonment**   A suspended sentence order is available where the court has imposed a sentence of imprisonment (or detention in YOI) for a period of at least 14 days and no more than two years, CJA 2003 s.189(1).

**Historic offences**   For offences pre-dating 4 April 2005, the court may impose a suspended sentence under PCC(S)A 2000, however old the offence, PCC(S)A 2000 s.118 and SI 2005/950 para.2 and Sch.2 para.5.

*Note: Orders under the PCC(S)A 2000 may not include community requirements.*

## Effect of the Order

A suspended sentence order will take effect where:

(a)   during a period specified in the order for the purposes of this paragraph ("*the operational period*") the defendant commits another offence in the UK (whether or not punishable with imprisonment); and

(b)   a court having power to do so subsequently orders the original sentence to take effect under CJA 2003 Sch.12 para.8, CJA 2003 s.189(1).

The order may also require the defendant to comply with requirements under the order, known as "*the supervision period*", CJA 2003 s.189(1A). This is not mandatory. Where requirements are included within the order, the order will also take effect where:

(a)   during the supervision period the defendant fails to comply with a requirement; and

(b)   a court having power to do so subsequently orders under CJA 2003 Sch.12 para.8 that the original sentence is to take effect, CJA 2003 s.189(1B).

## Making the Order

**Process**   There are distinctly two stages to imposing a suspended sentence order:

(1)   The court must first decide to impose a sentence of immediate imprisonment (or detention) upon the offender. This must be in accordance with

statutory obligations concerning custodial sentences, such as the requirement for custody to be of the shortest period commensurate with the seriousness of the offence, CJA 2003 s.153(2).

(2) Once the court has determined the appropriate length of immediate
imprisonment (or detention), having made any appropriate reductions, and
the sentence is between 14 days and two years, the court may impose a
suspended sentence order, CJA 2003 s.189(1).

**Operational period**   The court must fix the *"operational period"*. The operational
period must be at least six months and not more than two years, CJA 2003 s.189(3).

**Supervision period**   The supervision period must be at least six months and not
more than two years; the supervision period may not extend beyond the operational
period, but the operational period may extend beyond the end of the supervision
period, CJA 2003 s.189(3) and (4).

**Combining sentences**   If the court passes a suspended sentence, it may not impose
a community sentence in respect of that offence or any other offence for which the
offender is sentenced by the court, CJA 2003 s.189(5).

If a court imposes two sentences to be served consecutively, the power to suspend
the sentence is available only if the aggregate term does not exceed two years, CJA
2003 s.189(2).

A suspended sentence order cannot be combined with immediate custody,
*Sapiano* (1968) 52 Cr.App.R. 674.

**The requirements**   The community requirements which may be included in a
suspended sentence order are all of those which may be included in a community
order, subject to the same conditions as apply to a community order. (See **COM-
MUNITY ORDERS**, p.57.)

A suspended sentence order which includes one or more community requirements may provide for periodic review of the order by the court which made the
order, except where the requirement is a drug rehabilitation requirement, in which
case periodic reviews are provided for in the provisions governing the requirement itself, CJA 2003 s.191.

**Time on remand**   A suspended sentence order ordered to take effect is to be
treated for the purposes of CJA 2003 s.240ZA as a sentence of imprisonment, CJA
2003 s.240ZA(7).

A judge considering whether or not to impose a suspended sentence order should
take the fact that the defendant has spent time on remand into account at that stage,
*Mohammed* [2007] EWCA Crim 2756; [2008] 2 Cr.App.R. (S.) 14 (p.85).

Where time on remand would entirely *"swallow up"* the period of the suspended
sentence (if activated), a suspended sentence order should not usually be imposed,
*Rakib* [2011] EWCA Crim 870; [2012] 1 Cr.App.R. (S.) 1.

**Breach**

A *"breach"* of a suspended sentence order may occur either by a failure to comply with a community requirement during the supervision period, or by the commission of an offence during the operational period, CJA 2003 s.189(1) and (1A).

As these two periods may be different in any particular case, it will be important to ensure that the relevant event took place during the relevant period.

### Failure to comply with requirements

**Warning**  The responsible officer will first give the defendant a warning where he or she is of the opinion that the defendant has without reasonable excuse failed to comply with the order, CJA 2003 Sch.12 para.4(1).

**Failure to comply after warning**  If at any point in the 12 months following the date on which the warning was given, the responsible officer is of the opinion that the defendant has without reasonable excuse failed to comply with the order, breach proceedings are mandatory and the defendant will be brought before the court, CJA 2003 Sch.12 para.5.

**Powers upon breach**  If it is proved to the satisfaction of the court that the defendant has failed to comply with any of the community requirements of the order without reasonable excuse, the court must:

(a)   order the sentence to take effect with the original term unaltered; or
(b)   order the sentence to take effect with the term reduced, CJA 2003 Sch.12 para.8(3).

If the court considers it would be unjust in all the circumstances to activate the term in full or in part, it must state its reasons and take one of the following courses:

(a)   order the defendant to pay a fine not exceeding £2,500;
(b)   in the case of an order with community requirements:
    i)      impose more onerous community requirements;
    ii)     extend the supervision period (but not beyond the operational period and not exceeding the two-year maximum);
    iii)    extend the operational period (not exceeding the two year maximum);
(c)   in the case of an order without community requirements:
    (i)     extend the operational period (not exceeding the two year maximum), CJA 2003 Sch.12 para.8(2)–(4).

### Further offence

**Which court deals with the breach?**  If the offender is convicted of an offence committed during the operational period of a suspended sentence (other than one that has taken effect):

(a)   the Crown Court may deal with him in respect of the breach irrespective of which court made the original order;
(b)   the magistrates' court may deal with him in respect of the breach, only if the suspended sentence was passed by a magistrates' court; or
(c)   if the suspended sentence was passed by the Crown Court and the offender is convicted by a magistrates' court of the new offence, the magistrates' court may commit him to the Crown Court to be dealt with, CJA 2003 Sch.12 paras.8(1)(b) and 11.

If the magistrates' court does not commit the offender to the Crown Court, it must notify the Crown Court, and the Crown Court may issue process to secure his appearance before the Crown Court, CJA 2003 Sch.12 para.11(2).

**Powers on breach**   Where the court has power to deal with the breach of the suspended sentence order, the court must:

(a)   order the sentence to take effect with the original term unaltered; or

(b)   order the sentence to take effect with the term reduced, CJA 2003 Sch.12 para.8(3).

If the court considers it would be unjust in all the circumstances to activate the term in full or in part, it must state its reasons and take one of the following courses:

(a)   order the defendant to pay a fine not exceeding £2,500;

(b)   in the case of an order with community requirements:
    (i)   impose more onerous community requirements;
    (ii)   extend the supervision period (but not beyond the operational period and not exceeding the two-year maximum);
    (iii)   extend the operational period (not exceeding the two-year maximum);

(c)   in the case of an order without community requirements:
    (i)   extend the operational period (not exceeding the two-year maximum), CJA 2003 Sch.12 para.8(2)–(4).

**Presumption of consecutive sentences**   It is expected that the activated term of the suspended sentence is to run consecutively to any custodial sentence imposed for the new offence, *New Sentences: Criminal Justice Act 2003 Guideline* para.2.2.21.

**New offence does not need to carry imprisonment**   It is not necessary that the later offence should be punishable with imprisonment, however the court should consider whether it is appropriate to activate the suspended sentence order at all, *New Sentences: Criminal Justice Act 2003 Guideline* para.2.2.22.

**New offence less serious**   Where the new offence is less serious than the offence for which the suspended sentence order was imposed, it may justify activating the sentence of the suspended sentence order with a reduced term, or amending the order, *New Sentences: Criminal Justice Act 2003 Guideline* para.2.2.20.

**Cannot revoke the order**   There is no power to revoke the order and impose a custodial sentence of greater length than the sentence which was suspended, see CJA 2003 Sch.12.

**Conviction for offence committed before suspended sentence imposed**   Where an offender who is subject to a suspended sentence appears for sentence for an offence committed before the suspended sentence was imposed, the court has no power to order the suspended sentence to take effect, to impose more onerous requirements or extend the operational period, but may cancel the community requirement of the suspended sentence order on the application of the offender or responsible officer, CJA 2003 Sch.12 para.13(1).

# TIME IN CUSTODY ON REMAND

## CRIMINAL JUSTICE ACT 2003 s.240ZA

*References: Current Sentencing Practice A7, Archbold 5A-631*

### Applicability

These provisions apply to any person sentenced on or after 3 December 2012, irrespective of the date on which the offence was committed. For sentences imposed prior to that date, earlier legislation will need to be consulted.

### To which sentences does it apply?

These provisions apply to offenders serving:

(a)  a term of imprisonment (including an activated suspended sentence order);
(b)  an extended sentence of imprisonment or detention in a young offender institution under CJA 2003 ss.226A or 227;
(c)  a special custodial sentence for offenders of particular concern under CJA 2003 s.236A;
(d)  a determinate sentence of detention in a young offender institution under PCC(S)A 2000 s.96;
(e)  a determinate sentence of detention under PCC(S)A 2000 s.91; and
(f)  an extended sentence of detention under CJA 2003 ss.226B or 228, CJA 2003 s.240ZA(1)(a) and (11).

The provisions do not apply to offenders serving sentences of life imprisonment, custody for life, detention for life or detention and training orders.

### Extent of discount

If the offender has been remanded in custody for the offence or a related offence, the number of days for which the offender was remanded in custody count as time served as part of the sentence, CJA 2003 s.240ZA(3).

It is immaterial whether for all or part of the period during which the defendant was remanded in custody, the defendant was also remanded in custody in connection with other offences, however a day may be counted in relation to only one sentence, and only once in relation to that sentence, CJA 2003 s.240ZA(2) and (5).

If, on any day on which the offender was remanded in custody, the offender was also detained in connection with any other matter, that day is not to count as time served, CJA 2003 s.240ZA(4).

### Court does not make an order

It is not necessary for the sentencing court to make any order in relation to time spent in custody on remand.

### Related offences

A related offence is an offence with which the offender was charged and which was founded on the same facts or evidence as the offence for which the sentence was imposed, CJA 2003 s.240ZA(8).

### Extradition

If the offender has been extradited the court must specify in open court the number of days for which the offender was kept in custody while awaiting extradition. Such days are treated as counting as time served as part of the sentence. The court has no discretion to disallow any days spent in custody while awaiting extradition, CJA 2003 s.243(2) and (2A).

In circumstances where the reduction in sentence under s.243 does not apply, there is jurisdiction to make a reduction to an otherwise lawful sentence, however that jurisdiction is an exceptional one, *Prenga* [2017] EWCA Crim 2149; [2018] 1 Cr.App.R. (S.) 41.

**Young offenders**    Time spent in local authority accommodation does not equate to being remanded in custody as defined in s.242(2)(b) of the Criminal Justice Act 2003 (which refers to being "remanded to youth detention accommodation under s.91(4) of the Legal Aid, Sentencing and Punishment of Offenders Act 2012") and therefore is not automatically deducted. Where a court intended that such time be deducted from the sentence, it does not follow that on appeal, that reduction will be made, *Anderson* [2017] EWCA Crim 2604; [2018] 2 Cr.App.R. (S.) 21.

# TIME SPENT ON REMAND ON BAIL SUBJECT TO QUALIFYING CURFEW

## CRIMINAL JUSTICE ACT s.240A

*References: Current Sentencing Practice A7; Archbold 5A-632*

### Applicability

These provisions apply to offences committed before 4 April 2005, as well as to offences committed on or after that date.

### To which sentences does it apply?

These provisions apply to defendants serving:

(a)   a term of imprisonment (including an activated suspended sentence order);
(b)   an extended sentence of imprisonment or detention in a young offender institution under CJA 2003 ss.226A or 227;
(c)   a special custodial sentence for offenders of particular concern under CJA 2003 s.236A;
(d)   a determinate sentence of detention in a young offender institution under PCC(S)A 2000 s.96;
(e)   a determinate sentence of detention under PCC(S)A 2000 s.91; and
(f)   an extended sentence of detention under CJA 2003 ss.226B or 228; and the defendant was remanded on bail by a court in course of or in connection with proceedings for the offence, or any related offence, CJA 2003 s.240A(1) and (11).

The provisions do not apply to offenders serving sentences of life imprisonment, custody for life, detention for life or detention and training orders.

### Definitions

The discount applies only if the defendant's bail was subject to a qualifying curfew condition and an electronic monitoring condition, CJA 2003 s.240A(1)(c).

An *"electronic monitoring condition"* is any electronic monitoring requirement imposed under the BA 1976 for the purpose of securing the electronic monitoring of a person's compliance with a qualifying curfew condition, CJA 2003 s.240A(12).

A *"qualifying curfew condition"* means a condition of bail which requires the person granted bail to remain at one or more specified places for a total of not less than nine hours in any given day, CJA 2003 s.240A(12).

A *"related offence"* is an offence, other than the offence for which the sentence is imposed, with which the offender was charged and the charge for which was founded on the same facts or evidence as the offence for which the sentence is imposed.

[297]

## Mandatory order

Where the defendant is sentenced to a sentence of imprisonment (see above), was remanded on bail and was subject to a qualifying curfew condition and an electronic monitoring condition, the court must direct that the credit period is to count as time served by the offender as part of the sentence, CJA 2003 s.240A(1).

## Extent of credit

The credit period is calculated by taking the following steps.

*Step 1* — add up those days spent during the course of the qualifying curfew, including the first, but not the last day, if on the last day the defendant was taken into custody;

*Step 2* — deduct those days when the defendant was, at the same time, also (i) being monitored with a tag for compliance with a curfew requirement; and/or (ii) on temporary release from custody;

*Step 3* — deduct those days when the defendant had broken the curfew or the relevant tagging condition;

*Step 4* — divide the result by two; and

*Step 5* — if necessary, round up to the nearest whole number, CJA 2003 s.240A(3) and *Thorsby* [2015] EWCA Crim 1; [2015] 1 Cr.App.R. (S.) 63.

## Exceptions

A day of the credit period counts as time served in relation to only one sentence and only once in relation to that sentence, CJA 2003 s.240(3A).

## Form of words

In *Hoggard* [2013] EWCA Crim 1024; [2014] 1 Cr.App.R. (S.) 42, the court suggested the following form of words:

*"the defendant will receive full credit for half the time spent under curfew if the curfew qualified under the provisions of s.240A. On the information before me the total period is ... days (subject to the deduction of ... days that I have directed under Step(s) 2 and/or 3 making a total of ... days), but if this period is mistaken, this court will order an amendment of the record for the correct period to be recorded."*

## Guidance

In *Marshall* [2015] EWCA Crim 1999; [2016] 1 Cr.App.R. (S.) 45, the Court of Appeal gave guidance regarding the procedure in the magistrates' court, Crown Court and Court of Appeal, and underlined the importance of using the form of words suggested in *Hoggard* [2013] EWCA Crim 1024; [2014] 1 Cr.App.R. (S.) 42.

# TRAVEL RESTRICTION ORDERS

*References: Current Sentencing Practice C2-5450; Archbold 5A-908*

## General

**Applicability**   Where a court:

(a)  convicts an offender of a drug trafficking offence committed on or after 1 April 2002; and
(b)  determines that it would be appropriate to impose a sentence of imprisonment of four years or more; the court must consider whether it would be appropriate to make a travel restriction order in relation to the offender, CJPA 2001 s.33(1) and (2).

**Drug Trafficking Offence**   This means an offence under:

(a)  MDA 1971 s.4(2), 4(3), 20;
(b)  CEMA 1979 s.50(2), 50(3), 68(2), 170, in connection with a prohibition or restriction on importation or exportation, see MDA 1971 s.3;
(c)  CLA 1971 s.1 (or common law conspiracy) in respect of the offences listed in a) and b);
(d)  CAA 1981 s.1 in respect of the offences listed in a) and b);
(e)  MDA 1971 s.19 (or inciting at common law) of the offences listed in a) and b), CJPA 2001 s.34(1).

Possession with intent to supply, and money laundering offences, are not included.

## Making the Order

**Duty to make an order**   If the court determines that it would be appropriate to make an order, the court must make such travel restriction order as it thinks suitable in all the circumstances, CJPA 2001 s.33(1) and (2).

**Must give reasons if not making an order**   If the court determines that it is not appropriate to make a travel restriction order, it must state its reasons for not making one, CJPA 2001 s.33(1) and (2).

**Start date of the order**   The order begins on the day on which the offender is released from prison, CJPA 2001 s.33(3)(a).

**Minimum length**   A travel restriction order must be for at least two years, CJPA 2001 s.33(3)(b).

**Effect of the order**   A travel restriction order prohibits the offender from leaving the United Kingdom at any time during the period beginning with his release from custody and continuing to the end of the period specified by the court, CJPA 2001 s.33(3).

A travel restriction order may contain a direction to the offender to deliver up, or cause to be delivered up, to the court any UK passport held by him, CJPA 2001 s.33(4).

### Revoking or Amending the Order

The defendant may apply, to the court that imposed the order, for the order to be revoked or suspended, CJPA 2001 s.35(1).

**When may the application be made?**    The application may be made at any time which after the end of the minimum period, and not less than three months after the making of any previous application for the revocation of the prohibition, CJPA 2001 s.35(1).

**Minimum period**    The minimum period is:

    (a)   in the case of an order for four years or less, a period of two years;

    (b)   in the case of an order for more than four years but less than 10 years, a period of four years; and

    (c)   in any other case is a period of five years, CJPA 2001 s.35(7).

**Test: Revocation**    A court must not revoke a travel restriction order unless it considers that it is appropriate to do so in all the circumstances of the case and having regard, in particular the offender's character, his conduct since the making of the order, and the offences of which he was convicted on the occasion on which the order was made, CJPA 2001 s.35(2).

**Test: Suspension**    A court must not suspend a travel restriction order for any period unless it is satisfied that there are exceptional circumstances that justify the suspension on compassionate grounds, in particular having regard to the offender's character, his conduct since the making of the order, the offences of which he was convicted on the occasion on which the order was made and any other circumstances of the case that the court considers relevant, CJPA 2001 s.35(3) and (4).

# UNFIT TO PLEAD (CROWN COURT)

CRIMINAL PROCEDURE (INSANITY) ACT 1964 s.5

*References: Current Sentencing Practice E1-2150; Archbold 5A-1218*

## General

**Applicability**    Where findings are recorded that a person:

(a) is under a disability and that he did the act or made the omission charged against him; or
(b) a special verdict is returned that the accused is not guilty by reason of insanity; the court is limited in how it shall dispose of the indivudual, CP(I)A 1964 s.5(1).

**Disposals**    The court shall impose one of the following orders:

(a) a hospital order (with or without a restriction order);
(b) a supervision order; or
(c) an order for absolute discharge, CP(I)A 1964 s.5(2).

**Murder**    Where the offence to which the findings relate is an offence for which the sentence is fixed by law, and the court has power to make a hospital order, the court must make a hospital order with a restriction order, CP(I)A 1964 s.5(3).

## Supervision Order

**Definition**    *"Supervision order"* means an order which requires the person in respect of whom it is made (*"the supervised person"* to be under the supervision of a social worker, an officer of a local probation board or an officer of a provider of probation services (*"the supervising officer"* for a period specified in the order of not more than two years, CP(I)A 1964 Sch.1A para.1(1).

**Test**    The court must not make a supervision order unless it is satisfied that, having regard to all the circumstances of the case, the making of such an order is the most suitable means of dealing with the person, CP(I)A 1964 Sch.1A para.2(1).

**Requirements**    The court must not make a supervision order unless it is satisfied that the supervising officer intended to be specified in the order is willing to undertake the supervision, and that arrangements have been made for the treatment intended to be specified in the order, CP(I)A 1964 Sch.1A para.2(2).

**Treatment**    A supervision order may include a requirement that the supervised person shall, during the whole or part of the period specified in the order, submit to treatment by or under the direction of a registered medical practitioner with a view to the improvement of his mental condition.

A treatment requirement may be imposed only if the court is satisfied on the written or oral evidence of two or more registered medical practitioners that the mental condition of the supervised person is such as requires and may be susceptible to treatment, but is not such as to warrant the making of a hospital order.

The treatment required may be treatment as a non-resident patient at a specified institution or place and treatment by or under the direction of a specified registered medical practitioner, CP(I)A 1964 Sch.1A para.4(1)–(4).

**Residence**    A supervision order may include requirements as to the residence of the supervised person, CP(I)A 1964 Sch.1A para.3.

**Explaining the order**    Before making a supervision order, the court must explain in ordinary language the effect of the order and that a magistrates' court has power to review the order on the application either of the supervised person or of the supervising officer, CP(I)A 1964 Sch.1A para.3(2).

## Hospital Order

A hospital order under the CP(I)A 1964 s.5 has the same meaning as under the MHA 1983 s.37. CP(I)A 1964 s.5A makes some modifications to s.37 for the purposes of enabling a court to impose a hospital order following a finding as specified in s.5.

See **HOSPITAL ORDERS** p.183 for more details.

## Absolute Discharge

An order for absolute discharge may be made if the court considers it is the most suitable disposal in all the circumstances of the case, CP(I)A 1964 Sch.1A para.5A(6).

CP(I)A 1964 Sch.1A para.5A(6) makes slight modifications to the PCC(S) A 2000 s.12 for the purposes of imposing such an order following a finding as specified in s.5.

# UNLAWFUL PROFIT ORDERS

Prevention of Social Housing Fraud Act 2013 s.4

*References: Archbold 5A-919*

*Archbold 5A-919*

## Definition

An unlawful profit order is an order requiring the defendant to pay a landlord the profit from unlawfully sub-letting a tenancy, PSHFA 2013 s.4(3).

## Types of order

There are two types, one following a conviction and one on an application to the magistrates' court. This section only deals with post conviction orders.

## Availability

The order is available where the defendant had been convicted of an offence under PSHFA 2013 ss.1 or 2 (unlawfully sub-letting a secured tenancy or an assured tenancy), PSHFA 2013 s.4(1).

## Duty to consider making an order

The court by or before which the offender is convicted must, on application or otherwise, decide whether to make an unlawful profit order, PSHFA 2013 s.4(2)(a).

## Combining sentences

The court may, if it considers it appropriate to do so, make such an order, instead of or in addition to dealing with the offender in any other way, PSHFA 2013 s.4(2)(b).

When the court proposes to impose a fine and an unlawful profit order, but considers that the defendant has insufficient means to pay an appropriate amount under both orders, the court must give preference to making an unlawful profit order (though it may impose a fine as well), PSHFA 2013 s.4(8) and (9).

## Must give reasons when not making an order

If the court decides not to make an unlawful profit order, it must give reasons for that decision on passing sentence on the offender, PSHFA 2013 s.4(4).

## Determining the amount

The amount payable under an unlawful profit order must be such amount as the court considers appropriate, having regard to any evidence and to any representations that are made by or on behalf of the offender or the prosecutor, PSHFA 2013 s.4(5).

**Maximum amount**

The maximum amount payable under an unlawful profit order is calculated as follows:

*Step 1*   Determine the total amount the defendant received as a result of the conduct constituting the offence (or the best estimate of that amount).

*Step 2*   Deduct from the amount determined under step 1 the total amount, if any, paid by the defendant as rent to the landlord (including service charges) over the period during which the offence was committed, PSHFA 2013 s.4(6).

# YOUTH REHABILITATION ORDERS

CRIMINAL JUSTICE AND IMMIGRATION ACT 2008 s.1

*References: Current Sentencing Practice F3-100; Archbold 5A-975*

## General

**Applicability**    These provisions apply only to offences committed on or after 30 November 2009, SI 2009/3074 art.2(a).

**The different types of order**    There are three types of YRO, a basic order and two "*enhanced*" orders:

    (a)   the basic order, imposing one or more requirements (see below);
    (b)   YRO with Intensive Supervision and Surveillance; and
    (c)   a YRO with Fostering, CJIA 2008 s.1(1) and (3).

## Availability and Power to Order

A YRO is available where a person *under 18* is convicted of an offence, the court may make a youth rehabilitation order containing specified requirements, CJIA 2008 s.1(1).

A youth rehabilitation order may not be made where the court is required to impose a mandatory custodial sentence.

A court must not make a youth rehabilitation order in respect of an offender at a time when:

    (a)   another youth rehabilitation order; or
    (b)   a reparation order made under PCC(S)A 2000 s.73, is in force in respect of the offender, unless when it makes the order it revokes the earlier order, CJIA 2008 Sch.1 para.30(4).

**Basic order**    A youth rehabilitation order may be made only if the court is of the opinion that:

    (a)   the offence or the combination of the offence and one or more offences associated with it was serious enough to warrant a youth rehabilitation order, CJA 2003 s.148(1);
    (b)   the particular requirements forming part of the order are the most suitable for the offender, CJA 2003 s.148(2)(a); and
    (c)   the restrictions on liberty imposed by the order are commensurate with the seriousness of the offence or the combination of the offence and one or more offences associated with it, CJA 2003 s.148(2)(b).

**YRO with Fostering/Intensive Supervision and Surveillance**    These orders are available where:

[305]

(a) the court is dealing with the offender for an offence which is punishable with imprisonment;

(b) the court is of the opinion that the offence, or the combination of the offence and one or more offences associated with it, was so serious that, but for the availability of a YRO with Fostering or Intensive Supervision and Surveillance, a custodial sentence would be appropriate (or, if the offender was aged under 12 at the time of conviction, would be appropriate if the offender had been aged 12); and

(c) if the offender was aged under 15 at the time of conviction, the court is of the opinion that the offender is a persistent offender, CJIA 2008 s.1(4).

## Making the Order

**Reports**    Before making a youth rehabilitation order, the court must obtain and consider information about the offender's family circumstances and the likely effect of the order on those circumstances, CJIA 2008 Sch.1 para.28.

**Compatibility of requirements**    Before making an order with two or more requirements, or two or more orders in respect of associated offences, the court must consider whether the requirements are compatible with each other.

The requirements must so far as is practicable avoid conflict with the offender's religious beliefs, avoid any interference with the times at which the offender normally works or attends any school or educational establishment, and avoid any conflict with the requirements of any other youth rehabilitation order to which the offender is subject, CJIA 2008 Sch.1 para.29(1) and (3).

**Credit for remand time**    In determining the restrictions on liberty to be imposed by a youth rehabilitation order the court may have regard to any period for which the offender has been remanded in custody in connection with the offence or any other offence the charge for which was founded on the same facts or evidence, CJA 2003 s.149(1).

**Guilty plea**    Where a court is considering sentence for an offence for which a custodial sentence is justified, a guilty plea may be one of the factors that persuades a court that it can properly impose a youth rehabilitation order instead and no further adjustment to the sentence needs to be made to fulfil the obligation to give credit for that plea.

Where the provisional sentence is already a youth rehabilitation order, the necessary reduction for a guilty plea should apply to those requirements within the order that are primarily punitive rather than to those which are primarily rehabilitative, Overarching principles: *Sentencing Youths Guideline*, paras.10.7 and 10.8

**Length of the order**    A youth rehabilitation order must specify a date, not more than three years after the date on which the order takes effect, by which all the requirements in it must have been complied with.

An order which imposes two or more different requirements may also specify a date or dates in relation to compliance with any one or more of them; the last such date must be the date by which all the requirements must be satisfied.

In the case of a youth rehabilitation order with intensive supervision and surveillance, the date specified must not be earlier than six months after the date on which the order takes effect, CJIA 2008 Sch.1 para.32.

**Further proceedings**    Where the Crown Court makes a youth rehabilitation order, it may give a direction that further proceedings relating to the order should be in a youth court or other magistrates' court, CJIA 2008 Sch.1 para.36.

**Effect of the order**    A youth rehabilitation order takes effect on the day on which it is made.

If the offender is subject to a detention and training order, the court may order the youth rehabilitation order to take effect when the offender is released from custody under supervision, or at the expiry of the term of the detention and training order, CJIA 2008 Sch.1 para.30.

## The Enhanced Orders

**Intensive supervision and surveillance**    If the court makes a youth rehabilitation order with intensive supervision and surveillance, the order may include an extended activity requirement of not more than 180 days, and must make a supervision requirement and a curfew requirement with an electronic monitoring requirement, where such a requirement is required.

A youth rehabilitation order with intensive supervision and surveillance may include other types of requirement, except a fostering requirement, CJIA 2008 Sch.1 para.3.

**Fostering requirement**    A fostering requirement is a requirement that, for a period specified in the order, the offender must reside with a local authority foster parent.

A court may not impose a fostering requirement unless it has consulted the offender's parents or guardians (unless it is impracticable to do so), and it has consulted the local authority which is to place the offender with a local authority foster parent.

A youth rehabilitation order which imposes a fostering requirement must also impose a supervision requirement.

The period specified must end no later than 12 months beginning with the date on which the requirement first has effect and not include any period after the offender has reached the age of 18.

If at any time during the period of the requirement, the responsible officer notifies the offender that no suitable local authority foster parent is available, and that the responsible officer has applied or proposes to apply for the revocation or amendment of the order, the fostering requirement is, until the determination of the application, to be taken to require the offender to reside in accommodation provided by or on behalf of a local authority.

A court may not include a fostering requirement in a youth rehabilitation order unless the court has been notified by the Secretary of State that arrangements for implementing such a requirement are available in the area of the local authority which is to place the offender with a local authority foster parent.

A fostering requirement may not be made unless the offender was legally represented at the relevant time in court, or a right to representation funded by the Legal Services Commission for the purposes of the proceedings was withdrawn because of the offender's conduct, or the offender refused or failed to apply for representation after being informed of the right to apply and having had the opportunity to do so.

A fostering requirement may not be included in a youth rehabilitation order with intensive supervision and surveillance, CJIA 2008 Sch.1 paras.4, 18 and 19.

### Requirements

The following requirements may be included in a youth rehabilitation order:

**Activity requirement**   An activity requirement is a requirement that the offender must participate in specified activities at a specified place or places, or participate in one or more residential exercises for a continuous period or periods of the number or numbers of days to be specified in the order, or engage in activities in accordance with instructions of the responsible officer on the number of days specified in the order.

The total number of days specified in an activity requirement must not in aggregate exceed 90, CJIA 2008 Sch.1 para.6.

**Attendance centre requirement**   An attendance centre requirement is a requirement that the offender must attend at an attendance centre specified in the order for such number of hours as may be so specified.

If the offender is aged 16 or over at the time of conviction, the aggregate number of hours for which the offender may be required to attend at an attendance centre must be not less than 12, and not more than 36.

If the offender is aged 14 or over but under 16 at the time of conviction, the aggregate number of hours for which the offender may be required to attend at an attendance centre must be not less than 12, and not more than 24.

If the offender is aged under 14 at the time of conviction, the aggregate number of hours for which the offender may be required to attend at an attendance centre must not be more than 12.

A court may not include an attendance centre requirement in a youth rehabilitation order unless it has been notified by the Secretary of State that an attendance centre is available for persons of the offender's description, and provision can be made at the centre for the offender. The court must be satisfied that the attendance centre proposed is reasonably accessible to the offender, having regard to the means of access available to the offender and any other circumstances, CJIA 2008 Sch.1 para.12.

**Curfew requirement**  A curfew requirement is a requirement that the offender must remain, for periods specified in the order, at a place so specified. A curfew requirement may specify different places or different periods for different days, but may not specify periods which amount to less than two hours or more than 16 hours (12 hours if the offence was committed before 3 December 2012) in any day.

A curfew requirement may not specify periods which fall outside the period of 12 months (six months if the offence was committed before 3 December 2012) beginning with the day on which the requirement first takes effect.

Before making a youth rehabilitation order imposing a curfew requirement, the court must obtain and consider information about the place proposed to be specified in the order (including information as to the attitude of persons likely to be affected by the enforced presence there of the offender).

Where a curfew requirement is made, the order must also include an electronic monitoring requirement, unless the court considers it inappropriate for the order to include an electronic monitoring requirement, or it will not be practicable to secure that the monitoring takes place, without the consent of some person other than the offender, and that person does not consent to the inclusion of the electronic monitoring requirement, CJIA 2008 Sch.1 paras.2 and 14.

**Drug testing requirement**  A drug testing requirement is a requirement that the offender must, during the treatment period of a drug treatment requirement, provide samples in accordance with instructions given by the responsible officer or the treatment provider for the purpose of ascertaining whether there is any drug in the offender's body.

A court may not include a drug testing requirement in a youth rehabilitation order unless:

(a)  the court has been notified by the Secretary of State that arrangements for implementing drug testing requirements are in force in the local justice area in which the offender resides or is to reside;

(b)  the order also imposes a drug treatment requirement; and

(c)  the offender has expressed willingness to comply with the requirement.

A drug testing requirement must specify for each month the minimum number of occasions on which samples are to be provided, and may specify times at which and circumstances in which the responsible officer or treatment provider may require samples to be provided, and descriptions of the samples which may be so required.

A drug testing requirement must provide for the results of tests carried out otherwise than by the responsible officer on samples provided by the offender in pursuance of the requirement to be communicated to the responsible officer, CJIA 2008 Sch.1 para.22 and 23.

**Drug treatment requirement**  A drug treatment requirement is a requirement that the offender must submit, during a period or periods specified in the order, to treatment, by or under the direction of a treatment provider with a view to the reduction or elimination of the offender's dependency on, or propensity to misuse, drugs.

A court may not include a drug treatment requirement in a youth rehabilitation order unless it is satisfied that the offender is dependent on, or has a propensity to misuse, drugs, and that the offender's dependency or propensity is such as requires and may be susceptible to treatment.

The treatment required may be treatment as a resident in such institution or place as may be specified in the order, or treatment as a non-resident at such institution or place, and at such intervals, as may be so specified. The nature of the treatment is not specified in the order.

A court must not make a drug treatment requirement unless:

(a)   the court has been notified by the Secretary of State that arrangements for implementing drug treatment requirements are in force in the local justice area in which the offender resides or is to reside; and

(b)   the court is satisfied that arrangements have been or can be made for the treatment intended to be specified in the order;

(c)   the requirement has been recommended to the court as suitable for the offender by a member of a youth offending team, an officer of a local probation board or an officer of a provider of probation services; and

(d)   the offender must express willingness to comply with the requirement, CJIA 2008 Sch.1 para.22.

**Education requirement**   An education requirement is a requirement that the offender must comply, during a period or periods specified in the order, with approved education arrangements made for the time being by the offender's parent or guardian, and approved by the local education authority specified in the order.

A court may not include an education requirement in a youth rehabilitation order unless:

(a)   it has consulted the local education authority proposed to be specified in the order with regard to the proposal to include the requirement;

(b)   it is satisfied that, in the view of that local education authority, arrangements exist for the offender to receive efficient full-time education suitable to the offender's age, ability, aptitude and special educational needs (if any); and

(c)   that, having regard to the circumstances of the case, the inclusion of the education requirement is necessary for securing the good conduct of the offender or for preventing the commission of further offences.

Any period specified in a youth rehabilitation order as a period during which an offender must comply with approved education arrangements must not include any period after the offender has ceased to be of compulsory school age, CJIA 2008 Sch.1 para.25.

**Electronic monitoring requirement**   An electronic monitoring requirement is a requirement for securing the electronic monitoring of the offender's compliance with other requirements imposed by the order during a period specified in the order or determined by the responsible officer in accordance with the order.

Where it is proposed to make an electronic monitoring requirement, but there is a person (other than the offender) without whose co-operation it will not be practicable to secure that the monitoring takes place, the requirement may not be included in the order without that person's consent.

A youth rehabilitation order which imposes an electronic monitoring requirement must include provision for making a person of a description specified in an order made by the Secretary of State responsible for the monitoring.

A court may not make an electronic monitoring requirement unless the court has been notified by the Secretary of State that arrangements for electronic monitoring of offenders are available in the local justice area proposed to be specified in the order, and in the area in which the relevant place is situated, and is satisfied that the necessary provision can be made under the arrangements currently available.

An electronic monitoring requirement must be made where the court makes either a curfew requirement or an exclusion requirement, unless the court considers it inappropriate for the order to include an electronic monitoring requirement, or it will not be practicable to secure that the monitoring takes place, without the consent of some person other than the offender, and that person does not consent to the inclusion of the electronic monitoring requirement, CJIA 2008 Sch.1 para.2 and 26.

**Exclusion requirement** An exclusion requirement is a provision prohibiting the offender from entering a place or area specified in the order for a period so specified, which must not exceed three months.

An exclusion requirement may provide for the prohibition to operate only during the periods specified in the order, and may specify different places for different periods or days.

Where an exclusion requirement is made, the order must also include an electronic monitoring requirement, unless the court considers it inappropriate for the order to include an electronic monitoring requirement, or it will not be practicable to secure that the monitoring takes place, without the consent of some person other than the offender, and that person does not consent to the inclusion of the electronic monitoring requirement, CJIA 2008 Sch.1 para.25.

**Intoxicating substance treatment requirement** An intoxicating substance treatment requirement is a requirement that the offender must submit, during a period or periods specified in the order, to treatment, by or under the direction of a specified qualified person with a view to the reduction or elimination of the offender's dependency on or propensity to misuse intoxicating substances.

A court may not include an intoxicating substance treatment requirement in a youth rehabilitation order unless it is satisfied that the offender is dependent on, or has a propensity to misuse, intoxicating substances, and that the offender's dependency or propensity is such as requires and may be susceptible to treatment.

The treatment required must be treatment as a resident in an institution or place specified in the order, or treatment as a non-resident in a specified institution or place, at specified intervals. The nature of the treatment is not specified.

A court may not make an intoxicating substance treatment requirement unless the court is satisfied that arrangements have been or can be made for the treatment intended to be specified in the order, the requirement has been recommended to the court as suitable for the offender by a member of a youth offending team, an officer of a local probation board or an officer of a provider of probation services, and the offender has expressed willingness to comply with the requirement, CJIA 2008 Sch.1 para.24.

**Local authority residence requirement**  A local authority residence requirement is a requirement that, during the period specified in the order, the offender must reside in accommodation provided by or on behalf of a local authority specified in the order for the purposes of the requirement.

The period for which the offender must reside in local authority accommodation must not be longer than six months, and must not include any period after the offender has reached the age of 18.

An order containing a local authority residence requirement may also stipulate that the offender is not to reside with a person specified in the order.

A court may not make a local authority residence requirement unless it is satisfied that the behaviour which constituted the offence was due to a significant extent to the circumstances in which the offender was living, and that the imposition of that requirement will assist in the offender's rehabilitation.

A court may not include a local authority residence requirement in a youth rehabilitation order unless it has consulted a parent or guardian of the offender (unless it is impracticable to consult such a person), and the local authority which is to receive the offender.

A local authority residence requirement may not be made unless:

(a)  the offender was legally represented at the relevant time in court;
(b)  a right to representation for the purposes of the proceedings was withdrawn because of the offender's conduct;
(c)  the offender refused or failed to apply for representation after being informed of the right to apply and having had the opportunity to do so.

A local authority residence requirement must specify, as the local authority which is to receive the offender, the local authority in whose area the offender resides or is to reside, CJIA 2008 Sch.1 paras.17 and 19.

**Mental health treatment requirement**  A mental health treatment requirement is a requirement that the offender must submit, during a period or periods specified in the order, to treatment by or under the direction of a registered medical practitioner or a chartered psychologist (or both, for different periods) with a view to the improvement of the offender's mental condition.

The treatment required must be treatment as a resident patient in an independent hospital or care home, or a hospital within the meaning of the MHA 1983, but not in hospital premises where high security psychiatric services are provided, treatment as a non-resident patient at such institution or place as may be specified in the order, or treatment by or under the direction of such registered medical practitioner or chartered psychologist (or both) as may be so specified. The nature of the treatment is not specified in the order.

A court may not make a mental health treatment requirement unless:

(a)  the court is satisfied that the mental condition of the offender:
    (i)  is such as requires and may be susceptible to treatment; but
    (ii)  is not such as to warrant the making of a hospital order or guardianship order within the meaning of that Act.
(b)  the court is satisfied that arrangements have been or can be made for the treatment intended to be specified in the order (including, where the offender is to be required to submit to treatment as a resident patient, arrangements for the reception of the offender); and
(c)  the offender has expressed willingness to comply with the requirement, CJIA 2008 Sch.1 para.20.

**Programme requirement**  A programme requirement is a requirement that the offender must participate in a systematic programme of activities specified in the order at a place or places so specified on such number of days as may be so specified.

A programme requirement may require the offender to reside at any place specified in the order for any period so specified if it is necessary for the offender to reside there for that period in order to participate in the programme.

A court may not include a programme requirement in a youth rehabilitation order unless the programme has been recommended to the court by:

(a)  a member of a youth offending team;
(b)  an officer of a local probation board; or
(c)  an officer of a provider of probation services, as being suitable for the offender, and the court is satisfied that the programme is available at the place or places proposed to be specified.

A court may not include a programme requirement in a youth rehabilitation order if compliance with that requirement would involve the co-operation of a person other than the offender and the offender's responsible officer, unless that other person consents to its inclusion, CJIA 2008 Sch.1 para.11.

**Prohibited activity requirement**  A prohibited activity requirement is a requirement that the offender must refrain from participating in activities specified in the order, on a day or days specified in the during a period specified in the order.

A court may not include a prohibited activity requirement in a youth rehabilitation order unless it has consulted a member of a youth offending team, an officer of a local probation board, or an officer of a provider of probation services.

The requirements that may be included in a youth rehabilitation order include a requirement that the offender does not possess, use or carry a firearm, CJIA 2008 Sch.1 para.13.

The primary function is not to punish the offender but to prevent, or at least to reduce, the risk of further offending, *Jacob* [2008] EWCA Crim 2002.

**Residence requirement**  A residence requirement is a requirement that, during the period specified in the order, the offender must reside with an individual specified in the order, or at a place specified in the order.

A residence requirement that the offender reside with an individual may not be made unless that individual has consented to the requirement.

A requirement that the offender reside at a specified place may not be made unless the offender was aged 16 or over at the time of conviction.

Before making a requirement that the offender reside at a specified place, the court must consider the home surroundings of the offender. The court may not specify a hostel or other institution as the place where an offender must reside except on the recommendation of a member of a youth offending team, an officer of a local probation board, an officer of a provider of probation services, or a social worker of a local authority.

A requirement that the offender reside at a specified place may provide that the offender may reside, with the prior approval of the responsible officer, at a place other than that specified in the order, CJIA 2008 Sch.1 para.16.

**Supervision requirement**    A supervision requirement is a requirement that the offender must attend appointments with the responsible officer or another person determined by the responsible officer, at such times and places as may be determined by the responsible officer, CJIA 2008 Sch.1 para.9.

**Unpaid work requirement**    An unpaid work requirement is a requirement that the offender must perform unpaid work.

An unpaid work requirement may be made only if the offender is 16 or 17 at the time of conviction. The number of hours or work must be not less than 40, and not more than 240.

A court may not impose an unpaid work requirement unless:

(a)   after hearing (if the court thinks necessary) an appropriate officer, the court is satisfied that the offender is a suitable person to perform work under such a requirement; and

(b)   the court is satisfied that provision for the offender to work under such a requirement can be made existing local arrangements.

The work must be performed at such times as the responsible officer may specify in instructions. The work must be performed during the period of 12 months beginning with the day on which the order takes effect. A youth rehabilitation order imposing an unpaid work requirement remains in force until the offender has worked under it for the number of hours specified in it, unless the order is revoked, CJIA 2008 Sch.1 para.10.

### Revocation of Order

**Application**    If an application is made by the offender or responsible officer to the appropriate court, and it appears to the court to be in the interests of justice to do so, having regard to circumstances which have arisen since the order was made, the court may either revoke the order, or revoke the order, and deal with the offender, for the offence in respect of which the order was made, in any way in which the court could have dealt with the offender for that offence, CJIA 2008 Sch.2 para.11(1) and (2).

**Good progress**  The circumstances in which a youth rehabilitation order may be revoked include the offender's making good progress or responding satisfactorily to supervision or treatment, CJIA 2008 Sch.2 para.11(3).

**Partial compliance**  If the court revokes the order and deals with the offender for the original offence, the court must take into account the extent to which the offender has complied with the requirements of the order, CJIA 2008 Sch.2 para.11(4).

### Breach: Failure to Comply

An order can be "breached" either by a failure to comply with a requirement imposed under the order, or by a conviction for an offence committed during the currency of the order.

**Requirements involving treatment**  If the order imposes a mental health treatment requirement, a drug treatment requirement, or an intoxicating substance treatment requirement, the offender is not to be treated as having failed to comply with the order on the ground only that the offender had refused to undergo any surgical, electrical or other treatment, if in the opinion of the court, the refusal was reasonable having regard to all the circumstances, CJIA 2008 Sch.2 para.9.

**Youth Court**  If it is proved to the satisfaction of a youth court or magistrates court that an offender subject to a youth rehabilitation order has failed without reasonable excuse to comply with the youth rehabilitation order, the court may deal with the offender by:

(a)  ordering the offender to pay a fine not exceeding £2,500 (except where the failure took place before 3 December 2012);

(b)  by amending the terms of the order so as to impose any requirement which could have been included in the order when it was made in addition to, or in substitution for any requirement or requirements already imposed by the order; or

(c)  by dealing with the offender, for the offence in respect of which the order was made, in any way in which the court could have dealt with the offender for that offence, CJIA 2008 Sch.2 para.6(2).

If the court *amends the order* and imposes a new requirement, the period for compliance with the order may be extended by up to six months, unless the period has previously been extended, CJIA 2008 Sch.2 para.6(6)-(6D).

If the order does not contain an unpaid work requirement, the court may add an unpaid work requirement with a requirement to perform between 20 and 240 hours' work, CJIA 2008 Sch.2 para.6(7).

The court may not add to an existing youth rehabilitation order an extended activity requirement, or a fostering requirement, if the order does not already impose such a requirement, CJIA 2008 Sch.2 para.6(8).

If the order imposes a fostering requirement, the court may impose a new fostering requirement ending not later than 18 months from the date on which the original order was made, CJIA 2008 Sch.2 para.6(9).

If the court *resentences* the offender for the offence (under para c) above, the court must take into account the extent to which the offender has complied with the order. The order must be revoked, CJIA 2008 Sch.2 para.6(4).

If the court is resentencing the offender and the offender has wilfully and persistently failed to comply with a YRO, the court may impose a youth rehabilitation order with intensive supervision and surveillance, CJIA 2008 Sch.2 para.6(12) and (13).

If the original order is a youth rehabilitation order with intensive supervision and surveillance, and the offence for which it was imposed was punishable with imprisonment, the court may impose a custodial sentence notwithstanding the general restrictions on imposing discretionary custodial sentences, CJIA 2008 Sch.2 para.6(12) and (14).

If the order is a youth rehabilitation order with intensive supervision and surveillance which was imposed following the breach of an earlier order, and the original offence was not punishable with imprisonment, the court may deal with the offender by making a detention and training order for a term not exceeding four months, CJIA 2008 Sch.2 para.6(12) and (15).

**Crown Court**   If the order made by the Crown Court contains a direction that further proceedings should be in the youth court or magistrates' court, the youth court or magistrates' court may commit the offender in custody or on bail, to be brought or appear before the Crown Court, CJIA 2008 Sch.2 para.7.

Where an offender appears or is brought before the Crown Court and it is proved to the satisfaction of that court that the offender has failed without reasonable excuse to comply with the youth rehabilitation order, the court may:

(a)   order the offender to pay a fine not exceeding £2,500 (except where the failure took place before 3 December 2012);

(b)   amend the terms of the order so as to impose any requirement which could have been included in the order when it was made, in addition to, or in substitution for, any requirement or requirements already imposed by the order; or

(c)   deal with the offender, for the offence in respect of which the order was made, in any way in which the Crown Court could have dealt with the offender for that offence, CJIA 2008 Sch.2 para.8(2).

If the court *amends the order* and imposes a new requirement, the period for compliance with the order may be extended by up to six months, unless the period has previously been extended, CJIA 2008 Sch.2 paras.(6)– (6D).

If the original order imposes a fostering requirement, the court may substitute a new fostering requirement ending not later than 18 months from the date on which the original order was made, CJIA 2008 Sch.2 para.8(9).

If the court *resentences* the offender for the offence, it must take into account the extent to which the offender has complied with the order. The order must be revoked, CJIA 2008 Sch.2 para.8(2) and (10).

If the order does not contain an unpaid work requirement, the court may add an unpaid work requirement requiring the offender to perform between 20 and 240 hours work. The court may not impose an extended activity requirement, or a fostering requirement, if the order does not already impose such a requirement, CJIA 2008 Sch.2 para.8(7) and (8).

If the offender has wilfully and persistently failed to comply with an order, and the court is dealing with the offender for the original offence, the court may impose a youth rehabilitation order with intensive supervision and surveillance, CJIA 2008 Sch.2 para.8(11) and (12).

If the order is a youth rehabilitation order with intensive supervision and surveillance, and the offence for which it was imposed was punishable with imprisonment, the court may impose a custodial sentence notwithstanding the general restrictions on imposing discretionary custodial sentences, CJIA 2008 Sch.2 para.8(11) and (13).

If the order is a youth rehabilitation order with intensive supervision and surveillance which was imposed following the breach of an earlier order, and the original offence was not punishable with imprisonment, the court may deal with the offender by making a detention and training order for a term not exceeding four months, CJIA 2008 Sch.2 para.8(11) and (14).

### Breach: Conviction of Further Offence

**Youth Court**   Where an order:

(a)   is in force and;
(b)   the offender is convicted of an offence by a youth court or other magistrates' court;
(c)   and the order was made by a youth court or other magistrates' court, or was made by the Crown Court with a direction that further proceedings should be in the youth court or magistrates court; and
(d)   the court is dealing with the offender for the further offence, the court may revoke the order and may deal with the offender, for the offence in respect of which the order was made, in any way in which it could have dealt with the offender for that offence, CJIA 2008 Sch.2 para.18(1)–(4).

The court must not revoke the order and deal with the offender for the original offence, unless it considers that it would be in the interests of justice to do so, having regard to circumstances which have arisen since the youth rehabilitation order was made, CJIA 2008 Sch.2 para.18(5).

The sentencing court must take into account the extent to which the offender has complied with the order, CJIA 2008 Sch.2 para.18(6).

If the youth rehabilitation order was made by the Crown Court, the youth court or magistrates' court may commit the offender in custody, or on bail to the Crown Court, CJIA 2008 Sch.2 para.18(8) and (9).

**Crown Court**   If an offender:

(a)   appears before the Crown Court while an *order is in force*, having been committed by the magistrates' court to the Crown Court for sentence; or

(b)  is convicted by the Crown Court of an offence *while an order is in force*, the Crown Court may revoke the order and may deal with the offender, for the offence in respect of which the order was made, in any way in which the court which made the order could have dealt with the offender for that offence, CJIA 2008 Sch.2 para.19(1)–(3).

The Crown Court must not deal with the offender for the original offence unless it considers that it would be in the interests of justice to do so, having regard to circumstances which have arisen since the youth rehabilitation order was made, CJIA 2008 Sch.2 para.19(4).

The Crown Court must take into account the extent to which the offender has complied with the order, CJIA 2008 Sch.2 para.19(5).

If the offender has been committed to the Crown Court to be dealt with in respect of a youth rehabilitation order following a conviction by a youth court or magistrates' court, the Crown Court may deal with the offender for the later offence in any way which the youth court or magistrates' court' could have dealt with the offender for that offence, CJIA 2008 Sch.2 para.19 (6).

# PART 2: MAXIMUM SENTENCES (INDICTABLE OFFENCES)

# ASSAULTS ON EMERGENCY WORKERS (OFFENCES) ACT 2018

Section 1 (common assault and battery)                    *2 years*

# AVIATION SECURITY ACT 1982

Section 1 (hijacking)                                      *Life*
Section 2 (destroying aircraft)                            *Life*
Section 3 (endangering safety of aircraft)                *Life*
Section 4 (possessing dangerous article)                  *5 years*
Section 6 (inducing offence)                              *Life*

# BAIL ACT 1976

Section 6 (failing to surrender)        *12 months (on indictment)*
                                        *3 months (summarily)\**

Note
*Where an offender is dealt with by the Crown Court for a bail offence, otherwise than on a committal by a magistrates' court under BA 1976 s.6(6) they are to be dealt with as if the bail offence were a contempt of court. In the youth court, an offender under the age of 18 may not be committed to custody for a bail offence.

# BRIBERY ACT 2010

Section 1 (bribery of another person)                              *10 years*
Section 2 (requesting, agreeing to accept or accepting a bribe)    *10 years*
Section 6 (bribery of foreign public official)                     *10 years*
Section 7 (failure of commercial organization to prevent bribery)  *Fine*

# CHILD ABDUCTION ACT 1984

Section 1 (taking out of United Kingdom without consent)    *7 years*
Section 2 (taking child out of lawful control)              *7 years*
Penalty provision: Section 4

# CHILDREN AND YOUNG PERSONS ACT 1933

Section 1 (ill-treatment or neglect etc.)                   *10 years\**

Section 25 (procuring child to go abroad by false representation)                    *2 years*

Note
\* If the offence is committed on or after 29 September 1988; otherwise two years.

## COMPANIES ACT 2006

Section 993 (fraudulent trading)                    *10 years\**

Note
\* The offence may be charged where a relevant event occurs before that date and another relevant event occurs after that date. If so, the maximum sentence is seven years. See SI 2007/2194 para.46.

## COMPUTER MISUSE ACT 1990

Section 1 (securing unauthorised access)                    *2 years\**
Section 2 (unauthorised access with intent)                    *5 years*
Section 3 (unauthorised modification)                    *10 years\*\**
Section 3ZA (unauthorised acts with serious damage)                    *14 years*
Section 3ZA (unauthorised acts with serious damage to national security or human welfare of types in (3)(a) or (b)                    *Life*
Section 3A (providing tools for unauthorised access)                    *2 years*

Note
\* (if offence committed on or after 1 October 2008).
\*\* (if offence committed on or after 1 October 2008; otherwise five years).

## CONTEMPT OF COURT ACT 1981

Section 14 (contempt of superior court)                    *2 years*

## COPYRIGHT DESIGNS AND PATENTS ACT 1988

Offences under s.107(1)(a), (b), (d)(iv) or (e)                    *10 years*
Offences under s.107(2A)                    *2 years*

## CRIME AND DISORDER ACT 1998

Section 29(1)(a) (racially or religiously aggravated unlawful wounding)                    *7 years*
Section 29(1)(b) (racially or religiously aggravated assault occasioning actual bodily harm)                    *7 years*

| | |
|---|---|
| Section 29(1)(c) (racially or religiously aggravated common assault) | *2 years* |
| Section 30 (racially or religiously aggravated criminal damage) | *14 years* |
| Section 31(1)(a) (racially or religiously aggravated causing fear of violence) | *2 years* |
| Section 31(1)(b) (racially or religiously aggravated intentional harassment) | *2 years* |
| Section 32(1)(a) (racially or religiously aggravated harassment) | *2 years* |
| Section 32(1)(b) (racially or religiously aggravated causing fear of violence) | *14 years** |

Note
* If committed on or after 3 April 2017; otherwise seven years.
An offence under s.31(1)(a) or (b) is a specified offence (Criminal Justice Act 2003 Sch.15).

## CRIMINAL ATTEMPTS ACT 1981

| | |
|---|---|
| Section 1 (attempted murder) | *Life* |
| Section 1 (attempting indictable offence) | *As for offence in question* |

Note
Special provisions apply to attempted incest. See Sexual Offences Act 1956.
An attempt to commit an offence which is a specified offence (Criminal Justice Act 2003 Sch.15), or a scheduled offence (SOA 2003 Schs.3 or 5) is also a specified offence or a scheduled offence.

## CRIMINAL DAMAGE ACT 1971

| | |
|---|---|
| Section 1(1) (criminal damage) | *10 years** |
| Section 1(2) (criminal damage with intent to endanger life) | *Life* |
| Section 1(3) (arson) | *Life* |
| Section 2 (threatening to damage property) | *10 years* |
| Section 3 (possession with intent) | *10 years* |
| Penalty provision: Section 4 | |

Note
* If the value of the damage does not exceed £5,000 and the matter comes before the Crown Court under CJA 1988 ss.40 or 41, or PCC(S)A 2000 s.6, the maximum sentence is three months.

## CRIMINAL JUSTICE ACT 1925

| | |
|---|---|
| Section 36(1) (making false statement to procure passport) | *2 years* |

# CRIMINAL JUSTICE ACT 1961

Section 22 (harbouring escaped prisoner)                    *10 years**

Note
* If committed on or after 16 May 1992; otherwise two years.

# CRIMINAL JUSTICE ACT 1988

Section 134 (torture)                                       *Life*
Section 139 (possessing sharp bladed or pointed instrument) *4 years*
(if offence was committed before 12 February, 2007; two years)
Section 139A (possessing offensive weapon on school premises) *4 years**
Section 139AA (threatening with article with a blade or point or
offensive weapon)                                           *4 years*
Section 160 (possessing indecent photograph of child)       *5 years***

Note
* If an offence under ss.(1) was committed before 12 February 2007 the maximum is two years.
** If an offence was committed before 11 January 2001, the offence is summary only with a maximum
sentence of six months.

# CRIMINAL JUSTICE ACT 1993

Section 52 (insider dealing)                                *7 years*

# CRIMINAL JUSTICE (INTERNATIONAL CO-OPERATION) ACT 1990

Section 12 (manufacturing or supplying scheduled substance) *14 years*
Section 19 (having possession of a Class A controlled drug on
a ship)                                                     *Life*
Section 19 (having possession of a Class B or temporary class
controlled drug on a ship)                                  *14 years*
Section 19 (having possession of a Class C controlled drug on
a ship)                                                     *14 years**

Note
* If offence committed on or after 29 January 2004; otherwise five years.
Offences under ss.12 and 19 are drug trafficking offences for the purposes of the Drug Trafficking Act
1994 and the Proceeds of Crime Act 2002 Sch.2.

# CRIMINAL JUSTICE AND PUBLIC ORDER ACT 1994

Section 51 (intimidating witness)                           *5 years*

# CRIMINAL LAW ACT 1967

Section 4 (assisting offender)

| | |
|---|---|
| Sentence for principal offence fixed by law | *10 years* |
| Maximum sentence for principal offence 14 years | *7 years* |
| Maximum sentence for principal offence 10 years | *5 years* |
| Otherwise (normally five years) | *3 years* |

# CRIMINAL LAW ACT 1977

| | |
|---|---|
| Section 1 (conspiracy to commit offence punishable by life imprisonment) | *Life* |
| Section 1 (conspiracy to commit offence for which no maximum is provided) | *Life* |
| Section 1 (conspiracy to commit offence with specified maximum term) | *Maximum term for offence in question* |
| Section 51 (bomb hoax) | *7 years\** |

Note
* If committed on or after 31 October 1991; otherwise five years.

# CUSTOMS AND EXCISE MANAGEMENT ACT 1979

| | |
|---|---|
| Section 50 (importing undutied or prohibited goods) | *7 years* |
| Section 68 (evading prohibition of exportation) | *7 years* |
| Section 170 (evading duty, or prohibition) | *7 years* |
| Section 170B (taking preparatory steps) | *7 years* |

Note
Where an offence under ss.50, 68 or 170 relates to Class A drugs, a temporary class, the maximum is life imprisonment; where the offence relates to Class B or Class C drugs, the maximum is 14 years (if the offence relates to class C drug committed before 29 January 2004, the maximum is five years).
Where an offence under ss.50, 68 or 170 relates to goods prohibited by the Forgery and Counterfeiting Act 1981 ss.20 or 21, the maximum sentence is 10 years.
Where an offence under s.50, s.69 or s.170 relates to nuclear materials, the maximum is 14 years.
Where an offence under ss.50, 68 or 170 relates to certain prohibited weapons within the meaning of the Firearms Act 1968 s.5(1) (excluding weapons falling within ss.5(1)(b) or 5(1A)(b) to (g)), the maximum sentence is life (if committed on or after 14 July 2014; otherwise 10 years).
Offences involving the importation or exportation of controlled drugs are drug trafficking offences for the purposes of the Drug Trafficking Act 1994 and the Proceeds of Crime Act 2002 Sch.2.

# DOMESTIC VIOLENCE, CRIME AND VICTIMS ACT 2004

| | |
|---|---|
| Section 5 (causing or allowing death of child/vulnerable adult) | *14 years* |
| Section 5 (causing or allowing serious injury of child/vulnerable adult) | *10 years* |

## EXPLOSIVE SUBSTANCES ACT 1883

| | |
|---|---|
| Section 2 (causing explosion likely to endanger life) | *Life* |
| Section 3 (attempting to cause explosion, or possessing explosive substance with intent) | *Life* |
| Section 4 (making or possessing explosive substance) | *Life\** |

Note
* If offence is committed on or after 13 April 2015; otherwise 14 years.

## FIREARMS ACT 1968

| | |
|---|---|
| Section 1 (possessing firearm without certificate) | *5 years* |
| Section 1 (possessing shortened shotgun) | *7 years* |
| Section 2 (possessing shotgun without certificate) | *5 years* |
| Section 3 (selling firearm, etc.) | *5 years* |
| Section 4 (shortening shotgun) | *7 years* |
| Section 5(1) and (1A) (possessing, etc., prohibited weapon) | *10 years* |
| Section 5 (2A) (manufacturing or distributing firearms) | *Life* |
| Section 16 (possessing firearm with intent to endanger life) | *Life* |
| Section 16A (possessing firearm with intent to cause fear of violence) | *10 years* |
| Section 17 (using firearm to prevent arrest, or while committing scheduled offence) | *Life* |
| Section 18 (carrying firearm with intent to commit offence) | *Life* |
| Section 19 (carrying firearm other than an airweapon in public place) | *7 years* |
| Section 20 (trespassing with firearm) | *7 years* |
| Section 21 (possessing firearm as former prisoner, etc.) | *5 years* |

Penalty provision: Schedule 6.

## FORGERY AND COUNTERFEITING ACT 1981

| | |
|---|---|
| Section 1 (making false instrument with intent) | *10 years* |
| Section 2 (making copy of false instrument with intent) | *10 years* |
| Section 3 (using false instrument with intent) | *10 years* |
| Section 4 (using copy of false instrument) | *10 years* |
| Section 5(1) (custody or control of false instrument with intent) | *10 years* |
| Section 5(2) (custody or control of false instrument, no intent) | *2 years* |
| Section 5(3) (making machine, etc., with intent) | *10 years* |
| Section 5(4) (making machine, etc., no intent) | *2 years* |

Penalty provision: Section 6.

# FRAUD ACT 2006

| | |
|---|---|
| Section 1 (fraud) | *10 years* |
| Section 6 (possession of article for use in fraud) | *5 years* |
| Section 7 (making or supplying article for use in fraud) | *10 years* |

# IDENTITY DOCUMENTS ACT 2010

| | |
|---|---|
| Section 4 (possession of false identity document with improper intent) | *10 years* |
| Section 5 (possession of apparatus etc. with improper intent) | *10 years* |
| Section 6 (possession of false identity document) | *2 years* |

# IMMIGRATION ACT 1971

| | |
|---|---|
| Section 24A (obtaining admission by deception) | *2 years* |
| Section 25 (facilitating illegal entry) | *14 years* |
| Section 25A (assisting asylum seeker) | *14 years* |
| Section 25B (assisting entry in breach of deportation order) | *14 years* |

# INCITEMENT TO DISAFFECTION ACT 1934

| | |
|---|---|
| Section 1 (seducing member of forces from duty) | *2 years* |
| Section 2 (possessing document, etc.) | *2 years* |
| Penalty provision: Section 3. | |

# INDECENCY WITH CHILDREN ACT 1960

| | |
|---|---|
| Section 1 (gross indecency with child) | *10 years* |

(If the offence was committed on or after 1 October 1997; otherwise two years).

This Act was repealed by the SOA 2003 with effect from 1 May 2004, but its practical effect has been preserved by the Interpretation Act 1978 s.16. See note to Sexual Offences Act 1956.

# INDECENT DISPLAYS (CONTROL) ACT 1981

| | |
|---|---|
| Section 1 (displaying indecent matter) | *2 years* |

Penalty provision: Section 4.

## INFANTICIDE ACT 1938

Section 1 (infanticide)                                    *Life*

## INFANT LIFE (PRESERVATION) ACT 1929

Section 1 (child destruction)                              *Life*

## KNIVES ACT 1997

Section 1 (marketing combat knife)                         *2 years*
Section 2 (publishing material)                            *2 years*

## MENTAL HEALTH ACT 1983

Section 126 (possession of false document)                 *2 years*
Section 127 (ill-treating patient)                         *5 years*
(if the offence was committed on or after 1 October 2007;
otherwise two years)
Section 128 (assisting absconded patient)                  *2 years*

## MERCHANT SHIPPING ACT 1995

Section 58 (endangering ship)                              *2 years*

## MISUSE OF DRUGS ACT 1971

Section 4(2) (producing Class A drug)                      *Life*
Section 4(2) (producing Class B drug)                      *14 years*
Section 4(2) (producing Class C drug)                      *14 years**
Section 4(3) (supplying Class A drug)                      *Life*
Section 4(3) (supplying Class B drug)                      *14 years*
Section 4(3) (supplying Class C drug)                      *14 years**
Section 5(2) (possessing Class A drug)                     *7 years*
Section 5(2) (possessing Class B drug)                     *5 years*

| | |
|---|---|
| Section 5(2) (possessing Class C drug) | *2 years* |
| Section 5(3) (possessing Class A drug with intent to supply) | *Life* |
| Section 5(3) (possessing Class B drug with intent to supply) | *14 years* |
| Section 5(3) (possessing Class C drug with intent to supply) | *14 years\** |
| Section 6(2) (cultivating cannabis plant) | *14 years* |
| Section 8 (occupier of premises permitting supply, etc. of Class A drugs) | *14 years* |
| Section 8 (occupier of premises permitting supply, etc. of Class B drugs) | *14 years* |
| Section 8 (occupier of premises permitting supply, etc. of Class C drugs) | *14 years\** |
| Section 9 (opium) 14 years | *14 years* |
| Section 11(2)(contravention of directions) | *2 years* |
| Section 12(6) (contravention of prohibition on prescribing in relation to Class A drug) | *14 years* |
| Section 12(6) (contravention of prohibition on prescribing in relation to Class B drug) | *14 years* |
| Section 12(6) (contravention of prohibition on prescribing in relation to Class C drug) | *14 years\** |
| Section 13(3) (contravention of prohibition on supplying in relation to Class A drug) | *14 years* |
| Section 13(3) (contravention of prohibition on supplying in relation to Class B drug) | *14 years* |
| Section 13(3) (contravention of prohibition on supplying in relation to Class C drug) | *14 years\** |
| Section 17(4) (giving false information) | *2 years* |
| Section 18 (contravention of regulations, etc.) | *2 years* |
| Section 20 (assisting offence outside United Kingdom) | *14 years* |
| Section 23 (obstructing search) | *2 years* |
| Penalty provision: Schedule 4 | |

Note

* For all Class C drug offences it is 14 years (if committed on or after 29 January 2004; otherwise five years.

## MODERN SLAVERY ACT 2015

| | |
|---|---|
| Section 1 (slavery, servitude and forced or compulsory labour) | *Life* |
| Section 2 (human trafficking) | *Life* |
| Section 4 (committing an offence with intent to commit an offence under s.2) | *10 years\** |

Note

* Unless the offence under s.4 is committed by kidnapping/false imprisonment, then the maximum is life.

## OBSCENE PUBLICATIONS ACT 1959

Section 2 (publishing obscene article or having article for *5 years\**
publication)

Note
\* If the offence was committed on or after 26 January, 2009, otherwise three years.

## OFFENCES AGAINST THE PERSON ACT 1861

| | |
|---|---|
| Section 4 (soliciting to murder) | *Life* |
| Section 16 (threatening to kill) | *10 years* |
| Section 18 (wounding with intent to cause grievous bodily harm) | *Life* |
| Section 20 (unlawful wounding) | *5 years* |
| Section 21 (choking, etc., with intent) | *Life* |
| Section 22 (administering drug with intent) | *Life* |
| Section 23 (administering noxious thing to endanger life) | *10 years* |
| Section 24 (administering noxious thing to injure, aggrieve or annoy) | *5 years* |
| Section 27 (abandoning child) | *5 years* |
| Section 28 (causing grievous bodily harm by explosion) | *Life* |
| Section 29 (using explosives with intent, throwing corrosive substance with intent) | *Life* |
| Section 30 (placing explosive substance with intent) | *14 years* |
| Section 31 (setting spring gun, etc.) | *5 years* |
| Section 32 (endangering safety of railway passengers) | *Life* |
| Section 33 (throwing object with intent to endanger rail passenger) | *Life* |
| Section 34 (endangering rail passenger by neglect) | *2 years* |
| Section 35 (causing grievous bodily harm by wanton driving) | *2 years* |
| Section 36 (obstructing minister of religion) | *2 years* |
| Section 38 (assault with intent to resist arrest) | *2 years* |
| Section 47 (assault occasioning actual bodily harm) | *5 years* |
| Section 58 (procuring miscarriage) | *Life* |
| Section 59 (supplying instrument, etc.) | *5 years* |
| Section 60 (concealment of birth) | *2 years* |

## OFFICIAL SECRETS ACT 1911

| | |
|---|---|
| Section 1 (act prejudicial to safety of state) | *14 years* |

Penalty provision: Official Secrets Act 1920 s.8(1).

## OFFICIAL SECRETS ACT 1920

| | |
|---|---|
| Section 1(1) (gaining admission to prohibited place) | *2 years* |
| Section 1(2) (retaining document, etc.) | *2 years* |
| Section 3 (interfering with police officer or sentry) | *2 years* |

Penalty provision: Section 8(2).

## OFFICIAL SECRETS ACT 1989

| | |
|---|---|
| Section 1 (disclosing information) | *2 years* |
| Section 3 (Crown servant making disclosure) | *2 years* |
| Section 4 (unauthorised disclosure) | *2 years* |
| Section 5 (unauthorised disclosure by recipient) | *2 years* |
| Section 6 (unauthorised disclosure) | *2 years* |

Penalty provision: Section 10.

## PERJURY ACT 1911

| | |
|---|---|
| Section 1 (witness making untrue statement) | *7 years* |
| Section 1A (false statement for foreign proceedings) | *2 years* |

## PREVENTION OF CRIME ACT 1953

| | |
|---|---|
| Section 1 (possessing offensive weapon) | *4 years** |
| Section 1A (threatening with offensive weapon in public) | *4 years* |

Note
* If committed after 4 July 1996, otherwise two years.

## PRISON ACT 1952

| | |
|---|---|
| Section 39 (assisting escape) | *10 years* |
| Section 40B (bringing etc. list A article into prison) | *10 years* |
| Section 40C (bringing etc. list B article into prison) | *2 years* |
| Section 40CA (possession of knife in prison) | *4 years* |
| Section 40CB (throwing article into prison) | *2 years* |
| Section 40D (transmitting recordings in and out of prison) | *2 years* |

# PRISON SECURITY ACT 1992

| | |
|---|---|
| Section 1 (prison mutiny) | *10 years* |

# PROCEEDS OF CRIME ACT 2002

| | |
|---|---|
| Section 327 (concealing, etc.) | *14 years* |
| Section 328 (arrangements) | *14 years* |
| Section 329 (acquisition, use and possession) | *14 years* |
| Section 330 (failure to disclose: regulated sector) | *5 years* |
| Section 331(failure to disclose: nominated officers in the regulated sector) | *5 years* |
| Section 332(failure to disclose: other nominated officers) | *5 years* |

# PROTECTION FROM HARASSMENT ACT 1997

| | |
|---|---|
| Section 3 (breach of injunction) | *5 years* |
| Section 4 (causing fear of violence) | *10 years** |
| Section 4A (stalking involving fear of violence or serious alarm or distress) | *10 years** |

Note
* The maximum sentence is 10 years if the offence is committed on or after 3 April 2017; otherwise five years.

# PROTECTION OF CHILDREN ACT 1978

| | |
|---|---|
| Section 1 (taking, distributing, possessing, publishing indecent photograph of child) | *10 years** |

Penalty provision: Section 6.

# PUBLIC ORDER ACT 1936

| | |
|---|---|
| Section 2 (unlawful organisation) | *2 years* |

Penalty provision: Section 7.

# PUBLIC ORDER ACT 1986

| | |
|---|---|
| Section 1 (riot) | *10 years* |
| Section 2 (violent disorder) | *5 years* |
| Section 3 (affray) | *3 years* |

Section 18 (using words to stir up racial hatred)                   *7 years\**

Section 19 (distributing material to stir up racial hatred)         *7 years\**

Section 20 (performing play to stir up racial hatred)               *7 years\**

Section 21 (distributing recording to stir up racial hatred)        *7 years\**

Section 22 (broadcasting programme)                                 *7 years\**

Section 23 (possessing material to stir up racial hatred)           *7 years\**

Penalty provision: Sections 1-3, those sections. Sections 18-23
Section 27(3).

Note
\* The maximum penalty is seven years unless the offence was committed before 14 December 2001, in which case it is two years.

## REPRESENTATION OF THE PEOPLE ACT 1983

Section 60 (personation)                                            *2 years*

## SEXUAL OFFENCES ACT 2003

Section 1 (rape)                                                    *Life*

Section 2 (assault by penetration)                                 *Life*

Section 3 (sexual assault)                                         *10 years*

Section 4 (causing sexual activity with penetration)               *Life*

Section 4 (causing sexual activity without penetration)            *10 years*

Section 5 (penetration of child under 13)                          *Life*

Section 6 (assault of person under 13 by penetration)              *Life*

Section 7 (sexual assault on person under 13)                      *14 years*

Section 8 (causing person under 13 to engage in sexual activity
involving penetration)                                              *Life*

Section 8 (causing person under 13 to engage in sexual activity
without penetration)                                                *14 years*

Section 9 (sexual activity with person under 16)                   *14 years*

Section 10 (causing person under 16 to engage in sexual activity)  *14 years*

Section 11 (sexual activity in presence of person under 16)        *10 years*

Section 12 (causing person under 16 to watch sexual act)           *10 years*

Section 13 (child sex offence committed by person under 18)        *5 years*

Section 14 (arranging child sex offence)                           *14 years*

Section 15 (meeting person under 16 with intent following
grooming)                                                          *10 years*

Section 15A (sexual communication with a child)                    *2 years*

Section 16 (abuse of trust by sexual activity)                     *5 years*

Section 17 (abuse of trust by causing sexual activity)             *5 years*

Section 18 (abuse of trust by sexual activity in presence of child) *5 years*

Section 19 (abuse of trust by causing child to watch sexual act) *5 years*

Section 25 (sexual activity by person over 18 with family member under 18) *14 years*

Section 25 (sexual activity by person under 18 with family member under 18) *5 years*

Section 26 (person over 18 inciting family member under 18 to engage in sexual activity) *14 years*

Section 26 (person under 18 inciting family member under 18 to engage in sexual activity) *5 years*

Section 30 (sexual activity involving penetration with person with mental disorder) *Life*

Section 30 (sexual activity not involving penetration with person with mental disorder) *14 years*

Section 31 (causing or inciting sexual activity involving penetration by person with mental disorder) *Life*

Section 31 (causing or inciting sexual activity not involving penetration by person with mental disorder) *14 years*

Section 32 (engaging in sexual activity in presence of person with mental disorder) *10 years*

Section 33 (causing person with mental disorder to watch sexual act) *10 years*

Section 34 (offering inducement to person with mental disorder to engage in sexual act involving penetration) *Life*

Section 34 (offering inducement to person with mental disorder to engage in sexual act not involving penetration) *14 years*

Section 35 (inducing person with mental disorder to engage in sexual act involving penetration) *Life*

Section 35 (inducing person with mental disorder to engage in sexual act not involving penetration) *14 years*

Section 36 (causing person with mental disorder to watch sexual act by inducement etc.) *10 years*

Section 37 (causing person with mental disorder to watch third party sexual act by inducement etc.) *10 years*

Section 38 (sexual acts involving penetration by care worker with person with mental disorder) *14 years*

Section 38 (sexual acts not involving penetration by care worker with person with mental disorder) *10 years*

Section 39 (care worker inciting person with mental disorder engage in sexual act involving penetration) *14 years*

Section 39 (care worker inciting person with mental disorder engage in sexual act not involving penetration) *10 years*

Section 40 (care worker engaging in sexual act in presence of person with mental disorder) *7 years*

Section 41 (care worker causing person with mental disorder to watch sexual act) *7 years*

| | |
|---|---|
| Section 47 (paying for sexual service involving penetration by person under 13) | *Life* |
| Section 47 (paying for sexual service by person under 16) | *14 years* |
| Section 47 (paying for sexual service by person under 18) | *7 years* |
| Section 48 (causing person under 18 to become involved in prostitution or pornography) | *14 years* |
| Section 49 (controlling prostitution by person under 18) | *14 years* |
| Section 50 (facilitating prostitution by person under 18) | *14 years* |
| Section 52 (causing or inciting prostitution) | *7 years* |
| Section 53 (controlling prostitution for gain) | *7 years* |
| Section 57 (arranging arrival for purposes of prostitution) | *14 years\** |
| Section 58 (facilitating travel for purposes of prostitution) | *14 years\** |
| Section 59 (facilitating departure for purposes of prostitution) | *14 years\** |
| Section 59A (trafficking people for sexual exploitation) | *14 years\*\** |
| Section 61 (administering substance with intent to enable sexual activity) | *10 years* |
| Section 62 (committing offence with intent to commit sexual offence) | *10 years* |
| Section 63 (trespass with intent to commit sexual offence) | *10 years* |
| Section 64 (sexual penetration of adult relative) | *2 years* |
| Section 65 (consenting to sexual penetration by adult relative) | *2 years* |
| Section 66 (intentional exposure) | *2 years* |
| Section 67 (observing private act) | *2 years* |
| Section 69 (sexual act with animal) | *2 years* |
| Section 70 (sexual penetration of corpse) | *2 years* |

Note

\* These offences were repealed on 6 April 2013, see SI 2013/470 for transitional and saving provision.

\*\* This offence was repealed on 30 July 2015, see SI 2015/1476 for transitional and saving provision.

## ROAD TRAFFIC ACT 1988

| | |
|---|---|
| Section 1 (causing death by dangerous driving) | *14 years* |
| Section 1A (causing serious injury by dangerous driving) | *5 years* |
| Section 2 (dangerous driving) | *2 years* |
| Section 2B (causing death by careless or inconsiderate driving) | *5 years* |
| Section 3ZB (causing death by driving while unlicenced, disqualified or uninsured) | *2 years* |
| Section 3ZC (causing death by driving: disqualified drivers) | *10 years* |
| Section 3ZD (causing serious injury by driving: disqualified drivers) | *4 years* |
| Section 3A (causing death by careless driving, having consumed alcohol) | *14 years* |

Penalty provision: RTOA 1988 Sch. 2.

## SERIOUS CRIME ACT 2007

Section 44 (encouraging or assisting commission of offence) ... if the anticipated offence is murder, life imprisonment, otherwise the maximum sentence for the anticipated or reference offence.

Section 45 (encouraging or assisting commission of offence, believing it will be committed) ... if the anticipated offence is murder, life imprisonment, otherwise the maximum sentence for the anticipated or reference offence.

Section 46 (encouraging or assisting commission of one or more offences) ... if the anticipated or reference offence is murder, life imprisonment, otherwise the maximum sentence for the anticipated or reference offence.

## SEXUAL OFFENCES ACT 1956

Most sections of the Sexual Offences Act 1956 are repealed with effect from 1 May 2004, by the Sexual Offences Act 2003. References in other statutes (such as the PCC(S)A 2000 s.161) are also for the most part repealed by the Sexual Offences Act 2003. The liability of an offender to be sentenced for a sexual offence committed before 1 May 2004, depends on the Interpretation Act 1978 s.16, which provides:

"Without prejudice to section 15, where an Act repeals an enactment, the repeal does not, unless the contrary intention appears,—

(c) affect any right, privilege, obligation or liability acquired, accrued or incurred under that enactment;

(d) affect any penalty, forfeiture or punishment incurred in respect of any offence committed against that enactment;

(e) affect any investigation, legal proceeding or remedy in respect of any such right, privilege, obligation, liability, penalty, forfeiture or punishment; and any such investigation, legal proceeding or remedy may be instituted, continued or enforced, and any such penalty, forfeiture or punishment may be imposed, as if the repealing Act had not been passed."

This section therefore preserves the effect of the Sexual Offences Act 1956, and preserves the effect of statutory provisions referring to provisions of that Act, in respect of offences committed on or before 1 May 2004.

| | |
|---|---|
| Section 1 (rape) | *Life* |
| Section 2 (procurement of woman by threats) | *2 years* |
| Section 3 (procurement by false pretences) | *2 years* |
| Section 4 (administering drugs) | *2 years* |
| Section 5 (intercourse with girl under 13) | *Life* |

| | |
|---|---|
| Section 6 (unlawful sexual intercourse with girl under 16) | *2 years* |
| Section 7 (intercourse with defective) | *2 years* |
| Section 9 (procurement of defective) | *2 years* |
| Section 10 (incest by man with girl under 13) (attempt, seven years) | *Life* |
| Section 10 (incest by man) (attempt, two years) | *7 years* |
| Section 11 (incest by woman) (attempt, two years) | *7 years* |
| Section 12 (buggery with person under 16) | *Life* |
| Section 12 (buggery with animal) | *Life* |
| Section 12 (buggery of person under 18 by person over 21) | *5 years* |
| Section 12 (other forms of buggery) | *2 years* |
| Section 13 (indecency by man over 21 with man under 18) | *5 years* |
| Section 13 (indecency by males) | *2 years* |
| Section 14 (indecent assault on woman) | *10 years* |

(If the offence was committed on or after 16 September 1985: otherwise two years, unless the victim was under 13 and her age was stated in the indictment, in which case the maximum is five years).

| | |
|---|---|
| Section 15 (indecent assault on male) | *10 years* |
| Section 16 (assault with intent to bugger) | *10 years* |
| Section 17 (abduction) | *14 years* |
| Section 19 (abduction of girl under 18) | *2 years* |
| Section 20 (abduction of girl under 16) | *2 years* |
| Section 21 (abduction of defective) | *2 years* |
| Section 22 (causing prostitution) | *2 years* |
| Section 23 (procuring girl under 21) | *2 years* |
| Section 24 (detention in brothel) | *2 years* |
| Section 25 (permitting premises to be used by girl under 13) | *Life* |
| Section 26 (permitting premises to be used) | *2 years* |
| Section 27 (permitting defective to use premises) | *2 years* |
| Section 28 (causing prostitution of girl under 16) | *2 years* |
| Section 29 (causing prostitution of defective) | *2 years* |
| Section 30 (living on earnings of prostitution) | *7 years* |
| Section 31 (controlling prostitute) | *7 years* |
| Section 32 (man soliciting) | *2 years* |
| Section 33A (keeping brothel used for prostitution) | *7 years* |

## SEXUAL OFFENCES (AMENDMENT) ACT 2000

| | |
|---|---|
| Section 3 (abuse of position of trust) | *5 years* |

Note
This Act was repealed by the SOA 2003; but see the note to the Sexual Offences Act 1956.

## SUICIDE ACT 1961

Section 2 (aiding suicide)                                    *14 years*

## THEFT ACT 1968

Section 7 (theft)                                             *7 years*
Section 8 (robbery)                                           *Life*
Section 9 (burglary of dwelling)                             *14 years*
Section 9 (burglary of building other than dwelling)         *10 years*
Section 10 (aggravated burglary)                             *Life*
Section 11 (removing object from public place)               *5 years*
Section 12A (aggravated vehicle taking resulting in death)   *14 years*
Section 12A (aggravated vehicle taking not resulting in death) *2 years*

Note
If the offence is aggravated vehicle taking by reason of causing damage, and the value of the damage does not exceed £5,000, the offence will normally be dealt with as a summary offence and the maximum sentence is six months.

Section 13 (abstracting electricity)                         *5 years*
Section 15 (obtaining by deception)                          *10 years*
Section 15A (obtaining money transfer by deception)          *10 years*
Section 16 (obtaining pecuniary advantage)                   *5 years*
Section 17 (false accounting)                                *7 years*
Section 20 (destroying valuable security etc.)               *7 years*
Section 22 (handling)                                        *14 years*

Note
The definition of burglary is amended by the SOA 2003 to omit references to an intent to rape; offences which would formerly have been charged as burglary with intent to rape will now be charged as trespass with intent, contrary to s.63.

## THEFT ACT 1978

Section 1 (obtaining services)                               *5 years*
Section 2 (evading liability, etc.)                          *5 years*
Section 3 (making off without payment)                       *2 years*
Penalty provision: Section 4

## VALUE ADDED TAX ACT 1994

Section 72 (fraudulently evading VAT, etc.)                  *7 years*

## VIOLENT CRIME REDUCTION ACT 2006

Section 28 (using another to hide weapon etc.)

| | |
|---|---|
| If weapon is weapon to which CJA 1988 s.141 or 141A applies | *4 years* |
| If weapon is prohibited weapon (with exceptions) and offender is over 16 | *10 years* |
| Other cases | *5 years* |

# PART 3: SCHEDULES

**Specified violent offences**

1       Manslaughter.

2       Kidnapping.

3       False imprisonment.

4       An offence under section 4 of the Offences against the Person Act 1861 (soliciting murder).

5       An offence under section 16 of that Act (threats to kill).

6       An offence under section 18 of that Act (wounding with intent to cause grievous bodily harm).

7       An offence under section 20 of that Act (malicious wounding).

8       An offence under section 21 of that Act (attempting to choke, suffocate or strangle in order to commit or assist in committing an indictable offence).

9       An offence under section 22 of that Act (using chloroform etc. to commit or assist in the committing of any indictable offence).

10     An offence under section 23 of that Act (maliciously administering poison etc. so as to endanger life or inflict grievous bodily harm).

11     An offence under section 27 of that Act (abandoning children).

12     An offence under section 28 of that Act (causing bodily injury by explosives).

13     An offence under section 29 of that Act (using explosives etc. with intent to do grievous bodily harm).

14     An offence under section 30 of that Act (placing explosives with intent to do bodily injury).

15     An offence under section 31 of that Act (setting spring guns etc. with intent to do grievous bodily harm).

16     An offence under section 32 of that Act (endangering the safety of railway passengers).

17     An offence under section 35 of that Act (injuring persons by furious driving).

18     An offence under section 37 of that Act (assaulting officer preserving wreck).

19     An offence under section 38 of that Act (assault with intent to resist arrest).

20     An offence under section 47 of that Act (assault occasioning actual bodily harm).

21     An offence under section 2 of the Explosive Substances Act 1883 (causing explosion likely to endanger life or property).

22     An offence under section 3 of that Act (attempt to cause explosion, or making or keeping explosive with intent to endanger life or property).

| 22A | An offence under section 4 of that Act (making or possession of explosive under suspicious circumstances). |
| 23 | An offence under section 1 of the Infant Life (Preservation) Act 1929 (child destruction). |
| 24 | An offence under section 1 of the Children and Young Persons Act 1933 (c. 12) (cruelty to children). |
| 25 | An offence under section 1 of the Infanticide Act 1938 (infanticide). |
| 26 | An offence under section 16 of the Firearms Act 1968 (possession of firearm with intent to endanger life). |
| 27 | An offence under section 16A of that Act (possession of firearm with intent to cause fear of violence). |
| 28 | An offence under section 17(1) of that Act (use of firearm to resist arrest). |
| 29 | An offence under section 17(2) of that Act (possession of firearm at time of committing or being arrested for offence specified in Schedule 1 to that Act). |
| 30 | An offence under section 18 of that Act (carrying a firearm with criminal intent). |
| 31 | An offence under section 8 of the Theft Act 1968 (robbery or assault with intent to rob). |
| 32 | An offence under section 9 of that Act of burglary with intent to— |

(a) inflict grievous bodily harm on a person, or
(b) do unlawful damage to a building or anything in it.

| 33 | An offence under section 10 of that Act (aggravated burglary). |
| 34 | An offence under section 12A of that Act (aggravated vehicle-taking) involving an accident which caused the death of any person. |
| 35 | An offence of arson under section 1 of the Criminal Damage Act 1971. |
| 36 | An offence under section 1(2) of that Act (destroying or damaging property) other than an offence of arson. |
| 37 | An offence under section 1 of the Taking of Hostages Act 1982 (hostage-taking). |
| 38 | An offence under section 1 of the Aviation Security Act 1982 (hijacking). |
| 39 | An offence under section 2 of that Act (destroying, damaging or endangering safety of aircraft). |
| 40 | An offence under section 3 of that Act (other acts endangering or likely to endanger safety of aircraft). |
| 41 | An offence under section 4 of that Act (offences in relation to certain dangerous articles). |
| 42 | An offence under section 127 of the Mental Health Act 1983 (ill-treatment of patients). |
| 43 | An offence under section 1 of the Prohibition of Female Circumcision Act 1985 (prohibition of female circumcision). |
| 44 | An offence under section 1 of the Public Order Act 1986 (riot). |
| 45 | An offence under section 2 of that Act (violent disorder). |
| 46 | An offence under section 3 of that Act (affray). |

| | |
|---|---|
| 47 | An offence under section 134 of the Criminal Justice Act 1988 (torture). |
| 48 | An offence under section 1 of the Road Traffic Act 1988 (causing death by dangerous driving). |
| 48A | An offence under section 3ZC of that Act (causing death by driving: disqualified drivers). |
| 49 | An offence under section 3A of that Act (causing death by careless driving when under influence of drink or drugs). |
| 50 | An offence under section 1 of the Aviation and Maritime Security Act 1990 (endangering safety at aerodromes). |
| 51 | An offence under section 9 of that Act (hijacking of ships). |
| 52 | An offence under section 10 of that Act (seizing or exercising control of fixed platforms). |
| 53 | An offence under section 11 of that Act (destroying fixed platforms or endangering their safety). |
| 54 | An offence under section 12 of that Act (other acts endangering or likely to endanger safe navigation). |
| 55 | An offence under section 13 of that Act (offences involving threats). |
| 56 | An offence under Part II of the Channel Tunnel (Security) Order 1994 (S.I. 1994/570) (offences relating to Channel Tunnel trains and the tunnel system). |
| 57 | An offence under section 4 or 4A of the Protection from Harassment Act 1997 (putting people in fear of violence and stalking involving fear of violence or serious alarm or distress) |
| 58 | An offence under section 29 of the Crime and Disorder Act 1998 (c. 37) (racially or religiously aggravated assaults). |
| 59 | An offence falling within section 31(1)(a) or (b) of that Act (racially or religiously aggravated offences under section 4 or 4A of the Public Order Act 1986). |
| 59A | An offence under section 54 of the Terrorism Act 2000 (weapons training). |
| 59B | An offence under section 56 of that Act (directing terrorist organisation). |
| 59C | An offence under section 57 of that Act (possession of article for terrorist purposes). |
| 59D | An offence under section 59 of that Act (inciting terrorism over- seas). |
| 60 | An offence under section 51 or 52 of the International Criminal Court Act 2001 (genocide, crimes against humanity, war crimes and related offences), other than one involving murder. |
| 60A | An offence under section 47 of the Anti-terrorism, Crime and Security Act 2001 (use etc of nuclear weapons). |
| 60B | An offence under section 50 of that Act (assisting or inducing certain weapons-related acts overseas). |
| 60C | An offence under section 113 of that Act (use of noxious substance or thing to cause harm or intimidate). |
| 61 | An offence under section 1 of the Female Genital Mutilation Act 2003 (female genital mutilation). |

62      An offence under section 2 of that Act (assisting a girl to mutilate her own genitalia).

63      An offence under section 3 of that Act (assisting a non-UK person to mutilate overseas a girl's genitalia).

63A    An offence under section 5 of the Domestic Violence, Crime and Victims Act 2004 (causing or allowing a child or vulnerable adult to die or suffer serious physical harm).

63B    An offence under section 5 of the Terrorism Act 2006 (preparation of terrorist acts).

63C    An offence under section 6 of that Act (training for terrorism).

63D    An offence under section 9 of that Act (making or possession of radioactive device or material).

63E    An offence under section 10 of that Act (use of radioactive device or material for terrorist purposes etc).

63F    An offence under section 11 of that Act (terrorist threats relating to radioactive devices etc).

63G    An offence under section 1 of the Modern Slavery Act 2015 (slavery, servitude and forced or compulsory labour).

63H    An offence under section 2 of that Act (human trafficking) which is not within Part 2 of this Schedule.

64

(1)   Aiding, abetting, counselling or procuring the commission of an offence specified in the preceding paragraphs of this Part of this Schedule.

(2)   An attempt to commit such an offence.

(3)   Conspiracy to commit such an offence.

(4)   Incitement to commit such an offence.

(5)   An offence under Part 2 of the Serious Crime Act 2007 in relation to which an offence specified in the preceding paragraphs of this Part of this Schedule is the offence (or one of the offences) which the person intended or believed would be committed.

65

(1)   An attempt to commit murder.

(2)   Conspiracy to commit murder.

(3)   Incitement to commit murder.

(4)   An offence under Part 2 of the Serious Crime Act 2007 in relation to which murder is the offence (or one of the offences) which the person intended or believed would be committed.

## Specified sexual offences

66      An offence under section 1 of the Sexual Offences Act 1956 (rape).

67      An offence under section 2 of that Act (procurement of woman by threats).

68      An offence under section 3 of that Act (procurement of woman by false pretences).

| | |
|---|---|
| 69 | An offence under section 4 of that Act (administering drugs to obtain or facilitate intercourse). |
| 70 | An offence under section 5 of that Act (intercourse with girl under thirteen). |
| 71 | An offence under section 6 of that Act (intercourse with girl under 16). |
| 72 | An offence under section 7 of that Act (intercourse with a defective). |
| 73 | An offence under section 9 of that Act (procurement of a defective). |
| 74 | An offence under section 10 of that Act (incest by a man). |
| 75 | An offence under section 11 of that Act (incest by a woman). |
| 76 | An offence under section 14 of that Act (indecent assault on a woman). |
| 77 | An offence under section 15 of that Act (indecent assault on a man). |
| 78 | An offence under section 16 of that Act (assault with intent to commit buggery). |
| 79 | An offence under section 17 of that Act (abduction of woman by force or for the sake of her property). |
| 80 | An offence under section 19 of that Act (abduction of unmarried girl under eighteen from parent or guardian). |
| 81 | An offence under section 20 of that Act (abduction of unmarried girl under sixteen from parent or guardian). |
| 82 | An offence under section 21 of that Act (abduction of defective from parent or guardian). |
| 83 | An offence under section 22 of that Act (causing prostitution of women). |
| 84 | An offence under section 23 of that Act (procuration of girl under twenty-one). |
| 85 | An offence under section 24 of that Act (detention of woman in brothel). |
| 86 | An offence under section 25 of that Act (permitting girl under thirteen to use premises for intercourse). |
| 87 | An offence under section 26 of that Act (permitting girl under sixteen to use premises for intercourse). |
| 88 | An offence under section 27 of that Act (permitting defective to use premises for intercourse). |
| 89 | An offence under section 28 of that Act (causing or encouraging the prostitution of, intercourse with or indecent assault on girl under sixteen). |
| 90 | An offence under section 29 of that Act (causing or encouraging prostitution of defective). |
| 91 | An offence under section 32 of that Act (soliciting by men). |
| 92A | An offence under section 33A of that Act (keeping a brothel used for prostitution). |
| 93 | An offence under section 128 of the Mental Health Act 1959 (sexual intercourse with patients). |
| 94 | An offence under section 1 of the Indecency with Children Act 1960 (indecent conduct towards young child). |
| 95 | An offence under section 4 of the Sexual Offences Act 1967 (procuring others to commit homosexual acts). |

| | |
|---|---|
| 96 | An offence under section 5 of that Act (living on earnings of male prostitution). |
| 97 | An offence under section 9 of the Theft Act 1968 (c. 60) of burglary with intent to commit rape. |
| 98 | An offence under section 54 of the Criminal Law Act 1977 (c. 45) (inciting girl under sixteen to have incestuous sexual intercourse). |
| 99 | An offence under section 1 of the Protection of Children Act 1978 (c. 37) (indecent photographs of children). |
| 100 | An offence under section 170 of the Customs and Excise Management Act 1979 (c. 2) (penalty for fraudulent evasion of duty etc.) in relation to goods prohibited to be imported under section 42 of the Customs Consolidation Act 1876 (c. 36) (indecent or obscene articles). |
| 101 | An offence under section 160 of the Criminal Justice Act 1988 (c. 33) (possession of indecent photograph of a child). |
| 102 | An offence under section 1 of the Sexual Offences Act 2003 (c. 42) (rape). |
| 103 | An offence under section 2 of that Act (assault by penetration). |
| 104 | An offence under section 3 of that Act (sexual assault). |
| 105 | An offence under section 4 of that Act (causing a person to engage in sexual activity without consent). |
| 106 | An offence under section 5 of that Act (rape of a child under 13). |
| 107 | An offence under section 6 of that Act (assault of a child under 13 by penetration). |
| 108 | An offence under section 7 of that Act (sexual assault of a child under 13). |
| 109 | An offence under section 8 of that Act (causing or inciting a child under 13 to engage in sexual activity). |
| 110 | An offence under section 9 of that Act (sexual activity with a child). |
| 111 | An offence under section 10 of that Act (causing or inciting a child to engage in sexual activity). |
| 112 | An offence under section 11 of that Act (engaging in sexual activity in the presence of a child). |
| 113 | An offence under section 12 of that Act (causing a child to watch a sexual act). |
| 114 | An offence under section 13 of that Act (child sex offences committed by children or young persons). |
| 115 | An offence under section 14 of that Act (arranging or facilitating commission of a child sex offence). |
| 116 | An offence under section 15 of that Act (meeting a child following sexual grooming etc.) |
| 116A | An offence under section 15A of that Act (sexual communication with a child). |
| 117 | An offence under section 16 of that Act (abuse of position of trust: sexual activity with a child). |
| 118 | An offence under section 17 of that Act (abuse of position of trust: causing or inciting a child to engage in sexual activity). |

119    An offence under section 18 of that Act (abuse of position of trust: sexual activity in the presence of a child).

120    An offence under section 19 of that Act (abuse of position of trust: causing a child to watch a sexual act).

121    An offence under section 25 of that Act (sexual activity with a child family member).

122    An offence under section 26 of that Act (inciting a child family member to engage in sexual activity).

123    An offence under section 30 of that Act (sexual activity with a person with a mental disorder impeding choice).

124    An offence under section 31 of that Act (causing or inciting a person with a mental disorder impeding choice to engage in sexual activity).

125    An offence under section 32 of that Act (engaging in sexual activity in the presence of a person with a mental disorder impeding choice).

126    An offence under section 33 of that Act (causing a person with a mental disorder impeding choice to watch a sexual act).

127    An offence under section 34 of that Act (inducement, threat or deception to procure sexual activity with a person with a mental disorder).

128    An offence under section 35 of that Act (causing a person with a mental disorder to engage in or agree to engage in sexual activity by inducement, threat or deception).

129    An offence under section 36 of that Act (engaging in sexual activity in the presence, procured by inducement, threat or deception, of a person with a mental disorder).

130    An offence under section 37 of that Act (causing a person with a mental disorder to watch a sexual act by inducement, threat or deception).

131    An offence under section 38 of that Act (care workers: sexual activity with a person with a mental disorder).

132    An offence under section 39 of that Act (care workers: causing or inciting sexual activity).

133    An offence under section 40 of that Act (care workers: sexual activity in the presence of a person with a mental disorder).

134    An offence under section 41 of that Act (care workers: causing a person with a mental disorder to watch a sexual act).

135    An offence under section 47 of that Act (paying for sexual services of a child).

136    An offence under section 48 of that Act (causing or inciting child prostitution or pornography).

137    An offence under section 49 of that Act (controlling a child prostitute or a child involved in pornography).

138    An offence under section 50 of that Act (arranging or facilitating child prostitution or pornography).

139    An offence under section 52 of that Act (causing or inciting prostitution for gain).

140    An offence under section 53 of that Act (controlling prostitution for

gain).

141 An offence under section 57 of that Act (trafficking into the UK for sexual exploitation).

142 An offence under section 58 of that Act (trafficking within the UK for sexual exploitation).

143 An offence under section 59 of that Act (trafficking out of the UK for sexual exploitation).

143A An offence under section 59A of that Act (trafficking for sexual exploitation).

144 An offence under section 61 of that Act (administering a substance with intent).

145 An offence under section 62 of that Act (committing an offence with intent to commit a sexual offence).

146 An offence under section 63 of that Act (trespass with intent to commit a sexual offence).

147 An offence under section 64 of that Act (sex with an adult relative: penetration).

148 An offence under section 65 of that Act (sex with an adult relative: consenting to penetration).

149 An offence under section 66 of that Act (exposure).

150 An offence under section 67 of that Act (voyeurism).

151 An offence under section 69 of that Act (intercourse with an animal).

152 An offence under section 70 of that Act (sexual penetration of a corpse).

152A An offence under section 2 of the Modern Slavery Act 2015 (human trafficking) committed with a view to exploitation that consists of or includes behaviour within section 3(3) of that Act (sexual exploitation).

153 An offence of— (a) aiding, abetting, counselling, procuring or inciting the commission of an offence specified in this Part of this Schedule, (b) conspiring to commit an offence so specified, or (c) attempting to commit an offence so specified.

The following offences are listed in Part 1 of Schedule 15B:

1      Manslaughter.

2      An offence under section 4 of the Offences against the Person Act 1861 (soliciting murder).

3      An offence under section 18 of that Act (wounding with intent to cause grievous bodily harm).

3A      An offence under section 28 of that Act (causing bodily injury by explosives).

3B      An offence under section 29 of that Act (using explosives etc with intent to do grievous bodily harm).

3C      An offence under section 2 of the Explosive Substances Act 1883 (causing explosion likely to endanger life or property).

3D      An offence under section 3 of that Act (attempt to cause explosion, or making or keeping explosive with intent to endanger life or property).

3E      An offence under section 4 of that Act (making or possession of explosive under suspicious circumstances).

4      An offence under section 16 of the Firearms Act 1968 (possession of a firearm with intent to endanger life).

5      An offence under section 17(1) of that Act (use of a firearm to resist arrest).

6      An offence under section 18 of that Act (carrying a firearm with criminal intent).

7      An offence of robbery under section 8 of the Theft Act 1968 where, at some time during the commission of the offence, the offender had in his possession a firearm or an imitation firearm within the meaning of the Firearms Act 1968. Where the question arises whether a robbery committed was an "offence of robbery under section 8 of the Theft Act 1968 where, at some time during the commission of the offence, the offender had in his possession a firearm or an imitation firearm within the meaning of the Firearms Act 1968", it must be established or admitted that the offender was a party to the robbery which to his knowledge involved the possession of a firearm or imitation firearm by one or more of those involved in robbery.

8      An offence under section 1 of the Protection of Children Act 1978 (indecent images of children).

8A      An offence under section 54 of the Terrorism Act 2000 (weapons training).

9      An offence under section 56 of the Terrorism Act 2000 (directing terrorist organisation).

10      An offence under section 57 of that Act (possession of article for terrorist purposes).

11      An offence under section 59 of that Act (inciting terrorism overseas) if the offender is liable on conviction on indictment to imprisonment for life.

12      An offence under section 47 of the Anti-terrorism, Crime and Security Act 2001 (use etc. of nuclear weapons).

13      An offence under section 50 of that Act (assisting or inducing certain weapons-related acts overseas).

14      An offence under section 113 of that Act (use of noxious substance or thing to cause harm or intimidate).

15      An offence under section 1 of the Sexual Offences Act 2003 (rape).

16      An offence under section 2 of that Act (assault by penetration).

17      An offence under section 4 of that Act (causing a person to engage in sexual activity without consent) if the offender is liable on conviction on indictment to imprisonment for life.

18      An offence under section 5 of that Act (rape of a child under 13).

19      An offence under section 6 of that Act (assault of a child under 13 by penetration).

20      An offence under section 7 of that Act (sexual assault of a child under 13).

21      An offence under section 8 of that Act (causing or inciting a child under 13 to engage in sexual activity).

22      An offence under section 9 of that Act (sexual activity with a child).

23      An offence under section 10 of that Act (causing or inciting a child to engage in sexual activity).

24      An offence under section 11 of that Act (engaging in sexual activity in the presence of a child).

25      An offence under section 12 of that Act (causing a child to watch a sexual act).

26      An offence under section 14 of that Act (arranging or facilitating commission of a child sex offence).

27      An offence under section 15 of that Act (meeting a child following sexual grooming etc.).

28      An offence under section 25 of that Act (sexual activity with a child family member) if the offender is aged 18 or over at the time of the offence.

29      An offence under section 26 of that Act (inciting a child family member to engage in sexual activity) if the offender is aged 18 or over at the time of the offence.

30      An offence under section 30 of that Act (sexual activity with a person with a mental disorder impeding choice) if the offender is liable on conviction on indictment to imprisonment for life.

31      An offence under section 31 of that Act (causing or inciting a person with a mental disorder to engage in sexual activity) if the offender is liable on conviction on indictment to imprisonment for life.

32      An offence under section 34 of that Act (inducement, threat or deception to procure sexual activity with a person with a mental disorder) if

the offender is liable on conviction on indictment to imprisonment for life.

33    An offence under section 35 of that Act (causing a person with a mental disorder to engage in or agree to engage in sexual activity by inducement etc.) if the offender is liable on conviction on indictment to imprisonment for life.

34    An offence under section 47 of that Act (paying for sexual services of a child) against a person aged under 16.

35    An offence under section 48 of that Act (causing or inciting sexual exploitation of a child).

36    An offence under section 49 of that Act (controlling a child in relation to sexual exploitation).

37    An offence under section 50 of that Act (arranging or facilitating sexual exploitation of a child).

38    An offence under section 62 of that Act (committing an offence with intent to commit a sexual offence) if the offender is liable on conviction on indictment to imprisonment for life.

39    An offence under section 5 of the Domestic Violence, Crime and Victims Act 2004 (causing or allowing the death of a child or vulnerable adult).

40    An offence under section 5 of the Terrorism Act 2006 (preparation of terrorist acts).

40A   An offence under section 6 of that Act (training for terrorism).

41    An offence under section 9 of that Act (making or possession of radioactive device or materials).

42    An offence under section 10 of that Act (misuse of radioactive devices or material and misuse and damage of facilities).

43    An offence under section 11 of that Act (terrorist threats relating to radioactive devices, materials or facilities).

43A   An offence under section 1 of the Modern Slavery Act 2015 (slavery, servitude and forced or compulsory labour).

43B   An offence under section 2 of that Act (human trafficking).

44
    (1) An attempt to commit an offence specified in the preceding paragraphs of this Part of this Schedule ("a listed offence") or murder.
    (2) Conspiracy to commit a listed offence or murder.
    (3) Incitement to commit a listed offence or murder.
    (4) An offence under Part 2 of the Serious Crime Act 2007 in relation to which a listed offence or murder is the offence (or one of the offences) which the person intended or believed would be committed.
    (5) Aiding, abetting, counselling or procuring the commission of a listed offence. The following offences to the extent that they are offences under the law of England and Wales—

45    Murder.

46    Any offence that—

    (a) was abolished (with or without savings) before the coming into force of this Schedule, and

(b) would, if committed on the day on which the offender was convicted of that offence have constituted an offence specified in Part 1 of this Schedule.

"*Relevant day*", in relation to an offence, means—

(a) (a) for the purposes of this paragraph as it applies for the purposes of section 246A(2), the day on which the offender was convicted of that offence, and

(b) for the purposes of this paragraph as it applies for the purposes of sections 224A(4) and 226A(2), the day on which the offender was convicted of the offence referred to in section 224A(1)(a) or 226A(1)(a) (as appropriate).

47 An offence under section 70 of the Army Act 1955, section 70 of the Air Force Act 1955 or section 42 of the Naval Discipline Act 1957 as respects which the corresponding civil offence (within the meaning of the Act in question) is an offence specified in Part 1 or 2 of this Schedule.

48 An offence under section 42 of the Armed Forces Act 2006 as respects which the corresponding offence under the law of England and Wales (within the meaning given by that section) is an offence specified in Part 1 or 2 of this Schedule.

49 An offence for which the person was convicted in Scotland, Northern Ireland or a member State other than the United Kingdom and which, if committed in England and Wales at the time of the conviction, would have constituted an offence specified in Part 1 or 2 of this Schedule.

49A A member State service offence which, if committed in England and Wales at the time of the conviction, would have constituted an offence specified in Part 1 or 2 of this Schedule.

49B In this Part of this Schedule— "civilian offence" means an offence other than an offence described in Part 3 of this Schedule or a member State service offence; "member State service offence" means an offence which was the subject of proceedings under the law of a member State, other than the United Kingdom, governing all or any of the naval, military or air forces of that State.

50 In this Schedule "imprisonment for life" includes custody for life and detention for life.

1    An offence under section 4 of the Offences against the Person Act 1861 (soliciting murder) that has a terrorist connection.

2    An offence under section 28 of that Act (causing bodily injury by explosives) that has a terrorist connection.

3    An offence under section 29 of that Act (using explosives etc with intent to do grievous bodily harm) that has a terrorist connection.

4    An offence under section 2 of the Explosive Substances Act 1883 (causing explosion likely to endanger life or property) that has a terrorist connection.

5    An offence under section 3 of that Act (attempt to cause explosion, or making or keeping explosive with intent to endanger life or property) that has a terrorist connection.

6    An offence under section 4 of that Act (making or possession of explosive under suspicious circumstances) that has a terrorist connection.

7    An offence under section 54 of the Terrorism Act 2000 (weapons training).

8    An offence under section 56 of that Act (directing terrorist organisation).

9    An offence under section 57 of that Act (possession of article for terrorist purposes).

10    An offence under section 59 of that Act (inciting terrorism overseas).

11    An offence under section 47 of the Anti-terrorism, Crime and Security Act 2001 (use etc of nuclear weapons).

12    An offence under section 50 of that Act (assisting or inducing certain weapons-related acts overseas).

13    An offence under section 113 of that Act (use of noxious substance or thing to cause harm or intimidate).

14    An offence under section 5 of the Terrorism Act 2006 (preparation of terrorist acts).

15    An offence under section 6 of that Act (training for terrorism).

16    An offence under section 9 of that Act (making or possession of radioactive device or material).

17    An offence under section 10 of that Act (use of radioactive device or material for terrorist purposes etc).

18    An offence under section 11 of that Act (terrorist threats relating to radioactive devices etc).

19    An offence under section 5 of the SOA 2003 (rape of a child under 13).

20    An offence under section 6 of that Act (assault of a child under 13 by penetration).

21

    (1)   Aiding, abetting, counselling or procuring the commission of an offence specified in the preceding paragraphs of this Schedule (a "relevant offence").

    (2)   An attempt to commit a relevant offence.

    (3)   Conspiracy to commit a relevant offence.

(4) An offence under Part 2 of the SCA 2007 in relation to which a relevant offence is the offence (or one of the offences) which the person intended or believed would be committed.

22     An offence in the following list that has a terrorist connection—

    (a)  an attempt to commit murder,

    (b)  conspiracy to commit murder, and

    (c)  in offence under Part 2 of the SCA 2007 in relation to which murder is the offence (or one of the offences) which the person intended or believed would be committed.

23     An offence that—

    (a)  was abolished before the coming into force of section 236A, and

    (b)  if committed on the day on which the offender was convicted of the offence, would have constituted an offence specified in the preceding paragraphs of this Schedule.

24     For the purposes of this Schedule, an offence has a terrorist connection if a court has determined under section 30 of the Counter-Terrorism Act 2008 that the offence has such a connection.

1      An offence under section 1 of the Sexual Offences Act 1956 (rape).

2      An offence under section 5 of that Act (intercourse with girl under 13).

3      An offence under section 6 of that Act (intercourse with girl under 16), if the offender was 20 or over.

4      An offence under section 10 of that Act (incest by a man), if the victim or (as the case may be) other party was under 18.

5      An offence under section 12 of that Act (buggery) if—

      (a)   the offender was 20 or over, and
      (b)   the victim or (as the case may be) other party was under 18.

6      An offence under section 13 of that Act (indecency between men) if—

      (a)   the offender was 20 or over, and
      (b)   the victim or (as the case may be) other party was under 18.

7      An offence under section 14 of that Act (indecent assault on a woman) if—

      (a)   the victim or (as the case may be) other party was under 18, or
      (b)   the offender, in respect of the offence or finding, is or has been—
          (i)   sentenced to imprisonment for a term of at least 30 months; or
          (ii)  admitted to a hospital subject to a restriction order.

8      An offence under section 15 of that Act (indecent assault on a man) if—

      (a)   the victim or (as the case may be) other party was under 18, or
      (b)   the offender, in respect of the offence or finding, is or has been—
          (i)   sentenced to imprisonment for a term of at least 30 months; or
          (ii)  admitted to a hospital subject to a restriction order.

9      An offence under section 16 of that Act (assault with intent to commit buggery), if the victim or (as the case may be) other party was under 18.

10    An offence under section 28 of that Act (causing or encouraging the prostitution of, intercourse with or indecent assault on girl under 16).

11    An offence under section 1 of the Indecency with Children Act 1960 (indecent conduct towards young child).

12    An offence under section 54 of the Criminal Law Act 1977 (inciting girl under 16 to have incestuous sexual intercourse).

13    An offence under section 1 of the Protection of Children Act 1978 (indecent photographs of children), if the indecent photographs or pseudo-photographs showed persons under 16 and—

      (a)   the conviction, finding or caution was before the commencement of this Part, or
      (b)   the offender—
          (i)   was 18 or over, or
          (ii)  is sentenced in respect of the offence to imprisonment for a term of at least 12 months.

14      An offence under section 170 of the Customs and Excise Management Act 1979 (penalty for fraudulent evasion of duty etc.) in relation to goods prohibited to be imported under section 42 of the Customs Consolidation Act 1876 (indecent or obscene articles), if the prohibited goods included indecent photographs of persons under 16 and—

(a)   the conviction, finding or caution was before the commencement of this Part, or

(b)   the offender—

(i)   was 18 or over, or

(ii)   is sentenced in respect of the offence to imprisonment for a term of at least 12 months.

15      An offence under section 160 of the Criminal Justice Act 1988 (possession of indecent photograph of a child), if the indecent photographs or pseudo-photographs showed persons under 16 and—

(a)   the conviction, finding or caution was before the commencement of this Part, or

(b)   the offender—

(i)   was 18 or over, or

(ii)   is sentenced in respect of the offence to imprisonment for a term of at least 12 months.

16      An offence under section 3 of the Sexual Offences (Amendment) Act 2000 (abuse of position of trust), if the offender was 20 or over.

17      An offence under section 1 or 2 of this Act (rape, assault by penetration).

18      An offence under section 3 of this Act (sexual assault) if—

(a)   where the offender was under 18, he is or has been sentenced, in respect of the offence, to imprisonment for a term of at least 12 months;

(b)   in any other case—

(i)   the victim was under 18, or

(ii)   the offender, in respect of the offence or finding, is or has been—

(a)   sentenced to a term of imprisonment,

(b)   detained in a hospital, or

(c)   made the subject of a community sentence of at least 12 months.

19      An offence under any of sections 4 to 6 of this Act (causing sexual activity without consent, rape of a child under 13, assault of a child under 13 by penetration).

20      An offence under section 7 of this Act (sexual assault of a child under 13) if the offender—

(a)   was 18 or over, or

(b)   is or has been sentenced in respect of the offence to imprisonment for a term of at least 12 months.

21      An offence under any of sections 8 to 12 of this Act (causing or inciting a child under 13 to engage in sexual activity, child sex offences committed by adults).

22       An offence under section 13 of this Act (child sex offences committed by children or young persons), if the offender is or has been sentenced, in respect of the offence, to imprisonment for a term of at least 12 months.

23       An offence under section 14 of this Act (arranging or facilitating the commission of a child sex offence) if the offender—

    (a)   was 18 or over, or
    (b)   is or has been sentenced, in respect of the offence, to imprisonment for a term of at least 12 months.

24       An offence under section 15 of this Act (meeting a child following sexual grooming etc).

24A     An offence under section 15A (sexual communication with a child).

25       An offence under any of sections 16 to 19 of this Act (abuse of a position of trust) if the offender, in respect of the offence, is or has been—

    (a)   sentenced to a term of imprisonment,
    (b)   detained in a hospital, or
    (c)   made the subject of a community sentence of at least 12 months.

26       An offence under section 25 or 26 of this Act (familial child sex offences) if the offender—

    (a)   was 18 or over, or
    (b)   is or has been sentenced in respect of the offence to imprisonment for a term of at least 12 months.

27       An offence under any of sections 30 to 37 of this Act (offences against persons with a mental disorder impeding choice, inducements etc. to persons with mental disorder).

28       An offence under any of sections 38 to 41 of this Act (care workers for persons with mental disorder) if—

    (a)   where the offender was under 18, he is or has been sentenced in respect of the offence to imprisonment for a term of at least 12 months;
    (b)   in any other case, the offender, in respect of the offence or finding, is or has been—
        (i)   sentenced to a term of imprisonment,
        (ii)  detained in a hospital, or
        (iii) made the subject of a community sentence of at least 12 months.

29       An offence under section 47 of this Act (paying for sexual services of a child) if the victim or (as the case may be) other party was under 16, and the offender—

    (a)   was 18 or over, or
    (b)   is or has been sentenced in respect of the offence to imprisonment for a term of at least 12 months.

29A    An offence under section 48 of this Act (causing or inciting child prostitution or pornography) if the offender –

  (a) was 18 or over, or

  (b) is or has been sentenced in respect of the offence to imprisonment for a term of at least 12 months.

29B An offence under section 49 of this Act (controlling a child prostitute or a child involved in pornography) if the offender –

  (a) was 18 or over, or

  (b) is or has been sentenced in respect of the offence to imprisonment for a term of at least 12 months.

29C An offence under section 50 of this Act (arranging or facilitating child prostitution or pornography) if the offender –

  (a) was 18 or over, or

  (b) is or has been sentenced in respect of the offence to imprisonment for a term of at least 12 months

30 An offence under section 61 of this Act (administering a substance with intent).

31 An offence under section 62 or 63 of this Act (committing an offence or trespassing, with intent to commit a sexual offence) if—

  (a) where the offender was under 18, he is or has been sentenced in respect of the offence to imprisonment for a term of at least 12 months;

  (b) in any other case—

   (i) the intended offence was an offence against a person under 18, or

   (ii) the offender, in respect of the offence or finding, is or has been—

    (a) sentenced to a term of imprisonment,

    (b) detained in a hospital, or

    (c) made the subject of a community sentence of at least 12 months.

32 An offence under section 64 or 65 of this Act (sex with an adult relative) if —

  (a) where the offender was under 18, he is or has been sentenced in respect of the offence to imprisonment for a term of at least 12 months;

  (b) in any other case, the offender, in respect of the offence or finding, is or has been—

   (i) sentenced to a term of imprisonment, or

   (ii) detained in a hospital.

33 An offence under section 66 of this Act (exposure) if—

  (a) where the offender was under 18, he is or has been sentenced in respect of the offence to imprisonment for a term of at least 12 months;

  (b) in any other case—

   (i) the victim was under 18, or

   (ii) the offender, in respect of the offence or finding, is or has been—

(a)   sentenced to a term of imprisonment,

(b)   detained in a hospital, or

(c)   made the subject of a community sentence of at least 12 months.

34      An offence under section 67 of this Act (voyeurism) if—

(a)   where the offender was under 18, he is or has been sentenced in respect of the offence to imprisonment for a term of at least 12 months;

(b)   in any other case—

    (i)   the victim was under 18, or

    (ii)   the offender, in respect of the offence or finding, is or has been—

        (a)   sentenced to a term of imprisonment,

        (b)   detained in a hospital, or

        (c)   made the subject of a community sentence of at least 12 months.

35      An offence under section 69 or 70 of this Act (intercourse with an animal, sexual penetration of a corpse) if —

(a)   where the offender was under 18, he is or has been sentenced in respect of the offence to imprisonment for a term of at least 12 months;

(b)   in any other case, the offender, in respect of the offence or finding, is or has been—

    (i)   sentenced to a term of imprisonment, or

    (ii)   detained in a hospital.

35A    An offence under section 63 of the Criminal Justice and Immigration Act 2008 (possession of extreme pornographic images) if the offender—

(a)   was 18 or over, and

(b)   is sentenced in respect of the offence to imprisonment for a term of at least 2 years

35B    An offence under section 62(1) of the Coroners and Justice Act 2009 (possession of prohibited images of children) if the offender—

(a)   was 18 or over, and

(b)   is sentenced in respect of the offence to imprisonment for a term of at least 2 years

35C    An offence under section 69 of the Serious Crime Act 2015 (possession of paedophile manual) if the offender—

(a)   was 18 or over, or

(b)   is sentenced in respect of the offence to imprisonment for a term of at least 12 months.

Note: Paragraphs 36–92Y, concerning Scotland and Northern Ireland, have been omitted. For services offences, see paragraphs 93 and 93A.

*General*

94      A reference in a preceding paragraph to an offence includes—

(a) a reference to an attempt, conspiracy or incitement to commit that offence, and

(b) except in paragraphs 36 to 43, a reference to aiding, abetting, counselling or procuring the commission of that offence.

94A  A reference in a preceding paragraph to an offence includes—

(a) a reference to an attempt, conspiracy or incitement to commit that offence, and

(b) except in paragraphs 36 to 43, a reference to aiding, abetting, counselling or procuring the commission of that offence.

95  A reference in a preceding paragraph to a person's age is—

(a) in the case of an indecent photograph, a reference to the person's age when the photograph was taken;

(b) in any other case, a reference to his age at the time of the offence.

96  In this Schedule "community sentence" has—

(a) in relation to England and Wales, the same meaning as in the Powers of Criminal Courts (Sentencing) Act 2000, and

(b) in relation to Northern Ireland, the same meaning as in the Criminal Justice (Northern Ireland) Order 1996 (S.I. 1996/3160 (N.I. 24)).

97  For the purposes of paragraphs 14, 44 and 78—

(a) a person is to be taken to have been under 16 at any time if it appears from the evidence as a whole that he was under that age at that time;

(b) section 7 of the Protection of Children Act 1978 (c. 37) (interpretation), subsections (2) to (2C) and (8) to (10) of section 52 of the Civic Government (Scotland) Act 1982 (c. 45), and Article 2(2) and (3) of the Protection of Children (Northern Ireland) Order 1978 (S.I. 1978/1047 (N.I. 17)) (interpretation) (respectively) apply as each provision applies for the purposes of the Act or Order of which it forms part.

98  A determination under paragraph 60 constitutes part of a person's sentence, within the meaning of the Criminal Procedure (Scotland) Act 1995 (c. 46), for the purposes of any appeal or review.

1    Murder.

2    Manslaughter.

3    Kidnapping.

4    False imprisonment.

4A   Outraging public decency.

5    An offence under section 4 of the Offences against the Person Act 1861 (soliciting murder).

6    An offence under section 16 of that Act (threats to kill).

7    An offence under section 18 of that Act (wounding with intent to cause grievous bodily harm).

8    An offence under section 20 of that Act (malicious wounding).

9    An offence under section 21 of that Act (attempting to choke, suffocate or strangle in order to commit or assist in committing an indictable offence).

10   An offence under section 22 of that Act (using chloroform etc. to commit or assist in the committing of any indictable offence).

11   An offence under section 23 of that Act (maliciously administering poison etc. so as to endanger life or inflict grievous bodily harm).

12   An offence under section 27 of that Act (abandoning children).

13   An offence under section 28 of that Act (causing bodily injury by explosives).

14   An offence under section 29 of that Act (using explosives etc. with intent to do grievous bodily harm).

15   An offence under section 30 of that Act (placing explosives with intent to do bodily injury).

16   An offence under section 31 of that Act (setting spring guns etc. with intent to do grievous bodily harm).

17   An offence under section 32 of that Act (endangering the safety of railway passengers).

18   An offence under section 35 of that Act (injuring persons by furious driving).

19   An offence under section 37 of that Act (assaulting officer preserving wreck).

20   An offence under section 38 of that Act (assault with intent to resist arrest).

21   An offence under section 47 of that Act (assault occasioning actual bodily harm).

22   An offence under section 2 of the Explosive Substances Act 1883 (causing explosion likely to endanger life or property).

23   An offence under section 3 of that Act (attempt to cause explosion, or making or keeping explosive with intent to endanger life or property).

24   An offence under section 1 of the Infant Life (Preservation) Act 1929 (child destruction).

| 25 | An offence under section 1 of the Children and Young Persons Act 1933 (cruelty to children). |
| 26 | An offence under section 1 of the Infanticide Act 1938 (infanticide). |
| 27 | An offence under section 16 of the Firearms Act 1968 (possession of firearm with intent to endanger life). |
| 28 | An offence under section 16A of that Act (possession of firearm with intent to cause fear of violence). |
| 29 | An offence under section 17(1) of that Act (use of firearm to resist arrest). |
| 30 | An offence under section 17(2) of that Act (possession of firearm at time of committing or being arrested for offence specified in Schedule 1 to that Act). |
| 31 | An offence under section 18 of that Act (carrying a firearm with criminal intent). |
| 31A | An offence under section 1 of the Theft Act 1968 (theft). |
| 32 | An offence under section 8 of that Act (robbery or assault with intent to rob). |
| 33 | An offence under section 9(1)(a) of that Act (burglary with intent to steal, inflict grievous bodily harm or do unlawful damage). |
| 34 | An offence under section 10 of that Act (aggravated burglary). |
| 35 | An offence under section 12A of that Act (aggravated vehicle-taking) involving an accident which caused the death of any person. |
| 36 | An offence of arson under section 1 of the Criminal Damage Act 1971. |
| 37 | An offence under section 1(2) of that Act (destroying or damaging property) other than an offence of arson. |
| 38 | An offence under section 1 of the Taking of Hostages Act 1982 (hostage-taking). |
| 39 | An offence under section 1 of the Aviation Security Act 1982 (hijacking). |
| 40 | An offence under section 2 of that Act (destroying, damaging or endangering safety of aircraft). |
| 41 | An offence under section 3 of that Act (other acts endangering or likely to endanger safety of aircraft). |
| 42 | An offence under section 4 of that Act (offences in relation to certain dangerous articles). |
| 43 | An offence under section 127 of the MHA 1983 (ill-treatment of patients). |
| 43A | An offence under section 1 of the Child Abduction Act 1984 (offence of abduction of child by parent, etc). |
| 43B | An offence under section 2 of that Act (offence of abduction of child by other persons). |
| 44 | An offence under section 1 of the Prohibition of Female Circumcision Act 1985 (prohibition of female circumcision). |
| 45 | An offence under section 1 of the Public Order Act 1986 (riot). |
| 46 | An offence under section 2 of that Act (violent disorder). |
| 47 | An offence under section 3 of that Act (affray). |

| 48 | An offence under section 134 of the CJA 1988 (torture). |
|---|---|

48     An offence under section 134 of the CJA 1988 (torture).

49     An offence under section 1 of the Road Traffic Act 1988 (causing death by dangerous driving).

50     An offence under section 3A of that Act (causing death by careless driving when under influence of drink or drugs).

51     An offence under section 1 of the Aviation and Maritime Security Act 1990 (endangering safety at aerodromes).

52     An offence under section 9 of that Act (hijacking of ships).

53     An offence under section 10 of that Act (seizing or exercising control of fixed platforms).

54     An offence under section 11 of that Act (destroying fixed platforms or endangering their safety).

55     An offence under section 12 of that Act (other acts endangering or likely to endanger safe navigation).

56     An offence under section 13 of that Act (offences involving threats).

56A     An offence under section 2 or 2A of the Protection from Harassment Act 1997 (offences of harassment and stalking)

57     An offence under section 4 or 4A of that Act (putting people in fear of violence and stalking involving fear of violence or serious alarm or distress).

58     An offence under section 29 of the CDA 1998 (racially or religiously aggravated assaults).

59     An offence falling within section 31(1)(a) or (b) of that Act (racially or religiously aggravated offences under section 4 or 4A of the Public Order Act 1986).

60     An offence under Part II of the Channel Tunnel (Security) Order 1994 (S.I. 1994/570) (offences relating to Channel Tunnel trains and the tunnel system).

60ZA     An offence under section 53 or 54 of the Regulation of Investigatory Powers Act 2000 (contravention of notice relating to encrypted information or tipping off in connection with such a notice).

60A     An offence under section 85(3) or (4) of the Postal Services Act 2000 (prohibition on sending certain articles by post).

61     An offence under section 51 or 52 of the International Criminal Court Act 2001 (genocide, crimes against humanity, war crimes and related offences), other than one involving murder.

61A     An offence under section 127(1) of the Communications Act 2003 (improper use of public electronic communications network).

62     An offence under section 47 of this Act, where the victim or (as the case may be) other party was 16 or over.

63     An offence under any of sections 51 to 53 or 57 to 59A of this Act.

63A     An offence under section 5 of the Domestic Violence, Crime and Victims Act 2004 (causing or allowing a child or vulnerable adult to die or suffer serious physical harm).

63B     An offence under section 2 of the Modern Slavery Act 2015 (human trafficking).

Note: Paragraphs 64 to 171C, concerning Scotland and Northern Ireland, have been omitted. For service offences, see paragraphs 172 and 172A.

173    A reference in a preceding paragraph to an offence includes—

    (a)   a reference to an attempt, conspiracy or incitement to commit that offence, and

    (b)   a reference to aiding, abetting, counselling or procuring the commission of that offence.

173A   A reference in a preceding paragraph to an offence ("offence A") includes a reference to an offence under Part 2 of the SCA 2007 in relation to which offence A is the offence (or one of the offences) which the person intended or believed would be committed.

174    A reference in a preceding paragraph to a person's age is a reference to his age at the time of the offence.

### Drug trafficking

1(1) An offence under any of the following provisions of the Misuse of Drugs Act 1971—

(a)   section 4(2) or (3) (unlawful production or supply of controlled drugs);
(b)   section 5(3) (possession of controlled drug with intent to supply);
(ba)  section 6 (restriction of cultivation of cannabis plant);
(c)   section 8 (permitting etc. certain activities relating to controlled drugs);
(d)   section 20 (assisting in or inducing the commission outside the United Kingdom of an offence punishable under a corresponding law).

(2) An offence under any of the following provisions of the Customs and Excise Management Act 1979 if it is committed in connection with a prohibition or restriction on importation or exportation which has effect by virtue of section 3 of the Misuse of Drugs Act 1971—

(a)   section 50(2) or (3) (improper importation of goods);
(b)   section 68(2) (exportation of prohibited or restricted goods);
(c)   section 170 (fraudulent evasion of duty etc.).

(3) An offence under either of the following provisions of the Criminal Justice (International Co-operation) Act 1990—

(a)   section 12 (manufacture or supply of a substance for the time being specified in Schedule 2 to that Act);
(b)   section 19 (using a ship for illicit traffic in controlled drugs).

### Psychoactive substances

1ZA An offence under any of the following provisions of the Psychoactive Substances Act 2016—

(a)   section 4 (producing a psychoactive substance);
(b)   section 5 (supplying, or offering to supply, a psychoactive substance);
(c)   section 7 (possession of psychoactive substance with intent to supply);
(d)   section 8 (importing or exporting a psychoactive substance).

### Slavery etc

1A An offence under section 1 of the Modern Slavery Act 2015 (slavery, servitude and forced or compulsory labour).

### People trafficking

2(1) An offence under section 25, 25A or 25B of the Immigration Act 1971 (assisting unlawful immigration etc.).

(2) An offence under any of sections 57 to 59A of the Sexual Offences Act 2003 (trafficking for sexual exploitation).

(3) An offence under section 4 of the Asylum and Immigration (Treatment of Claimants, etc.) Act 2004 (c. 19) (trafficking people for exploitation).

## Firearms offences

3(1) An offence under any of the following provisions of the Firearms Act 1968—

  (a)  section 1(1) (possession etc of firearms or ammunition without certificate);
  (b)  section 2(1) (possession etc of shot gun without certificate);
  (c)  section 3(1) (dealing etc in firearms or ammunition by way of trade or business without being registered);
  (d)  section 5(1), (1A) or (2A) (possession, manufacture etc of prohibited weapons).

(2) An offence under either of the following provisions of the Customs and Excise Management Act 1979 if it is committed in connection with a firearm or ammunition—

  (a)  section 68(2) (exportation of prohibited or restricted goods);
  (b)  section 170 (fraudulent evasion of duty etc).

(3)(1) In sub-paragraph (2) "firearm" and "ammunition" have the same meanings as in section 57 of the Firearms Act 1968.

## Prostitution and child sex

4(1) An offence under section 33A of the Sexual Offences Act 1956 (c. 69) (keeping a brothel used for prostitution).

(2) An offence under any of the following provisions of the Sexual Offences Act 2003—

  (a)  section 14 (arranging or facilitating commission of a child sex offence);
  (b)  section 48 (causing or inciting sexual exploitation of a child);
  (c)  section 49 controlling a child in relation to sexual exploitation;
  (d)  section 50 (arranging or facilitating sexual exploitation of a child);
  (e)  section 52 (causing or inciting prostitution for gain);
  (f)  section 53 (controlling prostitution for gain).

## Armed robbery etc.

5(1) An offence under section 8(1) of the Theft Act 1968 (c. 60) (robbery) where the use or threat of force involves a firearm, an imitation firearm or an offensive weapon.

(2) An offence at common law of an assault with intent to rob where the assault involves a firearm, imitation firearm or an offensive weapon.

(3) In this paragraph—

"firearm" has the meaning given by section 57(1) of the Firearms Act 1968;
"imitation firearm" has the meaning given by section 57(4) of that Act;
"offensive weapon" means any weapon to which section 141 of the Criminal
Justice Act 1988 (offensive weapons) applies.

### Money laundering

6 An offence under any of the following provisions of the Proceeds of Crime Act
2002—

(a)   section 327 (concealing etc. criminal property);
(b)   section 328 (facilitating the acquisition etc. of criminal property by or on
behalf of another);
(c)   section 329 (acquisition, use and possession of criminal property).

### Fraud

7(1) An offence under section 17 of the Theft Act 1968 (false accounting).

(2) An offence under any of the following provisions of the Fraud Act 2006—

(a)   section 1 (fraud by false representation, failing to disclose information or
abuse of position);
(b)   section 6 (possession etc. of articles for use in frauds);
(c)   section 7 (making or supplying articles for use in frauds);
(d)   section 9 (participating in fraudulent business carried on by sole trader etc.);
(e)   section 11 (obtaining services dishonestly).

(3) An offence at common law of conspiracy to defraud.

### Offences in relation to public revenue

8(1) An offence under section 170 of the Customs and Excise Management Act
1979 (fraudulent evasion of duty etc.) so far as not falling within paragraph 1(2)(c)
or 3(1)(b) above.

(2) An offence under section 72 of the Value Added Tax Act 1994 (fraudulent
evasion of VAT etc.).

(3) An offence under section 106A of the Taxes Management Act 1970
(fraudulent evasion of income tax).

(4) An offence under section 35 of the Tax Credits Act 2002 (tax credit fraud).

(5) An offence at common law of cheating in relation to the public revenue.

### Bribery

9 An offence under any of the following provisions of the Bribery Act 2010—

(a)   section 1 (offences of bribing another person);
(b)   section 2 (offences relating to being bribed);
(c)   section 6 (bribery of foreign public officials).

### Counterfeiting

10 An offence under any of the following provisions of the Forgery and Counterfeiting Act 1981—

(a)   section 14 (making counterfeit notes or coins);
(b)   section 15 (passing etc. counterfeit notes or coins);
(c)   section 16 (having custody or control of counterfeit notes or coins);
(d)   section 17 (making or having custody or control of counterfeiting materials or implements).

11(1) An offence under section 21 of the Theft Act 1968 (blackmail).

(2) An offence under section 12(1) or (2) of the Gangmasters (Licensing) Act 2004 (acting as a gangmaster other than under the authority of a licence, possession of false documents, etc.).

### Computer misuse

11A An offence under any of the following provisions of the Computer Misuse Act 1990—

(a)   section 1 (unauthorised access to computer material);
(b)   section 2 (unauthorised access with intent to commit or facilitate commission of further offences);
(c)   section 3 (unauthorised acts with intent to impair, or with recklessness as to impairing, operation of computer etc);
(d)   section 3ZA (unauthorised acts causing, or creating risk of, serious damage to human welfare etc);
(e)   section 3A (making, supplying or obtaining articles for use in offence under section 1, 3 or 3ZA).

### Intellectual property

12(1) An offence under any of the following provisions of the Copyright, Designs and Patents Act 1988—

(a)   section 107(1)(a), (b), (d)(iv) or (e) (making, importing or distributing an article which infringes copyright);
(b)   section 198(1)(a), (b) or (d)(iii) (making, importing or distributing an illicit recording);
(c)   section 297A (making or dealing etc. in unauthorised decoders).

(2) An offence under section 92(1), (2) or (3) of the Trade Marks Act 1994 (unauthorised use of trade mark etc.).

Environment

13(1) An offence under section 1 of the Salmon and Freshwater Fisheries Act 1975 (fishing ... with prohibited implements etc.).

(2) An offence under section 14 of the Wildlife and Countryside Act 1981 (introduction of new species etc.).

(3) An offence under section 33 of the Environmental Protection Act 1990 (prohibition on unauthorised or harmful deposit, treatment or disposal etc. of waste).

(4) An offence under regulation 8 of the Control of Trade in Endangered Species (Enforcement) Regulations 1997 (S.I. 1997/1372) (purchase and sale etc. of endangered species and provision of false statements and certificates).

Organised crime

13A An offence under section 45 of the Serious Crime Act 2015 (participating in activities of organised crime group).

Financial sanctions legislation

13B(1) An offence under an instrument made under section 2(2) of the European Communities Act 1972 for the purpose of implementing, or otherwise in relation to, EU obligations created or arising by or under an EU financial sanctions Regulation.

(2) An offence under an Act or under subordinate legislation where the offence was created for the purpose of implementing a UN financial sanctions Resolution.

(3) An offence under paragraph 7 of Schedule 3 to the Anti-terrorism, Crime and Security Act 2001 (freezing orders).

(4) An offence under paragraph 30 or 30A of Schedule 7 to the Counter-Terrorism Act 2008 where the offence relates to a requirement of the kind mentioned in paragraph 13 of that Schedule.

(5) An offence under paragraph 31 of Schedule 7 to the Counter-Terrorism Act 2008.

(6) In this paragraph—

"*EU financial sanctions Regulation*" and "*UN financial sanctions Resolution*" have the same meanings as in Part 8 of the Policing and Crime Act 2017 (see section 143 of that Act);
"subordinate legislation" has the same meaning as in the Interpretation Act 1978.

Inchoate offences

14(1) An offence of attempting or conspiring the commission of an offence specified or described in this Part of this Schedule.

(2) An offence under Part 2 of this Act (encouraging or assisting) where the offence (or one of the offences) which the person in question intends or believes would be committed is an offence specified or described in this Part of this Schedule.

(3) An offence of aiding, abetting, counselling or procuring the commission of an offence specified or described in this Part of this Schedule.

(4) The references in sub-paragraphs (1) to (3) to offences specified or described in this Part of this Schedule do not include the offence at common law of conspiracy to defraud.

## Earlier offences

15(1) This Part of this Schedule (apart from paragraph 14(2)) has effect, in its application to conduct before the passing of this Act, as if the offences specified or described in this Part included any corresponding offences under the law in force at the time of the conduct.

(2) Paragraph 14(2) has effect, in its application to conduct before the passing of this Act or before the coming into force of section 59 of this Act, as if the offence specified or described in that provision were an offence of inciting the commission of an offence specified or described in this Part of this Schedule.

## Scope of offences

16 Where this Part of this Schedule refers to offences which are offences under the law of England and Wales and another country, the reference is to be read as limited to the offences so far as they are offences under the law of England and Wales.

*Note: The court may treat any other offence as if it were a specified offence if it considers the offence to be sufficiently serious to be treated as if it were a specified offence, SCA 2007 s.2(2)(b).*

*N.b. In addition to the offences listed in this SI, the unduly lenient sentence scheme applies to all offences triable only on indictment, CJA 1988 s.35(3)(b)(i).*

The list of cases to which the ULS scheme applies is as follows:

1    Any case tried on indictment—
    (a)   following a notice of transfer given under s.4 of the CJA 1987 (notices of transfer and designated authorities); or
    (b)   in which one or more of the counts in respect of which sentence is passed relates to a charge which was dismissed under s.6(1) of the CJA 1987 (applications for dismissal) and on which further proceedings were brought by means of preferment of a voluntary bill of indictment.

1A  Any case tried on indictment—
    (a)   following a notice given under s.51B of the CDA 1998 (notices in serious or complex fraud cases); or
    (b)   following such a notice, in which one or more of the counts in respect of which sentence is passed relates to a charge—
    (i)    which was dismissed under para.2 of Sch.3 to the CDA 1998 (applications for dismissal); and
    (ii)   on which further proceedings were brought by means of the preferment of a voluntary bill of indictment.

2    Any case in which sentence is passed on a person for one of the following offences:
    (a)   an offence under s.16 of the OaPA 1861 (threats to kill);
    (b)   an offence under s.5(1) of the CLAA 1885 (defilement of a girl between 14 and 17);
    (c)   an offence under s.1 of the CYPA 1933 (cruelty to persons under 16) or s.20 of the CYPA (NI) 1968 (cruelty to persons under 16);
    (d)   an offence under s.6 of the SOA 1956 (unlawful sexual intercourse with a girl under 16), ss.14 or 15 of that Act (indecent assault on a woman or on a man), s.52 of the OaPA 1861 (indecent assault upon a female), or art.21 of the CJ (NI) Order 2003 (indecent assault on a male);
    (e)   an offence under s.1 of the IWCA 1960 or s.22 of the CYPA (NI) 1968 (indecent conduct with a child);
    (f)   an offence under ss.4(2) or (3) (production or supply of a controlled drug), s.5(3)(possession of a controlled drug with intent to supply) or s.6(2) (cultivation of cannabis plant) of the MDA 1971;
    (g)   an offence under s.54 of the CLA 1977 or art.9 of the CJ (NI) Order 1980 (inciting a girl under 16 to have incestuous sexual intercourse);
    (h)   an offence under ss.50(2) or (3), s.68(2) or s.170(1) or (2) of the CEMA 1979, insofar as those offences are in connection with a prohibition or restriction on importation or exportation of either:
    (i)    a controlled drug within the meaning of s.2 of the MDA 1971, such prohibition or restriction having effect by virtue of s.3 of that Act; or

    (ii)    an article prohibited by virtue of s.42 of the CCA 1876 but only insofar as it relates to or depicts a person under the age of 16;

    (i)    offences under ss.29 to 32 of the CDA 1998 (racially or religiously aggravated assaults; racially or religiously aggravated criminal damage; racially or religiously aggravated public order offences; racially or religiously aggravated harassment etc);

    (j)    an offence under s.4 of the AI(ToC)A 2004 (trafficking people for exploitation);

    (k)    an offence under s.71 of the CoJA 2009 (slavery, servitude and forced or compulsory labour);

    (l)    an offence under s.1 (slavery, servitude and forced or compulsory labour), 2 (human trafficking) or 4 (committing an offence with intent to commit a human trafficking offence) of the MDA 2015.

3    Any case in which sentence is passed on a person for an offence under one of the following sections of the Sexual Offences Act 2003

    (t)    s.61 (administering a substance with intent).

    (sa)    s.59A (trafficking people for sexual exploitation);

    (sa)    s.59A (trafficking people for sexual exploitation);

    (s)    s.59 (trafficking out of the UK for sexual exploitation);

    (r)    s.58 (trafficking within the UK for sexual exploitation);

    (q)    s.57 (trafficking into the UK for sexual exploitation);

    (p)    s.52 (causing or inciting prostitution for gain);

    (o)    s.50 (arranging or facilitating sexual exploitation of a child);

    (n)    s.49 (controlling a child in relation to sexual exploitation);

    (m)    s.48 (causing or inciting sexual exploitation of a child);

    (l)    s.47 (paying for sexual services of a child);

    (k)    s.25 (sexual activity with a child family member);

    (i)    s.14 (arranging or facilitating commission of a child sex offence);

    (h)    s.12 (causing a child to watch a sexual act);

    (g)    s.11 (engaging in sexual activity in the presence of a child);

    (f)    s.10 (causing or inciting a child to engage in sexual activity);

    (e)    s.9 (sexual activity with a child);

    (d)    s.8 (causing or inciting a child under 13 to engage in sexual activity);

    (c)    s.7 (sexual assault of a child under 13);

    (b)    s.4 (causing a person to engage in sexual activity without consent);

    (a)    s.3 (sexual assault);

3A    (1) Any case in which sentence is passed on a person for an offence under one of the following—

    (a)    ss.11 or 12 of the TA 2000 (offences relating to proscribed organisations);

    (b)    ss.15 to 18 of the TA 2000 (offences relating to terrorist property);

    (ba)    ss.19 (disclosure of information: duty), 21A (failure to disclose: regulated sector) or 21D (tipping off: regulated sector) of the 2000 Act;

    (ca)    s.39 of the 2000 Act 9 (disclosure of information);

    (c)    s.38B of the TA 2000 (failure to disclose information about acts of terrorism);

    (d)    s.54 of the TA 2000 (weapons training);

(e)    ss.57 to 58A of the TA 2000 (possessing things, collecting information and eliciting, publishing or communicating information about members of the armed forces etc for the purposes of terrorism);

(f)    s.113 of the AT,CSA 2001 (use of noxious substances or things to cause harm or intimidate);

(g)    s.1 or 2 of the TA 2006 (encouragement of terrorism);

(h)    s.6 or 8 of the TA 2006 (training for terrorism);

(i)    s.54 of the Counter-Terrorism Act 2008 (offences relating to notification);

(j)    s.23 of the Terrorism Prevention and Investigation Measures Act 2011 14 (offence of contravening a TPIM notice);

(k)    s.10 of the Counter-Terrorism and Security Act 2015 (offences of contravening a Temporary Exclusion Order or not complying with a restriction after return).

(2)    Any case in which sentence is passed on a person for one of the following—

(a)    an offence under s.20 of the OAPA 1861(inflicting bodily harm);

(b)    an offence under the following provisions of the CDA 1971

(i)    s.1(1) (destroying or damaging property);

(ii)    s.1(1) and (3) (arson);

(iii)    s.2 (threats to destroy or damage property);

(c)    an offence under ss.1 to 5 of the FCA 1981; where there is jurisdiction in England and Wales by virtue of any of ss.63B to 63D of the TA 2000 (extra-territorial jurisdiction in respect of certain offences committed outside the United Kingdom for the purposes of terrorism etc).

3    Any case in which sentence is passed on a person for an offence under one of the following—

(a)    s.4 of the Aviation Security Act 1982 (offences in relation to certain dangerous articles);

(b)    s.114 of the Anti-Terrorism, Crime and Security Act 2001 (hoaxes involving noxious substances or things) where the court has determined that the offence has a terrorist connection under s.30 of the Counter-Terrorism Act 2008 (sentences for offences with a terrorist connection: England and Wales).

4    Any case in which sentence is passed on a person for—

(a)    attempting to commit a relevant offence;

(b)    inciting the commission of a relevant offence; or

(c)    an offence under ss.44 or 45 of the SCA 2007 (encouraging or assisting an offence) in relation to a relevant offence.

(2)    In this paragraph, "a relevant offence" means an offence set out in paragraph 2(a) to (h), (j) or (k) or paragraphs 3 or 3A

*Note: The SI was last amended on 29 January 2018 by SI 2017/1328.*

# PART 4: CHARTS AND TABLES

# DISQUALIFICATION FROM DRIVING

Begin by identifying the category to which the offence with which you are concerned belongs, and then follow the instructions. Repeat the process for each offence, but bear in mind the restrictions on imposing penalty points for offences committed on the same occasion and on imposing more than one disqualification in penalty point cases.

All disqualifications run concurrently.

| **Offences Subject To Obligatory Disqualilfication:** | |
| --- | --- |
| Causing death by dangerous driving | 3–11 |
| Causing serious injury by dangerous driving | 3–11 |
| Dangerous driving | 3–11 |
| Causing death by driving: unlicensed or uninsured drivers | 3–11 |
| Causing death by driving: disqualified drivers | 3–11 |
| Causing serious injury by driving: disqualified drivers | 3–11 |
| Causing death by careless driving while under the influence of drink or drugs | 3–11 |
| Driving or attempting to drive while unfit | 3–11 |
| Driving or attempting to drive with excess alcohol | 3–11 |
| Failing to provide a specimen for analysis (driving or attempting to drive) | 3–11 |
| Racing or speed trials | 3–11 |
| Manslaughter | 3–11 |
| Aggravated vehicle taking | 3–11 |
| *Go to "Obligatory Disqualification"* | |

| **Offences Subject to Discretionary Disqualification but not Endorsement:** |
| --- |
| Stealing or attempting to steal a motor vehicle |
| Taking a motor vehicle without consent, or being carried |
| Going equipped to steal a motor vehicle |
| *Go to "Discretionary Disqualification"* |

| **Offences Subject to Obligatory Endorsement (Selected; for Other Offences see Road Traffic Offenders Act 1988, Sch.2):** | |
| --- | --- |
| Careless driving | 3–9 |
| Being in charge of a vehicle when unfit to drive | 10 |
| Being in charge of a vehicle with excess alcohol level | 10 |
| Failing to provide a breath specimen | 4 |
| Failing to provide a specimen when disqualification not obligatory | 10 |
| Leaving vehicle in dangerous position | 3 |
| Failing to comply with directions or signs | 3 |
| Using vehicle in dangerous condition | 3 |

**Offences Subject to Obligatory Endorsement (Selected; for Other Offences see Road Traffic Offenders Act 1988, Sch.2):**

| | |
|---|---:|
| Driving without licence | 3–6 |
| Driving with uncorrected eyesight | 3 |
| Driving while disqualified | 6 |
| Using vehicle without insurance | 6–8 |
| Failing to stop after accident | 5–10 |
| Failing to give information as to driver | 3 |
| *Go to "Penalty Points"* | |

Note: *An offender convicted of any offence may be disqualified from driving under the PCC(S)A s.147.*

*All references are to the Road Traffic Offenders Act 1988 as amended.*

# OBLIGATORY DISQUALIFICATION

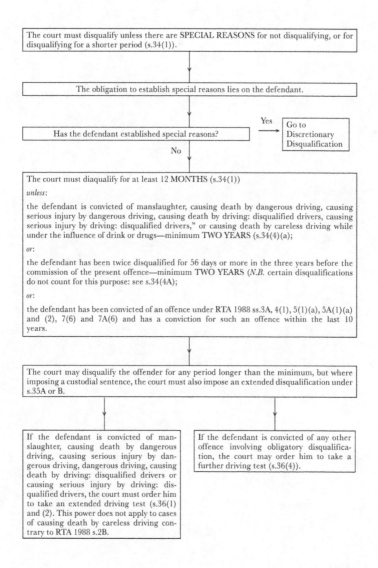

The court must disqualify unless there are SPECIAL REASONS for not disqualifying, or for disqualifying for a shorter period (s.34(1)).

The obligation to establish special reasons lies on the defendant.

Has the defendant established special reasons?

Yes → Go to Discretionary Disqualification

No

The court must diaqualify for at least 12 MONTHS (s.34(1))

*unless*:

the defendant is convicted of manslaughter, causing death by dangerous driving, causing serious injury by dangerous driving, causing death by driving: disqualified drivers, causing serious injury by driving: disqualified drivers," or causing death by careless driving while under the influence of drink or drugs—minimum TWO YEARS (s.34(4)(a);

*or*:

the defendant has been twice disqualified for 56 days or more in the three years before the commission of the present offence—minimum TWO YEARS (*N.B.* certain disqualifications do not count for this purpose: see s.34(4A);

*or*:

the defendant has been convicted of an offence under RTA 1988 ss.3A, 4(1), 5(1)(a), 5A(1)(a) and (2), 7(6) and 7A(6) and has a conviction for such an offence within the last 10 years.

The court may disqualify the offender for any period longer than the minimum, but where imposing a custodial sentence, the court must also impose an extended disqualification under s.35A or B.

If the defendant is convicted of man-slaughter, causing death by dangerous driving, causing serious injury by dangerous driving, dangerous driving, causing death by driving: disqualified drivers or causing serious injury by driving: disqualified drivers, the court must order him to take an extended driving test (s.36(1) and (2). This power does not apply to cases of causing death by careless driving contrary to RTA 1988 s.2B.

If the defendant is convicted of any other offence involving obligatory disqualification, the court may order him to take a further driving test (s.36(4)).

# PENALTY POINTS

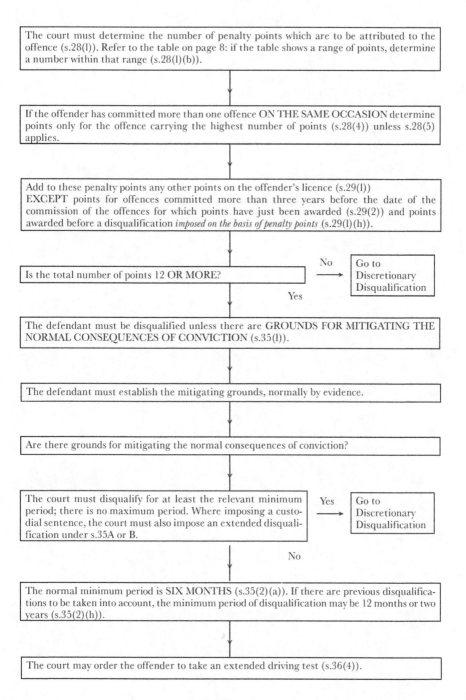

The court must determine the number of penalty points which are to be attributed to the offence (s.28(l)). Refer to the table on page 8: if the table shows a range of points, determine a number within that range (s.28(l)(b)).

If the offender has committed more than one offence ON THE SAME OCCASION determine points only for the offence carrying the highest number of points (s.28(4)) unless s.28(5) applies.

Add to these penalty points any other points on the offender's licence (s.29(l))
EXCEPT points for offences committed more than three years before the date of the commission of the offences for which points have just been awarded (s.29(2)) and points awarded before a disqualification *imposed on the basis of penalty points* (s.29(l)(h)).

Is the total number of points 12 OR MORE? → No → Go to Discretionary Disqualification

Yes

The defendant must be disqualified unless there are GROUNDS FOR MITIGATING THE NORMAL CONSEQUENCES OF CONVICTION (s.35(l)).

The defendant must establish the mitigating grounds, normally by evidence.

Are there grounds for mitigating the normal consequences of conviction?

The court must disqualify for at least the relevant minimum period; there is no maximum period. Where imposing a custodial sentence, the court must also impose an extended disqualification under s.35A or B. → Yes → Go to Discretionary Disqualification

No

The normal minimum period is SIX MONTHS (s.35(2)(a)). If there are previous disqualifications to be taken into account, the minimum period of disqualification may be 12 months or two years (s.35(2)(h)).

The court may order the offender to take an extended driving test (s.36(4)).

# DISCRETIONARY DISQUALIFICATION

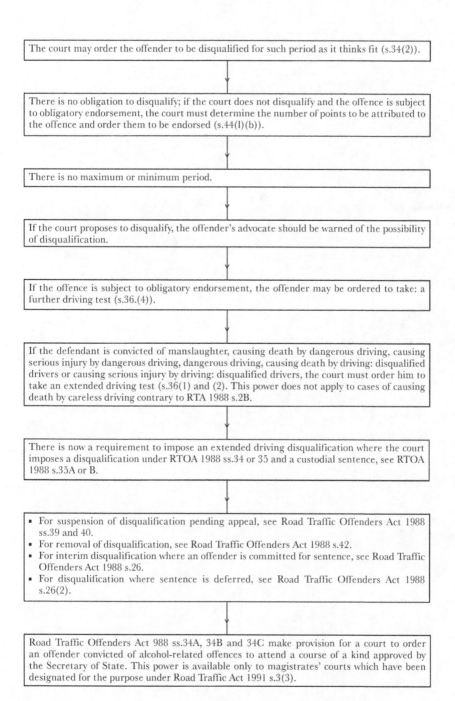

The court may order the offender to be disqualified for such period as it thinks fit (s.34(2)).

There is no obligation to disqualify; if the court does not disqualify and the offence is subject to obligatory endorsement, the court must determine the number of points to be attributed to the offence and order them to be endorsed (s.44(I)(b)).

There is no maximum or minimum period.

If the court proposes to disqualify, the offender's advocate should be warned of the possibility of disqualification.

If the offence is subject to obligatory endorsement, the offender may be ordered to take: a further driving test (s.36.(4)).

If the defendant is convicted of manslaughter, causing death by dangerous driving, causing serious injury by dangerous driving, dangerous driving, causing death by driving: disqualified drivers or causing serious injury by driving: disqualified drivers, the court must order him to take an extended driving test (s.36(1) and (2). This power does not apply to cases of causing death by careless driving contrary to RTA 1988 s.2B.

There is now a requirement to impose an extended driving disqualification where the court imposes a disqualification under RTOA 1988 ss.34 or 35 and a custodial sentence, see RTOA 1988 s.35A or B.

- For suspension of disqualification pending appeal, see Road Traffic Offenders Act 1988 ss.39 and 40.
- For removal of disqualification, see Road Traffic Offenders Act 1988 s.42.
- For interim disqualification where an offender is committed for sentence, see Road Traffic Offenders Act 1988 s.26.
- For disqualification where sentence is deferred, see Road Traffic Offenders Act 1988 s.26(2).

Road Traffic Offenders Act 988 ss.34A, 34B and 34C make provision for a court to order an offender convicted of alcohol-related offences to attend a course of a kind approved by the Secretary of State. This power is available only to magistrates' courts which have been designated for the purpose under Road Traffic Act 1991 s.3(3).

## SENTENCES FOR YOUNG OFFENDERS

| Age on date of conviction: | 10 | 11 | 12 | 13 | 14 | 15 | 16 | 17 | 18 | 19 | 20 |
|---|---|---|---|---|---|---|---|---|---|---|---|
| *Custodial sentences:* | | | | | | | | | | | |
| Detention s.91 | 1 | 1 | 1 | 1 | 1 | 1 | 1 | 1 | N | N | N |
| Detention and training order | N | N | 2 | 2 | 2 | Y | Y | Y | N | N | N |
| Detention in a young offender institution | N | N | N | N | N | N | N | N | Y | Y | Y |
| Extended sentence of detention | 3 | 3 | 3 | 3 | 3 | 3 | 3 | 3 | N | N | N |
| Extended sentence of detention in a young offender institution | N | N | N | N | N | N | N | N | 3 | 3 | 3 |

Note

Y = the order is available

N = the order is not available

1, 2 or 3 = refer to footnote

1 If convicted on indictment of an offence to which the PCC(S)A 2000 s.91 applies.

2 If a "persistent offender".

3 If s.91 is available, the offender has been convicted of a specified offence, and the court considers that there is a significant risk of serious harm to members of the public by the commission of further specified offences committed by him/her.

# MANDATORY SENTENCES: THE BASICS

This table lists all mandatory sentencing orders currently in force. It does not list automatic consequences of conviction, such as notification, or the statutory surcharge.

Readers should refer to the respective sections of Part 1 of this book for full details of each order. This table states the location of the trigger offence but does not state the other conditions which must be satisfied prior to the imposition of the order.

| Order | Trigger offence | Discount for guilty plea | Required length |
|---|---|---|---|
| Mandatory life (Murder) | Murder | None: a reduction may be made to the length of the minimum term. | None |
| Automatic life | CJA 2003 Sch.15B offence | | |
| Discretionary life | CJA 2003 Sch.15 offence | | |
| Third drug trafficking offence | POCA 2002 Sch.2 para.1 and 10 | Yes: but resultant sentence must not be less than 80% of the required minimum | 7 years |
| Posession of prohibited firearms | FA 1968:<br>i) s.5(1) (1)(a), (ab), (aba), (ac), (ad), (ae), (af) or (c); or<br>ii) s.5(1A)(a); or<br>iii) an offence under s.5(2A); s.16; s.16A; s.17; s.18; s.19; or s.20(1) in respect of a firearm or ammunition specified in s.5(1)(a), (ab), (aba), (ac), (ad), (ae), (af) or (c) | None | Age at conviction:<br>18+: 5 years<br>16–17: 3 years (s.91) |
| Minding weapons | VCRA 2006 s.28 | None | Age at conviction:<br>18+: 5 years<br>16–17: 3 years (s.91) |

| Order | Trigger offence | Discount for guilty plea | Required length |
|---|---|---|---|
| This domestic burglary offences | TA 1968 s.9 where specified as "domestic burglary" in the indictment | Yes: but resultant sentence must not be less than 80% of the required minimum | 3 years |
| Article with blade or point in a public place | CJA 1988 s.139 | | Age at conviction 18+: 6 months 16–17: 4-month DTO (unless the offender pleaded guilty, in which case the court may impose any sentence). |
| Article with blade or point on school premises | CJA 1988 s.139A | Yes: but where the offender is aged 18+ at conviction, the resultant sentence must not be less than 80% of the required minimum | |
| Threatening with article with blade or point or offensive weapon | CJA 1988 s.139AA | | |
| Possession of offensive weapon | PCA 1953 s.1 | | |
| Threatening with offensive weapon in public | PCA 1953 s.1A | Yes: but where the offender is aged 18+ at conviction, the resultant sentence must not be less than 80% of the required minimum. | Age at conviction: 18+: 6 months 16–17: 4-month DTO (unless the offender pleaded guilty, in which case the court may impose any sentence). |
| Offenders of particular concern | CJA 2003 Sch.18A | None: a reduction may be made to the length of the custodial sentence in the usual way. | - |

## MINIMUM SENTENCES: GUILTY PLEA REDUCTION

| Order | Discount for guilty plea | Minimum sentence with any guilty plea reduction |
|---|---|---|
| Third drug trafficking offence | Yes: but resultant sentence must not be less and 80% of the required minimum | 2,045 days (5 years 7.2 months) |
| Possession of prohibited firearms | None | – |
| Minding weapons | None | – |
| Third domestic burglary offence | Yes: But the resultant sentence must not be less than 80% of the required minimum | 876 days (2 years 4.8 months) |
| Article with blade or point in a public place | Yes: But where the defendant was aged 18+ conviction, the resultant sentence must not be less than 80% of the required minimum | Age at conviction: 18+: 146 days (4.8 months) 16–17: Any appropriate sentence* |
| Article with blade or point on school premises | | |
| Threatening with article with blade or point or offensive weapon | | |
| Possession of offensive weapon | | |
| Threatening with offensive weapon in public | | |

Note
* The minimum period required by the statute is a 4-month DTO. However, by virtue of CJA 2003 s.144(4), where a 16 or 17 year old has pleaded guilty, the minimum sentence provisions do not prevent the court from imposing any sentence it considers appropriate.

## GUILTY PLEA REDUCTION – PERCENTAGE TABLE

| Sentence in Years | Percentage reduction | | | |
|---|---|---|---|---|
| | 33% | 25% | 10% | 5% |
| 1 | 8 months | 9 months | 10.8 months | 11.4 months |
| 2 | 16 months | 18 months | 21.6 months | 22.8 months |
| 3 | 2 years | 2 years 3 months | 2 years 8.4 months | 2 years 10.2 months |
| 4 | 2 years 8 months | 3 years | 3 years 7.2 months | 3 years 9.6 months |
| 5 | 3 years 4 months | 3 years 9 months | 4 years 6 months | 4 years 9 months |
| 6 | 4 years | 4 years 6 months | 5 years 4.8 months | 5 years 8.4 months |
| 7 | 4 years 8 months | 5 years 3 months | 6 years 3.6 months | 6 years 7.8 months |
| 8 | 5 years 4 months | 6 years | 7 years 2.4 months | 7 years 7.2 months |
| 9 | 6 years | 6 years 9 months | 8 years 1.2 months | 8 years 6.6 months |
| 10 | 6 years 8 months | 7 years 6 months | 9 years | 9 years 6 months |
| 11 | 7 years 4 months | 8 years 3 months | 9 years 10.8 months | 10 years 5.4 months |
| 12 | 8 years | 9 years | 10 years 9.6 months | 11 years 4.8 months |
| 13 | 8 years 8 months | 9 years 9 months | 11 years 8.4 months | 12 years 4.2 months |
| 14 | 9 years 4 months | 10 years 6 months | 12 years 7.2 months | 13 years 3.6 months |
| 15 | 10 years | 11 years 3 months | 13 years 6 months | 14 years 3 months |
| 16 | 10 years 8 months | 12 years | 14 years 4.8 months | 15 years 2.5 months |
| 17 | 11 years 4 months | 12 years 9 months | 15 years 3.6 months | 16 years 1.8 months |
| 18 | 12 years | 13 years 6 months | 16 years 2.4 months | 17 years 1.2 months |
| 19 | 12 years 8 months | 14 years 3 months | 17 years 1.2 months | 18 years 0.6 months |
| 20 | 13 years 4 months | 15 years | 18 years | 19 years |

Note

All figures in this table have been rounded mathematically to one decimal place. These figures represent the precise reductions and of course, it is a matter for the individual judge to decide whether to increase or decrease that figure to the nearest whole month.

# LIST OF SENTENCING GUIDELINES

This table lists all sentencing guidelines currently in force, and the date on which they came into force. Guidelines are operative for all offences sentenced after the 'in force' date unless otherwise stated.

Unless otherwise stated, guidelines are issued by the Sentencing Council.

| Guideline topic | In force |
| --- | --- |
| Allocation, Offences Taken into Consideration and Totality | 1 March 2016 (Allocation) 11 June 2012 (TICs and Totality) |
| Assault | 13 June 2011 |
| Attempted murder (SGC) | 27 July 2009 |
| Bladed articles and offensive weapons | 1 June 2018 |
| Breach Offences | 1 October 2018 |
| Breach: Protective Order (SCG) | 18 December 2006 |
| Breach: ASBO (SGC) | 5 January 2009 |
| Burglary | 16 January 2012 |
| Causing death by driving (SGC) | 4 August 2008 |
| Child Cruelty Offences | 1 January 2019 |
| Dangerous dogs | 1 July 2016 |
| Domestic Abuse: Overarching principles | 24 May 2018 |
| Drug offences | 27 February 2012 |
| Environmental offences | 1 July 2014 |
| Failure to surrender to bail (SGC) | 10 December 2007 |
| Fraud, bribery and money laundering | 1 October 2014 |
| Guilty plea | 1 June 2017 (where the first hearing occurs on or after that date) |
| Health and safety offences, corporate manslaughter, food safety and hygiene offences | 1 February 2016 |
| Imposition of Community and Custodial Sentences | 1 February 2017 |
| Intimidatory Offences | 1 October 2018 |
| Magistrates' Court (SGC) | 4 August 2008 |
| Robbery | 1 April 2016 |
| Seriousness (SGC) | 16 December 2004 |
| Sexual Offences | 1 April 2014 |
| Terrorism Offences | 27 April 2018 |
| Theft | 1 February 2016 |
| Youths | 1 June 2017 |